All our dreams can come true if we have the courage to pursue them.

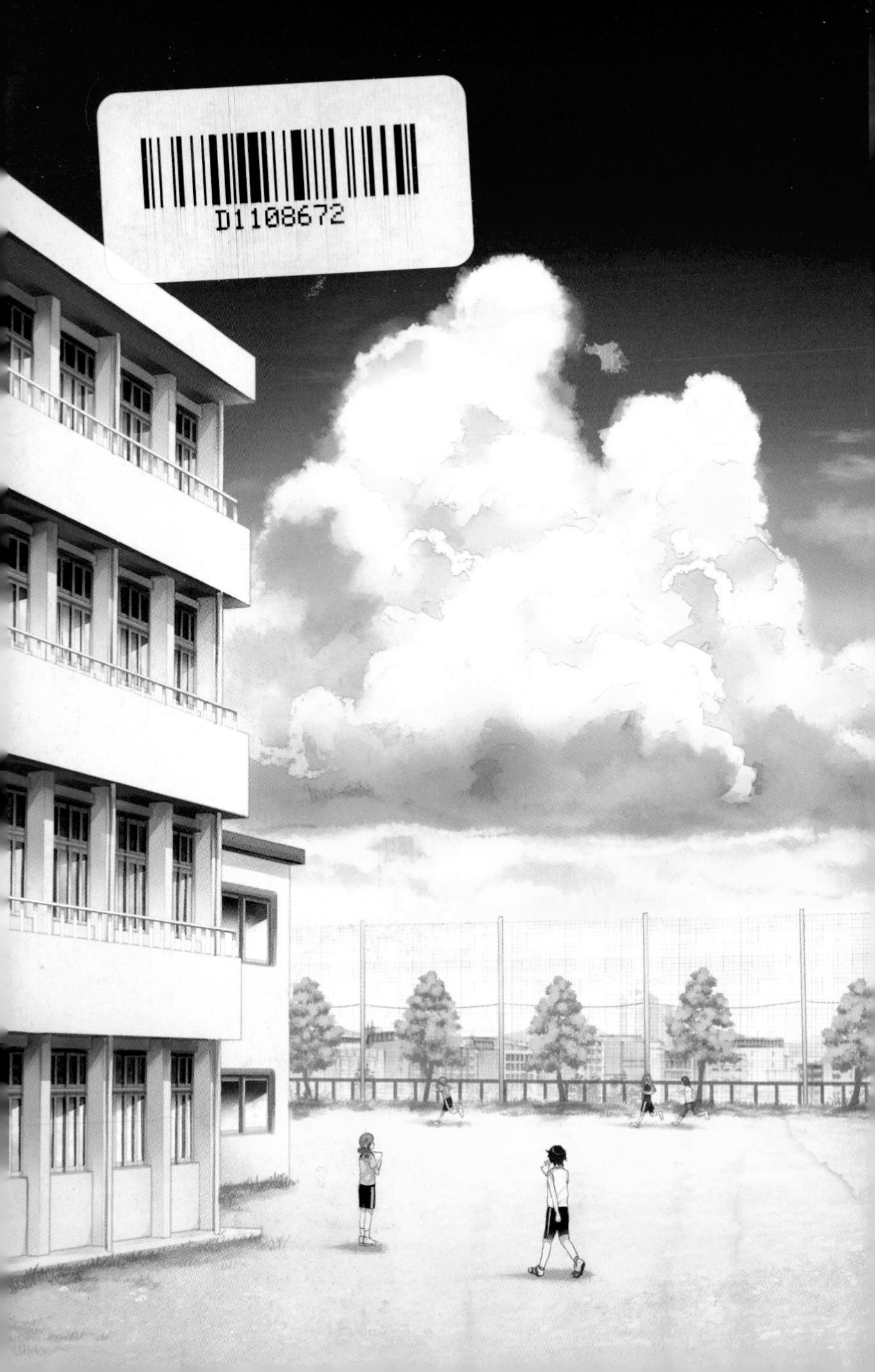

Kiss and White Lily for My Dearest Girl 4

Contents

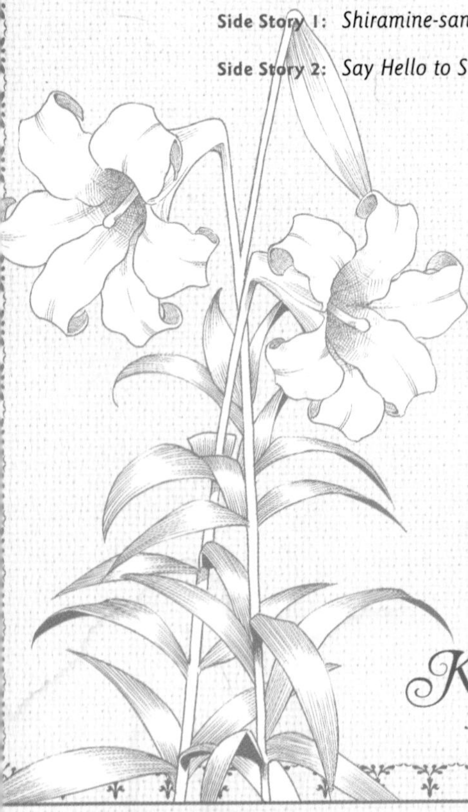

Kiss & White Lily for My Dearest Girl

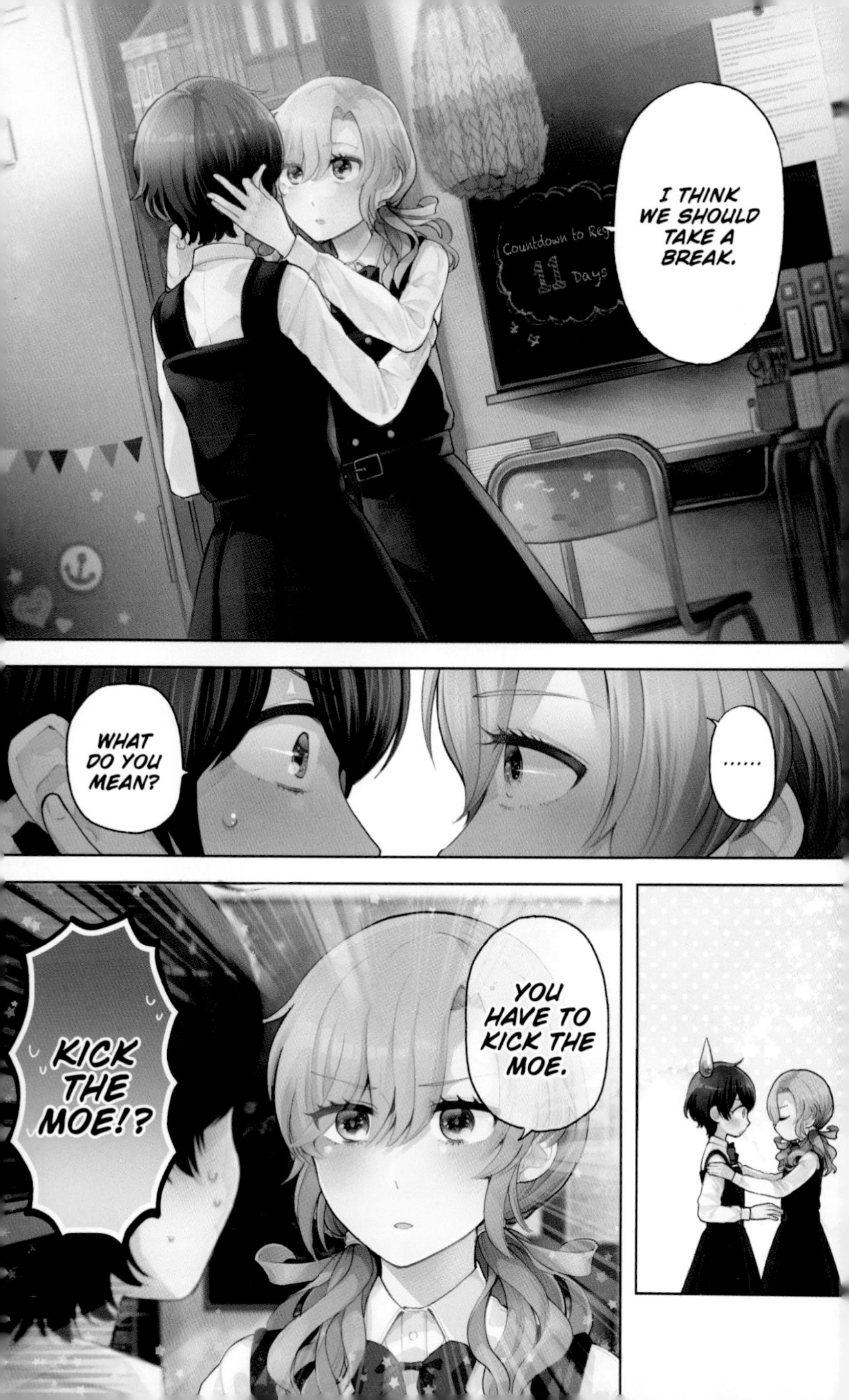
I THINK WE SHOULD TAKE A BREAK.
Countdown to
11 Days
......
WHAT DO YOU MEAN?
YOU HAVE TO KICK THE MOE.
KICK THE MOE!?

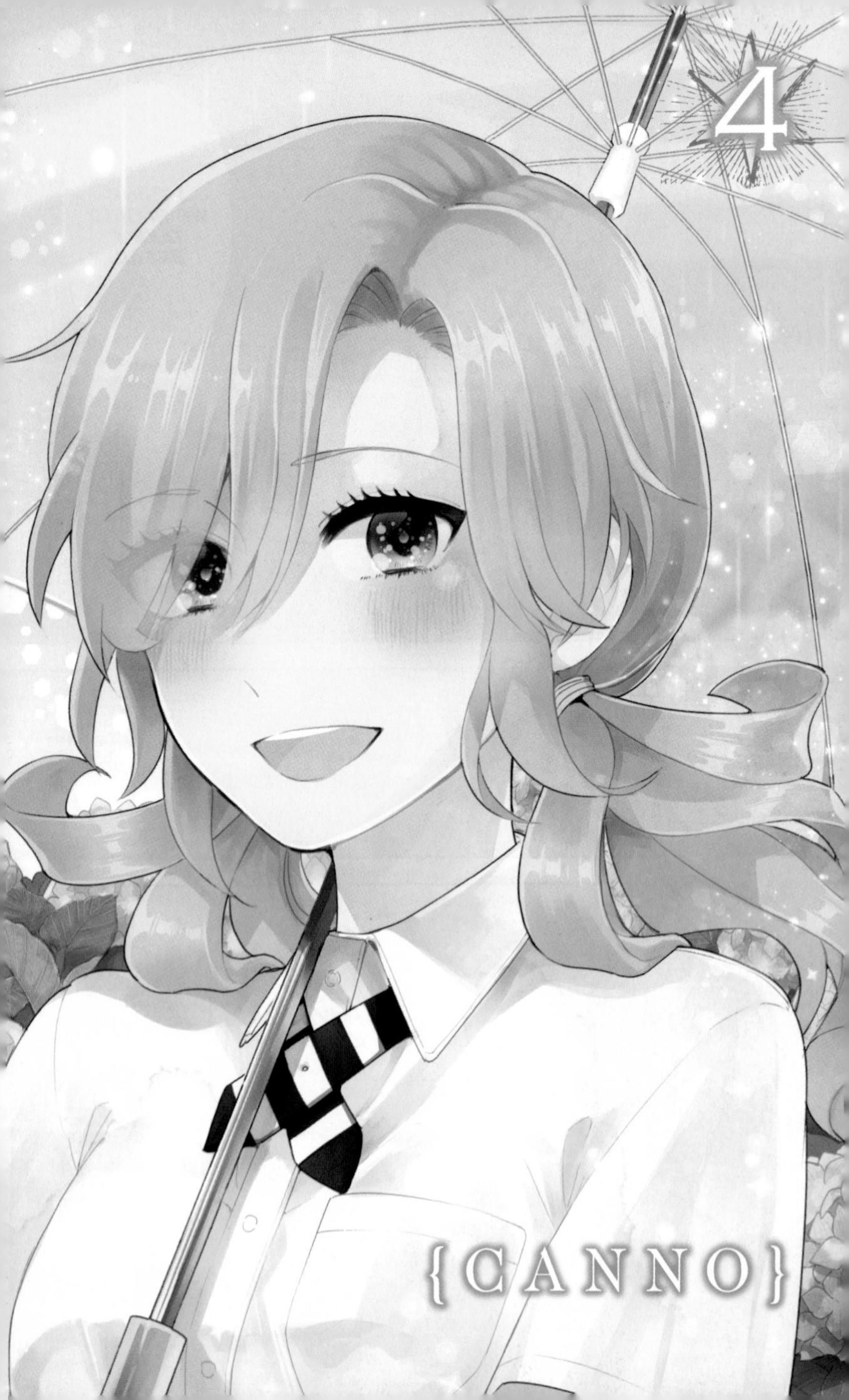
4
{CANNO}

Chapter 16: *Bluebird Drive*

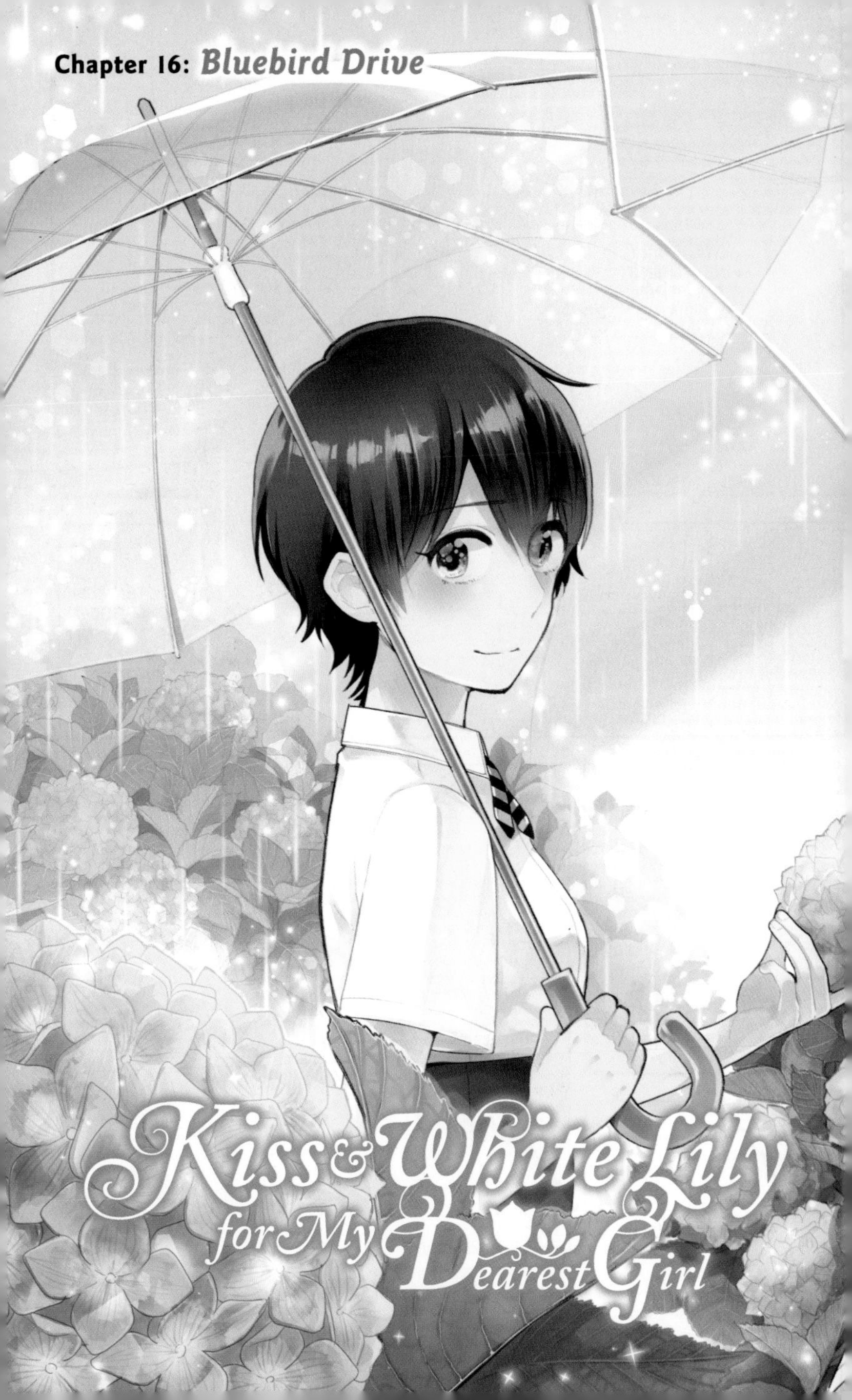
Kiss & White Lily for My Dearest Girl

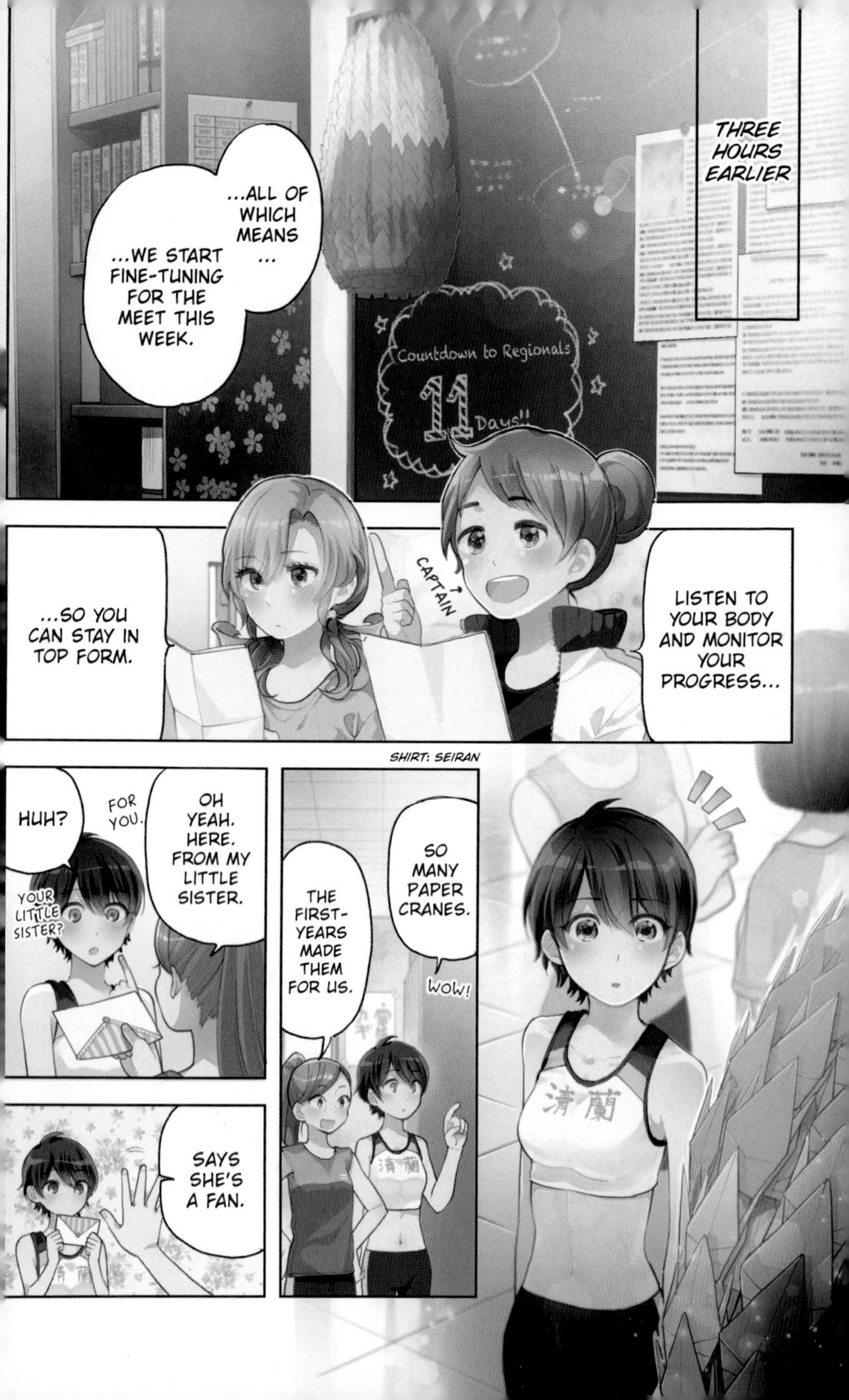
THREE HOURS EARLIER
...ALL OF WHICH MEANS ...
...WE START FINE-TUNING FOR THE MEET THIS WEEK.
Countdown to Regionals
11 Days!!
LISTEN TO YOUR BODY AND MONITOR YOUR PROGRESS...
CAPTAIN
...SO YOU CAN STAY IN TOP FORM.
SHIRT: SEIRAN
SO MANY PAPER CRANES.
WOW!
THE FIRST-YEARS MADE THEM FOR US.
OH YEAH. HERE. FROM MY LITTLE SISTER.
FOR YOU.
HUH?
YOUR LITTLE SISTER?
SAYS SHE'S A FAN.

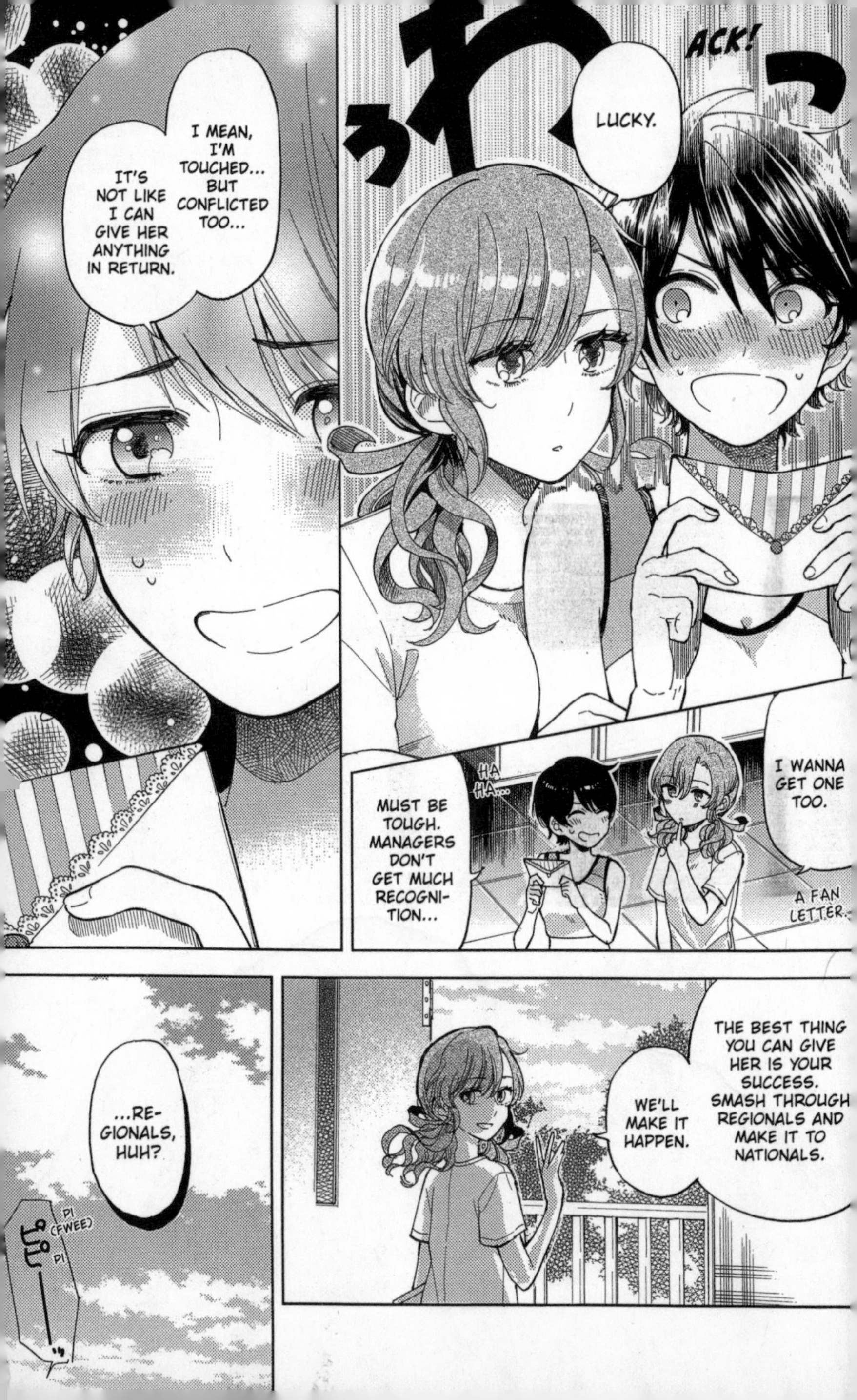
ACK!
LUCKY.
I WANNA GET ONE TOO.
A FAN LETTER.
HA HA...
MUST BE TOUGH. MANAGERS DON'T GET MUCH RECOGNI-TION...
I MEAN, I'M TOUCHED... BUT CONFLICTED TOO...
IT'S NOT LIKE I CAN GIVE HER ANYTHING IN RETURN.
THE BEST THING YOU CAN GIVE HER IS YOUR SUCCESS. SMASH THROUGH REGIONALS AND MAKE IT TO NATIONALS.
WE'LL MAKE IT HAPPEN.
...RE-GIONALS, HUH?
PI (FWEE) PI

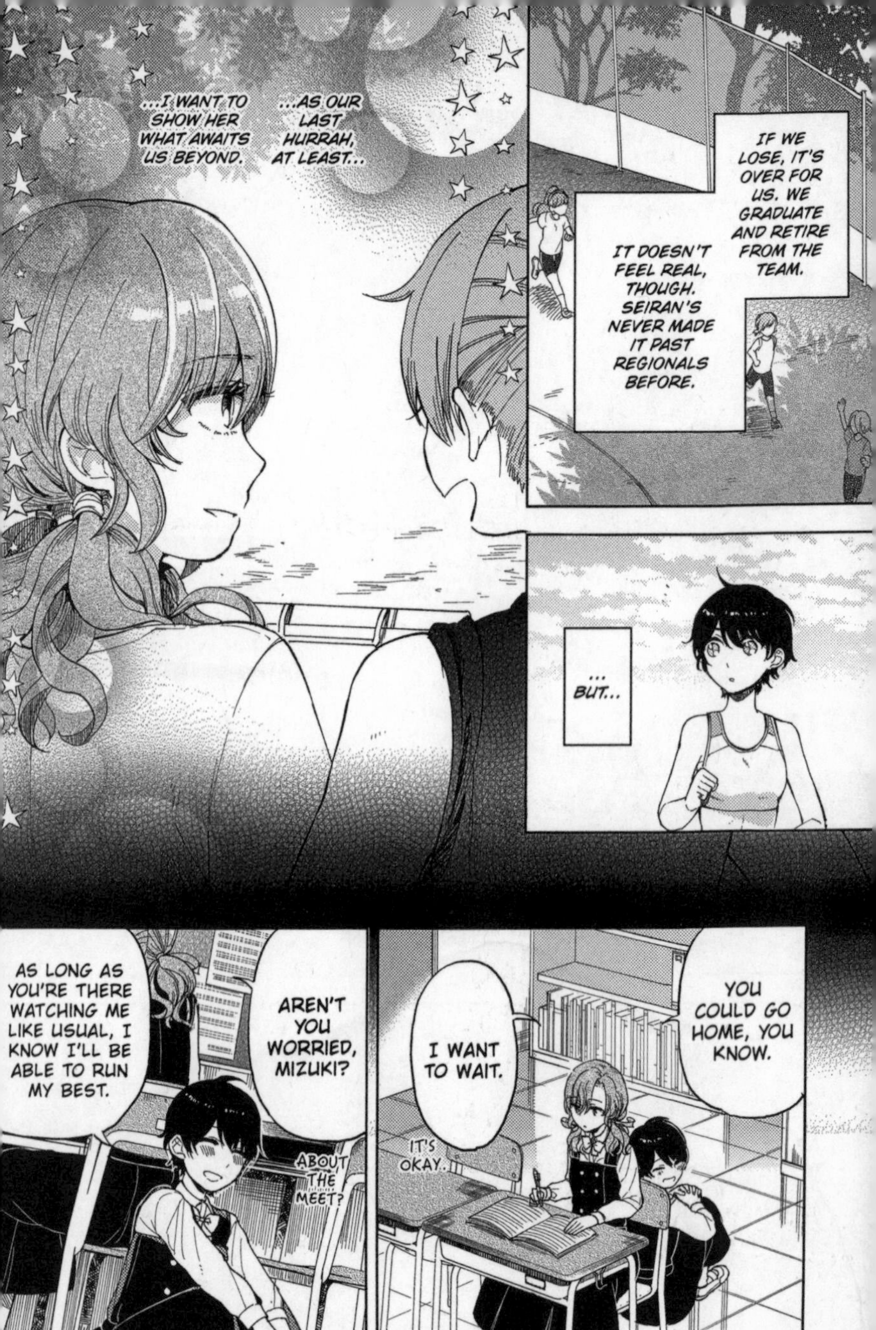
IF WE LOSE, IT'S OVER FOR US. WE GRADUATE AND RETIRE FROM THE TEAM.
IT DOESN'T FEEL REAL, THOUGH. SEIRAN'S NEVER MADE IT PAST REGIONALS BEFORE.
...BUT...
...AS OUR LAST HURRAH, AT LEAST...
...I WANT TO SHOW HER WHAT AWAITS US BEYOND.
YOU COULD GO HOME, YOU KNOW.
I WANT TO WAIT.
IT'S OKAY.
AREN'T YOU WORRIED, MIZUKI?
ABOUT THE MEET?
AS LONG AS YOU'RE THERE WATCHING ME LIKE USUAL, I KNOW I'LL BE ABLE TO RUN MY BEST.

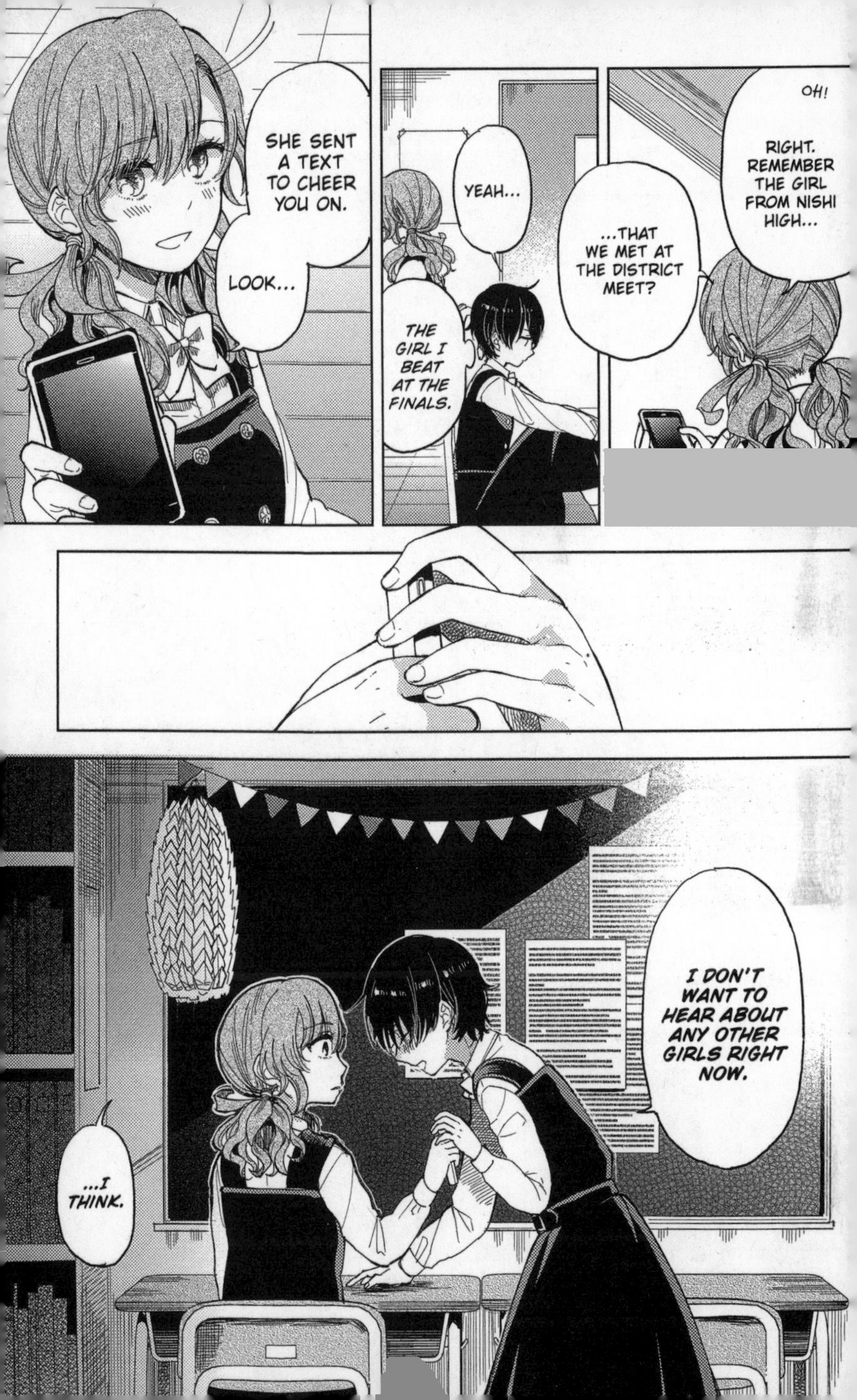
OH!
RIGHT. REMEMBER THE GIRL FROM NISHI HIGH...
...THAT WE MET AT THE DISTRICT MEET?
YEAH...
THE GIRL I BEAT AT THE FINALS.
SHE SENT A TEXT TO CHEER YOU ON.
LOOK...
I DON'T WANT TO HEAR ABOUT ANY OTHER GIRLS RIGHT NOW.
...I THINK.

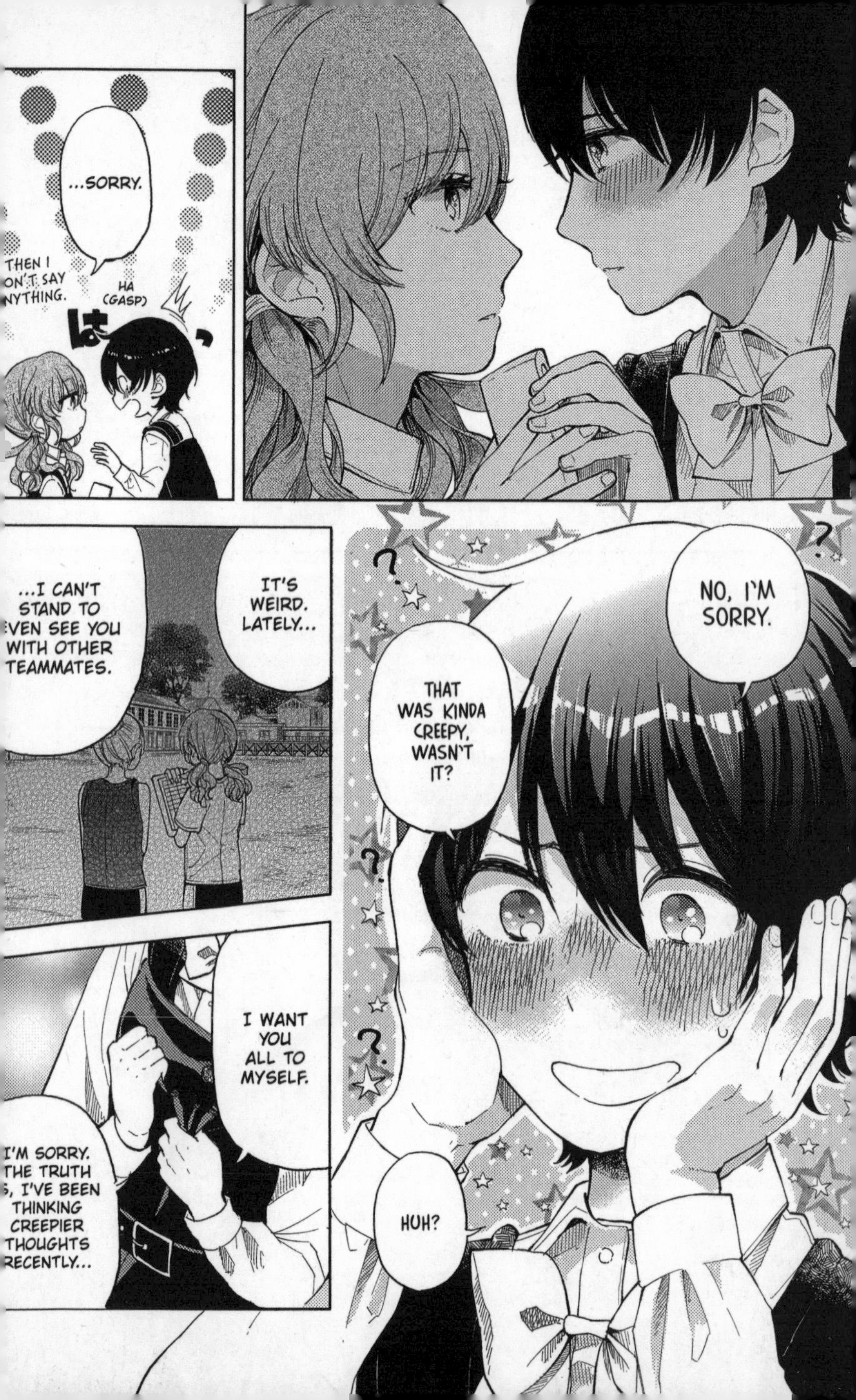
...SORRY.
HA (GASP)
はっ
THEN I ON'T SAY NYTHING.
NO, I'M SORRY.
THAT WAS KINDA CREEPY, WASN'T IT?
HUH?
IT'S WEIRD. LATELY...
...I CAN'T STAND TO VEN SEE YOU WITH OTHER TEAMMATES.
I WANT YOU ALL TO MYSELF.
I'M SORRY. THE TRUTH S, I'VE BEEN THINKING CREEPIER THOUGHTS RECENTLY...

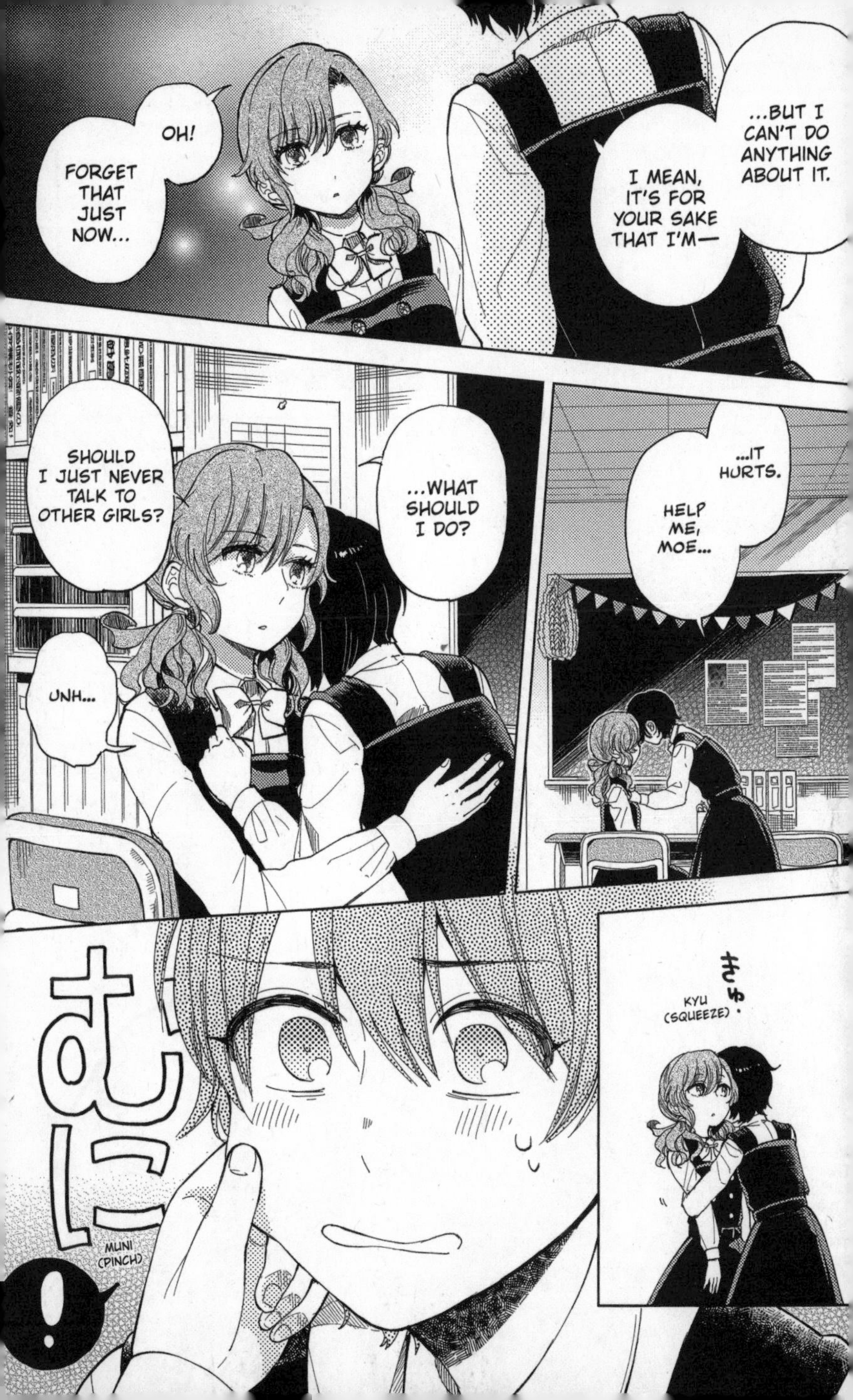
...BUT I CAN'T DO ANYTHING ABOUT IT.
I MEAN, IT'S FOR YOUR SAKE THAT I'M—
OH!
FORGET THAT JUST NOW...
...IT HURTS.
HELP ME, MOE...
...WHAT SHOULD I DO?
SHOULD I JUST NEVER TALK TO OTHER GIRLS?
UNH...
きゅ
KYU (SQUEEZE)
むに
MUNI (PINCH)
!

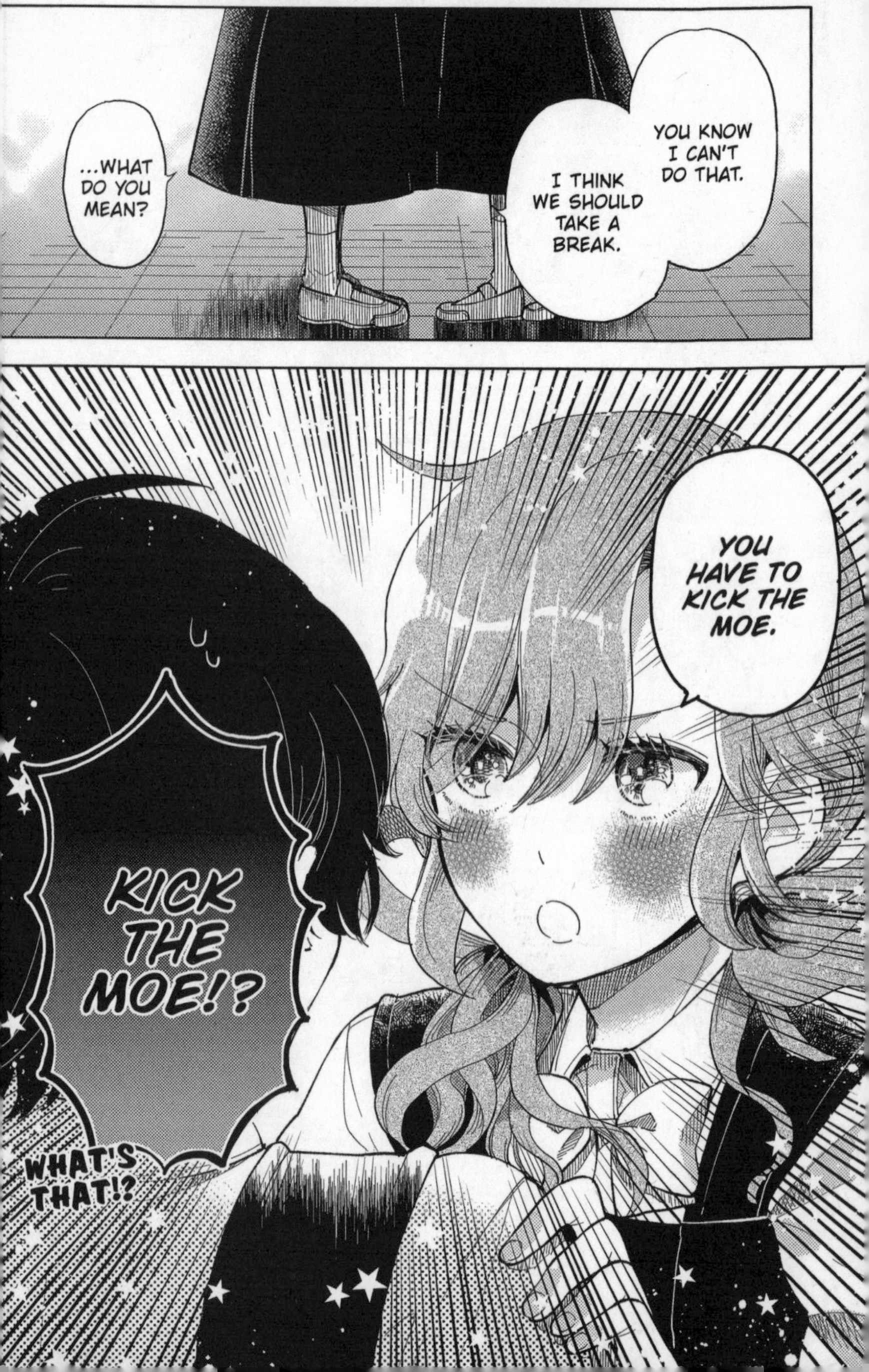
YOU KNOW I CAN'T DO THAT.
I THINK WE SHOULD TAKE A BREAK.
...WHAT DO YOU MEAN?
YOU HAVE TO KICK THE MOE.
KICK THE MOE!?
WHAT'S THAT!?

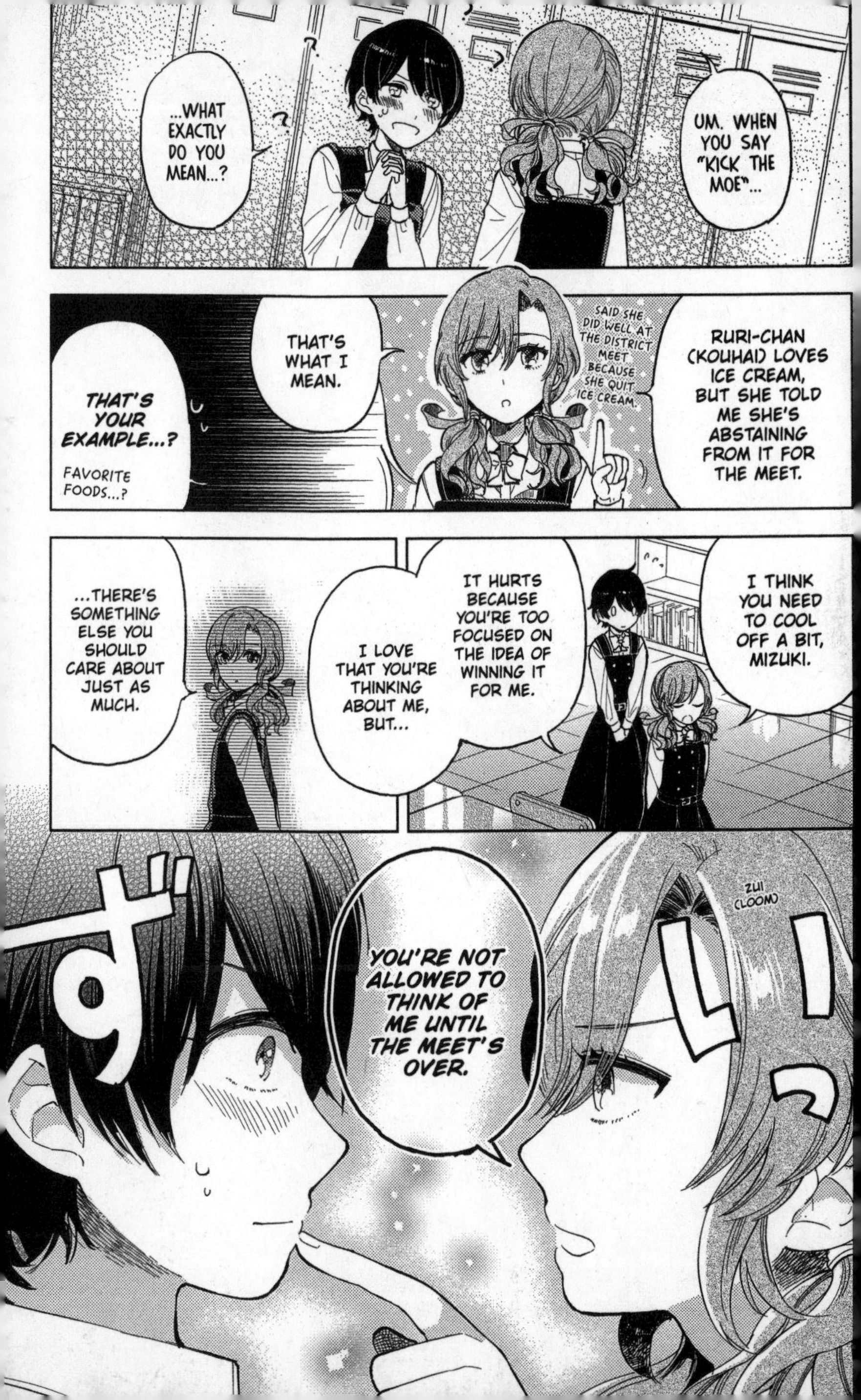
UM. WHEN YOU SAY "KICK THE MOE"...
...WHAT EXACTLY DO YOU MEAN...?
RURI-CHAN (KOUHAI) LOVES ICE CREAM, BUT SHE TOLD ME SHE'S ABSTAINING FROM IT FOR THE MEET.
SAID SHE DID WELL AT THE DISTRICT MEET BECAUSE SHE QUIT ICE CREAM.
THAT'S WHAT I MEAN.
THAT'S YOUR EXAMPLE...?
FAVORITE FOODS...?
I THINK YOU NEED TO COOL OFF A BIT, MIZUKI.
IT HURTS BECAUSE YOU'RE TOO FOCUSED ON THE IDEA OF WINNING IT FOR ME.
I LOVE THAT YOU'RE THINKING ABOUT ME, BUT...
...THERE'S SOMETHING ELSE YOU SHOULD CARE ABOUT JUST AS MUCH.
ずいっ
ZUI (LOOM)
YOU'RE NOT ALLOWED TO THINK OF ME UNTIL THE MEET'S OVER.

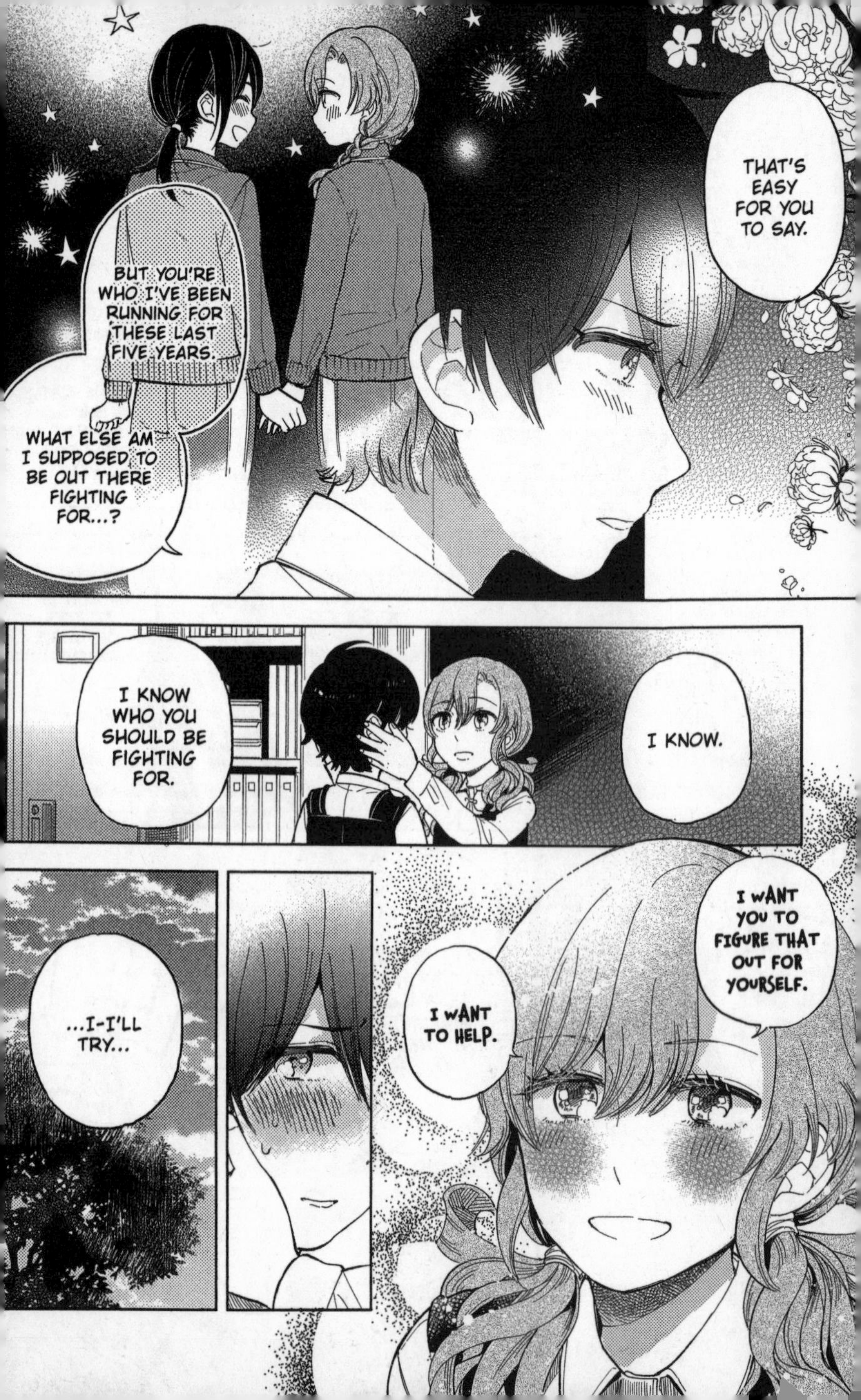
THAT'S EASY FOR YOU TO SAY.
BUT YOU'RE WHO I'VE BEEN RUNNING FOR THESE LAST FIVE YEARS.
WHAT ELSE AM I SUPPOSED TO BE OUT THERE FIGHTING FOR...?
I KNOW.
I KNOW WHO YOU SHOULD BE FIGHTING FOR.
I WANT YOU TO FIGURE THAT OUT FOR YOURSELF.
I WANT TO HELP.
...I-I'LL TRY...

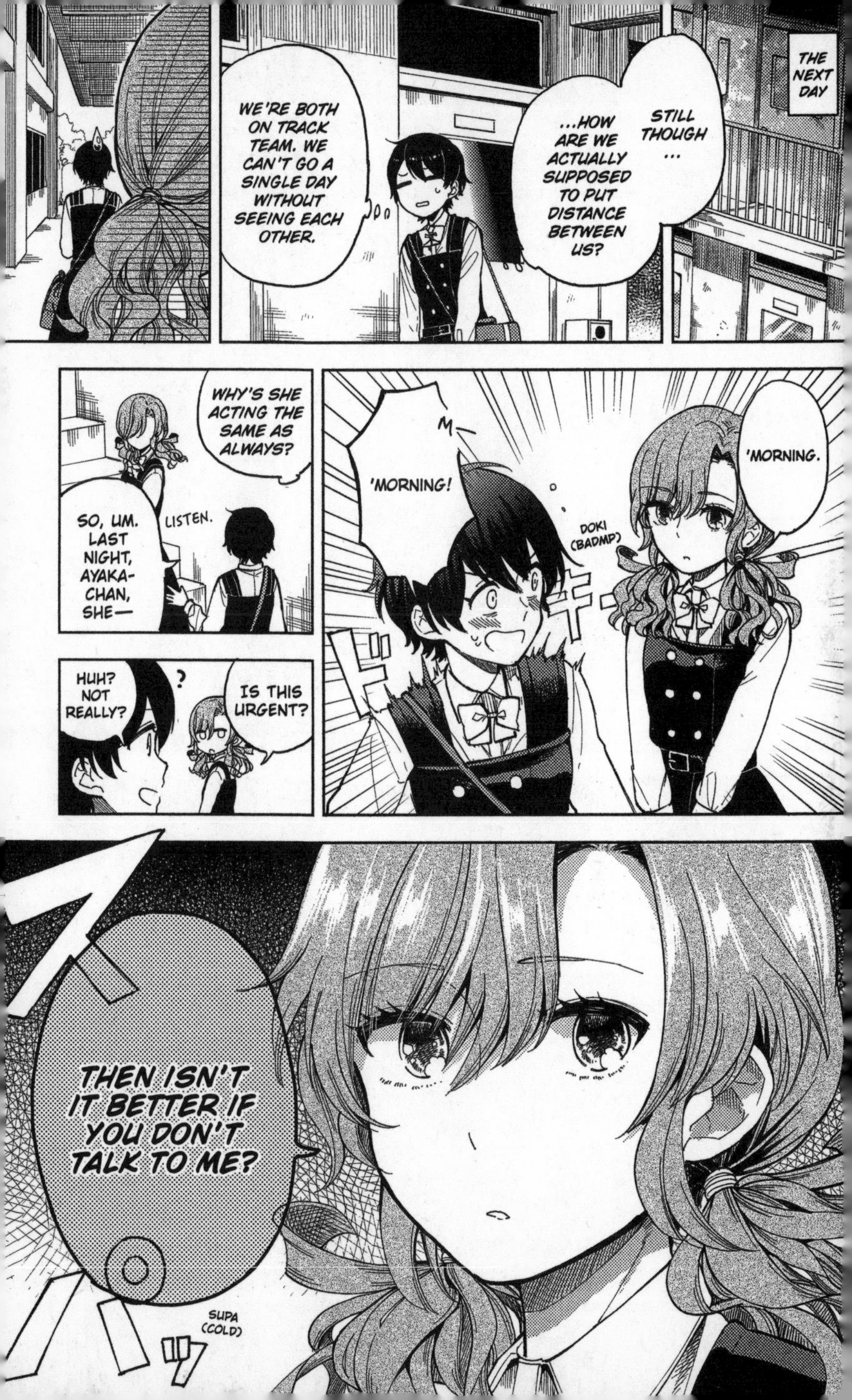
THE NEXT DAY
STILL THOUGH ...
...HOW ARE WE ACTUALLY SUPPOSED TO PUT DISTANCE BETWEEN US?
WE'RE BOTH ON TRACK TEAM. WE CAN'T GO A SINGLE DAY WITHOUT SEEING EACH OTHER.
'MORNING.
DOKI (BADMP)
M—
'MORNING!
WHY'S SHE ACTING THE SAME AS ALWAYS?
LISTEN.
SO, UM. LAST NIGHT, AYAKA-CHAN, SHE—
IS THIS URGENT?
?
HUH? NOT REALLY?
THEN ISN'T IT BETTER IF YOU DON'T TALK TO ME?
SUPA (COLD)

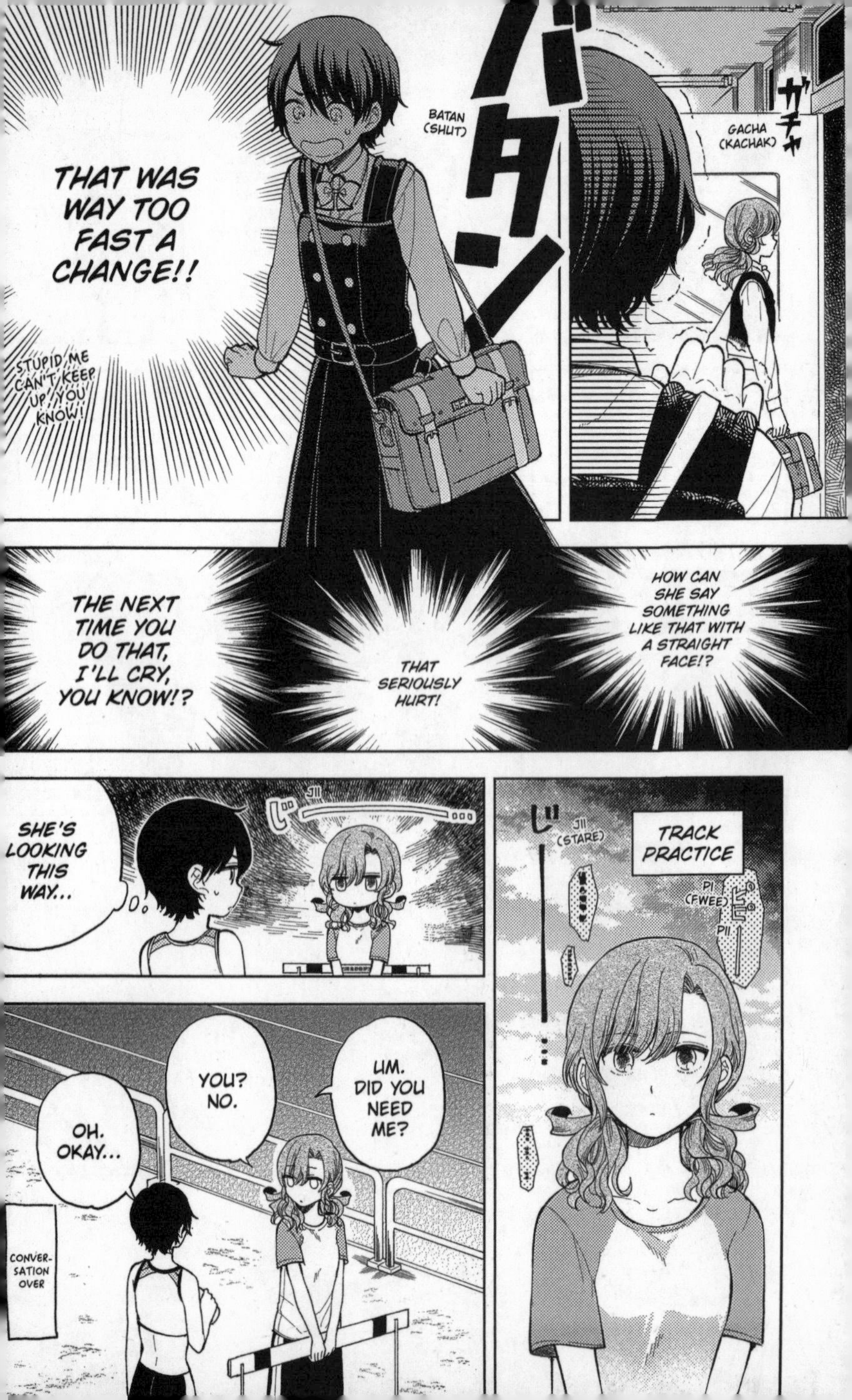
GACHA (KACHAK)
BATAN (SHUT)
THAT WAS WAY TOO FAST A CHANGE!!
STUPID ME CAN'T KEEP UP, YOU KNOW!
HOW CAN SHE SAY SOMETHING LIKE THAT WITH A STRAIGHT FACE!?
THAT SERIOUSLY HURT!
THE NEXT TIME YOU DO THAT, I'LL CRY, YOU KNOW!?
TRACK PRACTICE
PI (FWEE)
PII
JII (STARE)
JII
SHE'S LOOKING THIS WAY...
UM. DID YOU NEED ME?
YOU? NO.
OH. OKAY...
CONVERSATION OVER

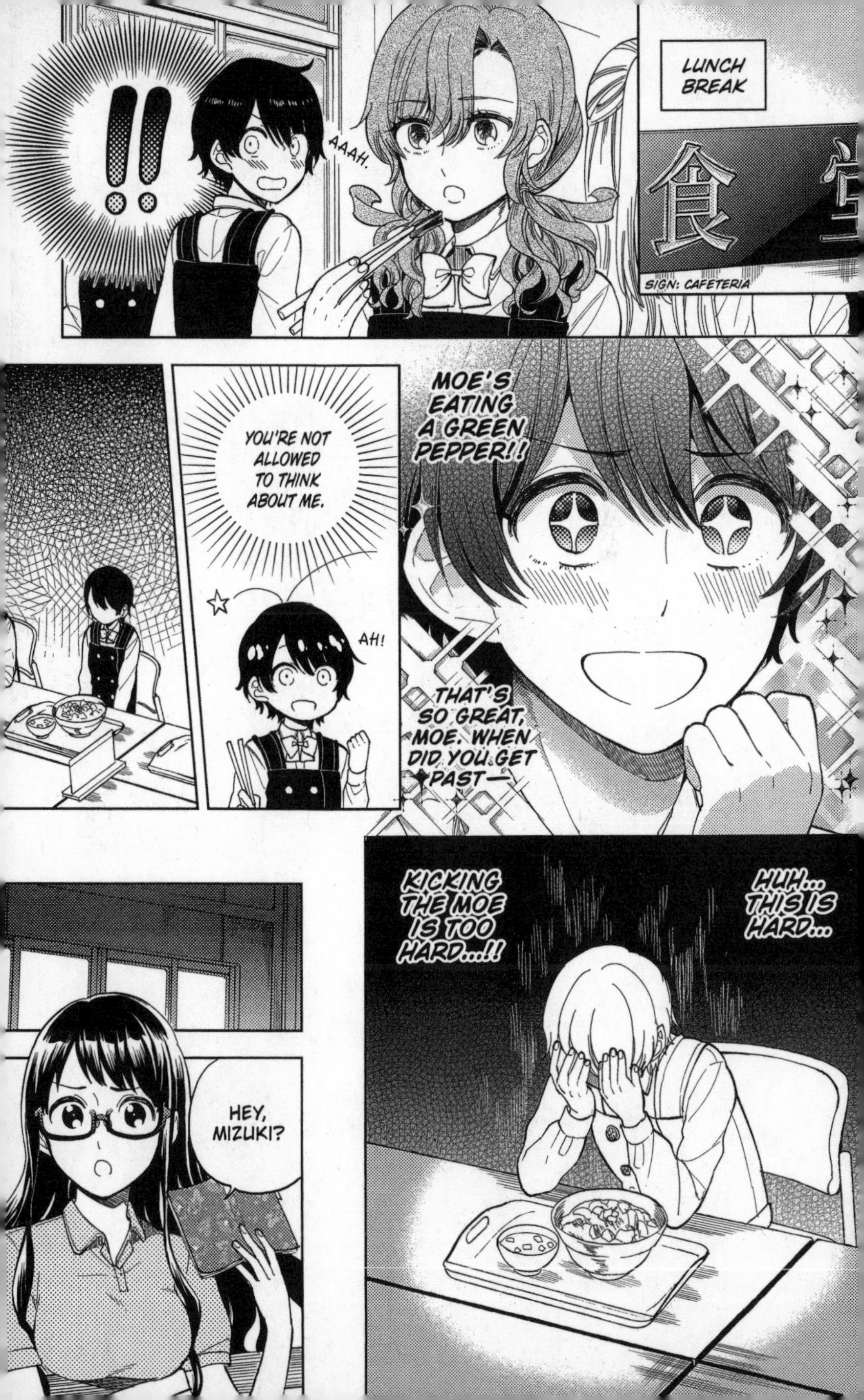
LUNCH BREAK
SIGN: CAFETERIA
AAAH.
!!
MOE'S EATING A GREEN PEPPER!!
THAT'S SO GREAT, MOE. WHEN DID YOU GET PAST—
YOU'RE NOT ALLOWED TO THINK ABOUT ME.
AH!
HUH... THIS IS HARD...
KICKING THE MOE IS TOO HARD...!!
HEY, MIZUKI?

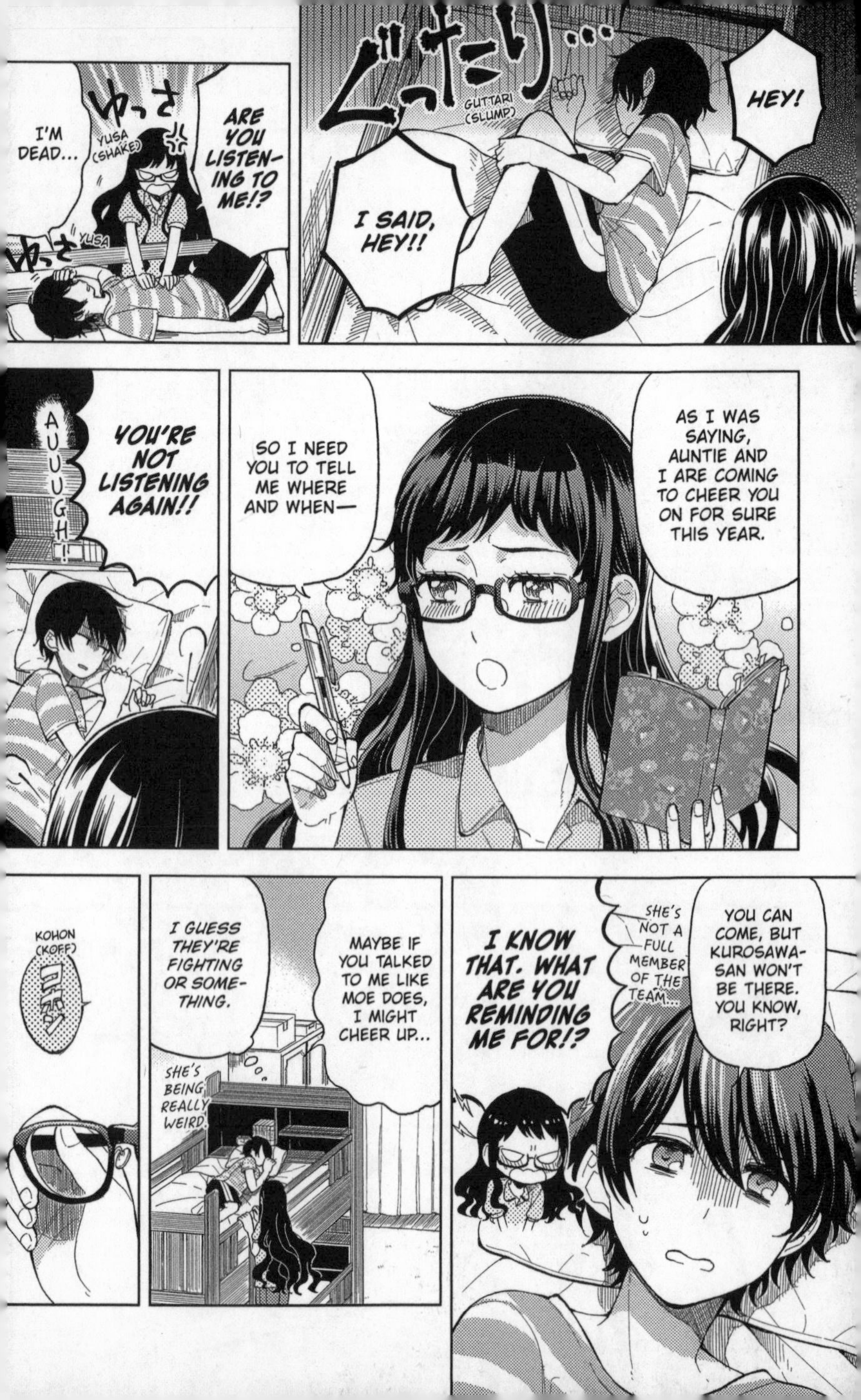
HEY!
ぐったり…
GUTTARI (SLUMP)
I SAID, HEY!!
ARE YOU LISTENING TO ME!?
ゆっさ
YUSA (SHAKE)
I'M DEAD…
ゆっさ
YUSA
AS I WAS SAYING, AUNTIE AND I ARE COMING TO CHEER YOU ON FOR SURE THIS YEAR.
SO I NEED YOU TO TELL ME WHERE AND WHEN—
YOU'RE NOT LISTENING AGAIN!!
AUUUGH!!
YOU CAN COME, BUT KUROSAWA-SAN WON'T BE THERE. YOU KNOW, RIGHT?
SHE'S NOT A FULL MEMBER OF THE TEAM…
I KNOW THAT. WHAT ARE YOU REMINDING ME FOR!?
MAYBE IF YOU TALKED TO ME LIKE MOE DOES, I MIGHT CHEER UP…
I GUESS THEY'RE FIGHTING OR SOMETHING.
SHE'S BEING REALLY WEIRD.
KOHON (KOFF)
コホン

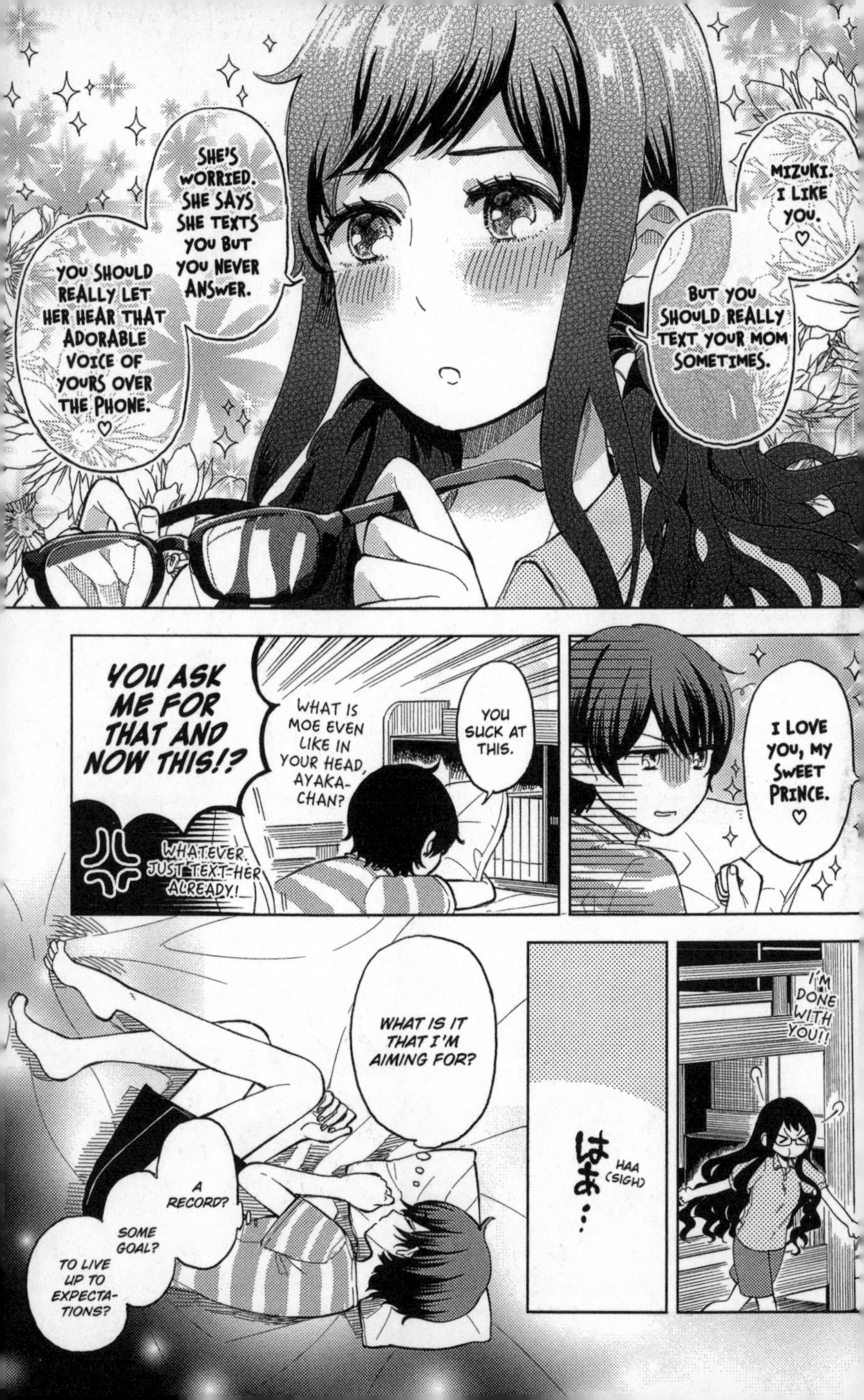
MIZUKI. I LIKE YOU. ♡
BUT YOU SHOULD REALLY TEXT YOUR MOM SOMETIMES.
SHE'S WORRIED. SHE SAYS SHE TEXTS YOU BUT YOU NEVER ANSWER.
YOU SHOULD REALLY LET HER HEAR THAT ADORABLE VOICE OF YOURS OVER THE PHONE. ♡
I LOVE YOU, MY SWEET PRINCE. ♡
YOU SUCK AT THIS.
WHAT IS MOE EVEN LIKE IN YOUR HEAD, AYAKA-CHAN?
YOU ASK ME FOR THAT AND NOW THIS!?
WHATEVER. JUST TEXT HER ALREADY!
I'M DONE WITH YOU!!
はぁ・・
HAA (SIGH)
WHAT IS IT THAT I'M AIMING FOR?
A RECORD?
SOME GOAL?
TO LIVE UP TO EXPECTATIONS?

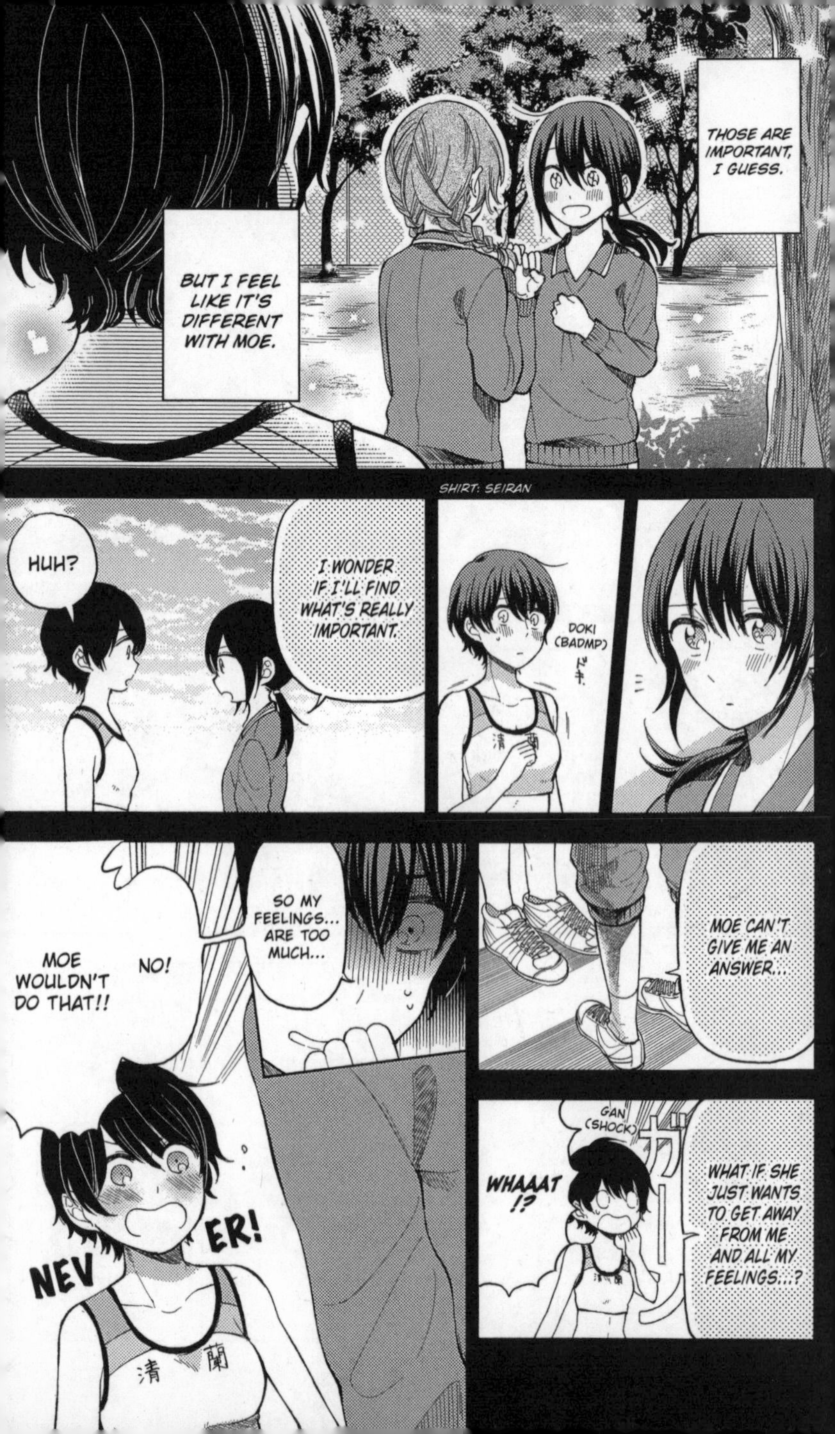
THOSE ARE IMPORTANT, I GUESS.
BUT I FEEL LIKE IT'S DIFFERENT WITH MOE.
SHIRT: SEIRAN
DOKI (BADMP)
ドキ
清蘭
I WONDER IF I'LL FIND WHAT'S REALLY IMPORTANT.
HUH?
MOE CAN'T GIVE ME AN ANSWER...
WHAT IF SHE JUST WANTS TO GET AWAY FROM ME AND ALL MY FEELINGS...?
GAN (SHOCK)
ガーン
WHAAAT!?
SO MY FEELINGS... ARE TOO MUCH...
NO!
MOE WOULDN'T DO THAT!!
NEVER!
清蘭

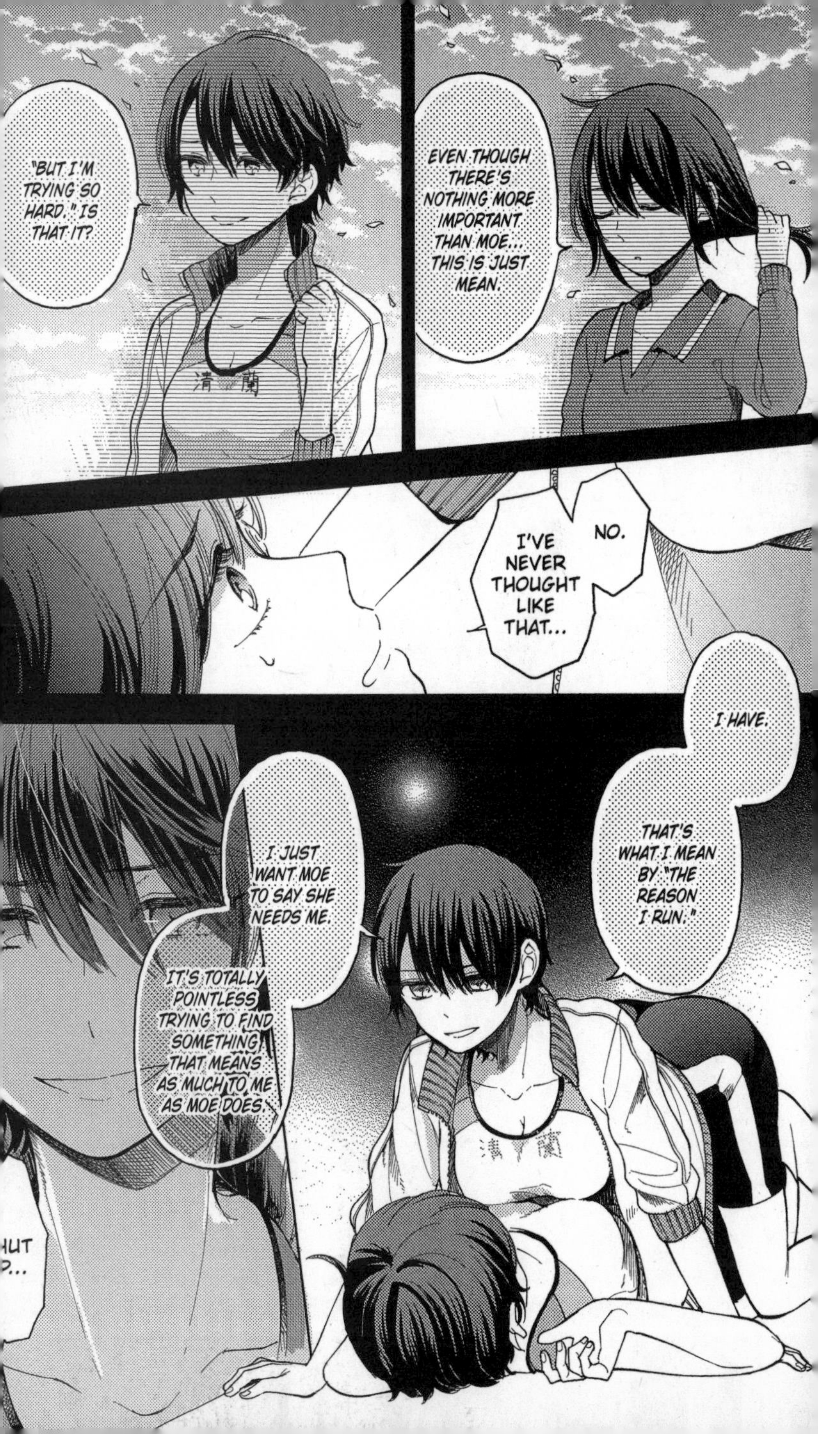
EVEN THOUGH THERE'S NOTHING MORE IMPORTANT THAN MOE... THIS IS JUST MEAN.
"BUT I'M TRYING SO HARD." IS THAT IT?
NO.
I'VE NEVER THOUGHT LIKE THAT...
I HAVE.
THAT'S WHAT I MEAN BY "THE REASON I RUN."
I JUST WANT MOE TO SAY SHE NEEDS ME.
IT'S TOTALLY POINTLESS TRYING TO FIND SOMETHING THAT MEANS AS MUCH TO ME AS MOE DOES.

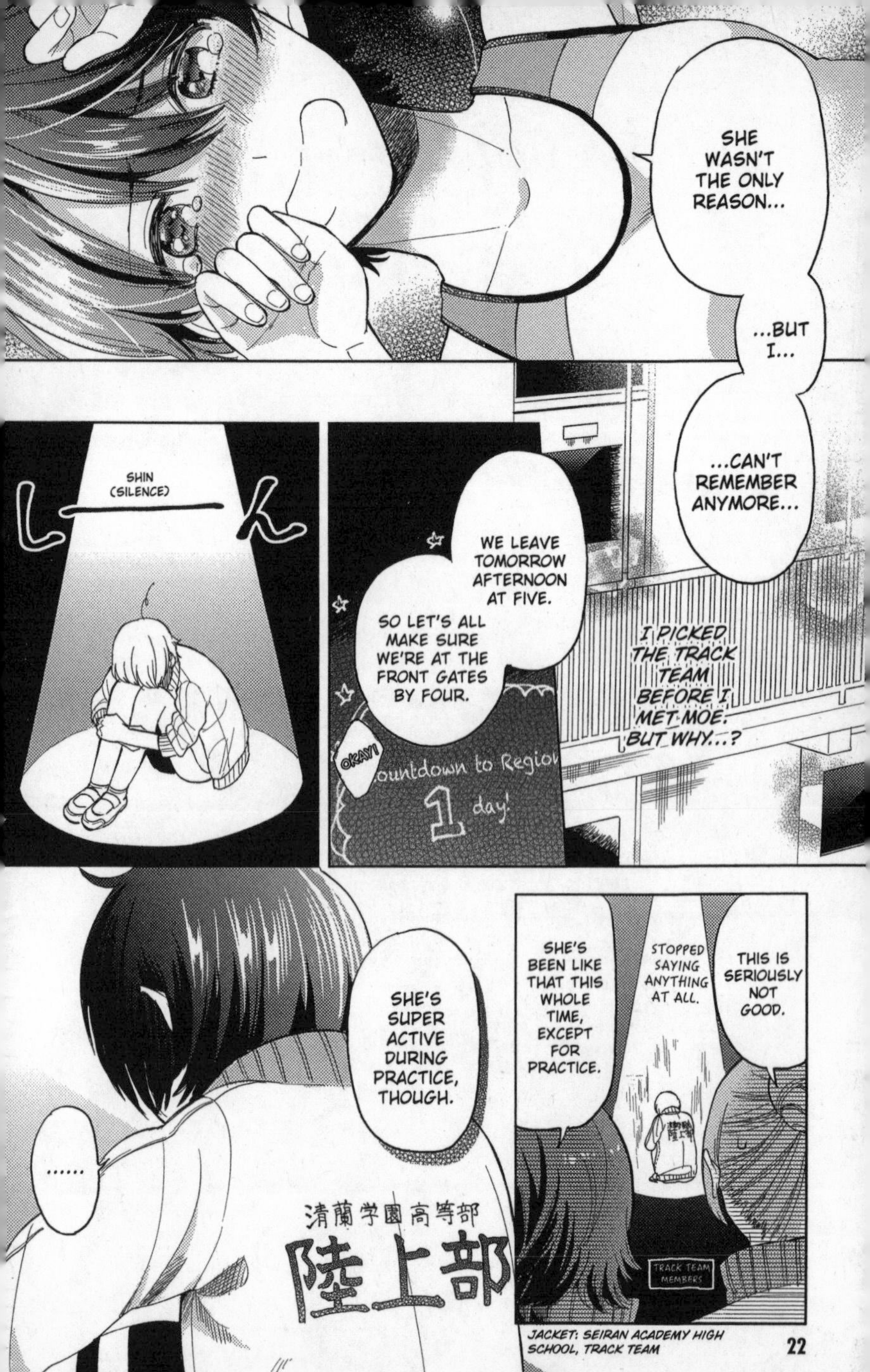
SHE WASN'T THE ONLY REASON...
...BUT I...
...CAN'T REMEMBER ANYMORE...
I PICKED THE TRACK TEAM BEFORE I MET MOE. BUT WHY...?
WE LEAVE TOMORROW AFTERNOON AT FIVE.
SO LET'S ALL MAKE SURE WE'RE AT THE FRONT GATES BY FOUR.
OKAY!
ountdown to Regio
1 day!
SHIN (SILENCE)
し——ん
THIS IS SERIOUSLY NOT GOOD.
STOPPED SAYING ANYTHING AT ALL.
SHE'S BEEN LIKE THAT THIS WHOLE TIME, EXCEPT FOR PRACTICE.
TRACK TEAM MEMBERS
SHE'S SUPER ACTIVE DURING PRACTICE, THOUGH.
......
清蘭学園高等部
陸上部

JACKET: SEIRAN ACADEMY HIGH SCHOOL, TRACK TEAM

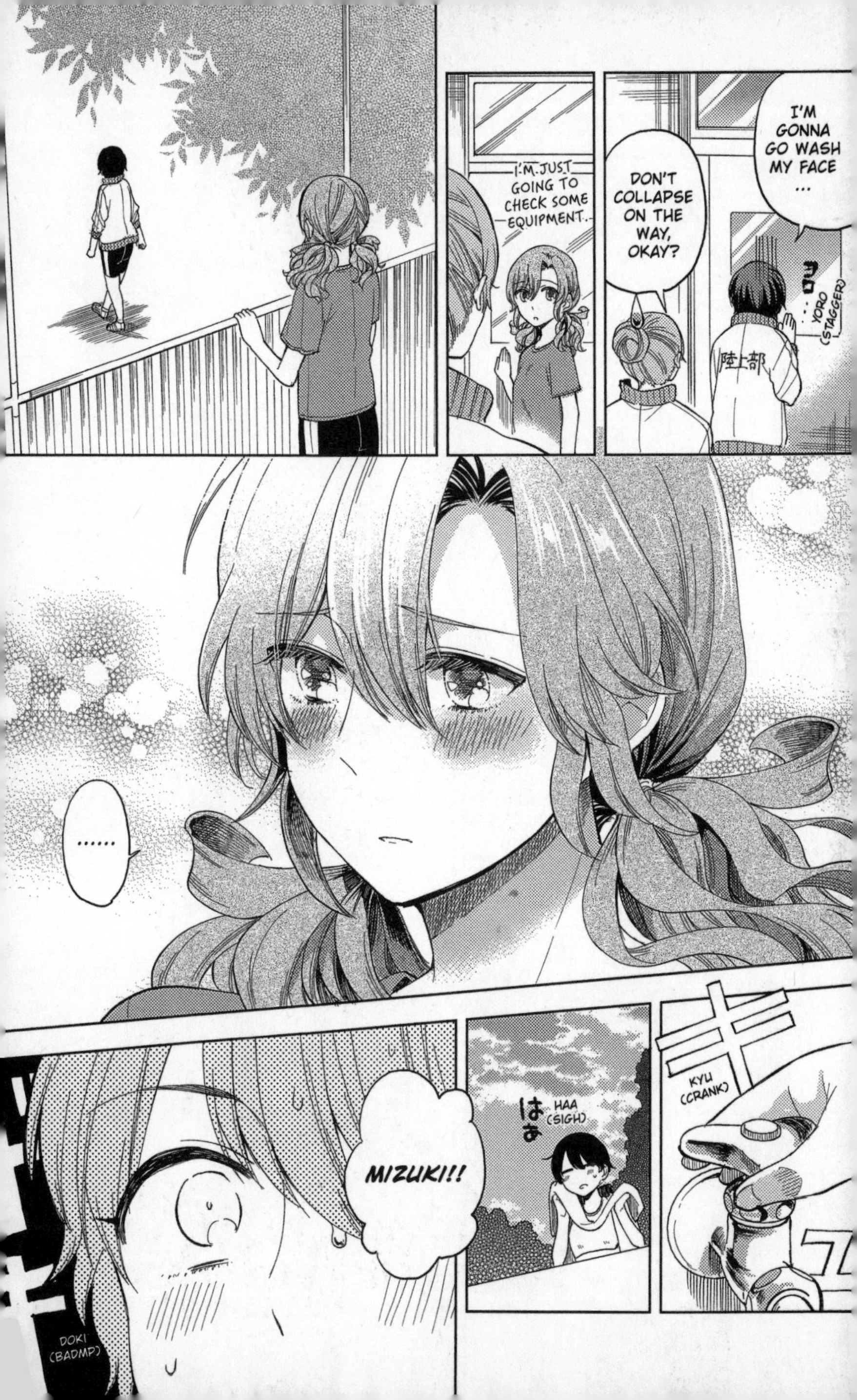
I'M GONNA GO WASH MY FACE ...
YORO (STAGGER)
陸上部
DON'T COLLAPSE ON THE WAY, OKAY?
I'M JUST GOING TO CHECK SOME EQUIPMENT.
......
KYU (CRANK)
はぁ
HAA (SIGH)
MIZUKI!!
DOKI (BADMP)

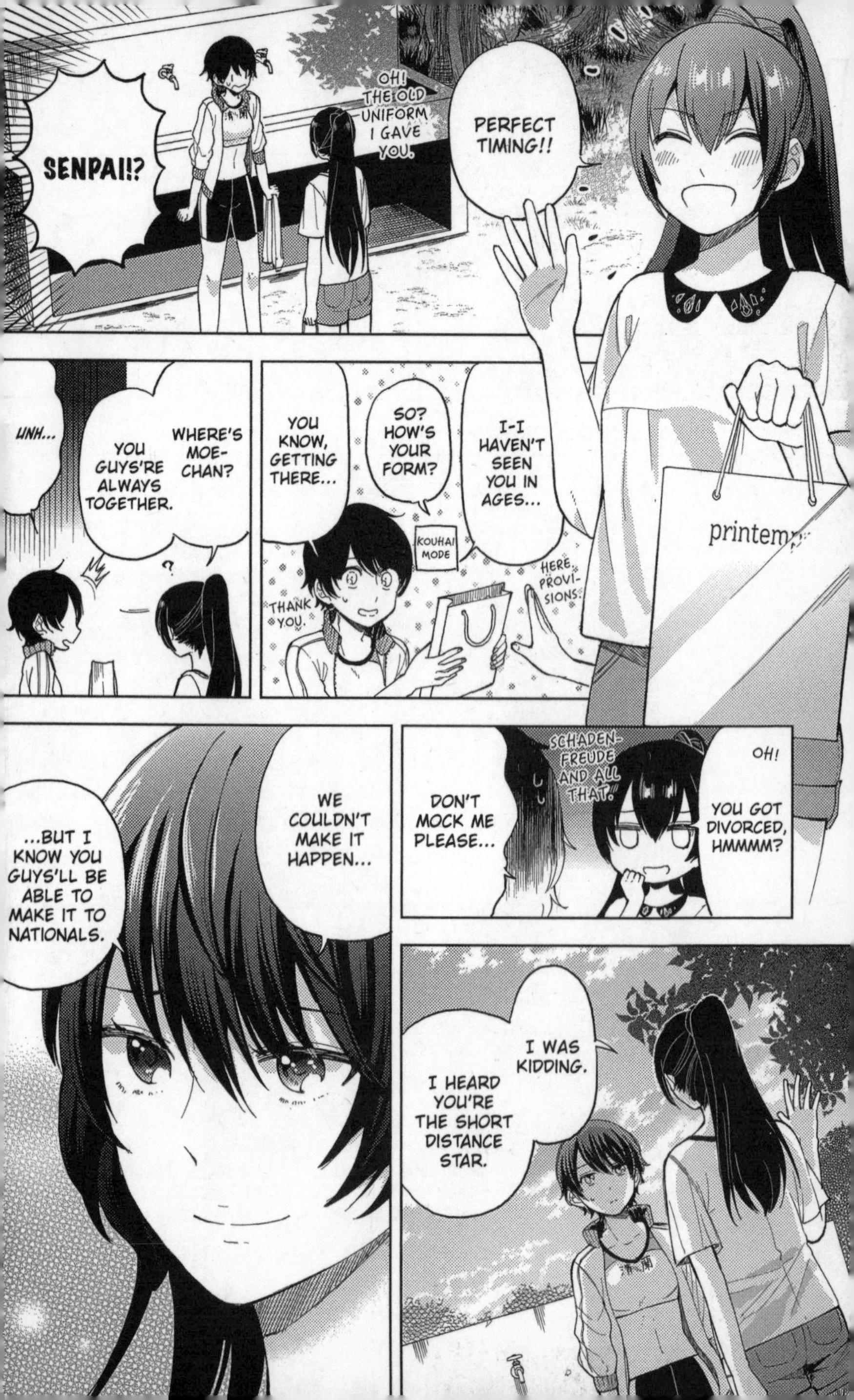
PERFECT TIMING!!
OH! THE OLD UNIFORM I GAVE YOU.
SENPAI!?
I-I HAVEN'T SEEN YOU IN AGES...
HERE. PROVISIONS.
KOUHAI MODE
SO? HOW'S YOUR FORM?
YOU KNOW, GETTING THERE...
THANK YOU.
WHERE'S MOE-CHAN?
YOU GUYS'RE ALWAYS TOGETHER.
UNH...
OH!
YOU GOT DIVORCED, HMMMM?
SCHADEN-FREUDE AND ALL THAT.
DON'T MOCK ME PLEASE...
I WAS KIDDING.
I HEARD YOU'RE THE SHORT DISTANCE STAR.
WE COULDN'T MAKE IT HAPPEN...
...BUT I KNOW YOU GUYS'LL BE ABLE TO MAKE IT TO NATIONALS.

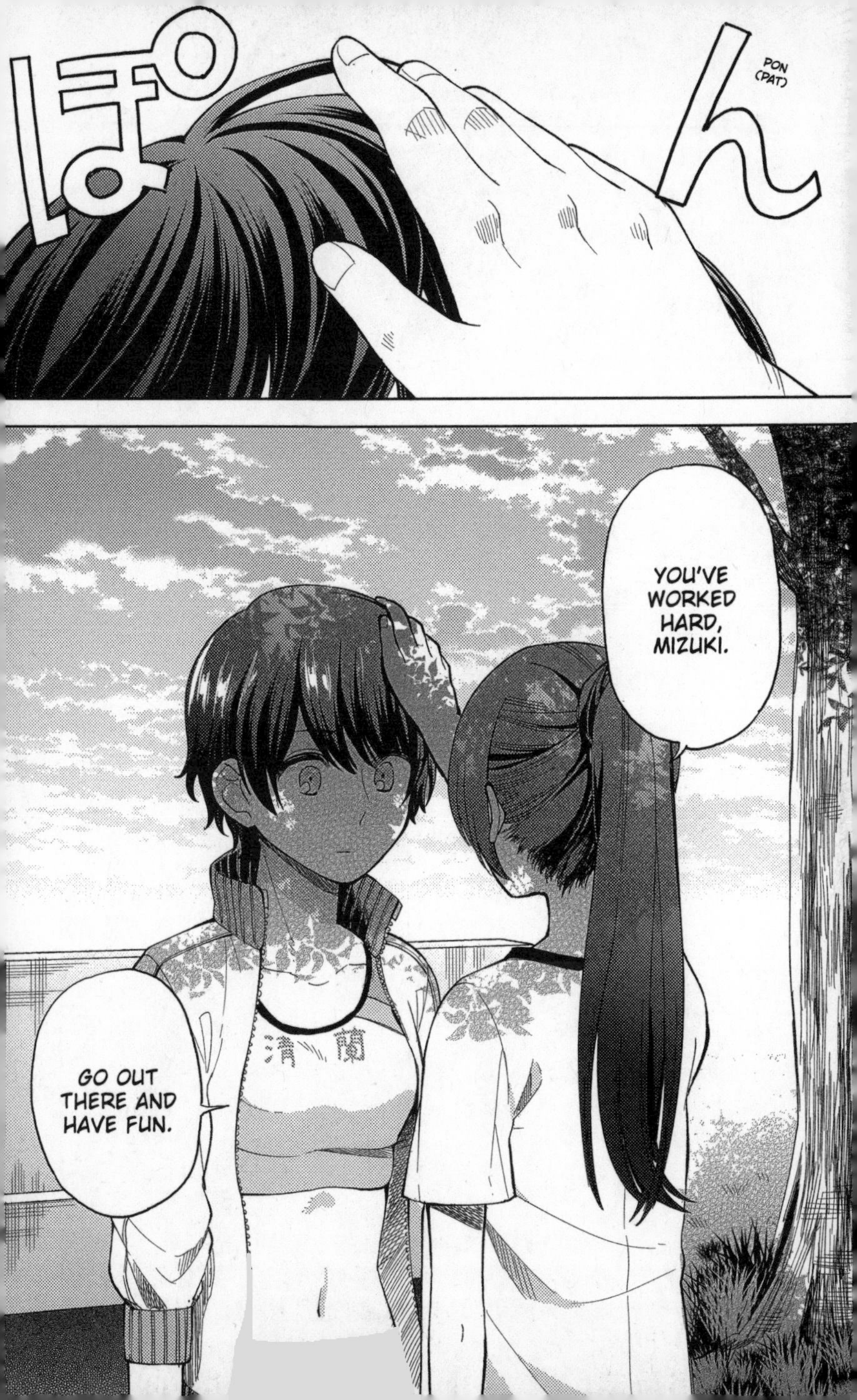
ぽん
PON (PAT)
YOU'VE WORKED HARD, MIZUKI.
清蘭
GO OUT THERE AND HAVE FUN.

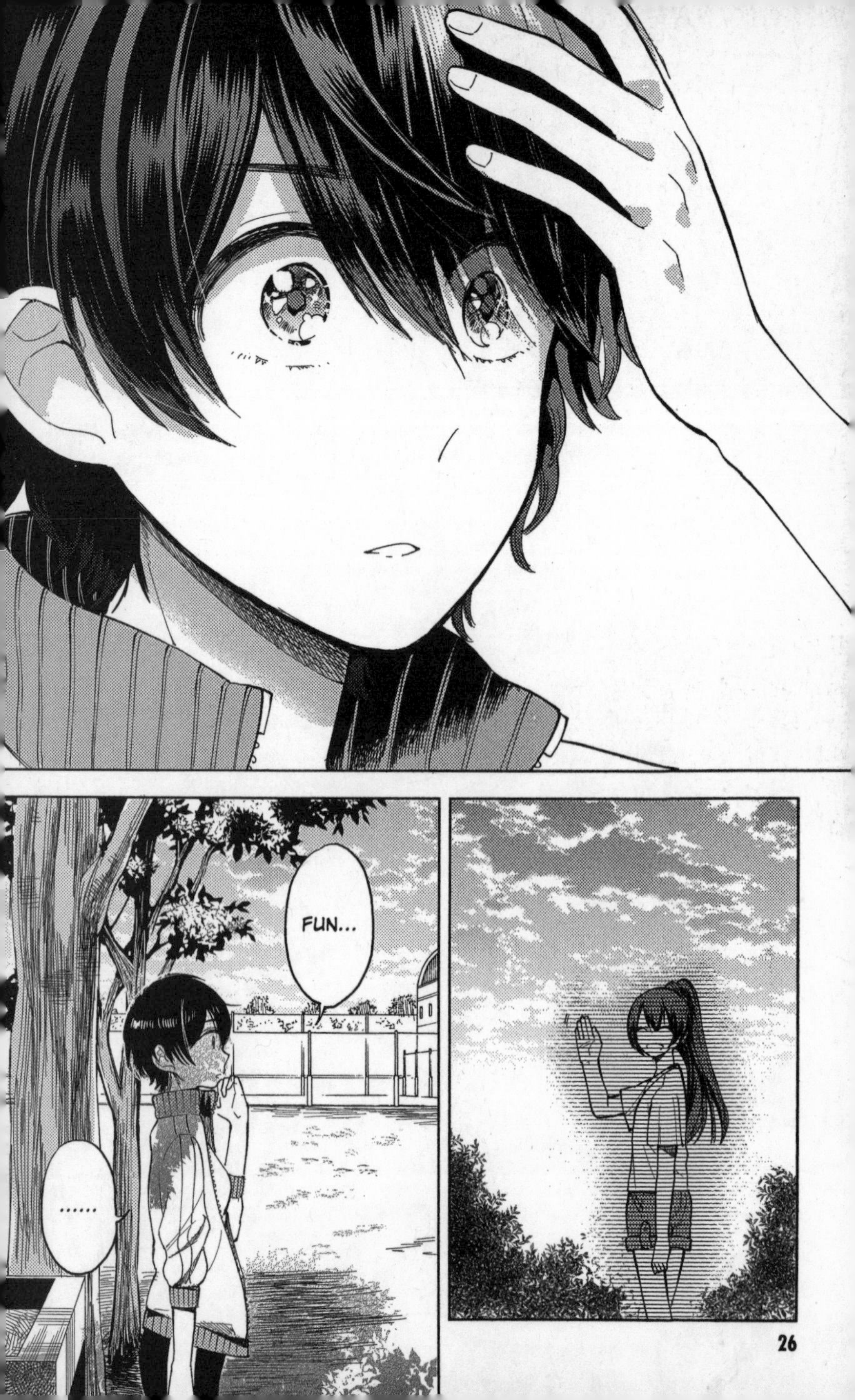
FUN...
......

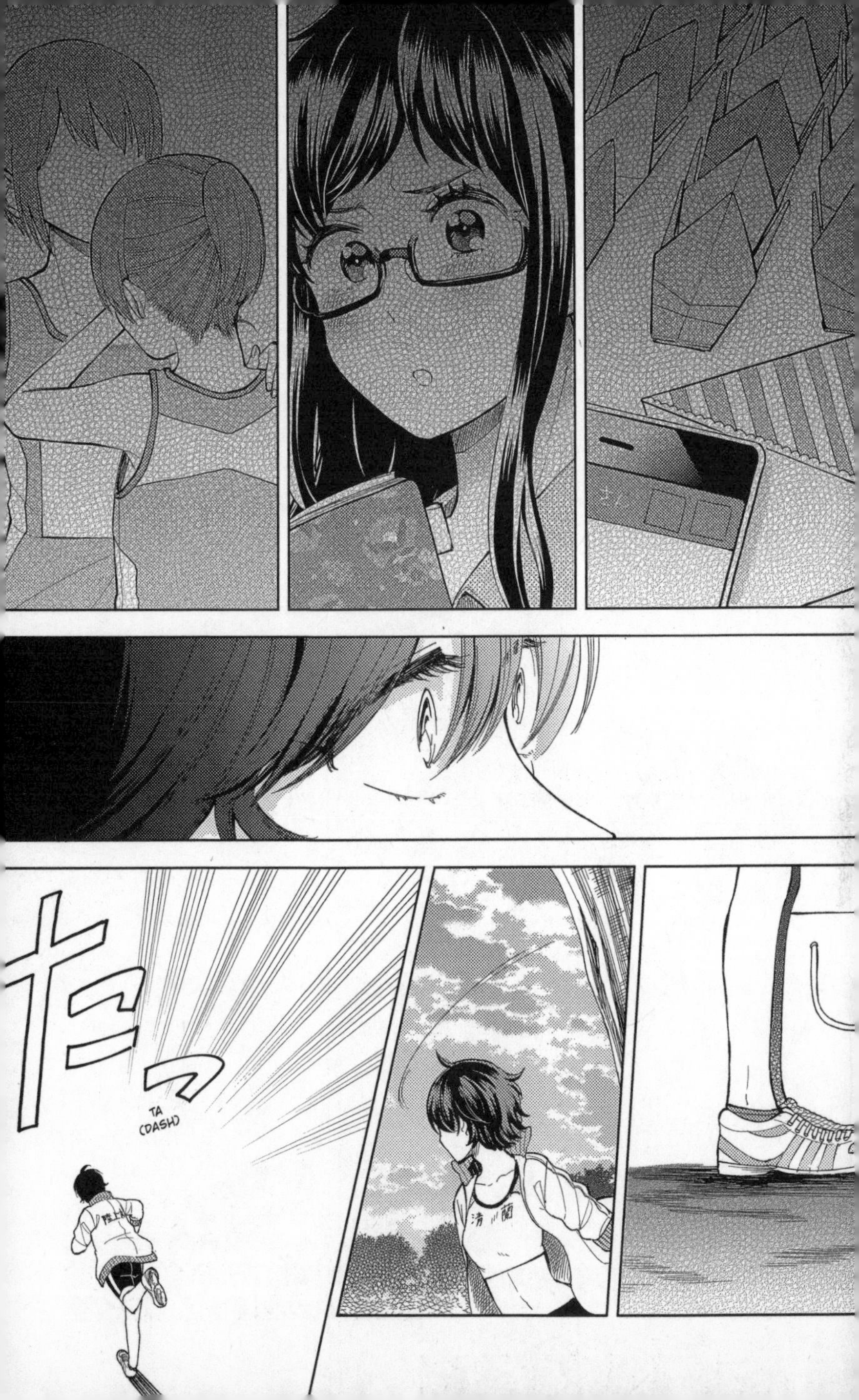
たっ
TA
(DASH)

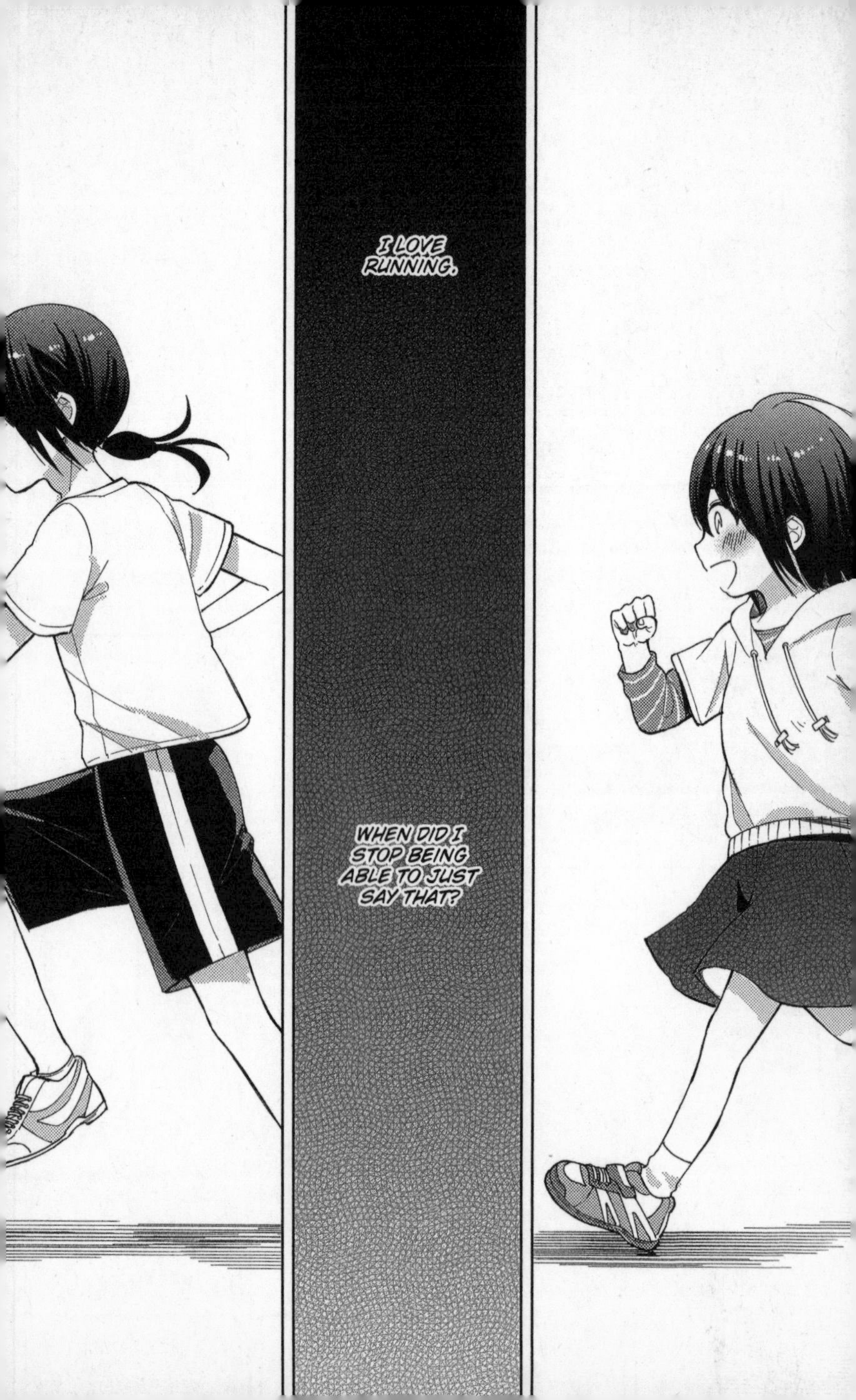
I LOVE RUNNING.
WHEN DID I STOP BEING ABLE TO JUST SAY THAT?

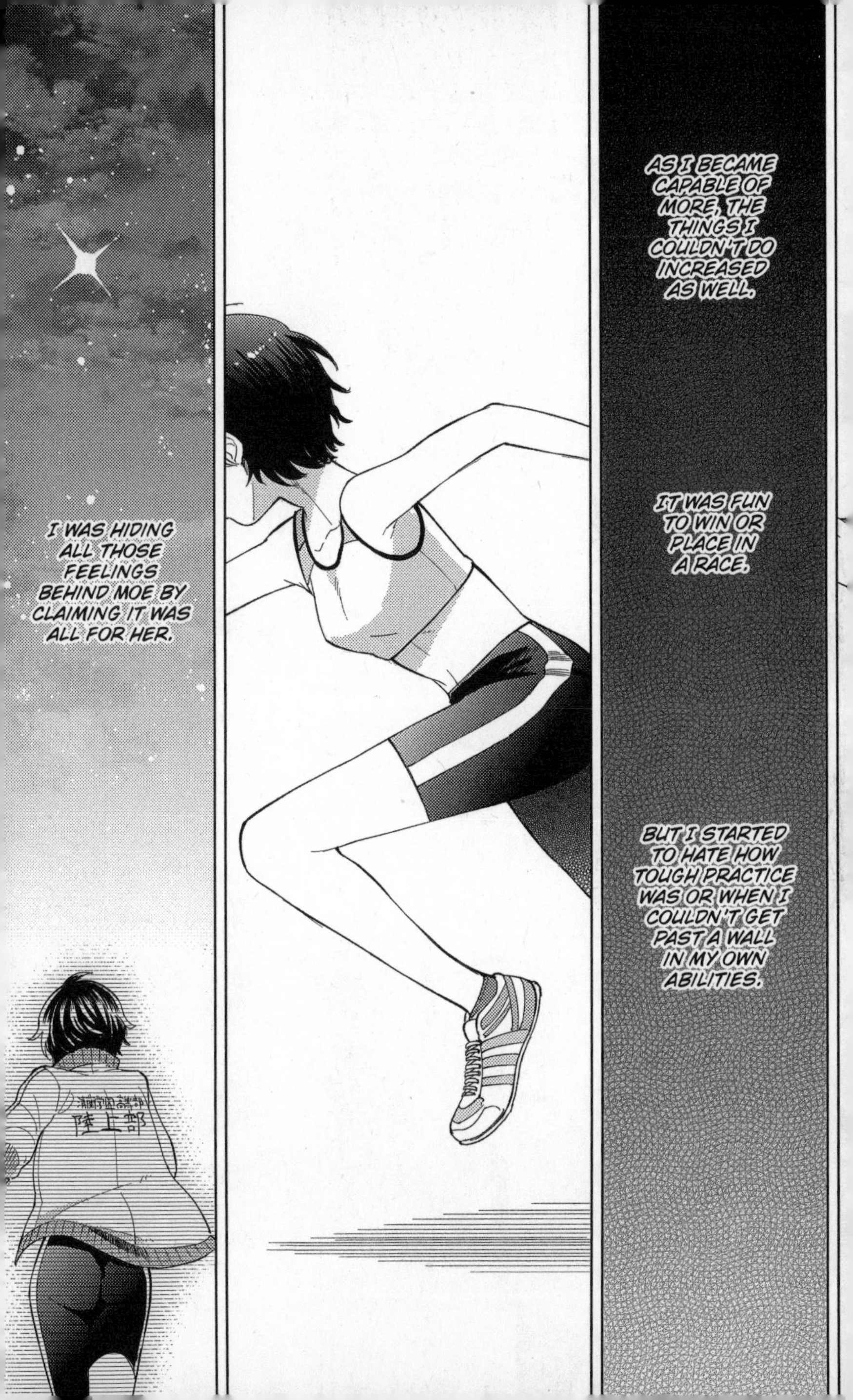
AS I BECAME CAPABLE OF MORE, THE THINGS I COULDN'T DO INCREASED AS WELL.
IT WAS FUN TO WIN OR PLACE IN A RACE.
BUT I STARTED TO HATE HOW TOUGH PRACTICE WAS OR WHEN I COULDN'T GET PAST A WALL IN MY OWN ABILITIES.
I WAS HIDING ALL THOSE FEELINGS BEHIND MOE BY CLAIMING IT WAS ALL FOR HER.
陸上部

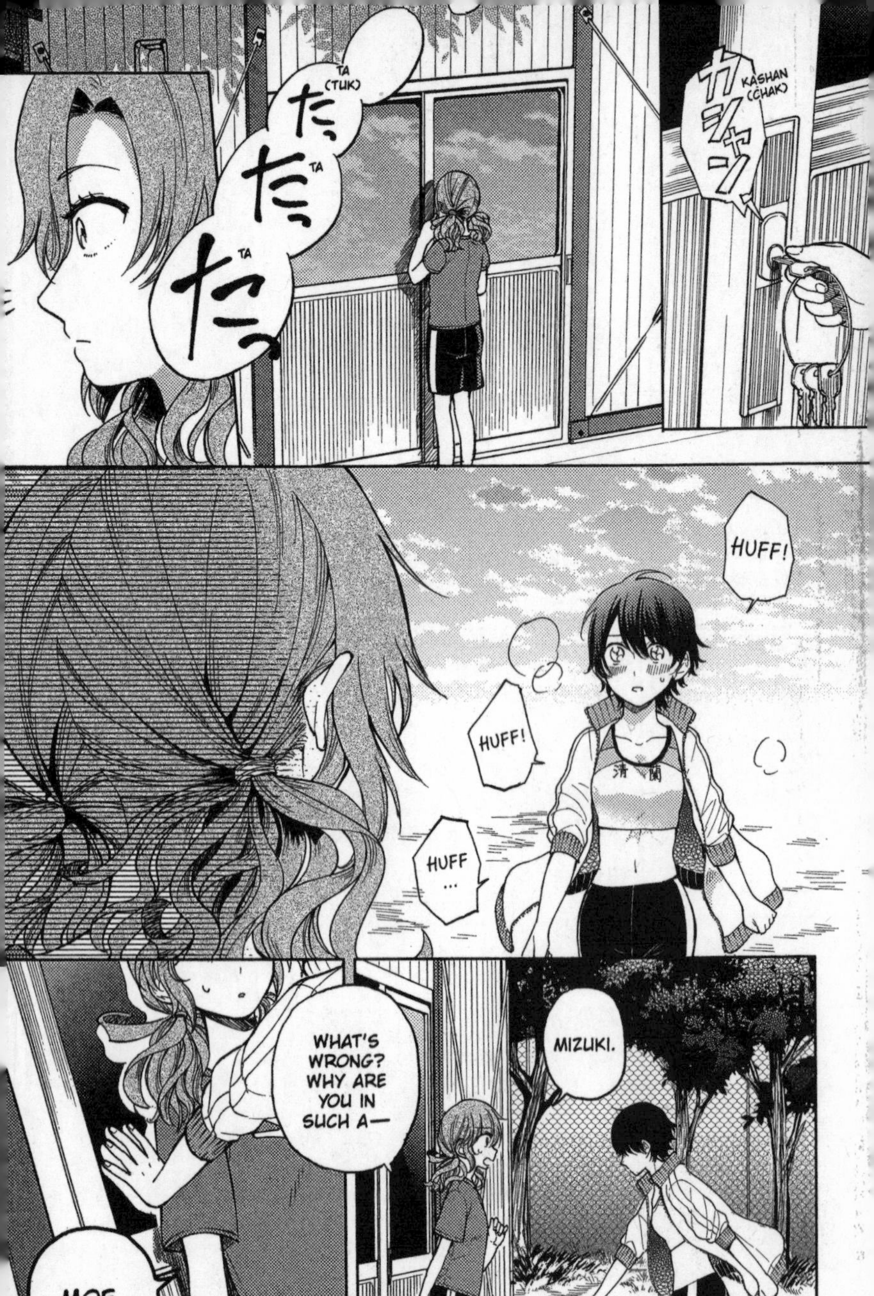
カシャン
KASHAN (CHAK)
た、
TA (TUK)
た、
TA
たっ
TA
HUFF!
HUFF!
HUFF ...
MIZUKI.
WHAT'S WRONG? WHY ARE YOU IN SUCH A—
MOE.

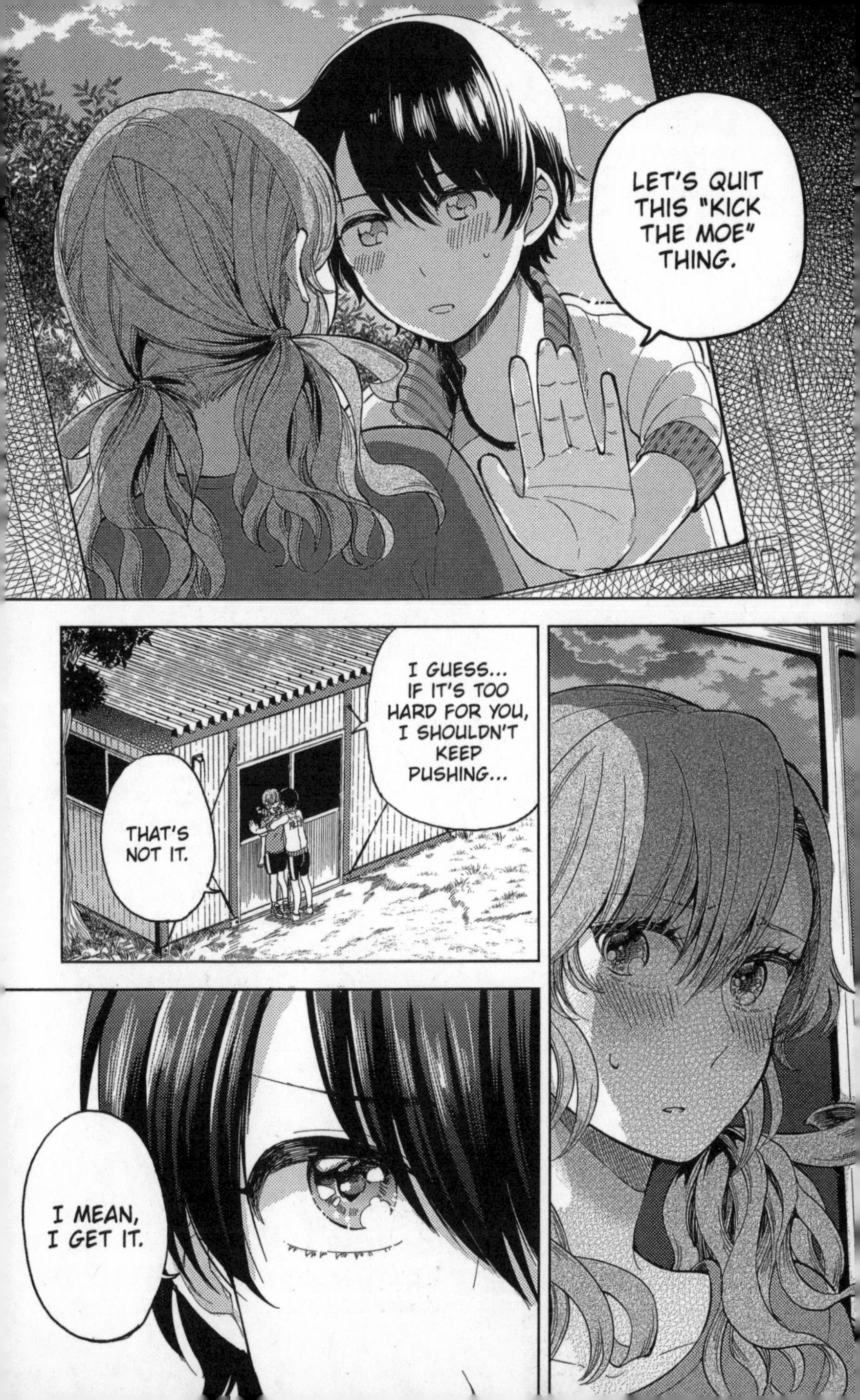
LET'S QUIT THIS "KICK THE MOE" THING.
I GUESS... IF IT'S TOO HARD FOR YOU, I SHOULDN'T KEEP PUSHING...
THAT'S NOT IT.
I MEAN, I GET IT.

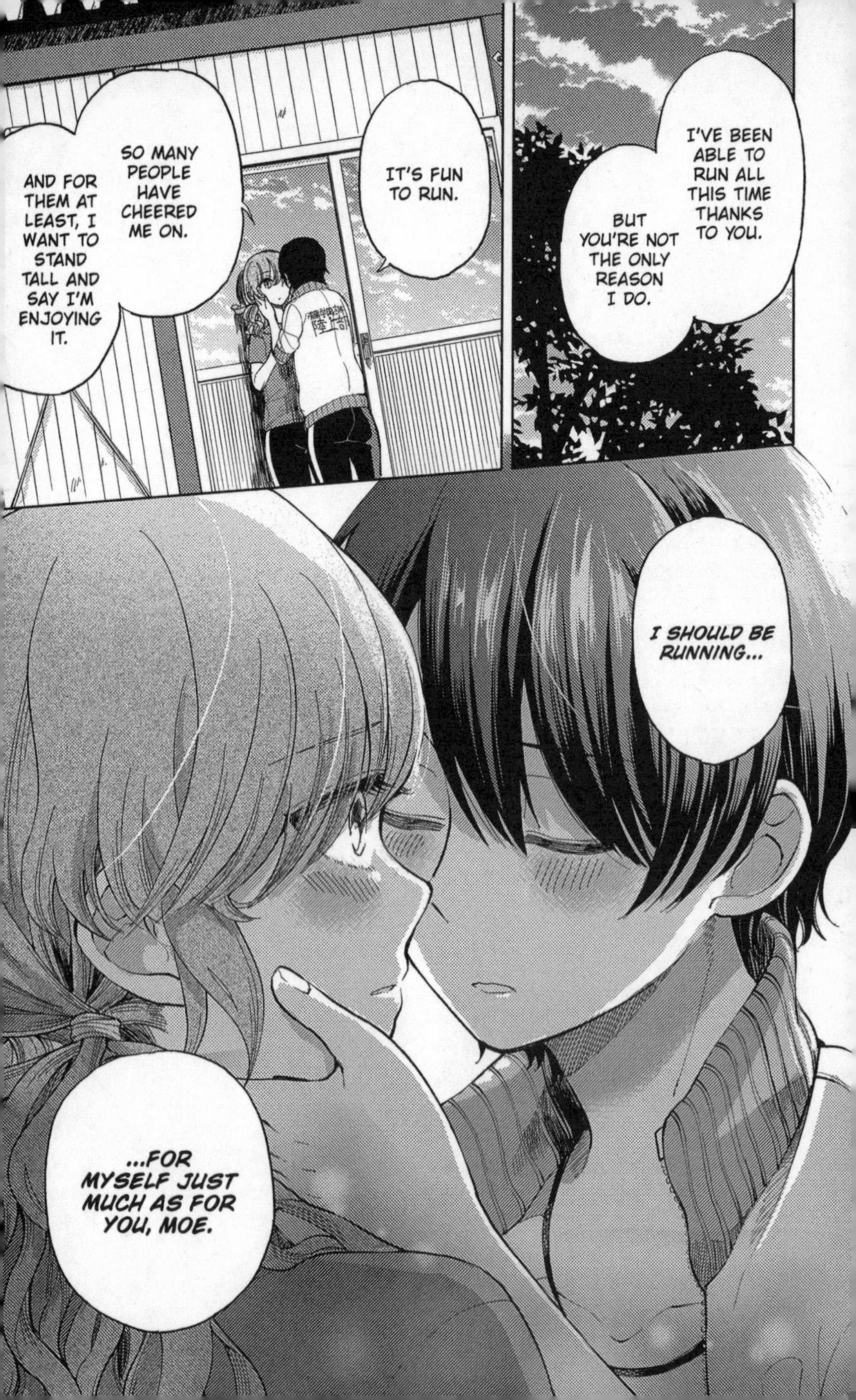
I'VE BEEN ABLE TO RUN ALL THIS TIME THANKS TO YOU.
BUT YOU'RE NOT THE ONLY REASON I DO.
IT'S FUN TO RUN.
SO MANY PEOPLE HAVE CHEERED ME ON.
AND FOR THEM AT LEAST, I WANT TO STAND TALL AND SAY I'M ENJOYING IT.
陸上部
I SHOULD BE RUNNING...
...FOR MYSELF JUST MUCH AS FOR YOU, MOE.

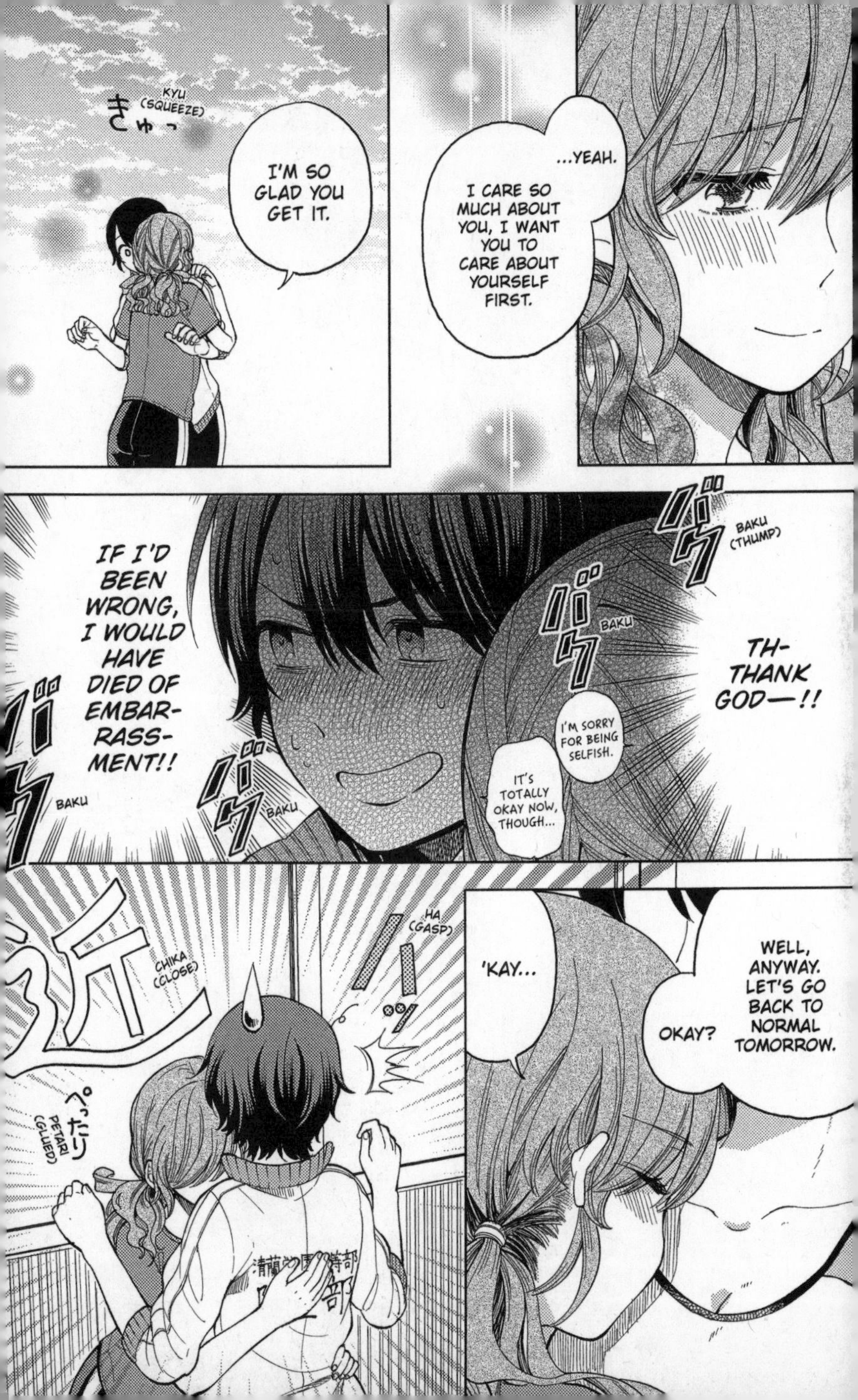
...YEAH.
I CARE SO MUCH ABOUT YOU, I WANT YOU TO CARE ABOUT YOURSELF FIRST.
I'M SO GLAD YOU GET IT.
KYU (SQUEEZE)
きゅっ
BAKU (THUMP)
BAKU
TH-THANK GOD—!!
I'M SORRY FOR BEING SELFISH.
IT'S TOTALLY OKAY NOW, THOUGH...
IF I'D BEEN WRONG, I WOULD HAVE DIED OF EMBARRASSMENT!!
BAKU
BAKU
WELL, ANYWAY. LET'S GO BACK TO NORMAL TOMORROW.
OKAY?
'KAY...
HA (GASP)
CHIKA (CLOSE)
ぺったり
PETARI (GLUED)

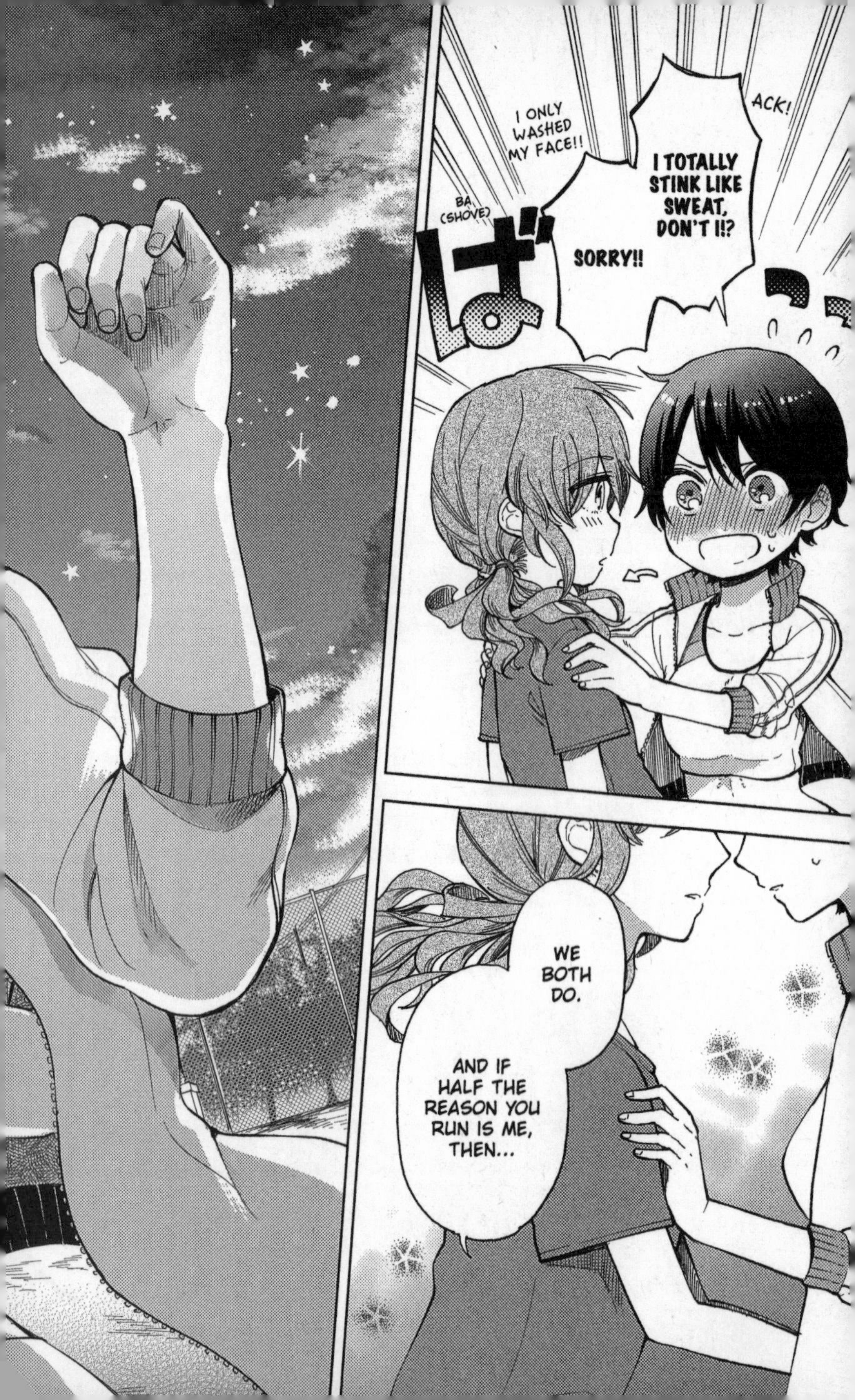
ACK!
I TOTALLY STINK LIKE SWEAT, DON'T I!?
SORRY!!
I ONLY WASHED MY FACE!!
BA (SHOVE)
ば
WE BOTH DO.
AND IF HALF THE REASON YOU RUN IS ME, THEN...

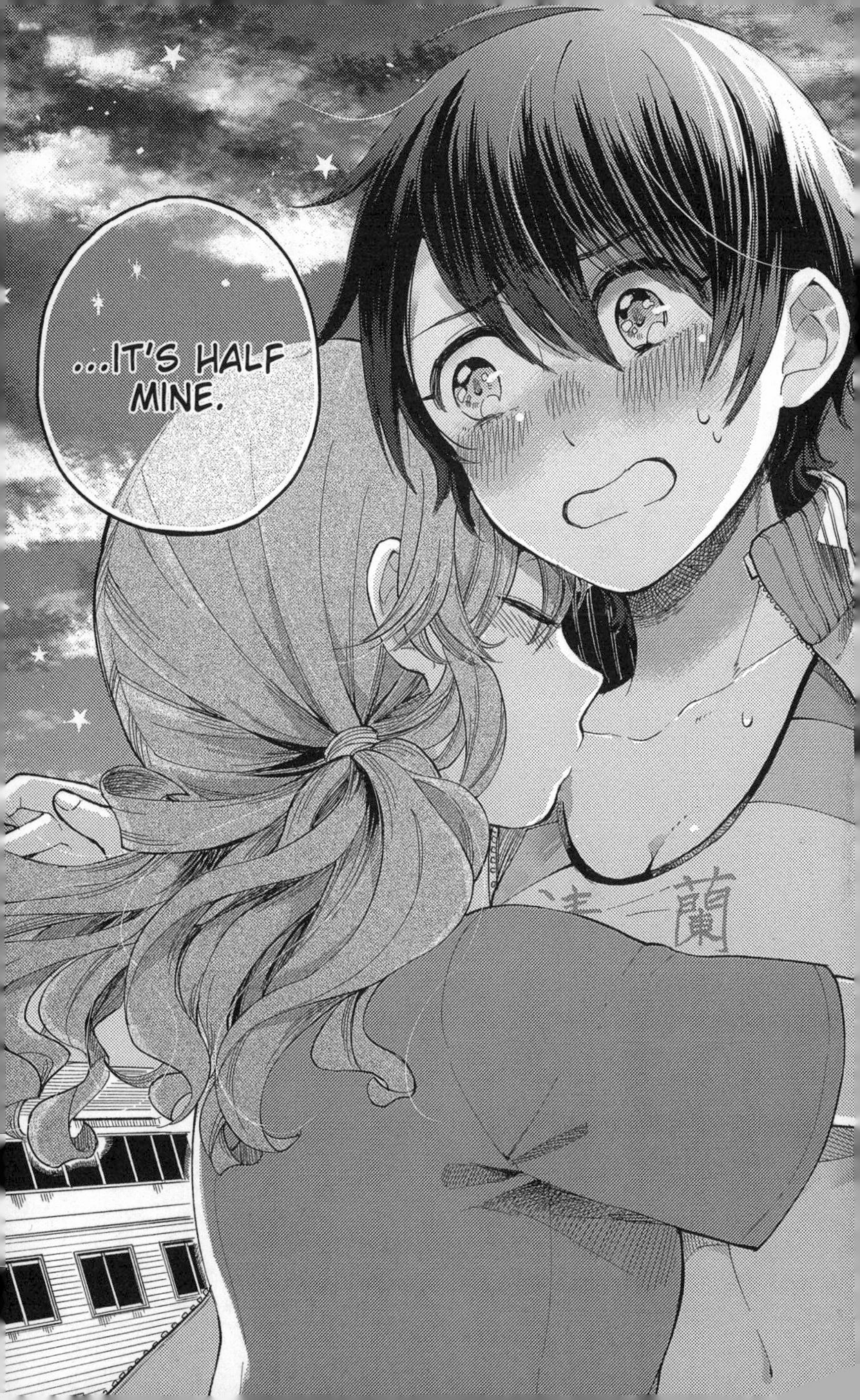
...IT'S HALF MINE.

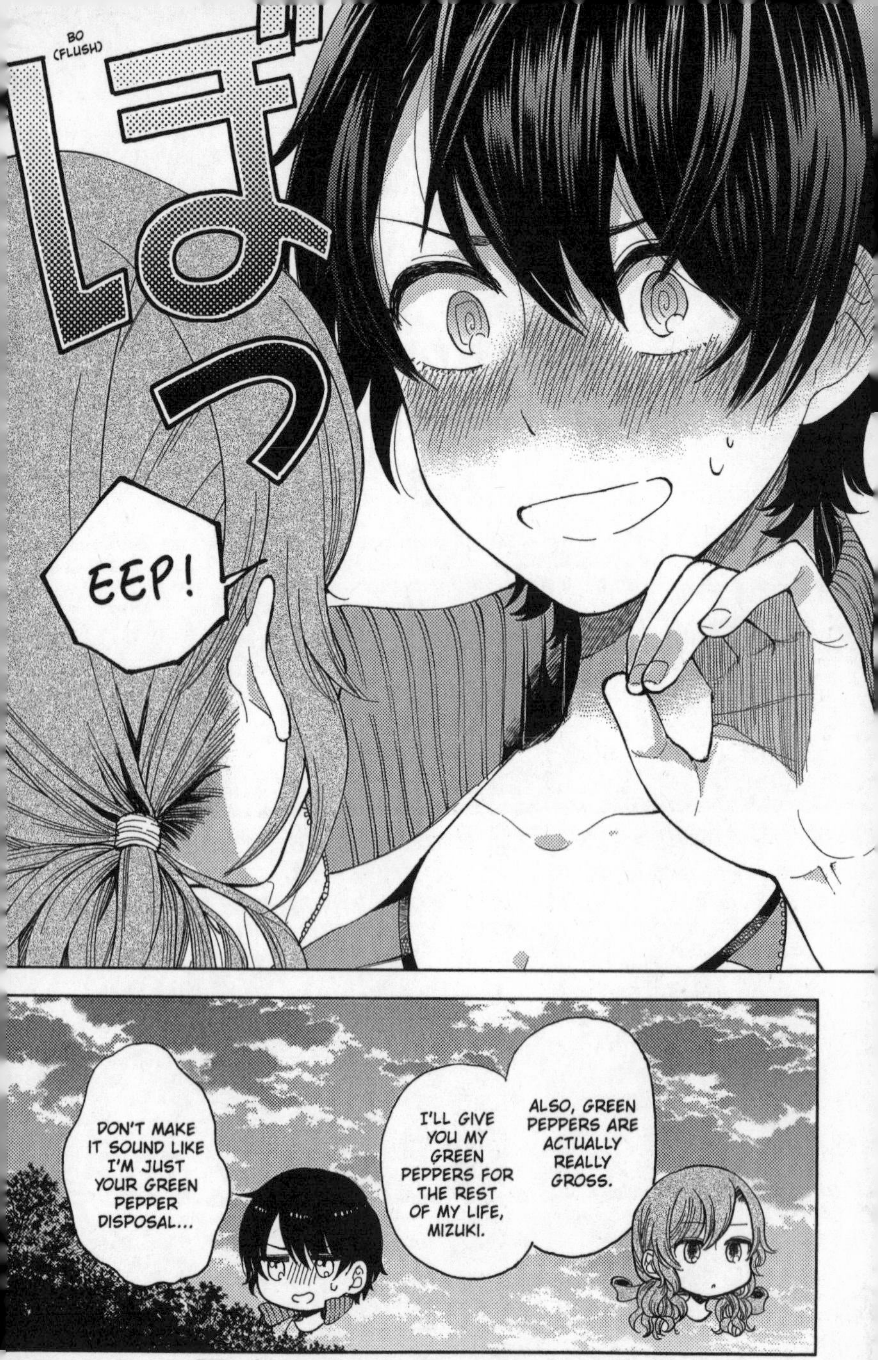
BO
(FLUSH)
EEP!
I'LL GIVE YOU MY GREEN PEPPERS FOR THE REST OF MY LIFE, MIZUKI.
ALSO, GREEN PEPPERS ARE ACTUALLY REALLY GROSS.
DON'T MAKE IT SOUND LIKE I'M JUST YOUR GREEN PEPPER DISPOSAL...

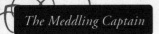

The Meddling Captain

HOMARE
THIRD-YEAR, TRACK TEAM. SHE'S SUNTANNED BEFORE SHE REALIZES...

YUI
THIRD-YEAR, TRACK AND FIELD CAPTAIN.

KISS THEATER: WHAT'S BEHIND THE STORY!? ✷ PEOPLE OTHER THAN THE MAIN CHARACTERS HAVE STORIES TOO. HERE, WE PRESENT THE "LITTLE LOVE" STORIES HAPPENING BEHIND THE SCENES.

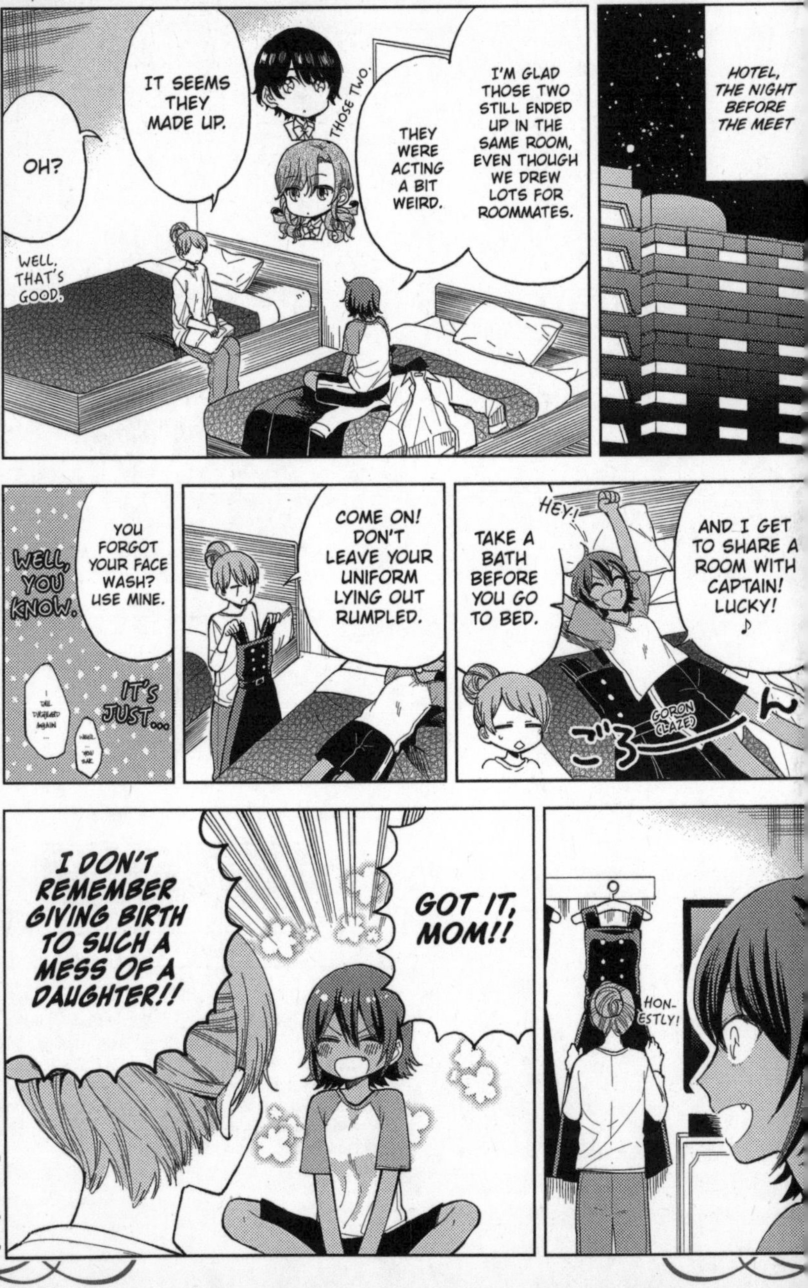
HOTEL, THE NIGHT BEFORE THE MEET
I'M GLAD THOSE TWO STILL ENDED UP IN THE SAME ROOM, EVEN THOUGH WE DREW LOTS FOR ROOMMATES.
THEY WERE ACTING A BIT WEIRD.
THOSE TWO.
IT SEEMS THEY MADE UP.
OH?
WELL, THAT'S GOOD.
AND I GET TO SHARE A ROOM WITH CAPTAIN! LUCKY! ♪
HEY-!
TAKE A BATH BEFORE YOU GO TO BED.
GORON (LAZE)
COME ON! DON'T LEAVE YOUR UNIFORM LYING OUT RUMPLED.
YOU FORGOT YOUR FACE WASH? USE MINE.
WELL, YOU KNOW.
IT'S JUST...
HON-ESTLY!
GOT IT, MOM!!
I DON'T REMEMBER GIVING BIRTH TO SUCH A MESS OF A DAUGHTER!!

Mizuki Senoo

Mizuki Senoo

Third-year student at Seiran Academy High School. Track team sprinter. With her boyish looks and her slightly pessimistic attitude, she is the prince of Seiran Academy. Even with the start of a new school year, Moe is number one as always. But given her looming retirement from the team and graduation from school, Mizuki seems to be thinking about things in her own way.

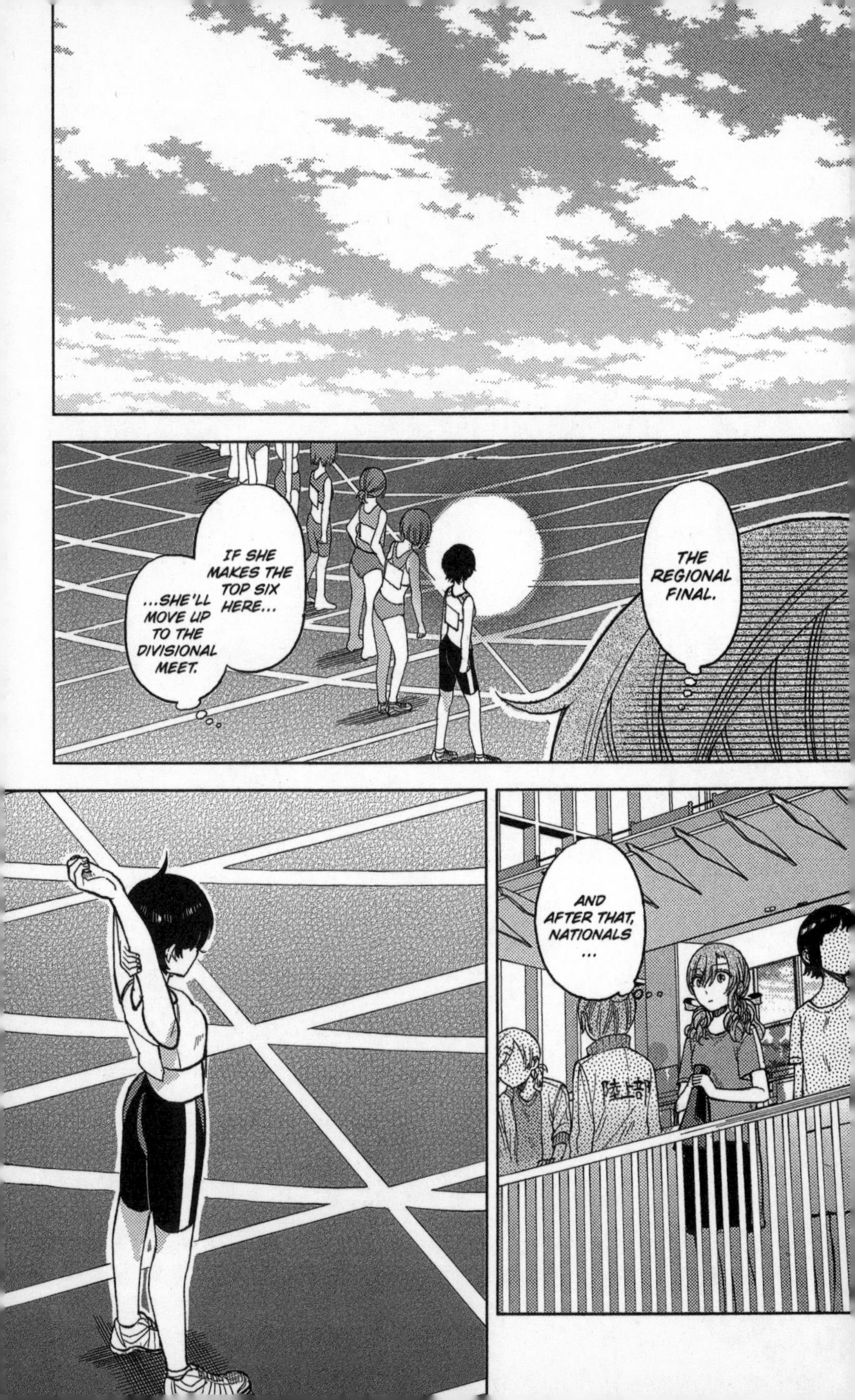
THE REGIONAL FINAL.
IF SHE MAKES THE TOP SIX HERE...
...SHE'LL MOVE UP TO THE DIVISIONAL MEET.
AND AFTER THAT, NATIONALS ...

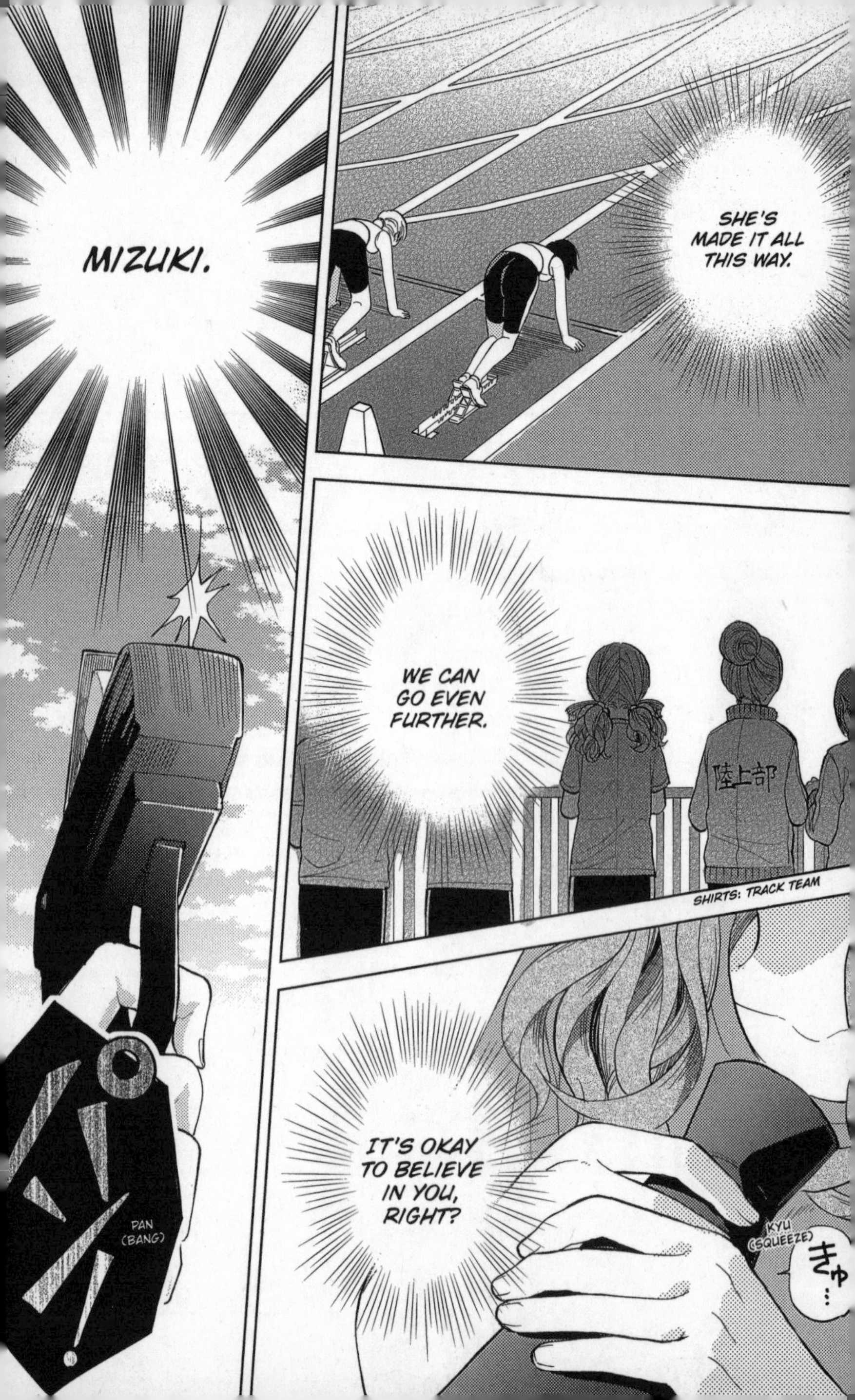
SHE'S MADE IT ALL THIS WAY.
WE CAN GO EVEN FURTHER.
陸上部
SHIRTS: TRACK TEAM
IT'S OKAY TO BELIEVE IN YOU, RIGHT?
きゅ…
KYU (SQUEEZE)
MIZUKI.
PAN (BANG)

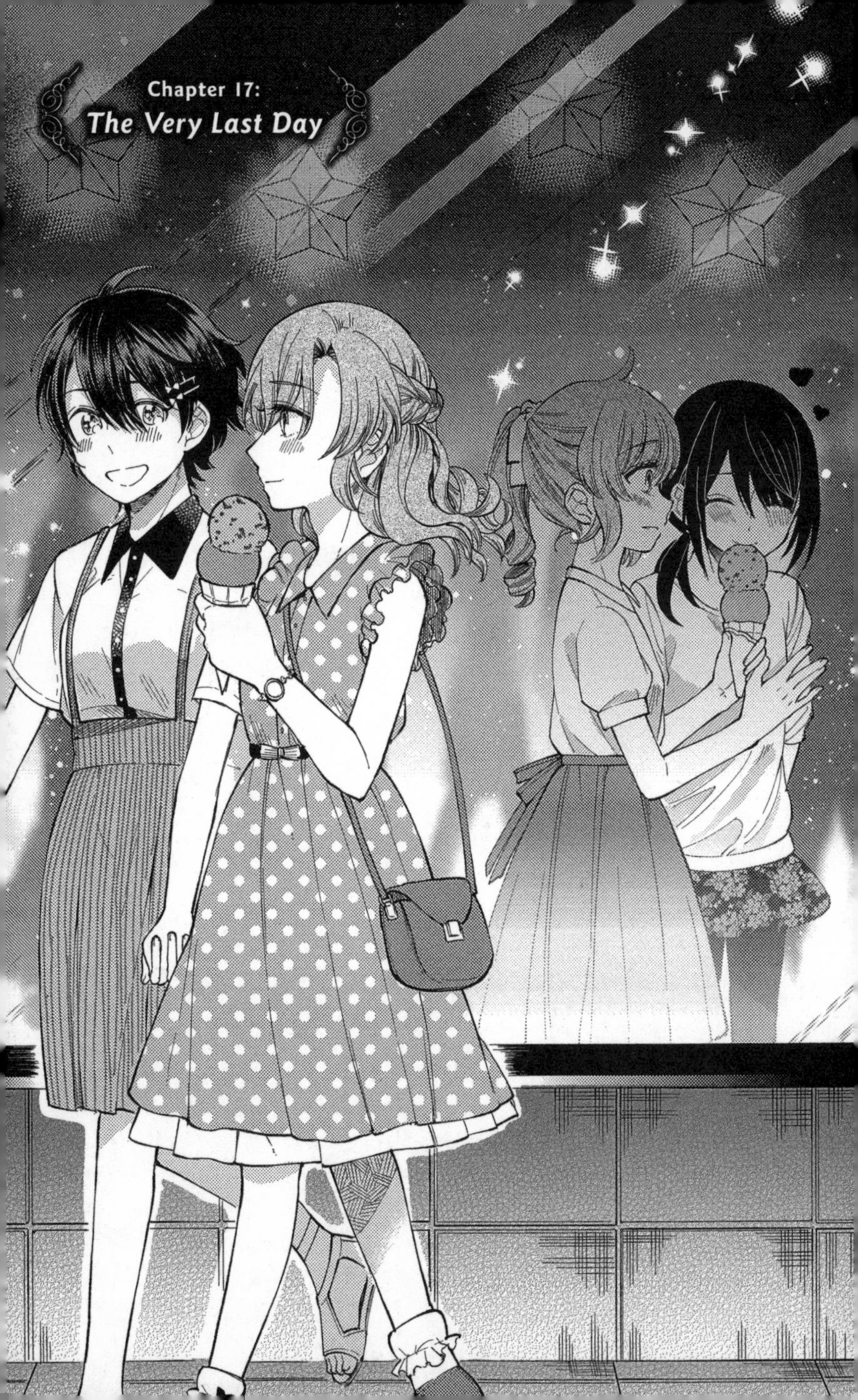
Chapter 17:
The Very Last Day

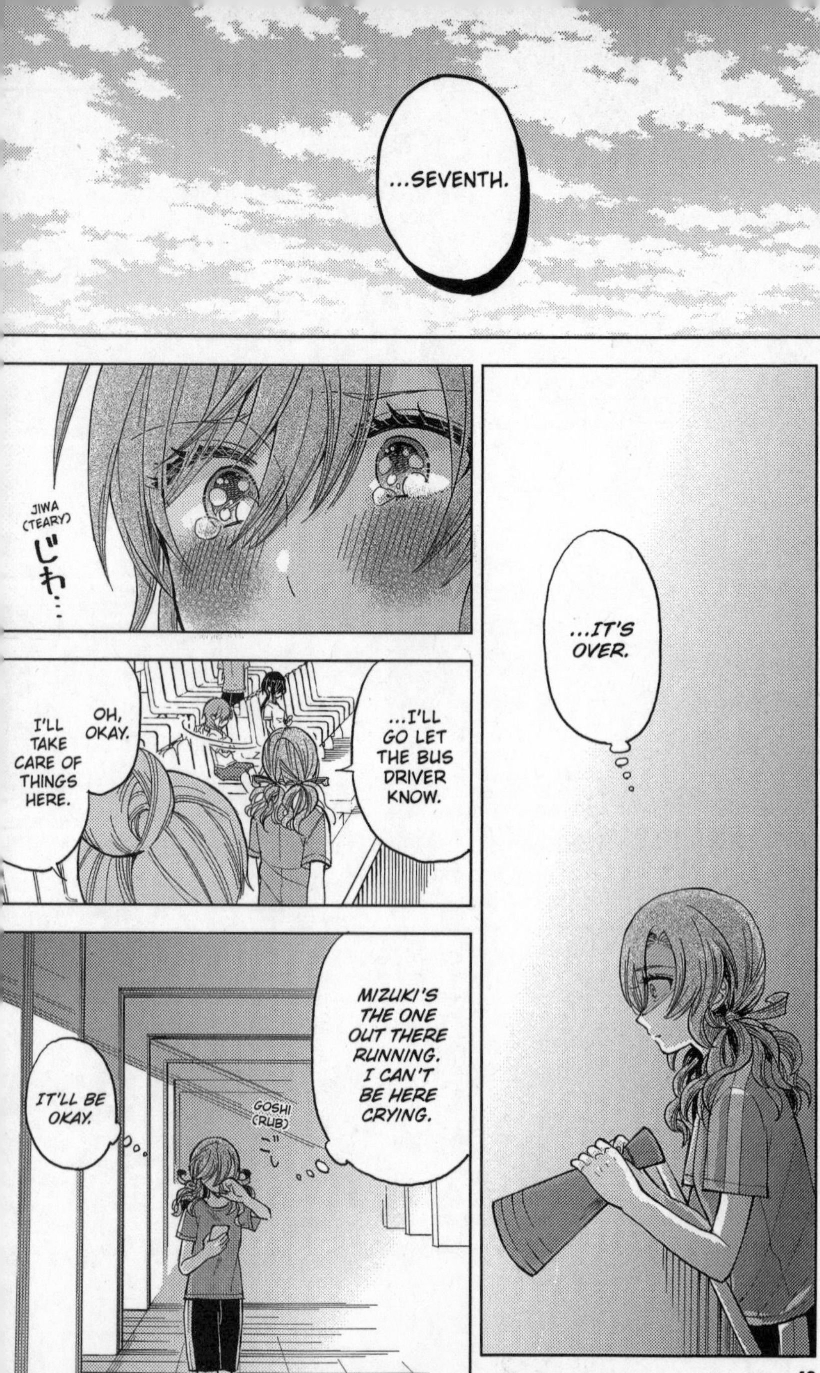
...SEVENTH.
...IT'S OVER.
JIWA (TEARY)
じわ…
...I'LL GO LET THE BUS DRIVER KNOW.
OH, OKAY.
I'LL TAKE CARE OF THINGS HERE.
MIZUKI'S THE ONE OUT THERE RUNNING. I CAN'T BE HERE CRYING.
GOSHI (RUB)
ごし
IT'LL BE OKAY.

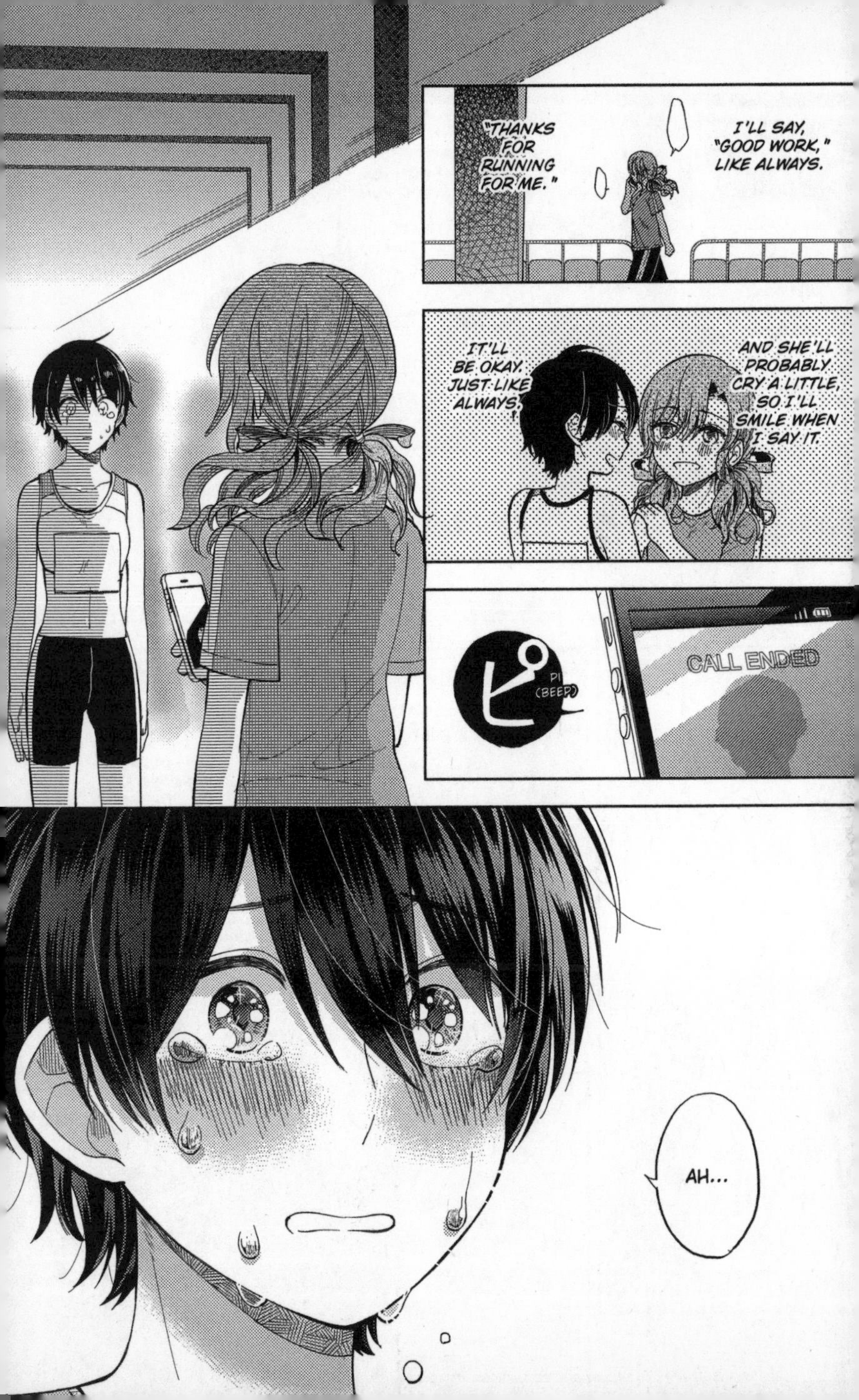
I'LL SAY, "GOOD WORK," LIKE ALWAYS.
"THANKS FOR RUNNING FOR ME."
AND SHE'LL PROBABLY CRY A LITTLE, SO I'LL SMILE WHEN I SAY IT.
IT'LL BE OKAY. JUST LIKE ALWAYS.
CALL ENDED
PI (BEEP)
AH...

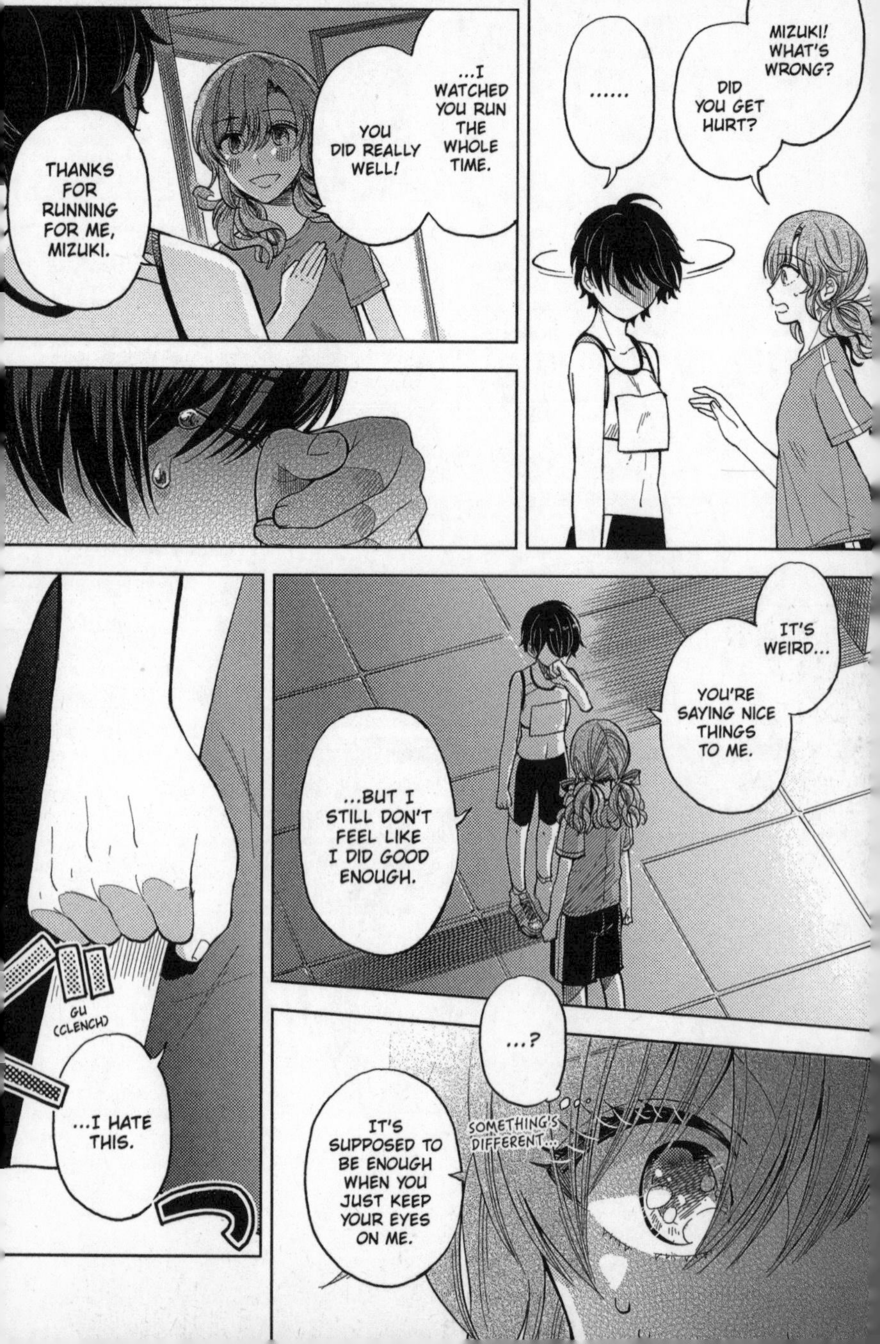
MIZUKI! WHAT'S WRONG? DID YOU GET HURT?
......
...I WATCHED YOU RUN THE WHOLE TIME.
YOU DID REALLY WELL!
THANKS FOR RUNNING FOR ME, MIZUKI.
IT'S WEIRD...
YOU'RE SAYING NICE THINGS TO ME.
...BUT I STILL DON'T FEEL LIKE I DID GOOD ENOUGH.
...?
SOMETHING'S DIFFERENT...
IT'S SUPPOSED TO BE ENOUGH WHEN YOU JUST KEEP YOUR EYES ON ME.
GU (CLENCH)
...I HATE THIS.

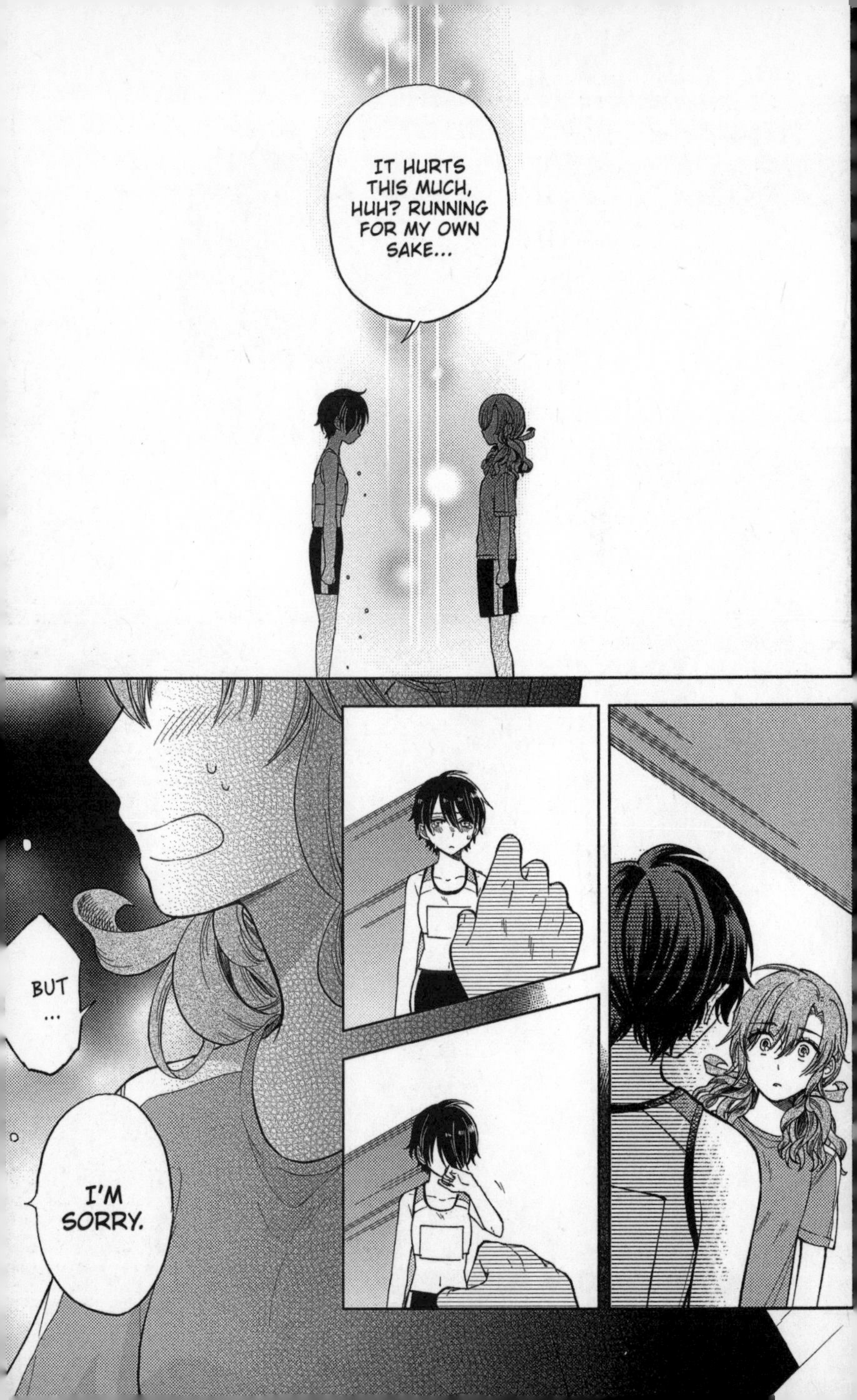
IT HURTS THIS MUCH, HUH? RUNNING FOR MY OWN SAKE...
BUT ...
I'M SORRY.

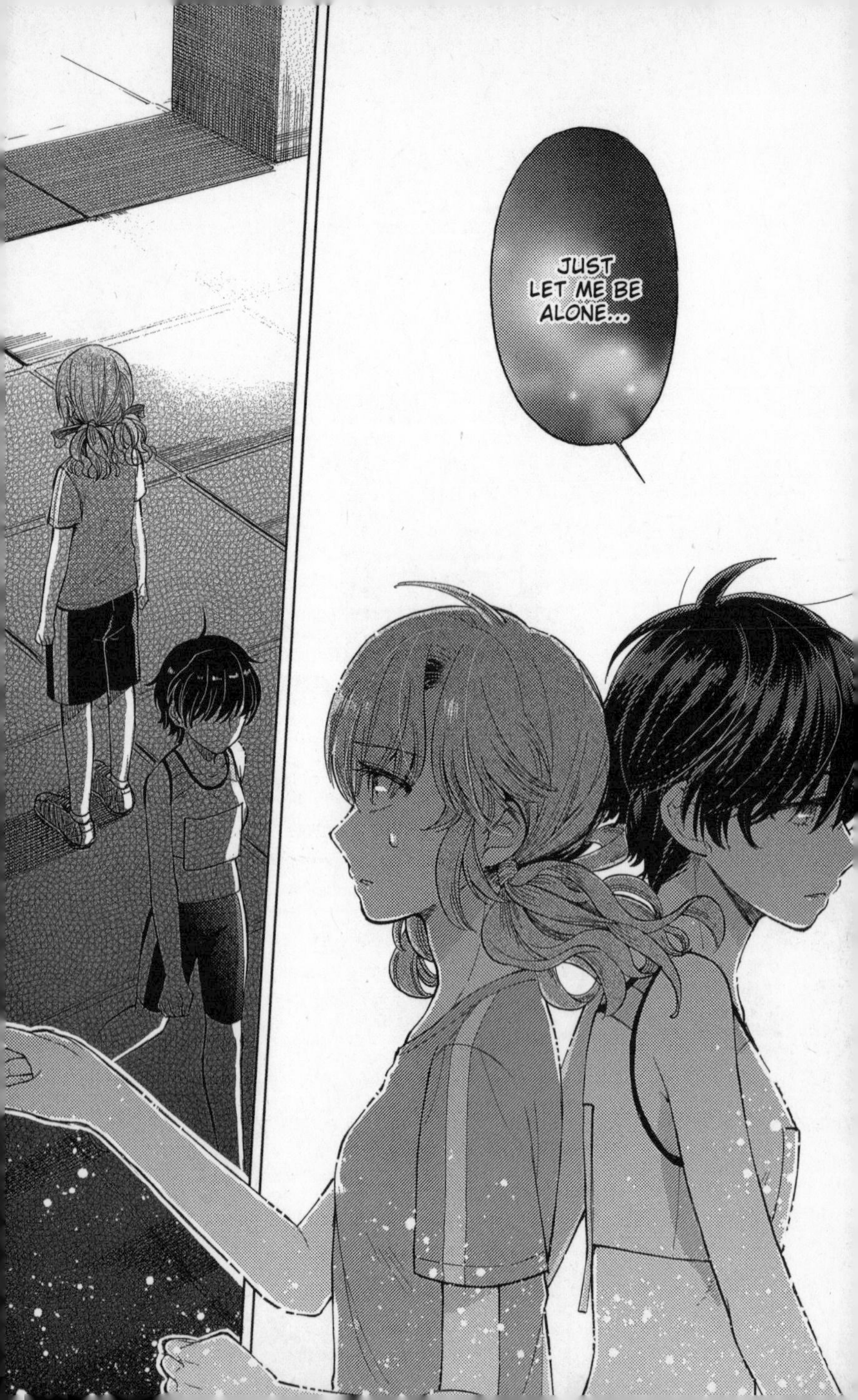
JUST LET ME BE ALONE...

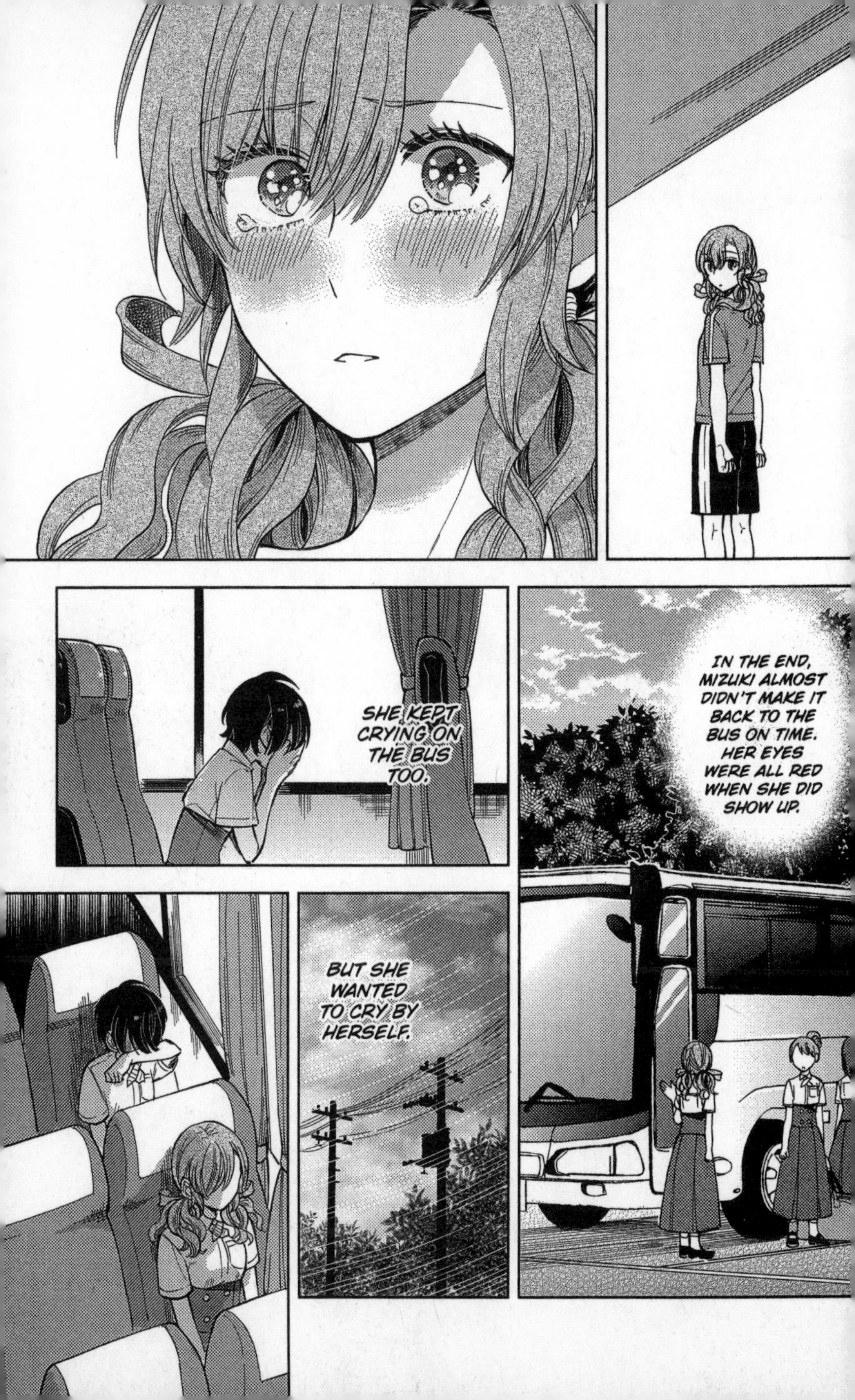
IN THE END, MIZUKI ALMOST DIDN'T MAKE IT BACK TO THE BUS ON TIME. HER EYES WERE ALL RED WHEN SHE DID SHOW UP.
SHE KEPT CRYING ON THE BUS TOO.
BUT SHE WANTED TO CRY BY HERSELF.

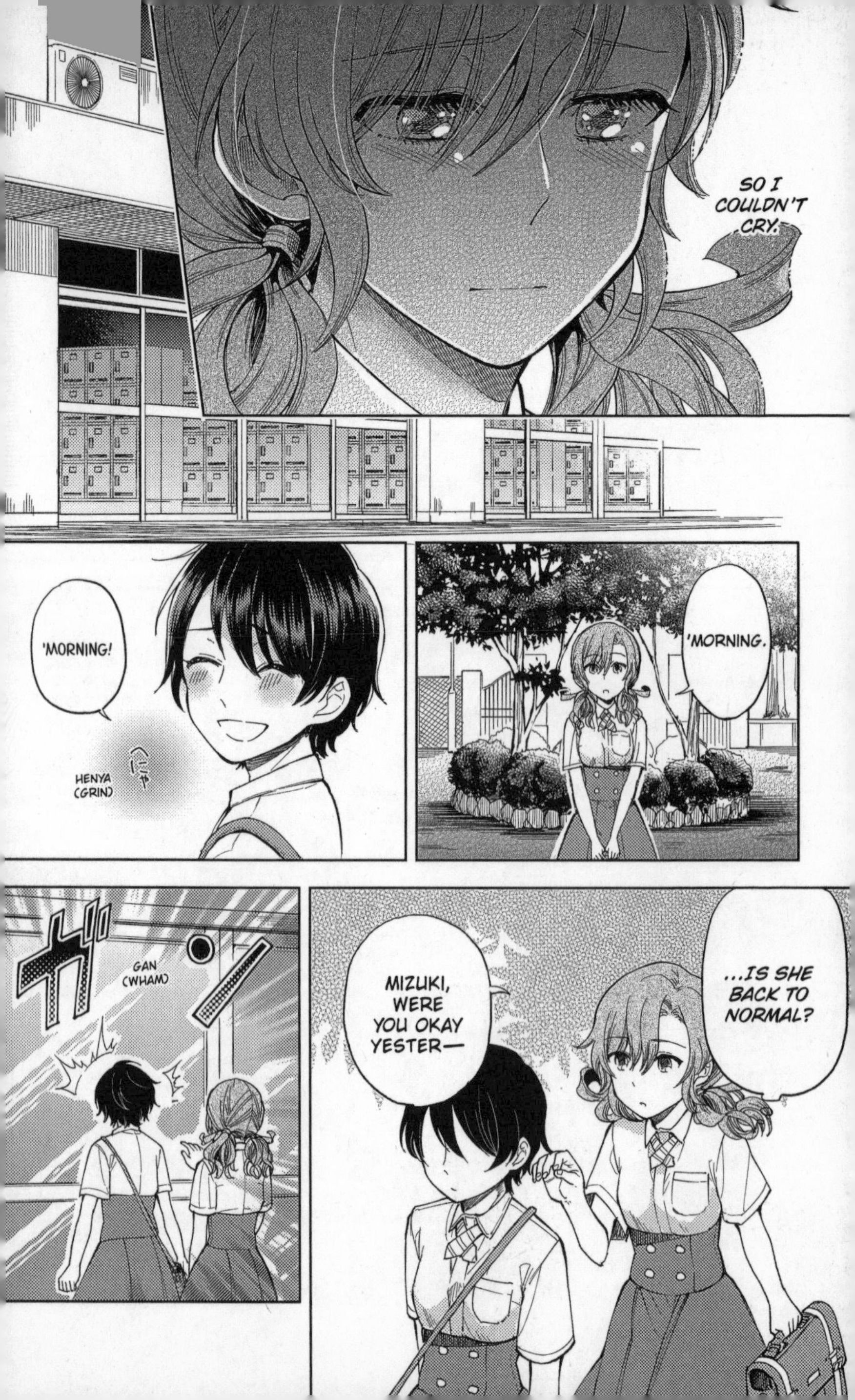
SO I COULDN'T CRY.
'MORNING.
'MORNING!
HENYA (GRIN)
...IS SHE BACK TO NORMAL?
MIZUKI, WERE YOU OKAY YESTER—
GAN (WHAM)

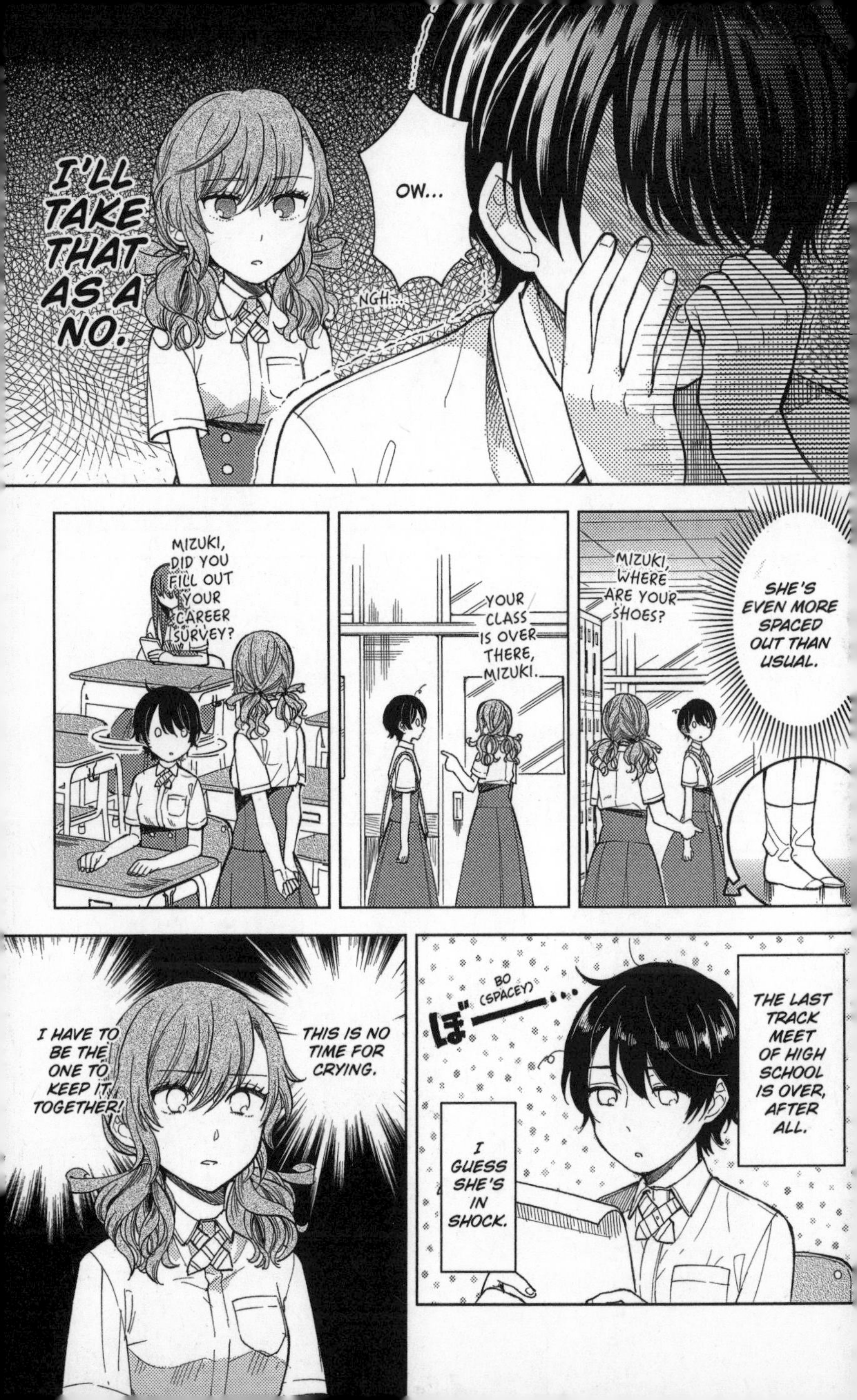
OW...
NGH...
I'LL TAKE THAT AS A NO.
SHE'S EVEN MORE SPACED OUT THAN USUAL.
MIZUKI, WHERE ARE YOUR SHOES?
YOUR CLASS IS OVER THERE, MIZUKI.
MIZUKI, DID YOU FILL OUT YOUR CAREER SURVEY?
THE LAST TRACK MEET OF HIGH SCHOOL IS OVER, AFTER ALL.
ぼー…
BO (SPACEY)
I GUESS SHE'S IN SHOCK.
THIS IS NO TIME FOR CRYING.
I HAVE TO BE THE ONE TO KEEP IT TOGETHER!

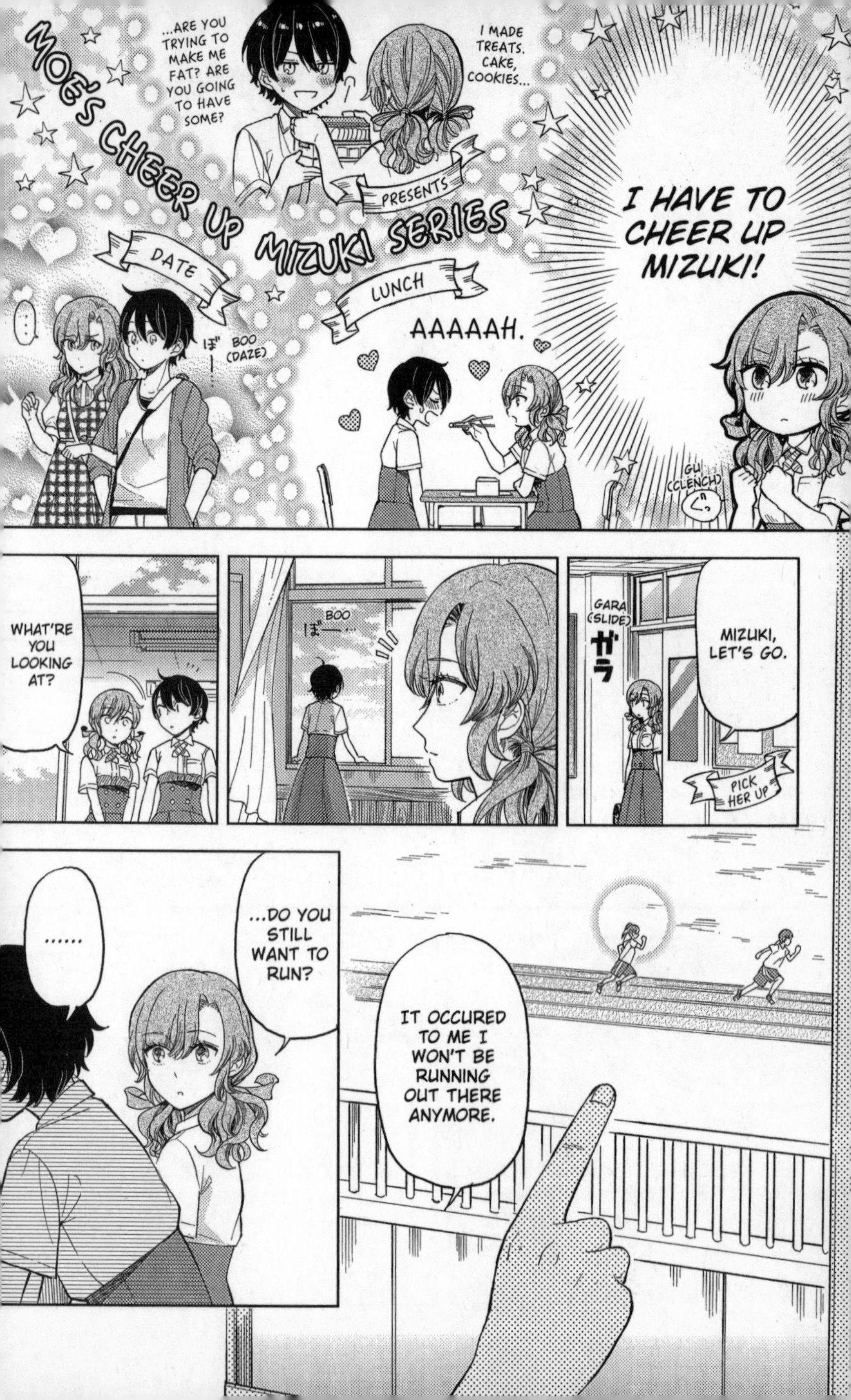
I HAVE TO CHEER UP MIZUKI!
GU (CLENCH)
ぐっ
MOE'S CHEER UP MIZUKI SERIES
PRESENTS
I MADE TREATS. CAKE, COOKIES...
...ARE YOU TRYING TO MAKE ME FAT? ARE YOU GOING TO HAVE SOME?
LUNCH
AAAAAH.
DATE
ぼ BOO (DAZE)
…
MIZUKI, LET'S GO.
GARA (SLIDE)
ガラ
PICK HER UP
BOO
ぼー…
WHAT'RE YOU LOOKING AT?
IT OCCURED TO ME I WON'T BE RUNNING OUT THERE ANYMORE.
...DO YOU STILL WANT TO RUN?
......

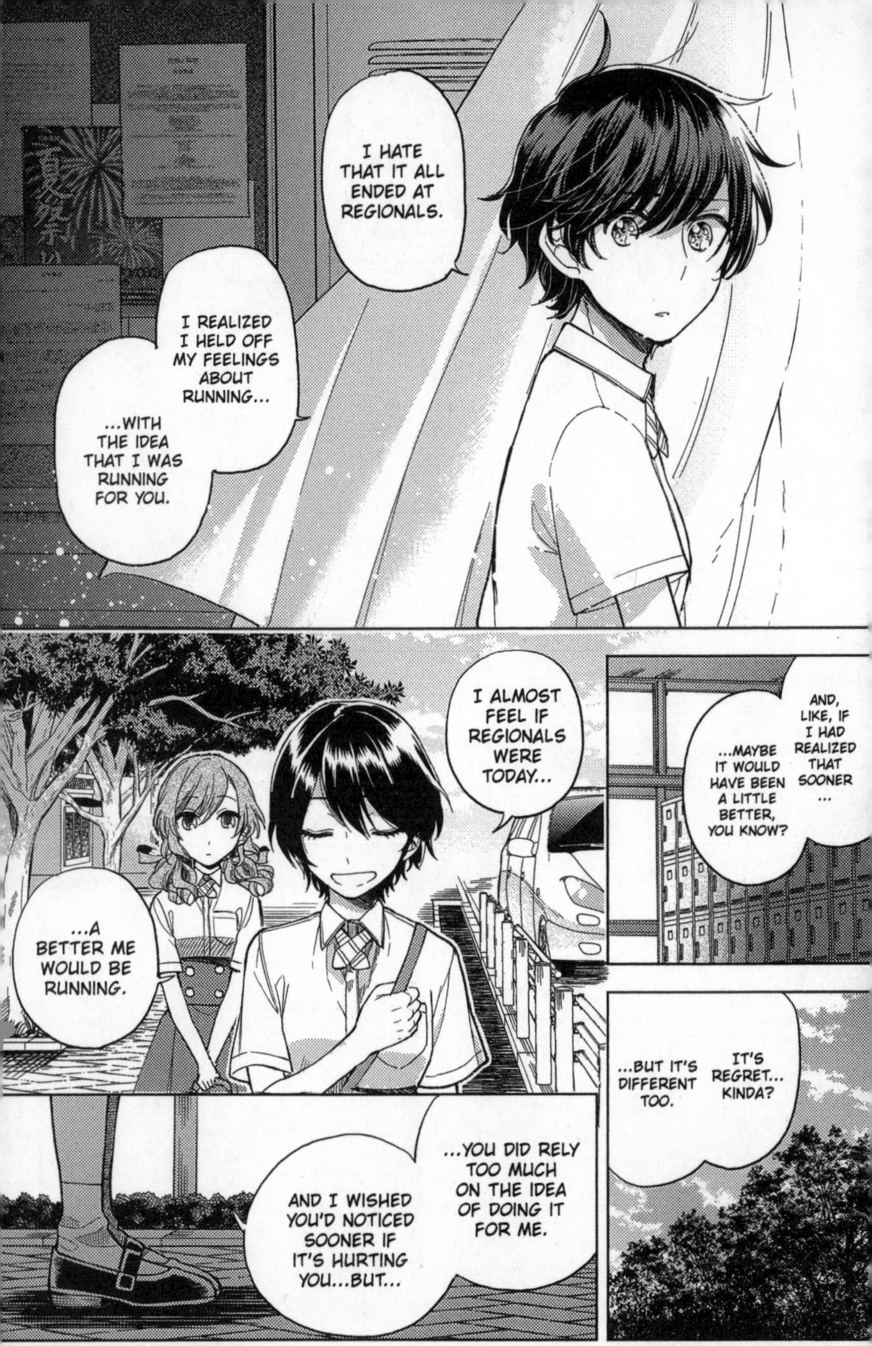
I HATE THAT IT ALL ENDED AT REGIONALS.
I REALIZED I HELD OFF MY FEELINGS ABOUT RUNNING...
...WITH THE IDEA THAT I WAS RUNNING FOR YOU.
AND, LIKE, IF I HAD REALIZED THAT SOONER...
...MAYBE IT WOULD HAVE BEEN A LITTLE BETTER, YOU KNOW?
I ALMOST FEEL IF REGIONALS WERE TODAY...
...A BETTER ME WOULD BE RUNNING.
IT'S REGRET... KINDA?
...BUT IT'S DIFFERENT TOO.
...YOU DID RELY TOO MUCH ON THE IDEA OF DOING IT FOR ME.
AND I WISHED YOU'D NOTICED SOONER IF IT'S HURTING YOU...BUT...

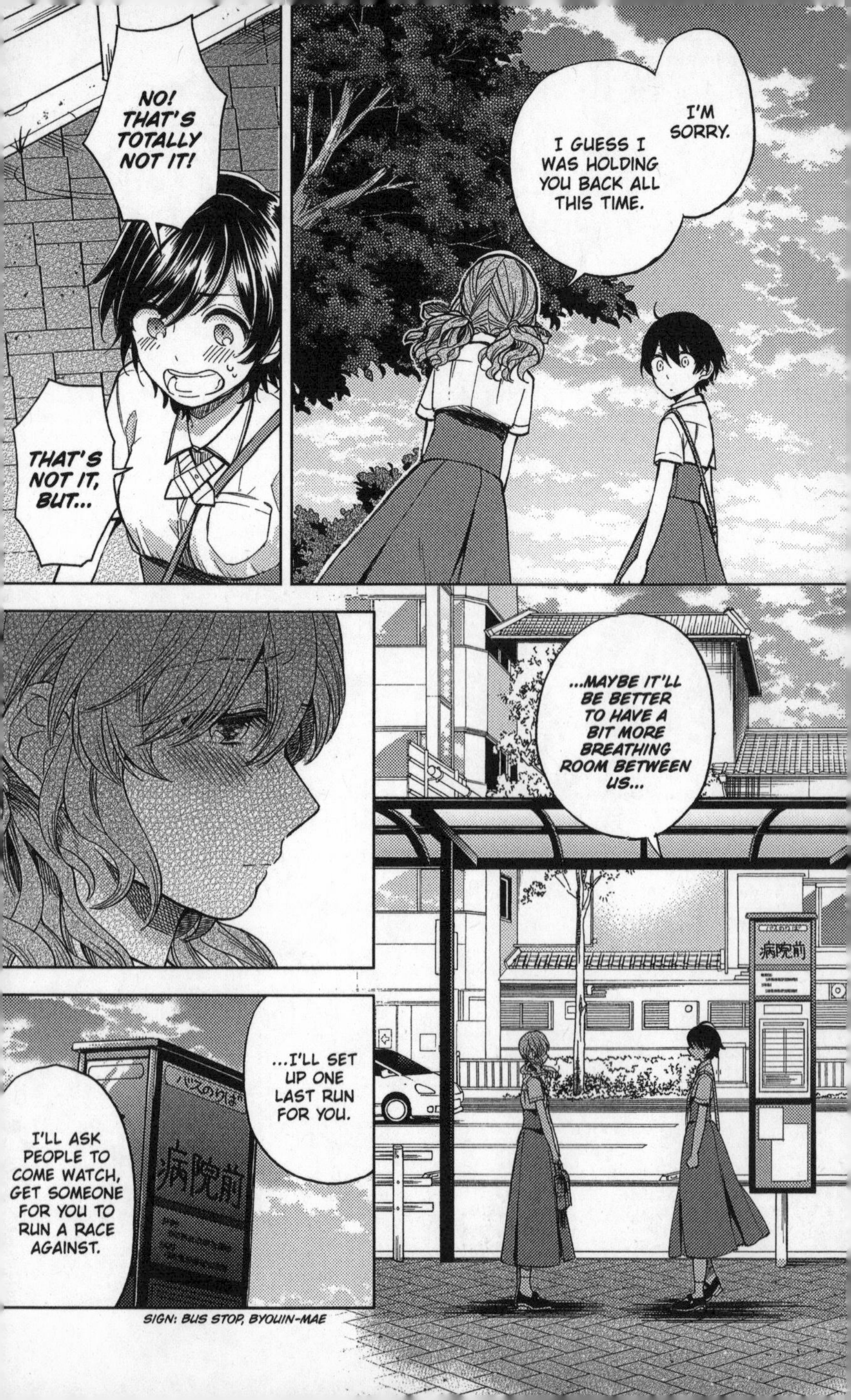
I'M SORRY.
I GUESS I WAS HOLDING YOU BACK ALL THIS TIME.
NO! THAT'S TOTALLY NOT IT!
THAT'S NOT IT, BUT...
...MAYBE IT'LL BE BETTER TO HAVE A BIT MORE BREATHING ROOM BETWEEN US...
病院前
...I'LL SET UP ONE LAST RUN FOR YOU.
I'LL ASK PEOPLE TO COME WATCH, GET SOMEONE FOR YOU TO RUN A RACE AGAINST.
病院前
SIGN: BUS STOP, BYOUIN-MAE

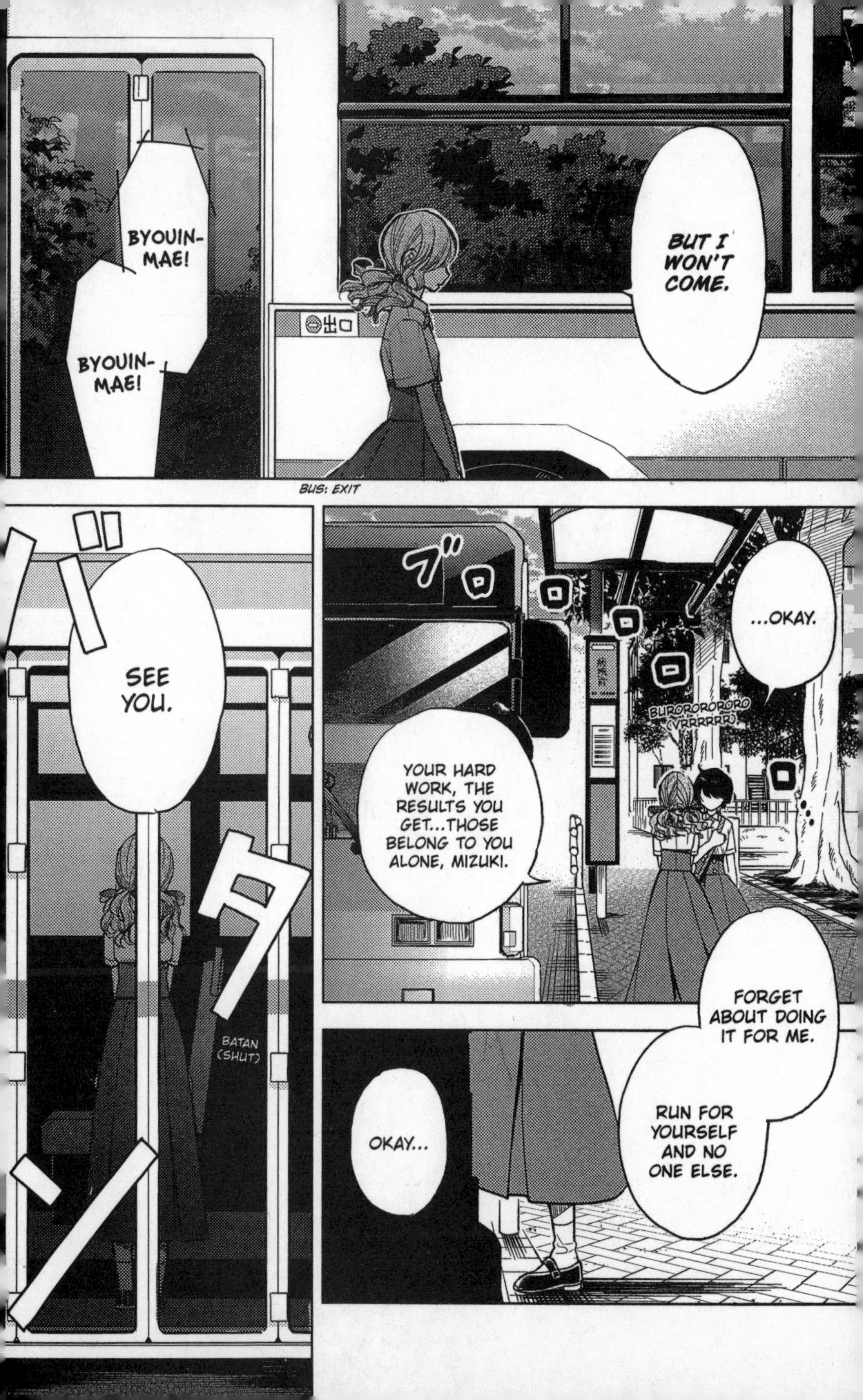
BUT I WON'T COME.
BYOUIN-MAE!
BYOUIN-MAE!
BUS: EXIT
...OKAY.
BURORORORO (VRRRRRR)
YOUR HARD WORK, THE RESULTS YOU GET...THOSE BELONG TO YOU ALONE, MIZUKI.
FORGET ABOUT DOING IT FOR ME.
RUN FOR YOURSELF AND NO ONE ELSE.
OKAY...
SEE YOU.
BATAN (SHUT)

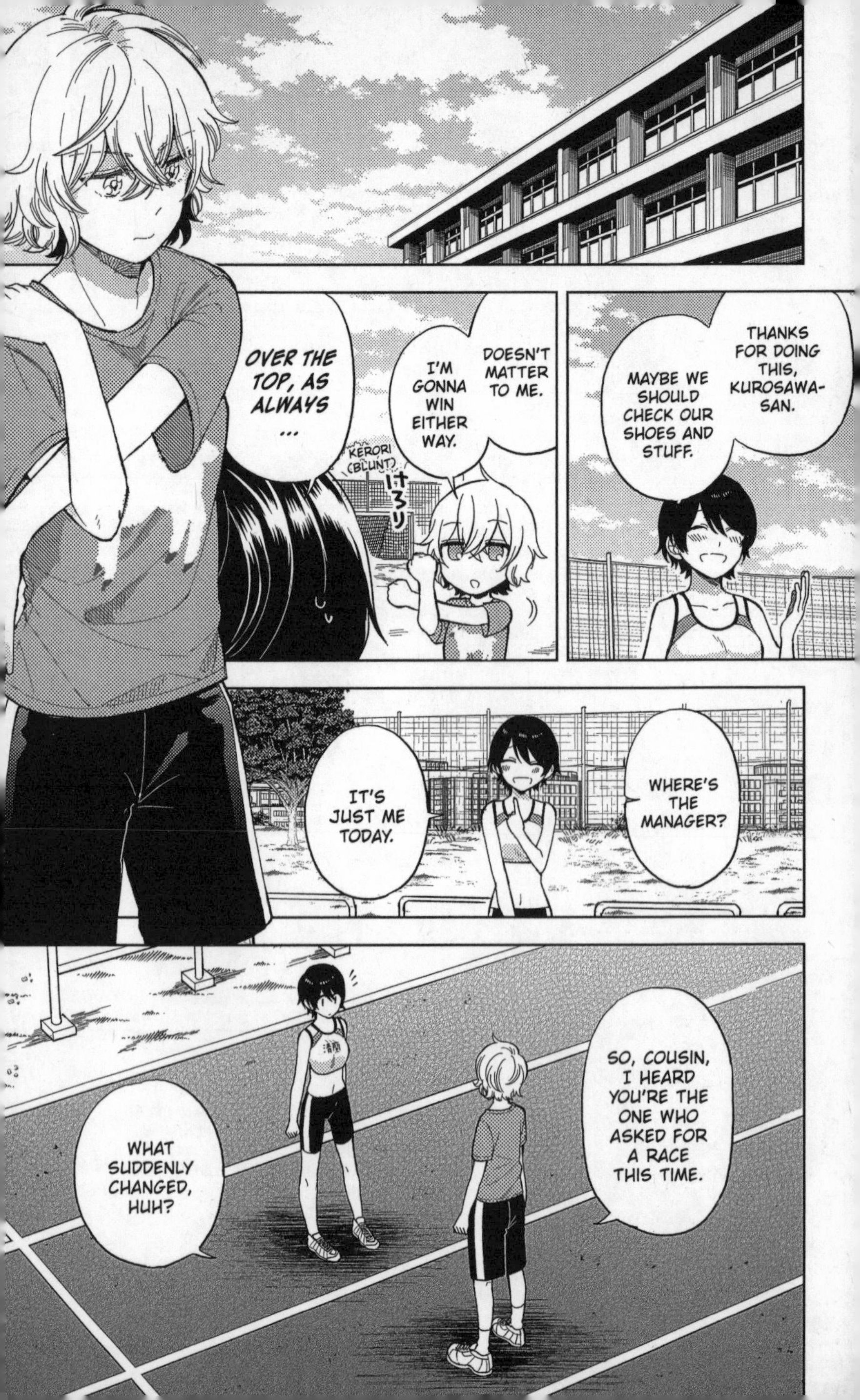
THANKS FOR DOING THIS, KUROSAWA-SAN.
MAYBE WE SHOULD CHECK OUR SHOES AND STUFF.
DOESN'T MATTER TO ME.
I'M GONNA WIN EITHER WAY.
KERORI (BLUNT)
けろり
OVER THE TOP, AS ALWAYS ...
WHERE'S THE MANAGER?
IT'S JUST ME TODAY.
SO, COUSIN, I HEARD YOU'RE THE ONE WHO ASKED FOR A RACE THIS TIME.
WHAT SUDDENLY CHANGED, HUH?

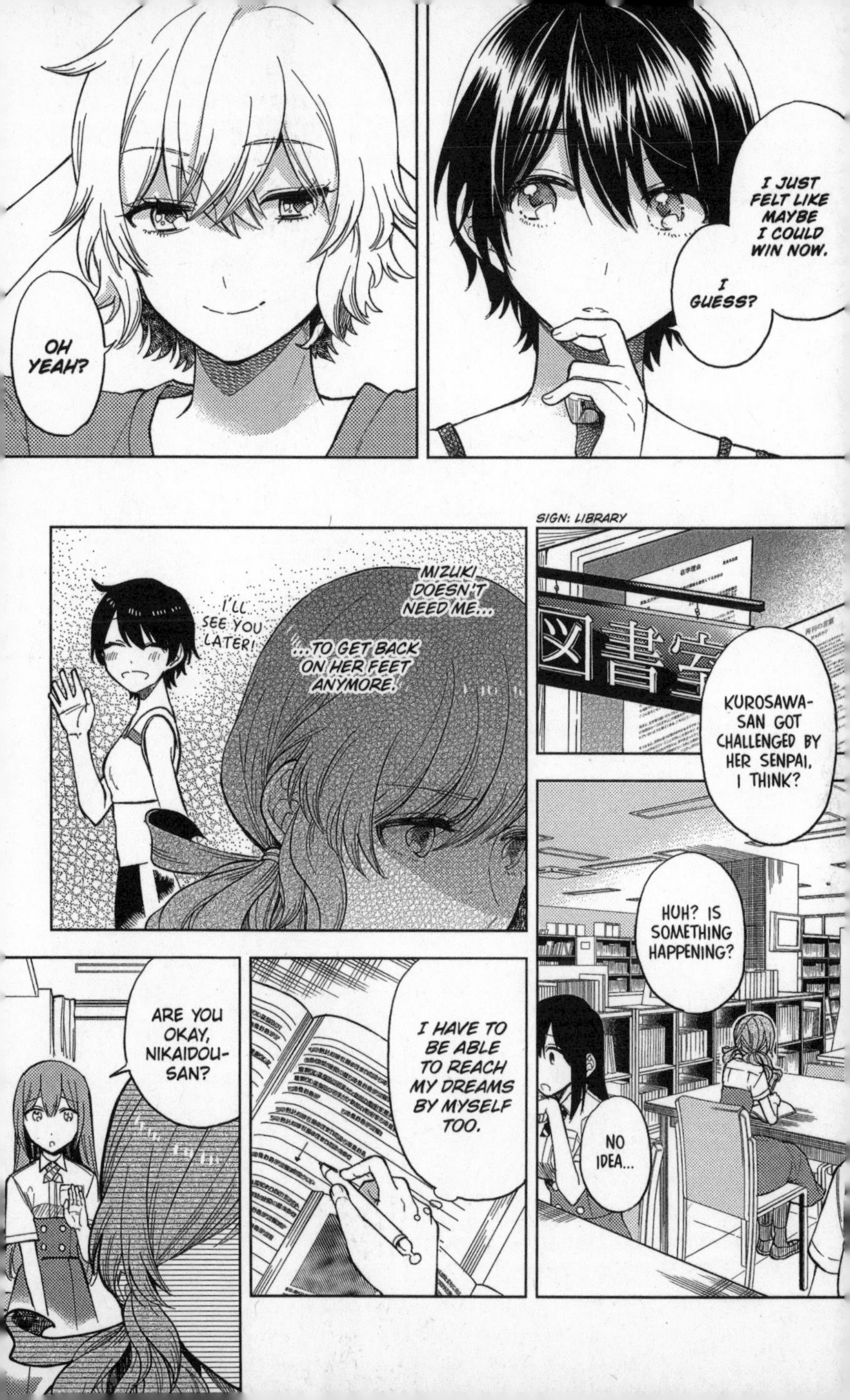
I JUST FELT LIKE MAYBE I COULD WIN NOW.
I GUESS?
OH YEAH?
SIGN: LIBRARY
図書室
KUROSAWA-SAN GOT CHALLENGED BY HER SENPAI, I THINK?
HUH? IS SOMETHING HAPPENING?
NO IDEA...
I'LL SEE YOU LATER!
MIZUKI DOESN'T NEED ME...
...TO GET BACK ON HER FEET ANYMORE.
I HAVE TO BE ABLE TO REACH MY DREAMS BY MYSELF TOO.
ARE YOU OKAY, NIKAIDOU-SAN?

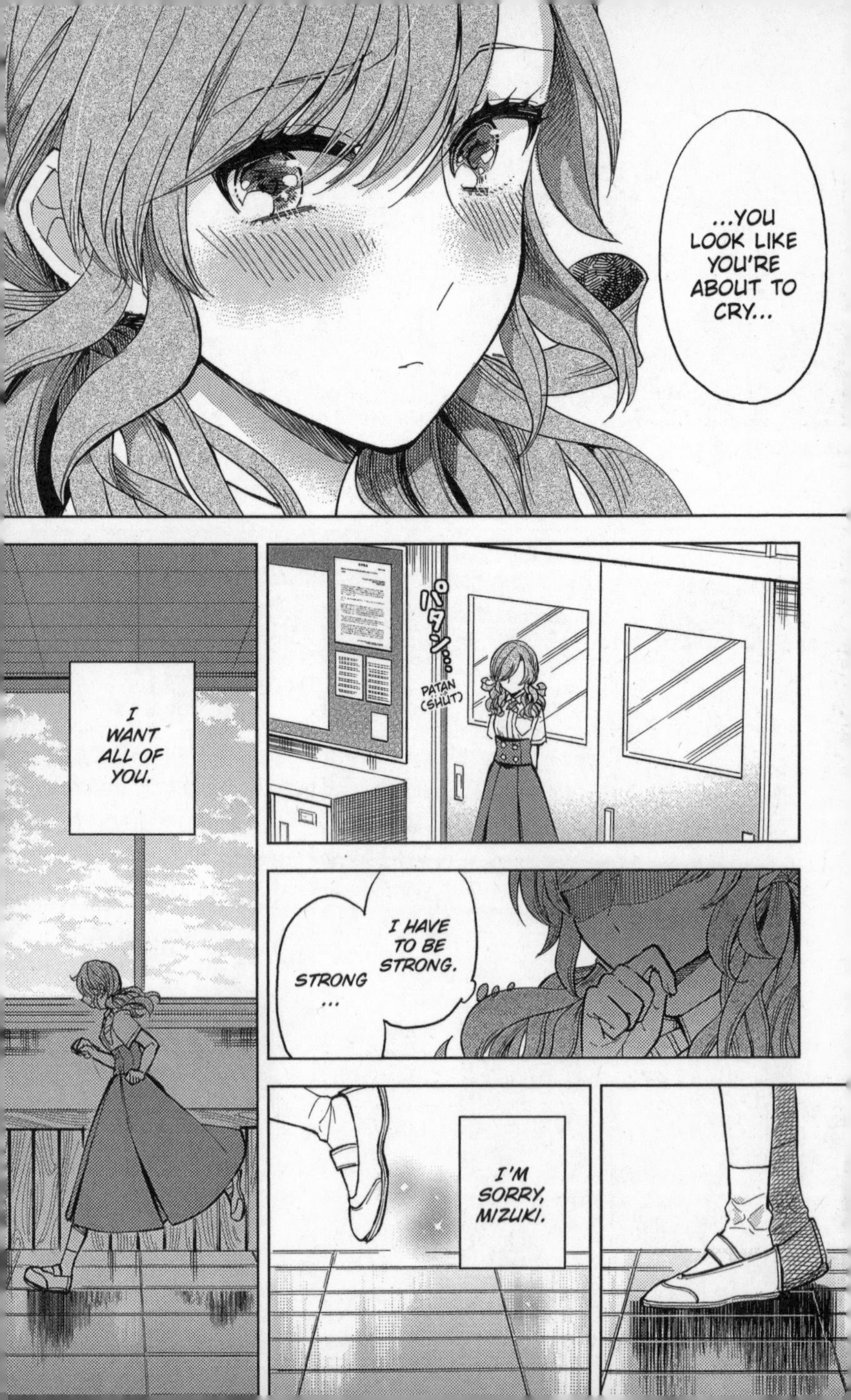
...YOU LOOK LIKE YOU'RE ABOUT TO CRY...
パタン…
PATAN (SHUT)
I HAVE TO BE STRONG.
STRONG...
I'M SORRY, MIZUKI.
I WANT ALL OF YOU.

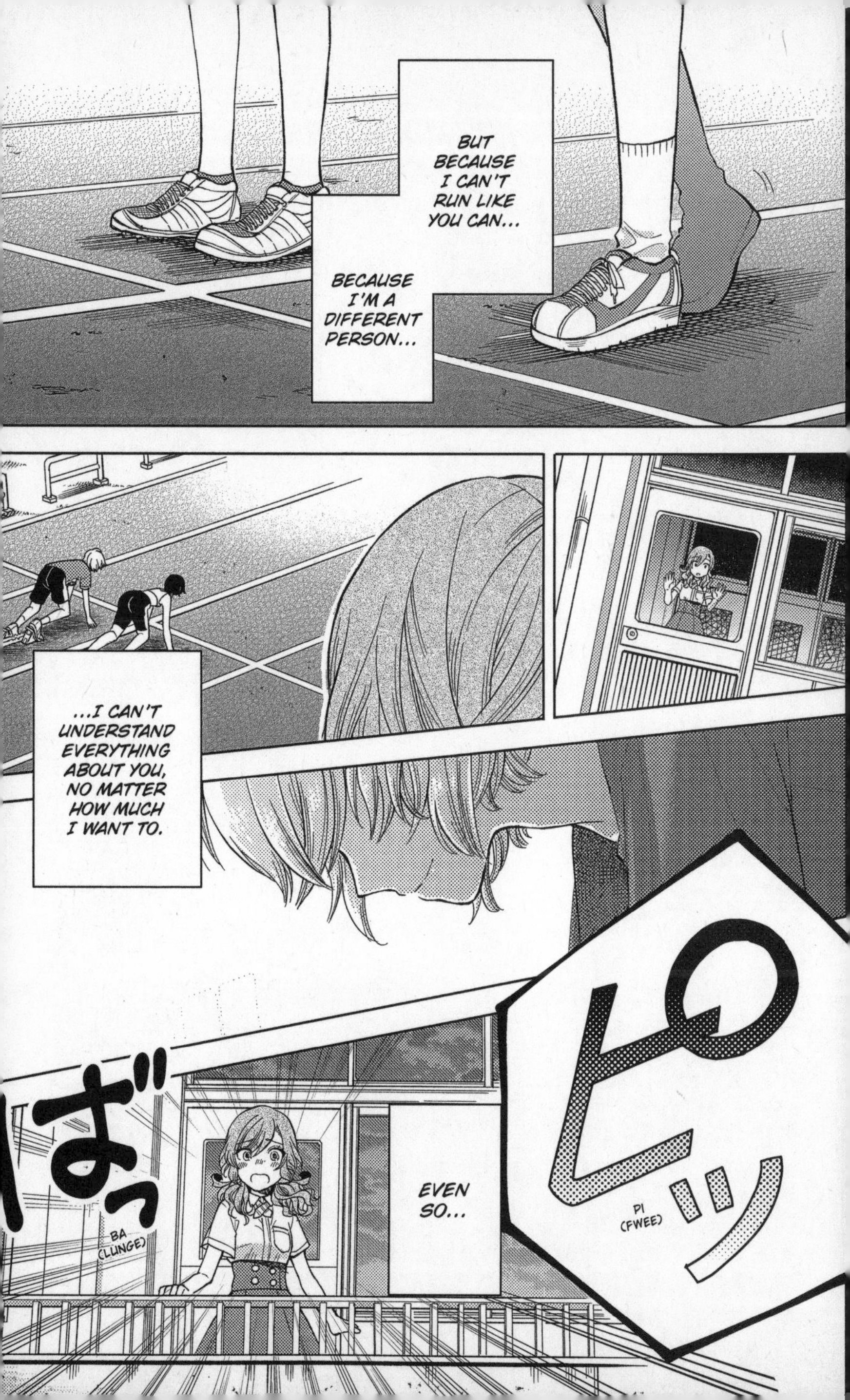
BUT BECAUSE I CAN'T RUN LIKE YOU CAN...
BECAUSE I'M A DIFFERENT PERSON...
...I CAN'T UNDERSTAND EVERYTHING ABOUT YOU, NO MATTER HOW MUCH I WANT TO.
ピッ
PI (FWEE)
EVEN SO...
ばっ
BA (LUNGE)

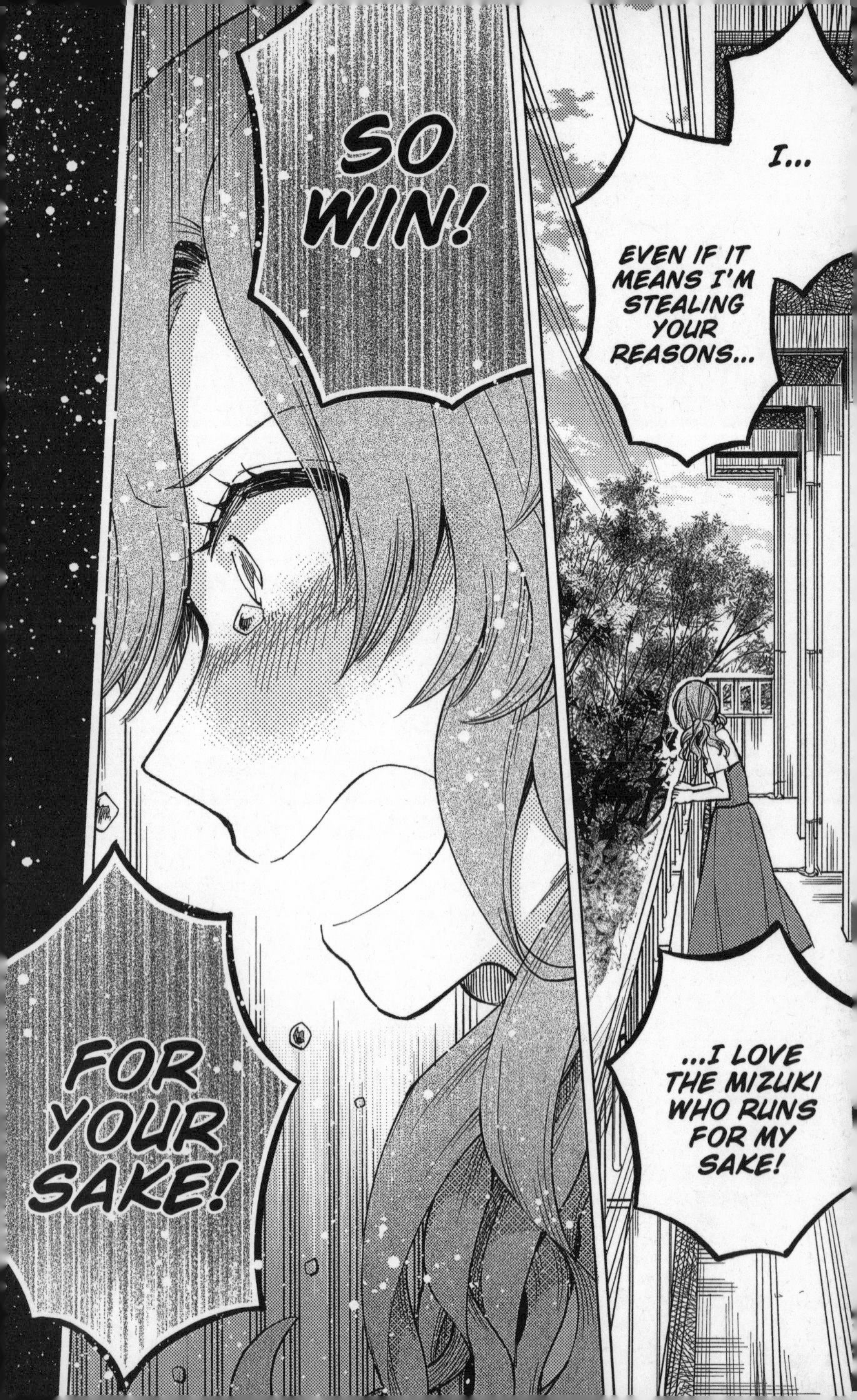
I...
EVEN IF IT MEANS I'M STEALING YOUR REASONS...
...I LOVE THE MIZUKI WHO RUNS FOR MY SAKE!
SO WIN!
FOR YOUR SAKE!

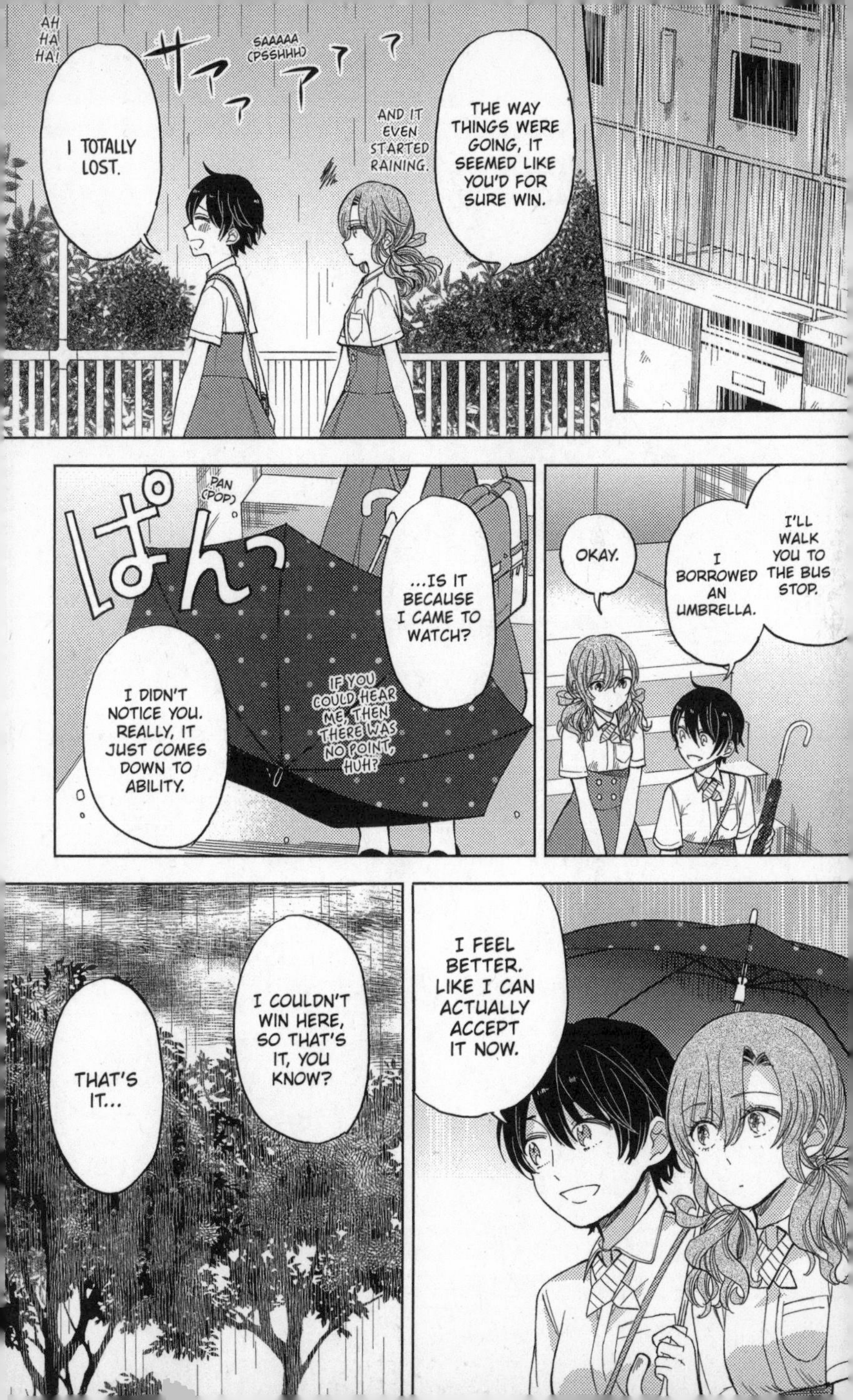
THE WAY THINGS WERE GOING, IT SEEMED LIKE YOU'D FOR SURE WIN.
AND IT EVEN STARTED RAINING.
SAAAAA (PSSHHH)
AH HA HA!
I TOTALLY LOST.
I'LL WALK YOU TO THE BUS STOP.
I BORROWED AN UMBRELLA.
OKAY.
PAN (POP)
...IS IT BECAUSE I CAME TO WATCH?
IF YOU COULD HEAR ME, THEN THERE WAS NO POINT, HUH?
I DIDN'T NOTICE YOU. REALLY, IT JUST COMES DOWN TO ABILITY.
I FEEL BETTER. LIKE I CAN ACTUALLY ACCEPT IT NOW.
I COULDN'T WIN HERE, SO THAT'S IT, YOU KNOW?
THAT'S IT...

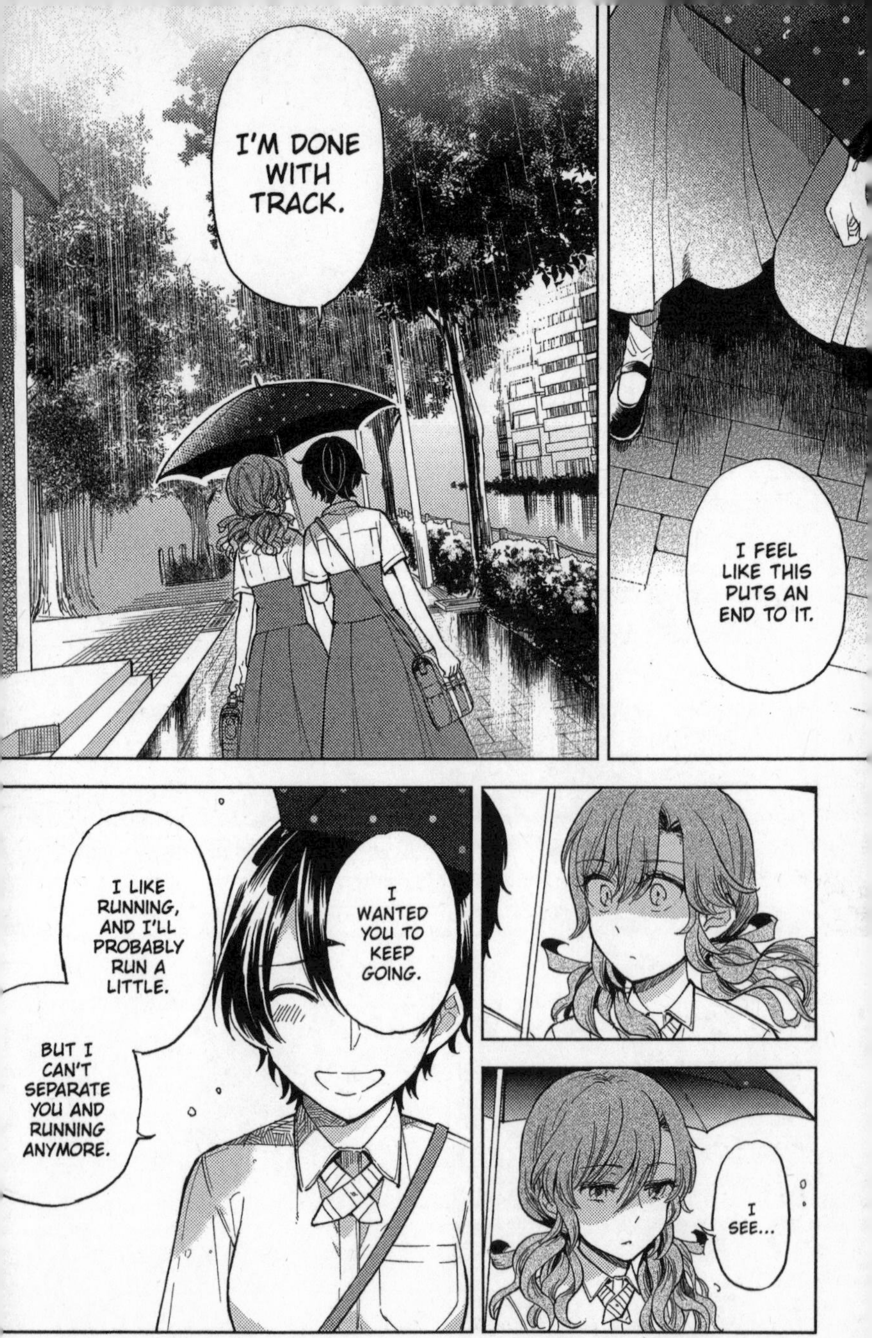
I FEEL LIKE THIS PUTS AN END TO IT.
I'M DONE WITH TRACK.
I SEE...
I WANTED YOU TO KEEP GOING.
I LIKE RUNNING, AND I'LL PROBABLY RUN A LITTLE.
BUT I CAN'T SEPARATE YOU AND RUNNING ANYMORE.

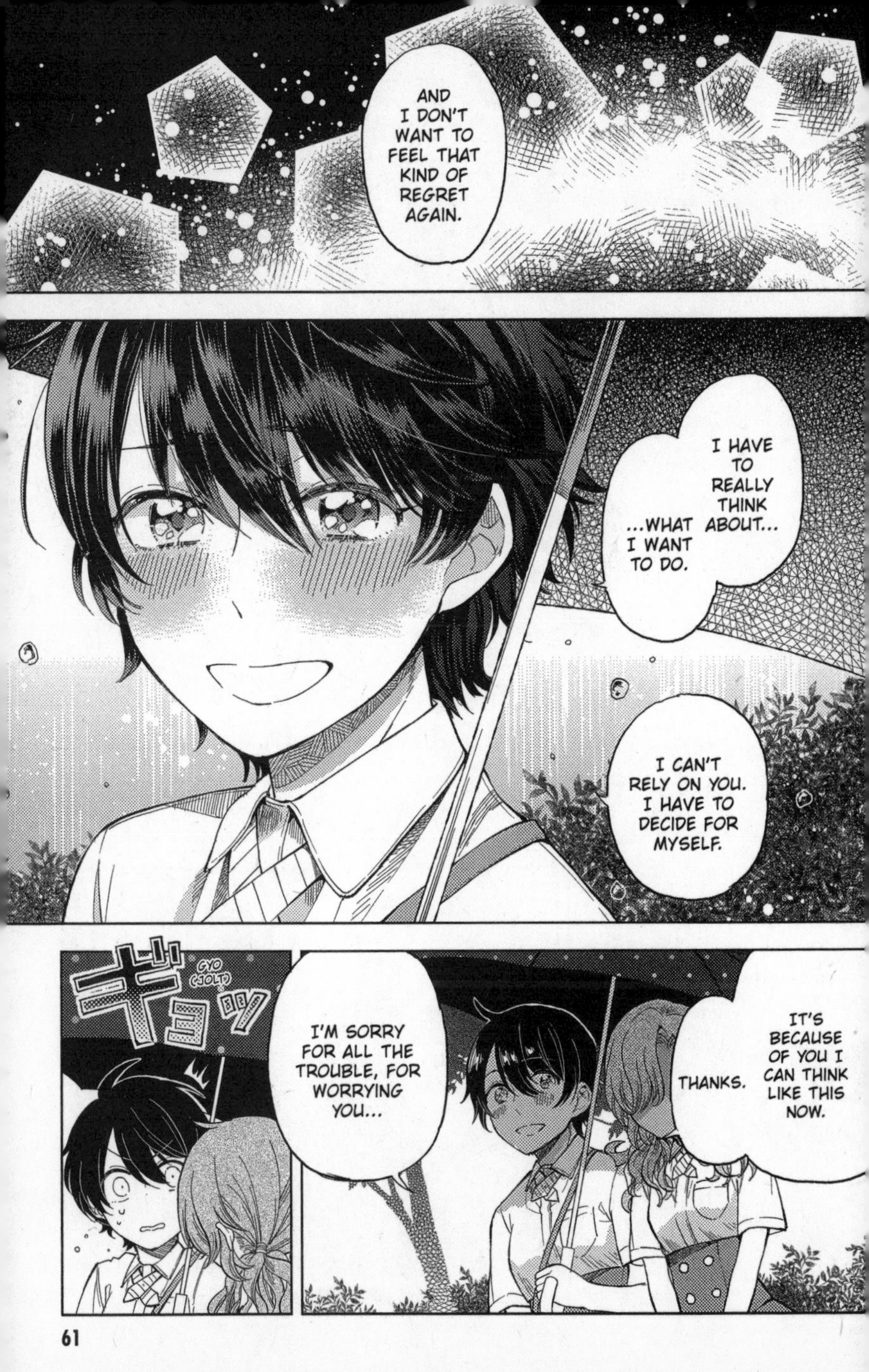
AND I DON'T WANT TO FEEL THAT KIND OF REGRET AGAIN.
I HAVE TO REALLY THINK ABOUT...
...WHAT I WANT TO DO.
I CAN'T RELY ON YOU. I HAVE TO DECIDE FOR MYSELF.
IT'S BECAUSE OF YOU I CAN THINK LIKE THIS NOW.
THANKS.
I'M SORRY FOR ALL THE TROUBLE, FOR WORRYING YOU...
GYO (JOLT)

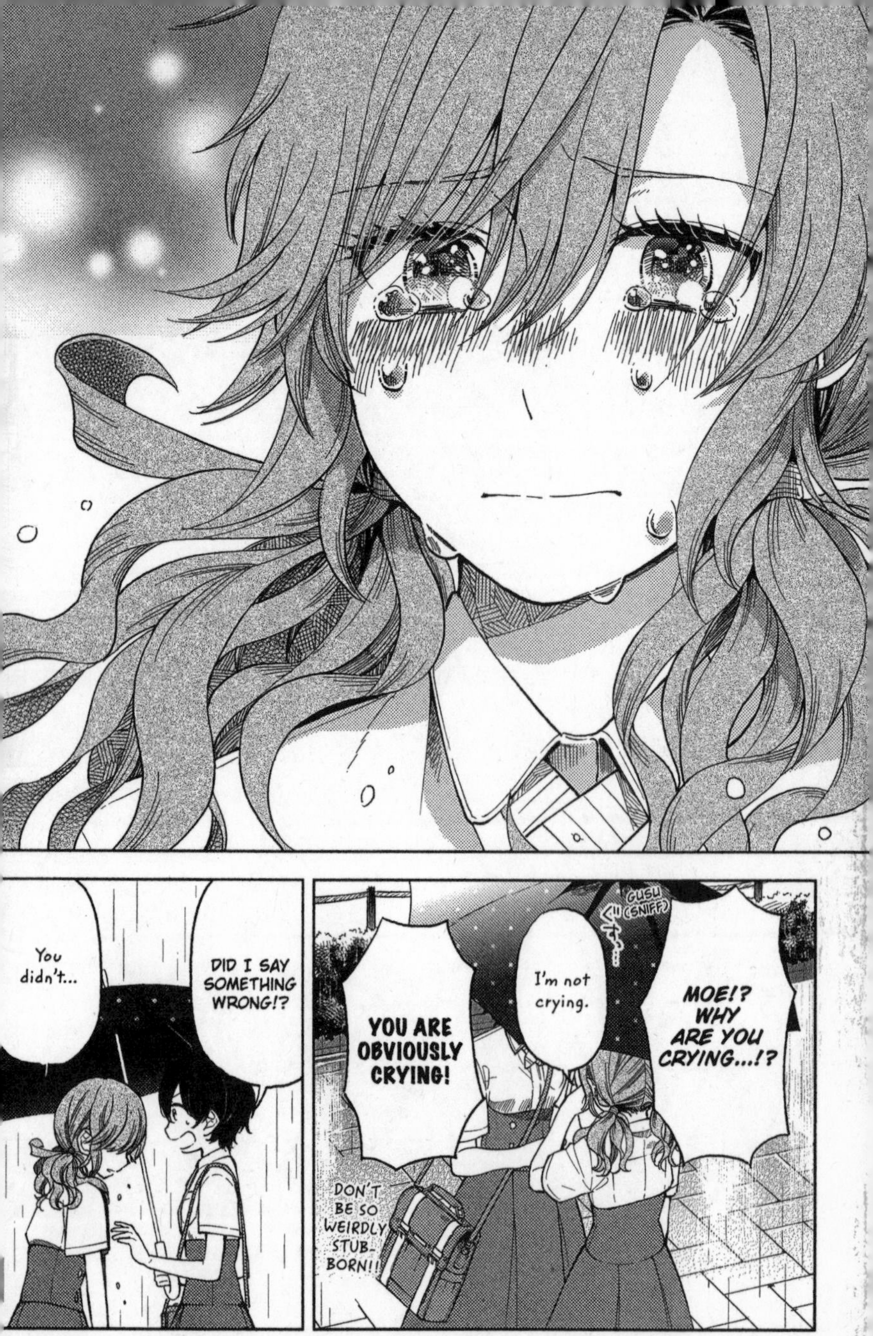
GUSU (SNIFF)
MOE!? WHY ARE YOU CRYING...!?
I'm not crying.
YOU ARE OBVIOUSLY CRYING!
DON'T BE SO WEIRDLY STUB-BORN!!
DID I SAY SOMETHING WRONG!?
You didn't...

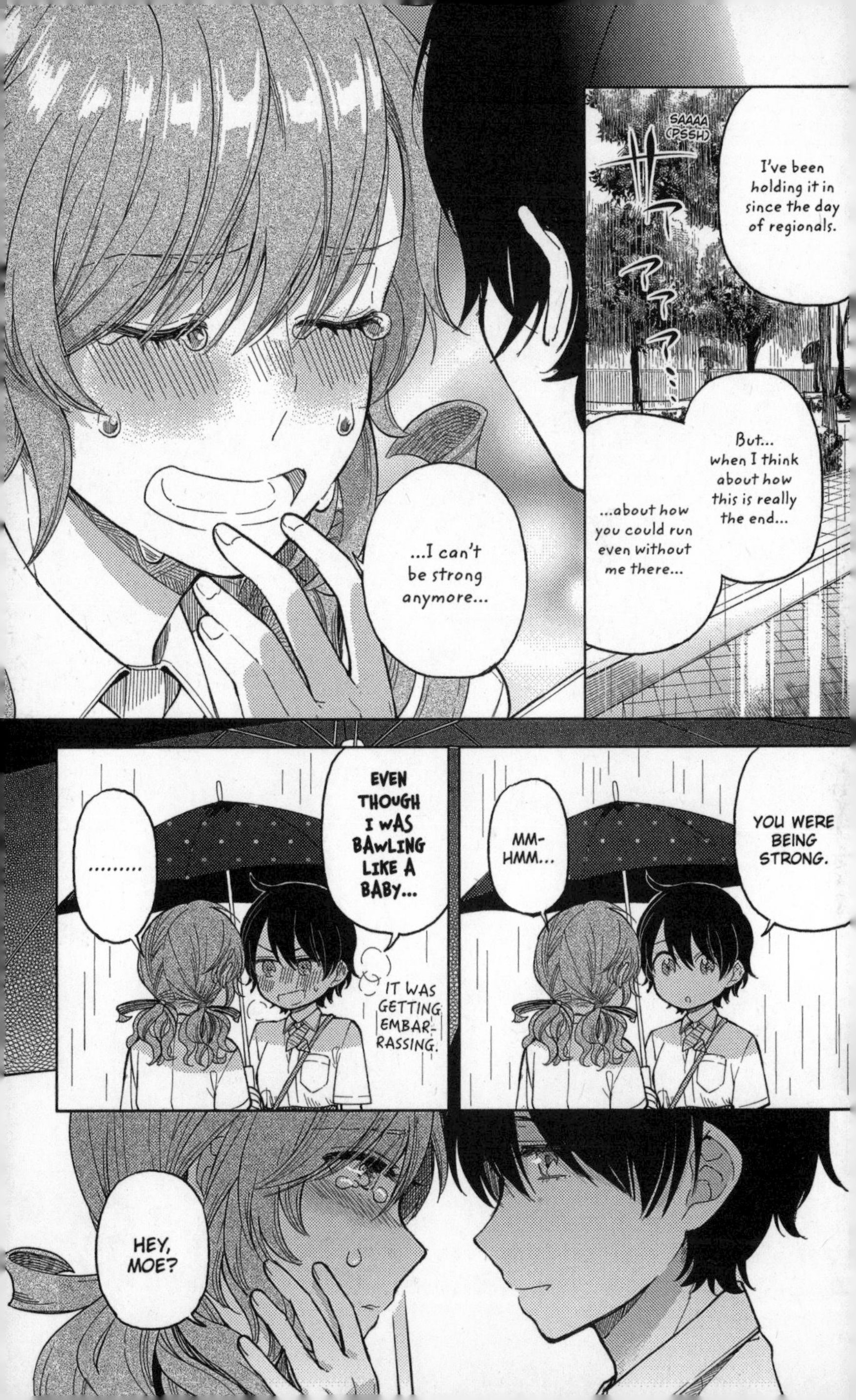
SAAAA (PSSH)
I've been holding it in since the day of regionals.
But... when I think about how this is really the end...
...about how you could run even without me there...
...I can't be strong anymore...
YOU WERE BEING STRONG.
MM-HMM...
EVEN THOUGH I WAS BAWLING LIKE A BABY...
IT WAS GETTING EMBARRASSING.
....
HEY, MOE?

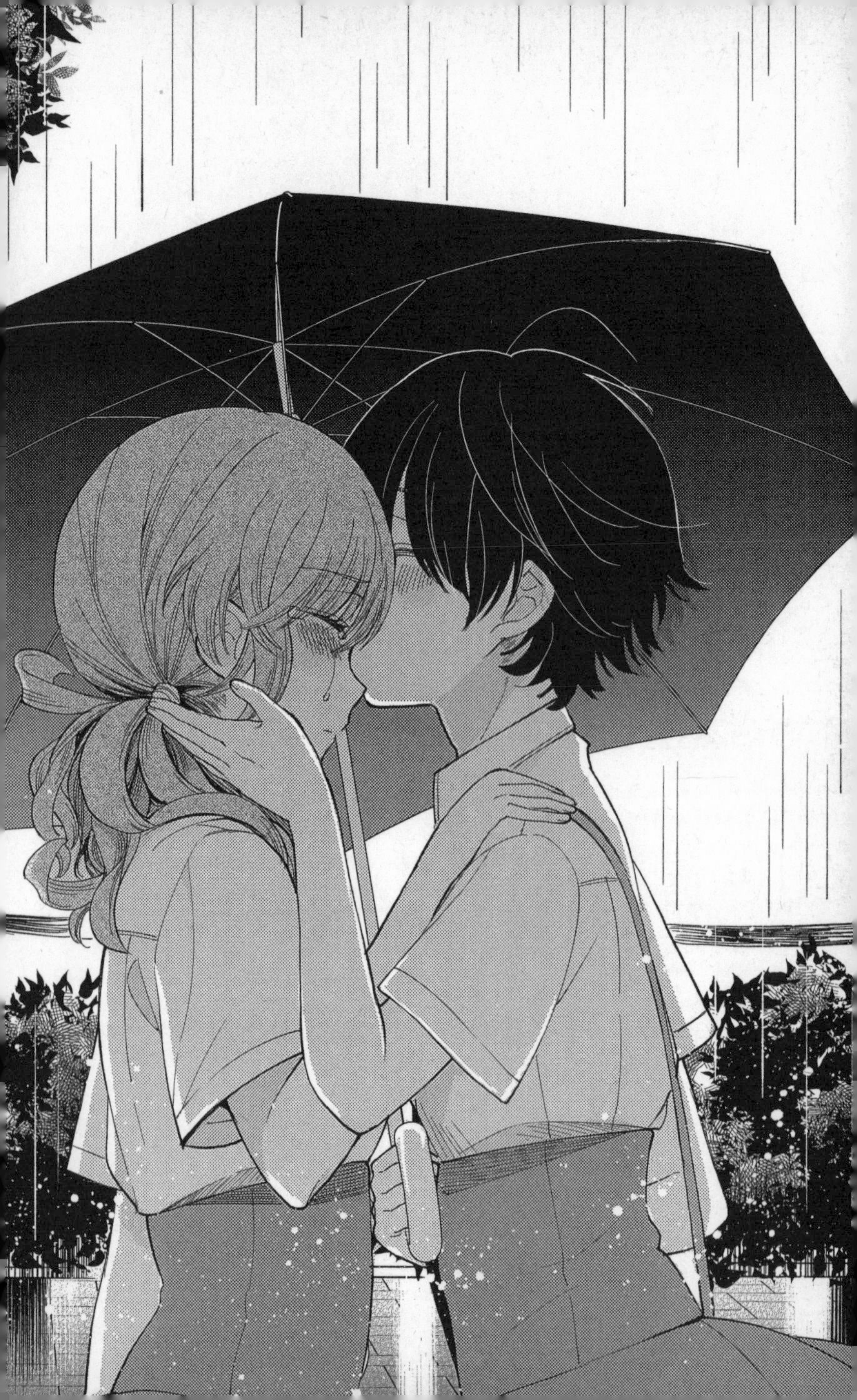

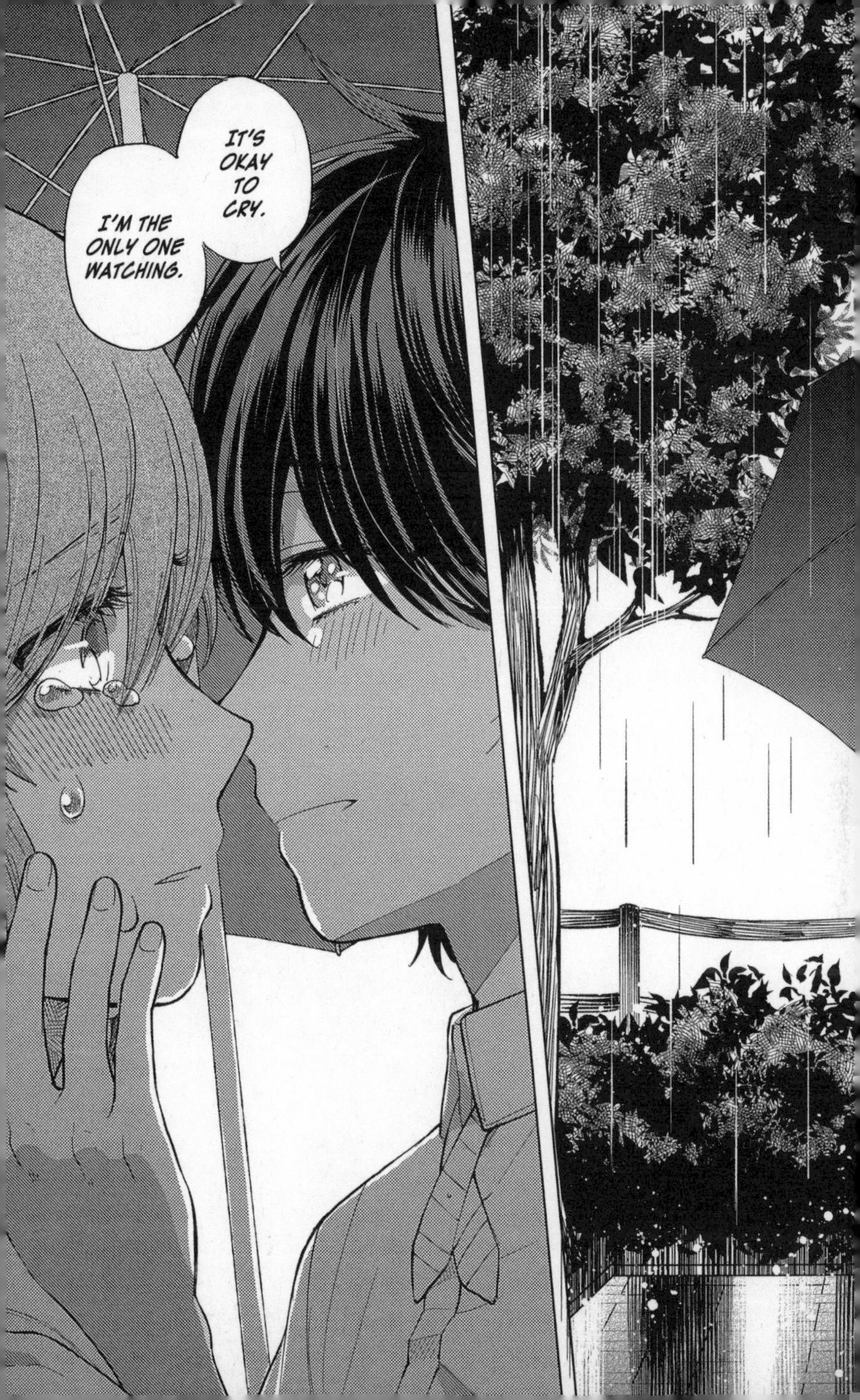
IT'S OKAY TO CRY.
I'M THE ONLY ONE WATCHING.

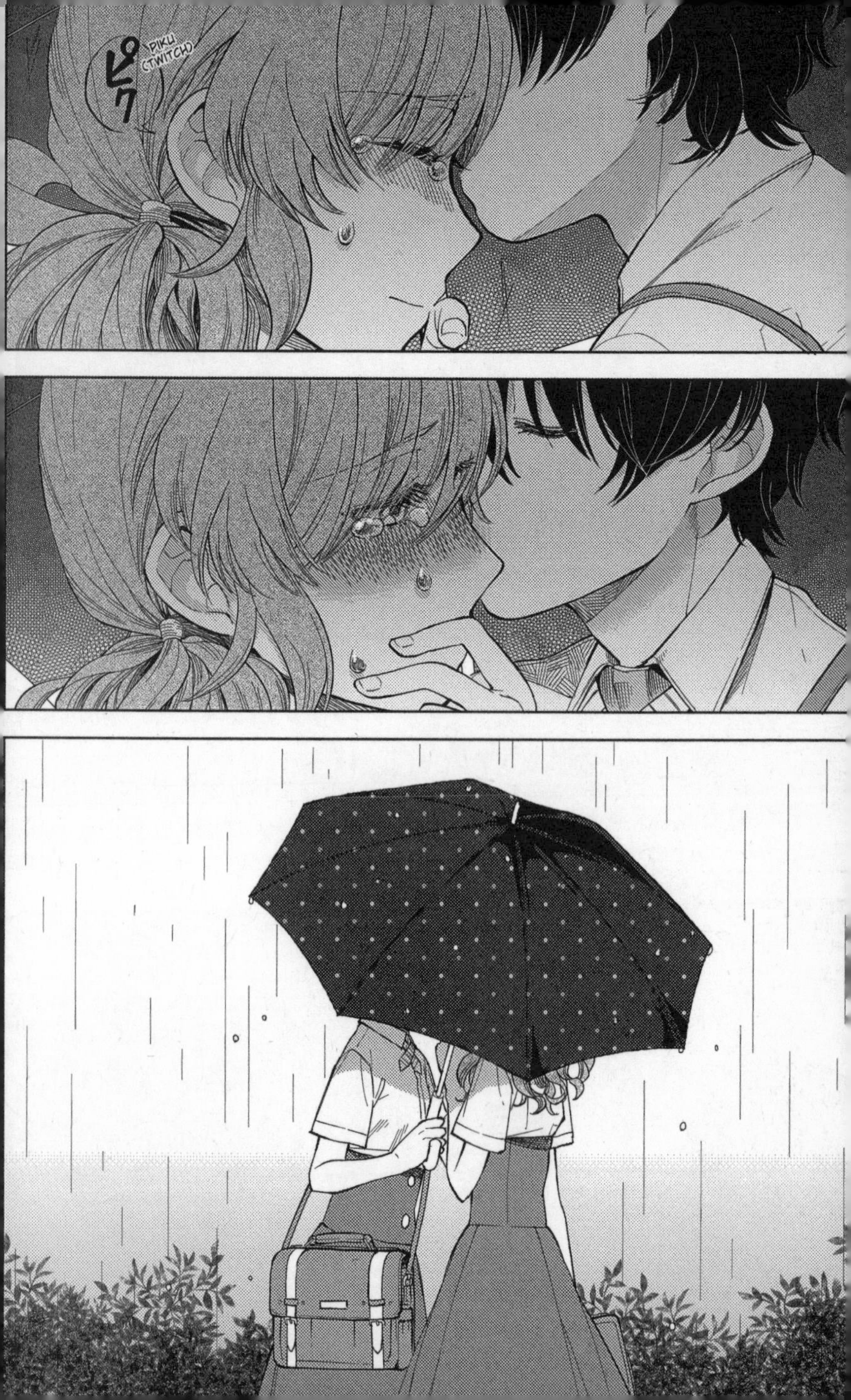
ピク
PIKU (TWITCH)

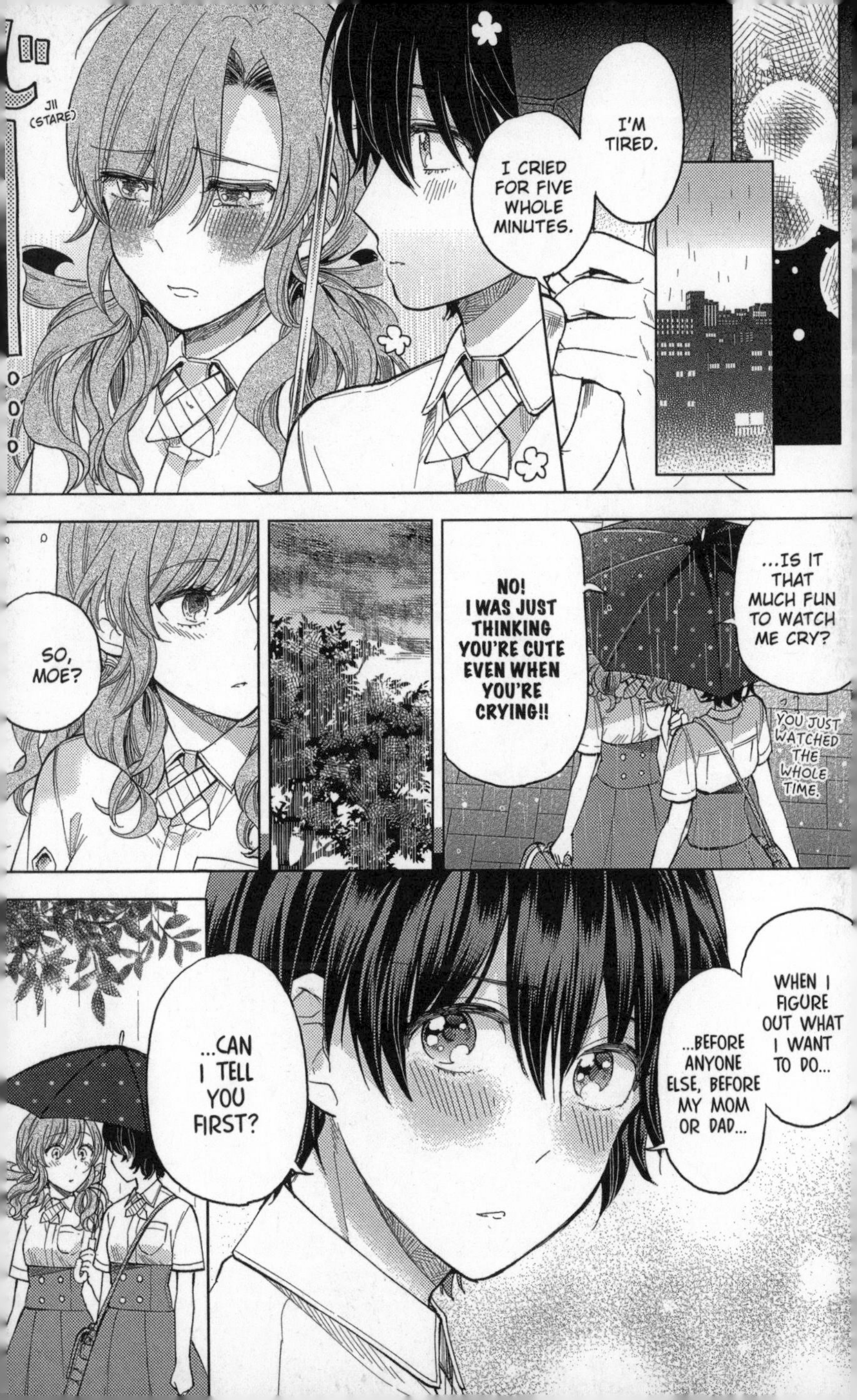
I'M TIRED.
I CRIED FOR FIVE WHOLE MINUTES.
JII (STARE)
...IS IT THAT MUCH FUN TO WATCH ME CRY?
NO! I WAS JUST THINKING YOU'RE CUTE EVEN WHEN YOU'RE CRYING!!
YOU JUST WATCHED THE WHOLE TIME.
SO, MOE?
WHEN I FIGURE OUT WHAT I WANT TO DO...
...BEFORE ANYONE ELSE, BEFORE MY MOM OR DAD...
...CAN I TELL YOU FIRST?

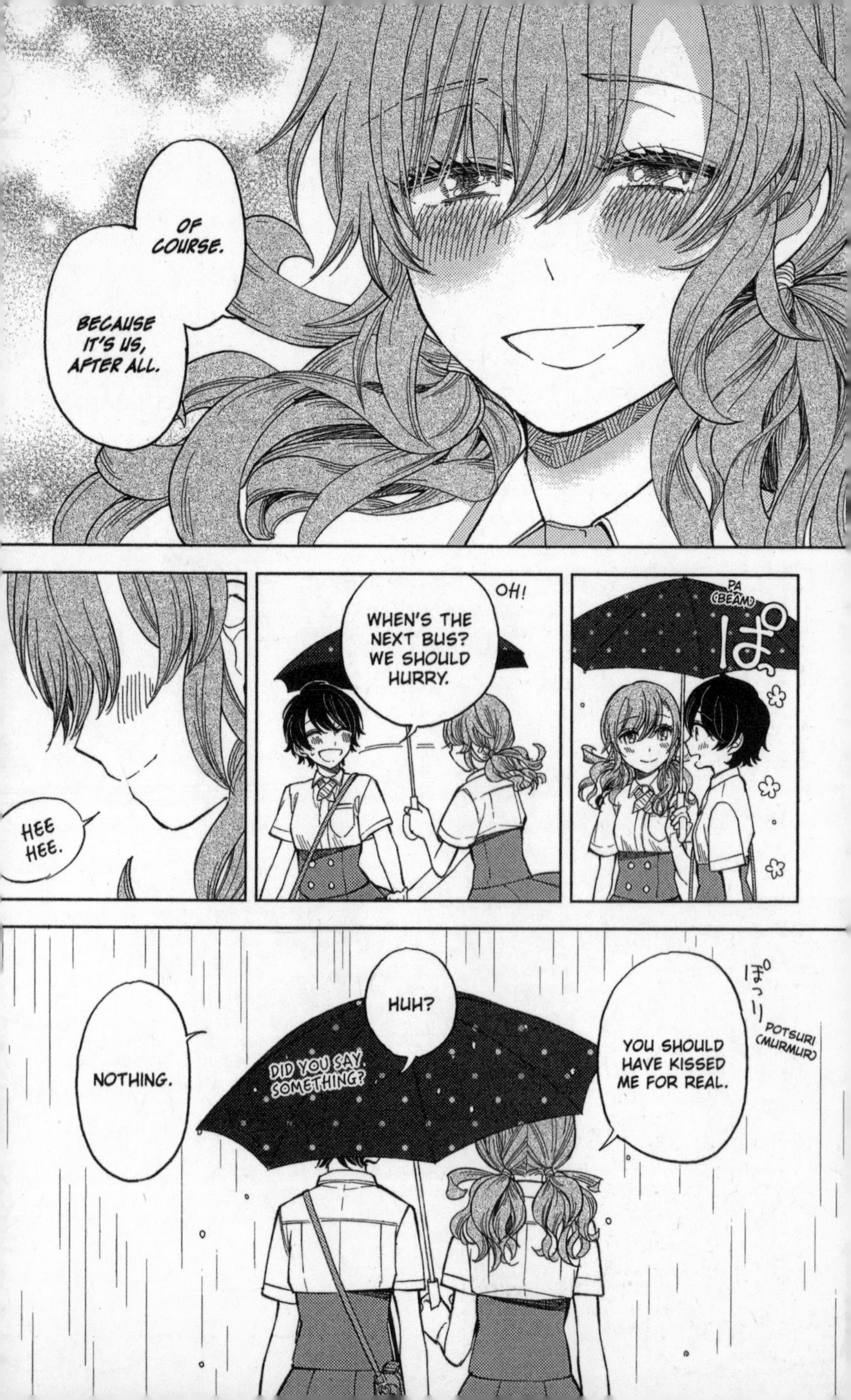
OF COURSE.
BECAUSE IT'S US, AFTER ALL.
ぱっ
PA (BEAM)
OH!
WHEN'S THE NEXT BUS? WE SHOULD HURRY.
HEE HEE.
ぽつり
POTSURI (MURMUR)
YOU SHOULD HAVE KISSED ME FOR REAL.
HUH?
DID YOU SAY SOMETHING?
NOTHING.

One More Regional

MAHO
THIRD-YEAR, SEIRAN ACADEMY HIGH SCHOOL, TRACK TEAM. QUIET AND CALM.

YUMEKO
SECOND-YEAR, PUBLIC CO-ED SCHOOL. HAS KNOWN MAHO FOR SOME TIME.

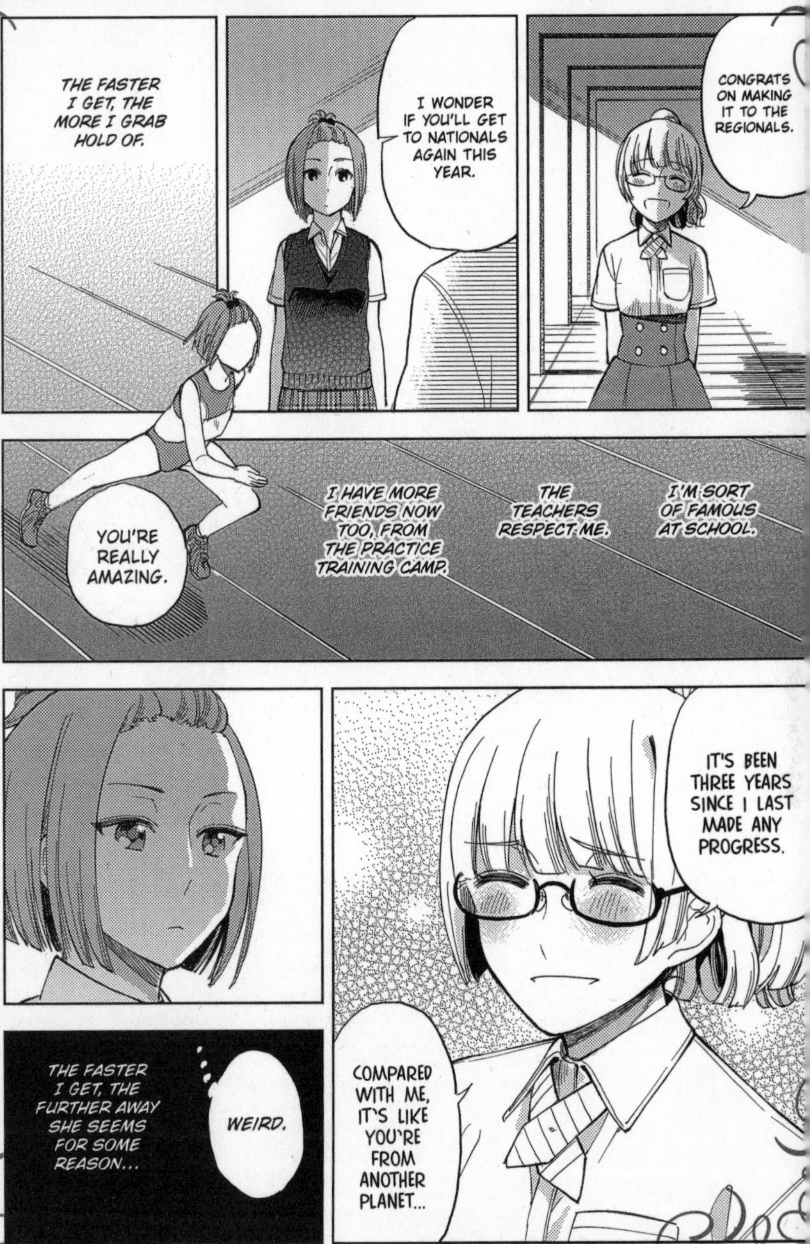

CONGRATS ON MAKING IT TO THE REGIONALS.
I WONDER IF YOU'LL GET TO NATIONALS AGAIN THIS YEAR.
THE FASTER I GET, THE MORE I GRAB HOLD OF.
I'M SORT OF FAMOUS AT SCHOOL.
THE TEACHERS RESPECT ME.
I HAVE MORE FRIENDS NOW TOO, FROM THE PRACTICE TRAINING CAMP.
YOU'RE REALLY AMAZING.
IT'S BEEN THREE YEARS SINCE I LAST MADE ANY PROGRESS.
COMPARED WITH ME, IT'S LIKE YOU'RE FROM ANOTHER PLANET...
WEIRD.
THE FASTER I GET, THE FURTHER AWAY SHE SEEMS FOR SOME REASON...

KISS THEATER: WHAT'S BEHIND THE STORY!?

PEOPLE OTHER THAN THE MAIN CHARACTERS HAVE STORIES TOO. HERE, WE PRESENT THE "LITTLE LOVE" STORIES HAPPENING BEHIND THE SCENES.

✳ *Moe Nikaidou* ✳

Moe Nikaidou

Third-year student at Seiran Academy High School and manager of the track team. By appearances she's a cool beauty, but she has an aggressive personality that complements more timid friends. Even though it's a new school year, she's still glued to Mizuki, but she's slightly bewildered by the way her friend is changing on her own.

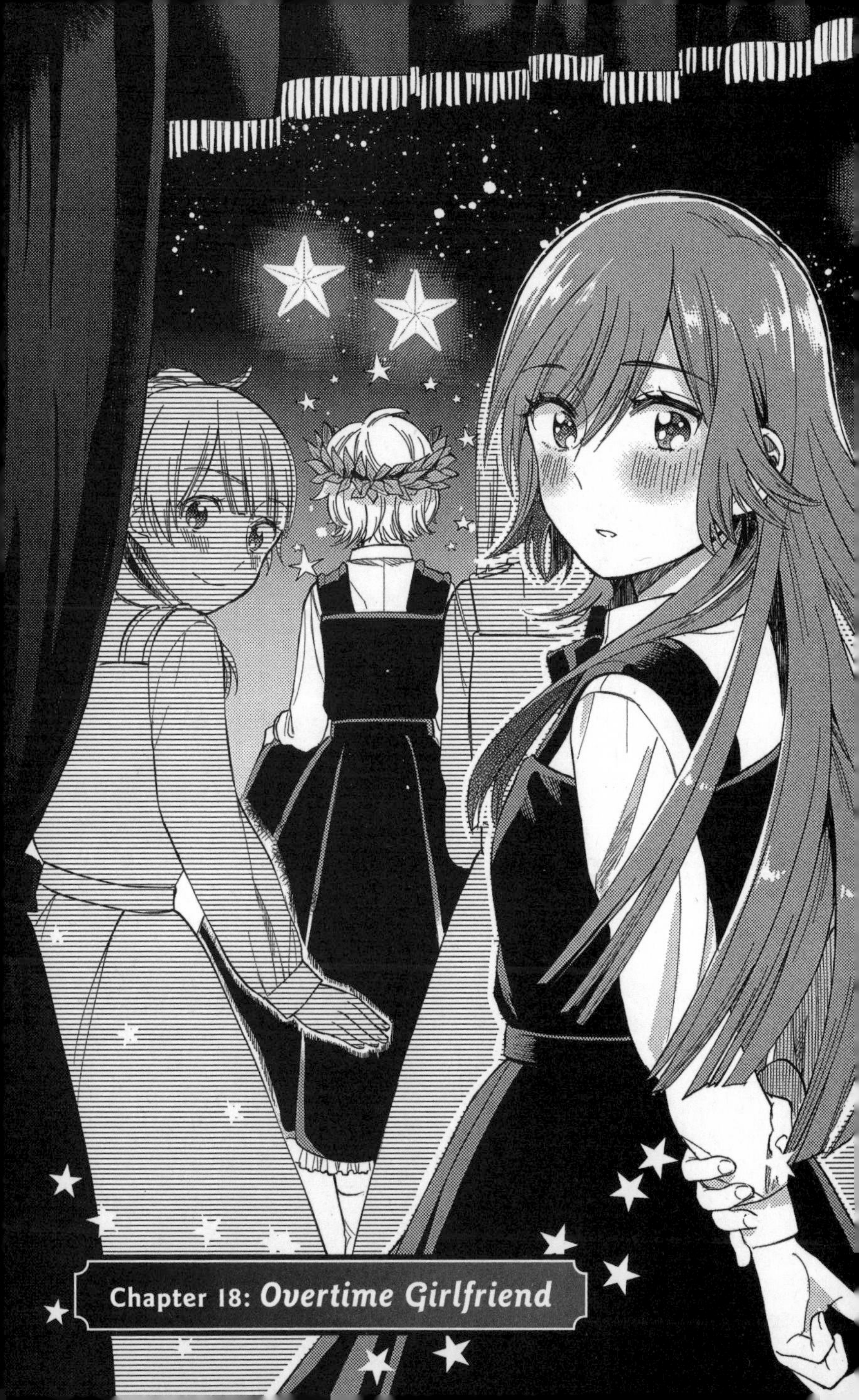
Chapter 18: Overtime Girlfriend

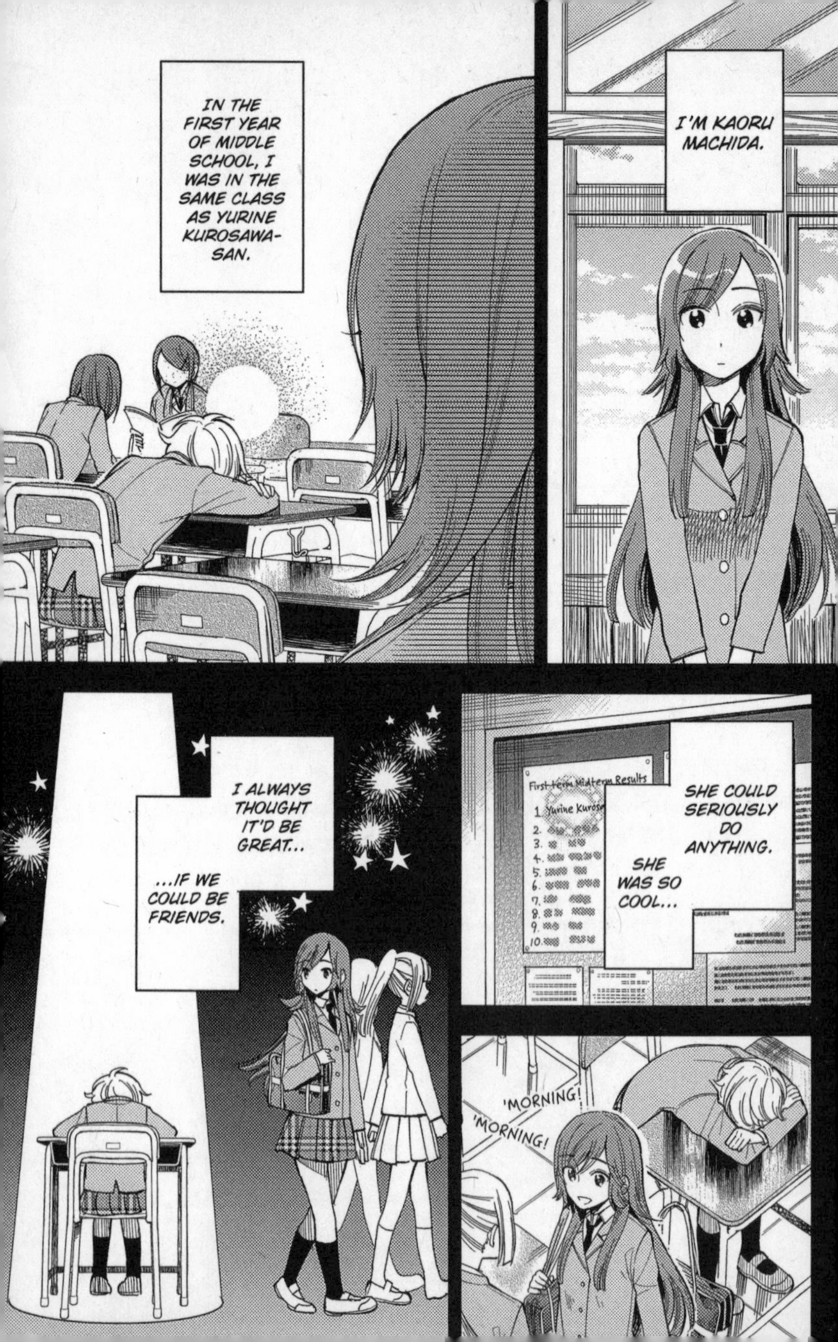
I'M KAORU MACHIDA.
IN THE FIRST YEAR OF MIDDLE SCHOOL, I WAS IN THE SAME CLASS AS YURINE KUROSAWA-SAN.
First-term Midterm Results
SHE COULD SERIOUSLY DO ANYTHING.
SHE WAS SO COOL...
'MORNING!
'MORNING!
I ALWAYS THOUGHT IT'D BE GREAT...
...IF WE COULD BE FRIENDS.

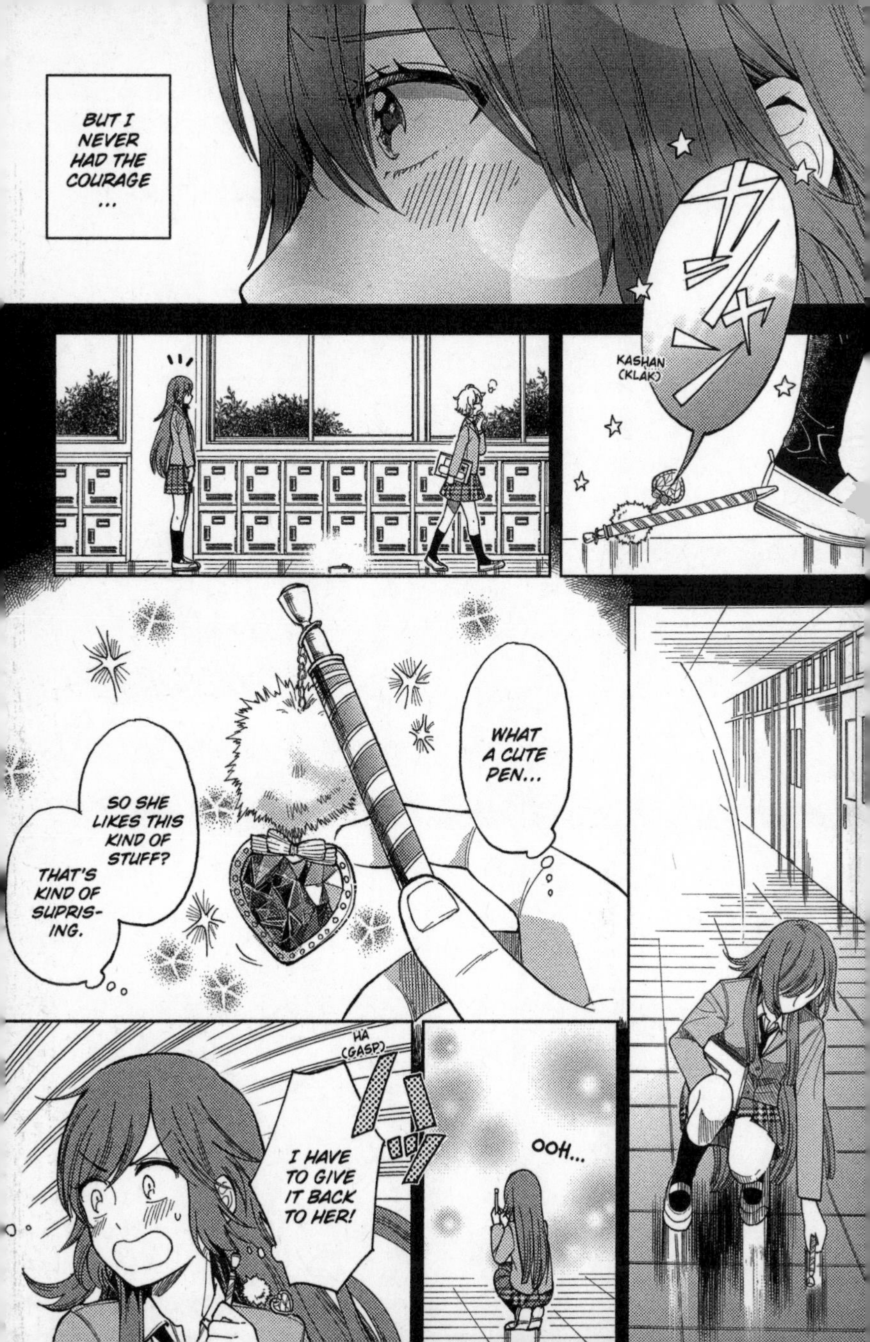
BUT I NEVER HAD THE COURAGE ...
KASHAN (KLAK)
WHAT A CUTE PEN...
SO SHE LIKES THIS KIND OF STUFF?
THAT'S KIND OF SUPRIS-ING.
OOH...
HA (GASP)
I HAVE TO GIVE IT BACK TO HER!

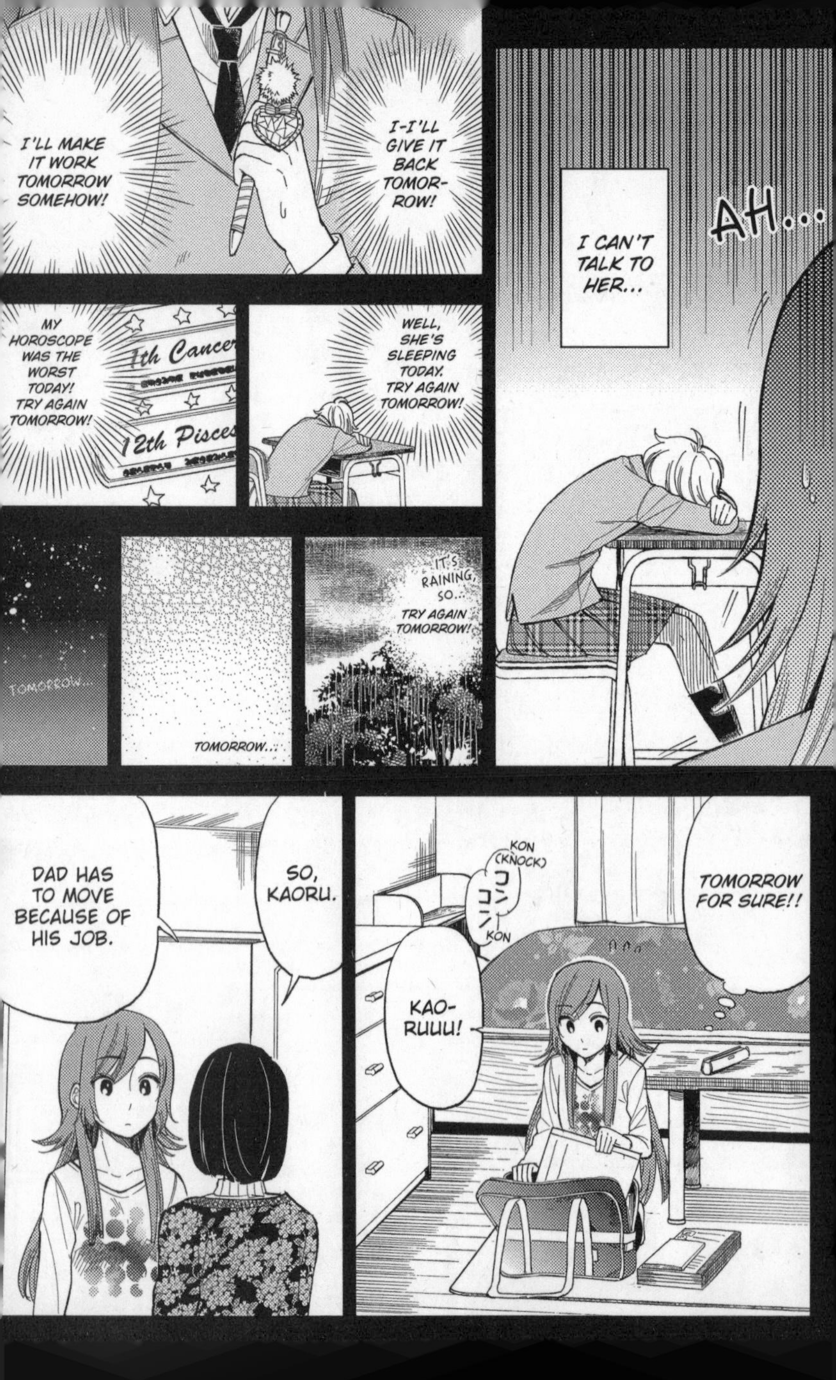

AH...
I CAN'T TALK TO HER...
I-I'LL GIVE IT BACK TOMORROW!
I'LL MAKE IT WORK TOMORROW SOMEHOW!
WELL, SHE'S SLEEPING TODAY. TRY AGAIN TOMORROW!
1th Cancer
12th Pisces
MY HOROSCOPE WAS THE WORST TODAY! TRY AGAIN TOMORROW!
IT'S RAINING, SO... TRY AGAIN TOMORROW!
TOMORROW...
TOMORROW...
TOMORROW FOR SURE!!
KON (KNOCK) コン コン KON
KAO-RUUU!
SO, KAORU.
DAD HAS TO MOVE BECAUSE OF HIS JOB.

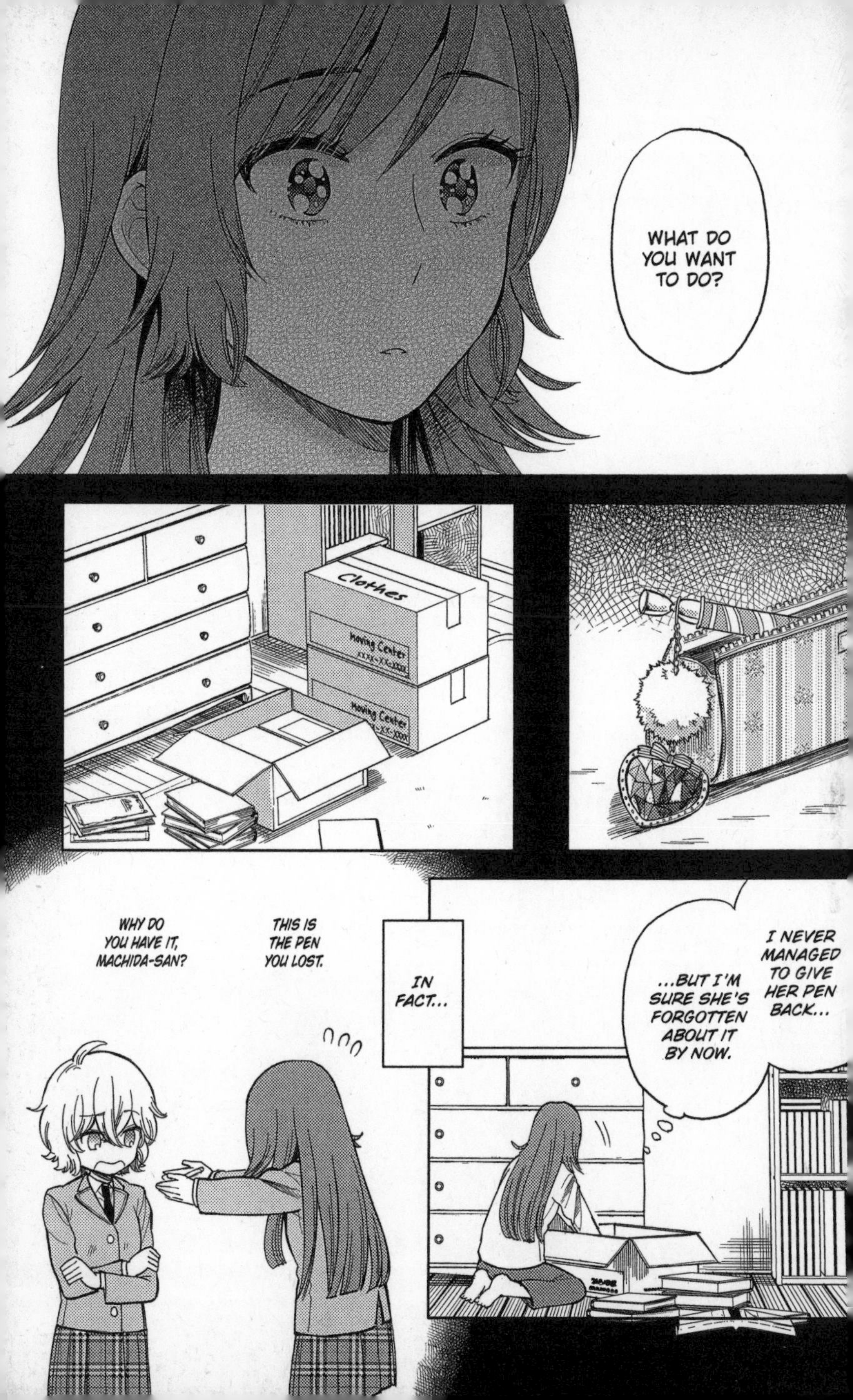
WHAT DO YOU WANT TO DO?
Clothes
Moving Center
Moving Center
I NEVER MANAGED TO GIVE HER PEN BACK...
...BUT I'M SURE SHE'S FORGOTTEN ABOUT IT BY NOW.
IN FACT...
THIS IS THE PEN YOU LOST.
WHY DO YOU HAVE IT, MACHIDA-SAN?

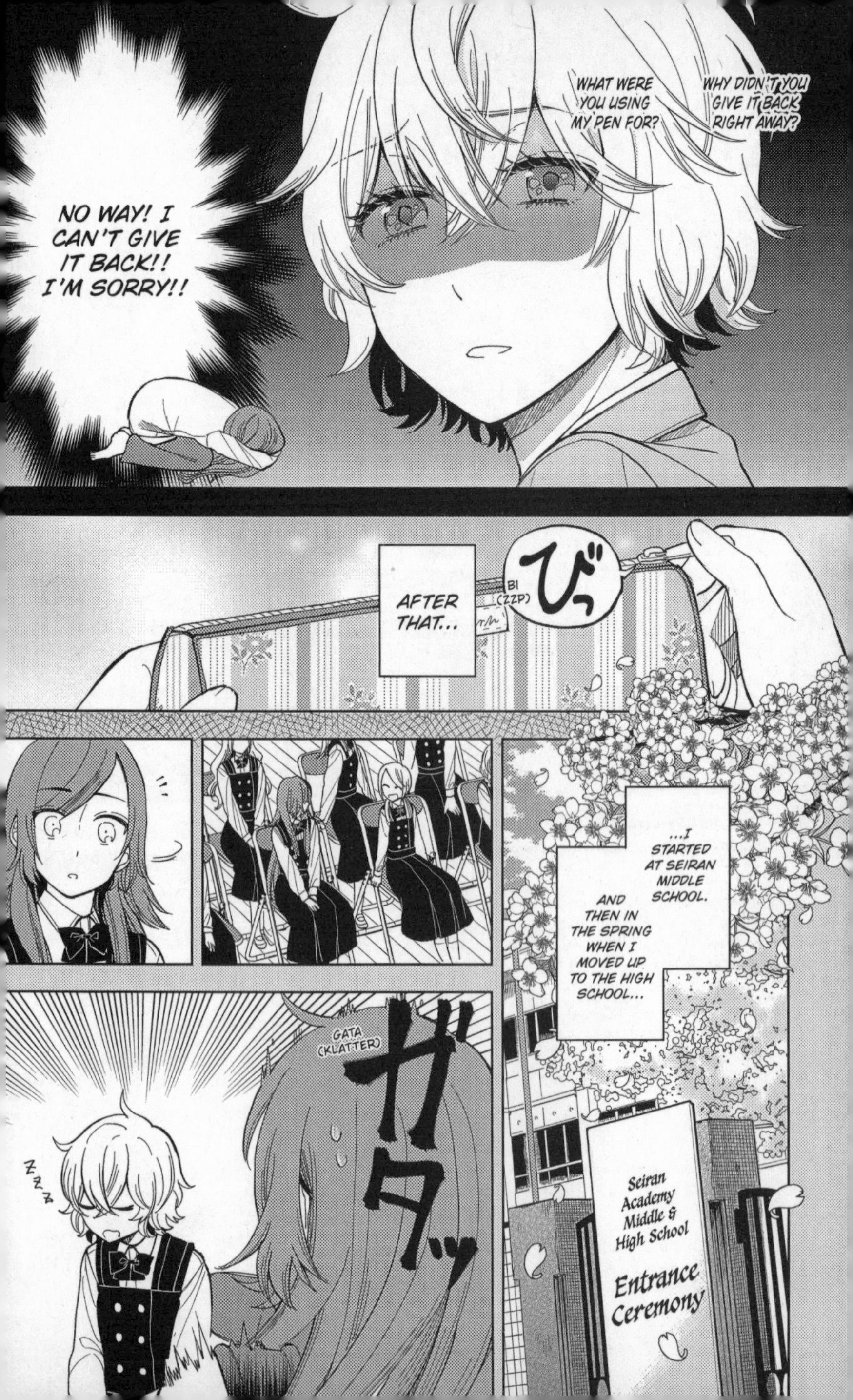
WHY DIDN'T YOU GIVE IT BACK RIGHT AWAY?
WHAT WERE YOU USING MY PEN FOR?
NO WAY! I CAN'T GIVE IT BACK!! I'M SORRY!!
びっ
BI (ZZP)
AFTER THAT...
...I STARTED AT SEIRAN MIDDLE SCHOOL.
AND THEN IN THE SPRING WHEN I MOVED UP TO THE HIGH SCHOOL...
Seiran Academy Middle & High School
Entrance Ceremony
ガタッ
GATA (KLATTER)
Z Z Z

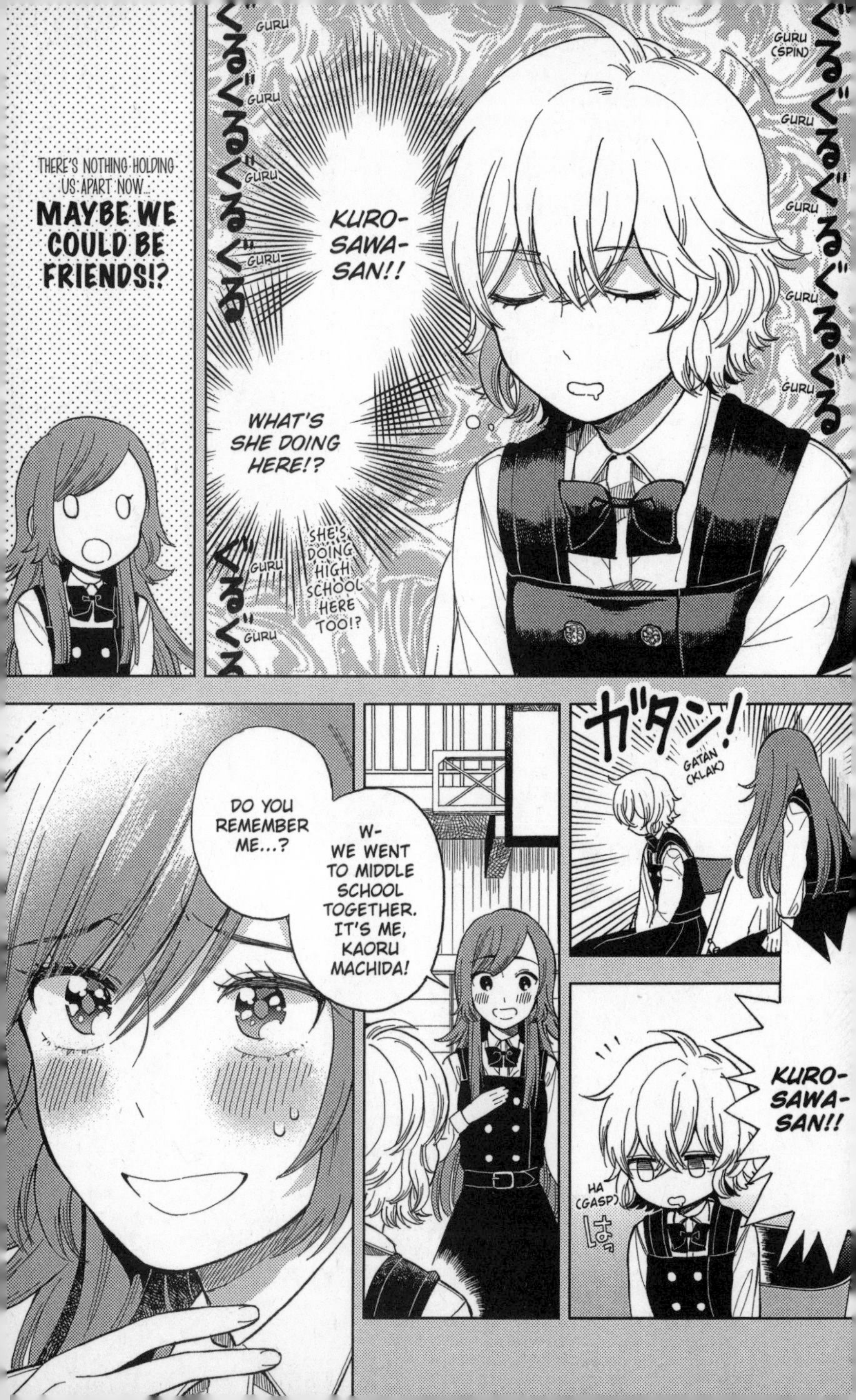

ぐるぐるぐるぐるぐる
GURU (SPIN)
GURU
GURU
GURU
GURU
KURO-SAWA-SAN!!
WHAT'S SHE DOING HERE!?
SHE'S DOING HIGH SCHOOL HERE TOO!?
ぐるぐるぐるぐる
GURU
GURU
GURU
GURU
GURU
GURU
THERE'S NOTHING HOLDING US APART NOW...
MAYBE WE COULD BE FRIENDS!?
ガタン!
GATAN (KLAK)
KURO-SAWA-SAN!!
HA (GASP)
はっ
W- WE WENT TO MIDDLE SCHOOL TOGETHER. IT'S ME, KAORU MACHIDA!
DO YOU REMEMBER ME...?

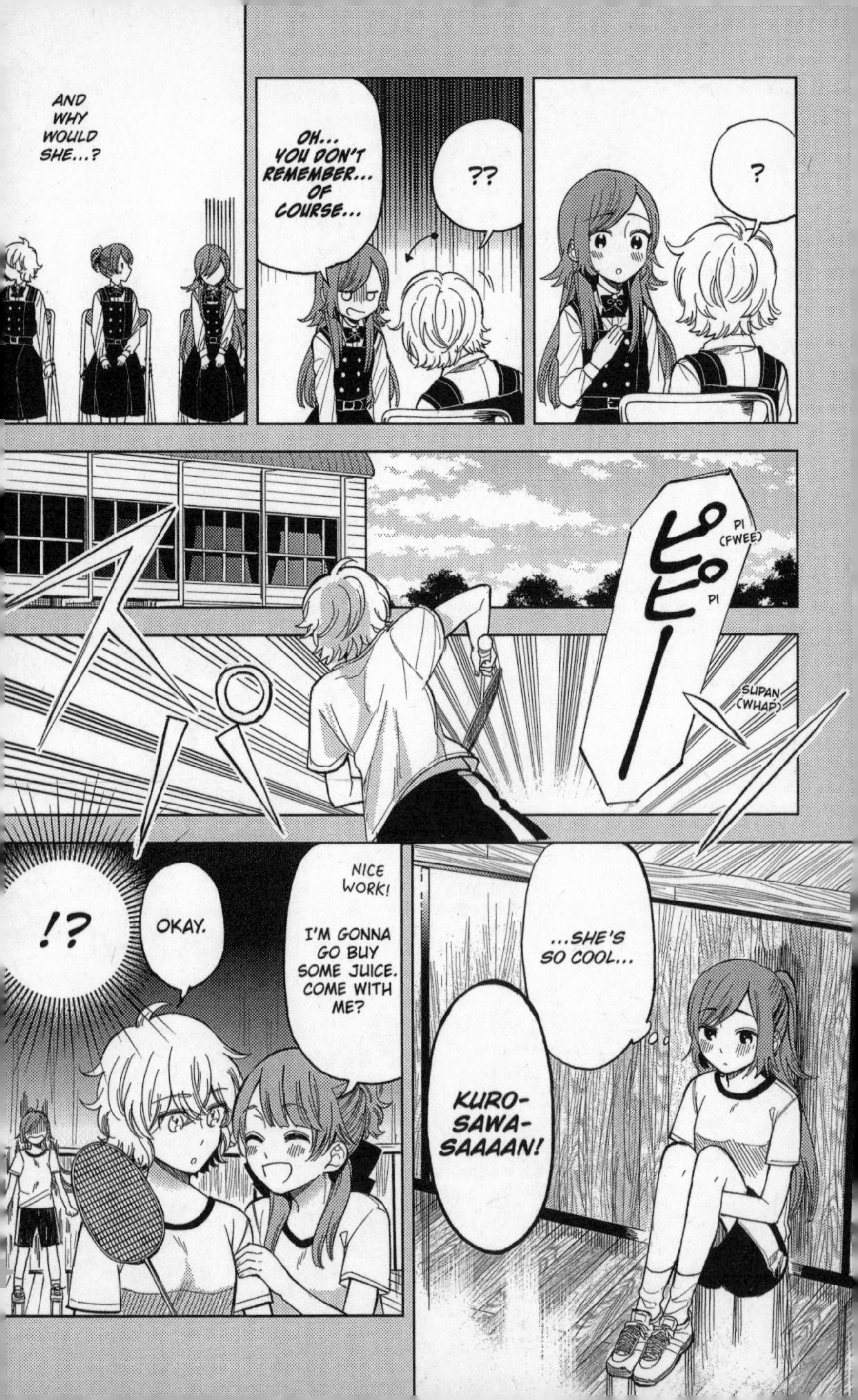
?
??
OH... YOU DON'T REMEMBER... OF COURSE...
AND WHY WOULD SHE...?
ピピー
PI (FWEE) PI
スパン
SUPAN (WHAP)
...SHE'S SO COOL...
KURO-SAWA-SAAAAN!
NICE WORK!
I'M GONNA GO BUY SOME JUICE. COME WITH ME?
OKAY.
!?

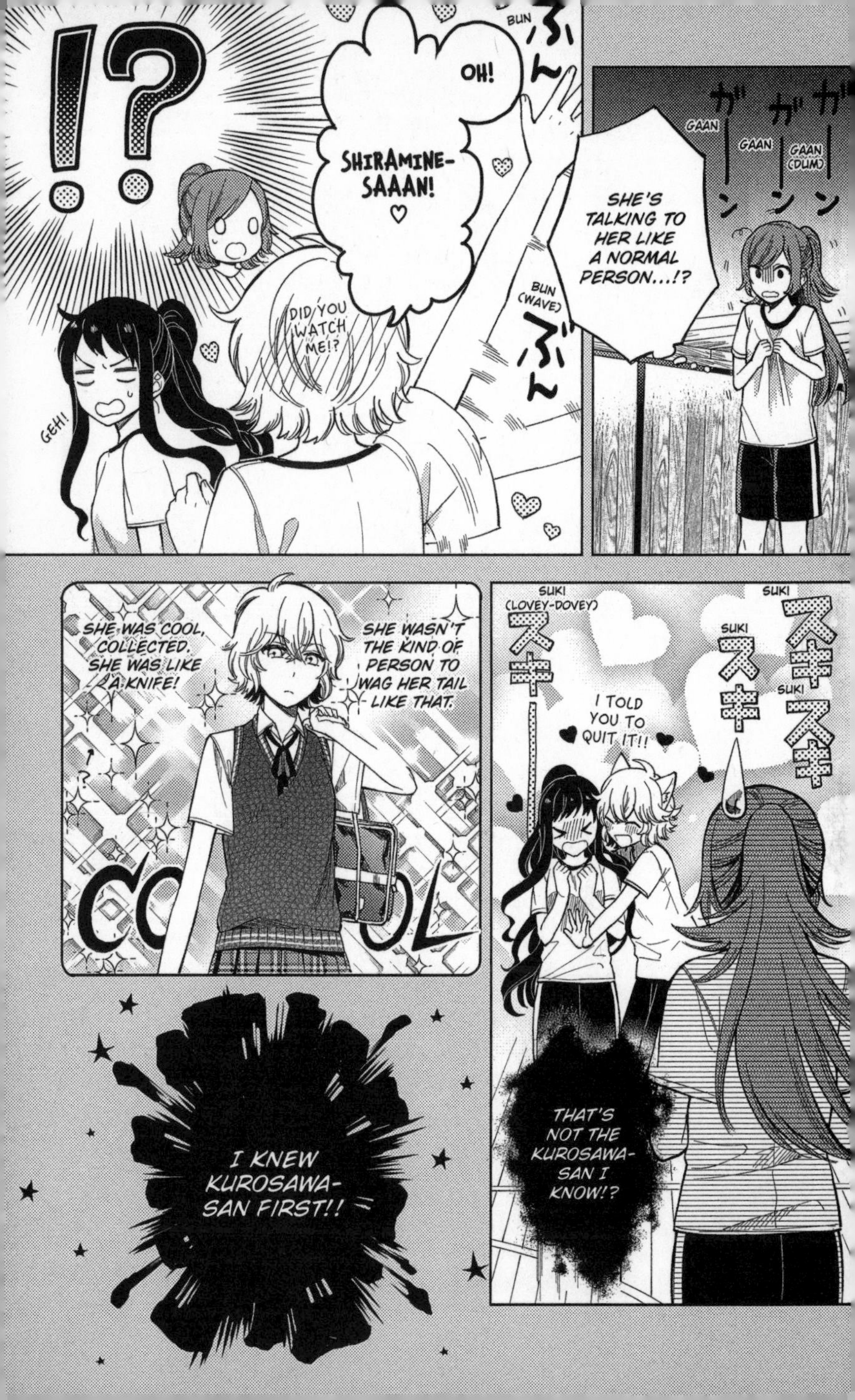

ガーン
GAAN
ガーン
GAAN
ガーン
GAAN (DUM)
SHE'S TALKING TO HER LIKE A NORMAL PERSON...!?
ぶん
BUN
OH!
SHIRAMINE-SAAAN! ♡
ぶん
BUN (WAVE)
DID YOU WATCH ME!?
!?
GEH!
スキ
SUKI
スキ
SUKI
スキ
SUKI
スキ
SUKI (LOVEY-DOVEY)
I TOLD YOU TO QUIT IT!!
THAT'S NOT THE KUROSAWA-SAN I KNOW!?
SHE WASN'T THE KIND OF PERSON TO WAG HER TAIL LIKE THAT.
SHE WAS COOL, COLLECTED. SHE WAS LIKE A KNIFE!
?
COOL
I KNEW KUROSAWA-SAN FIRST!!

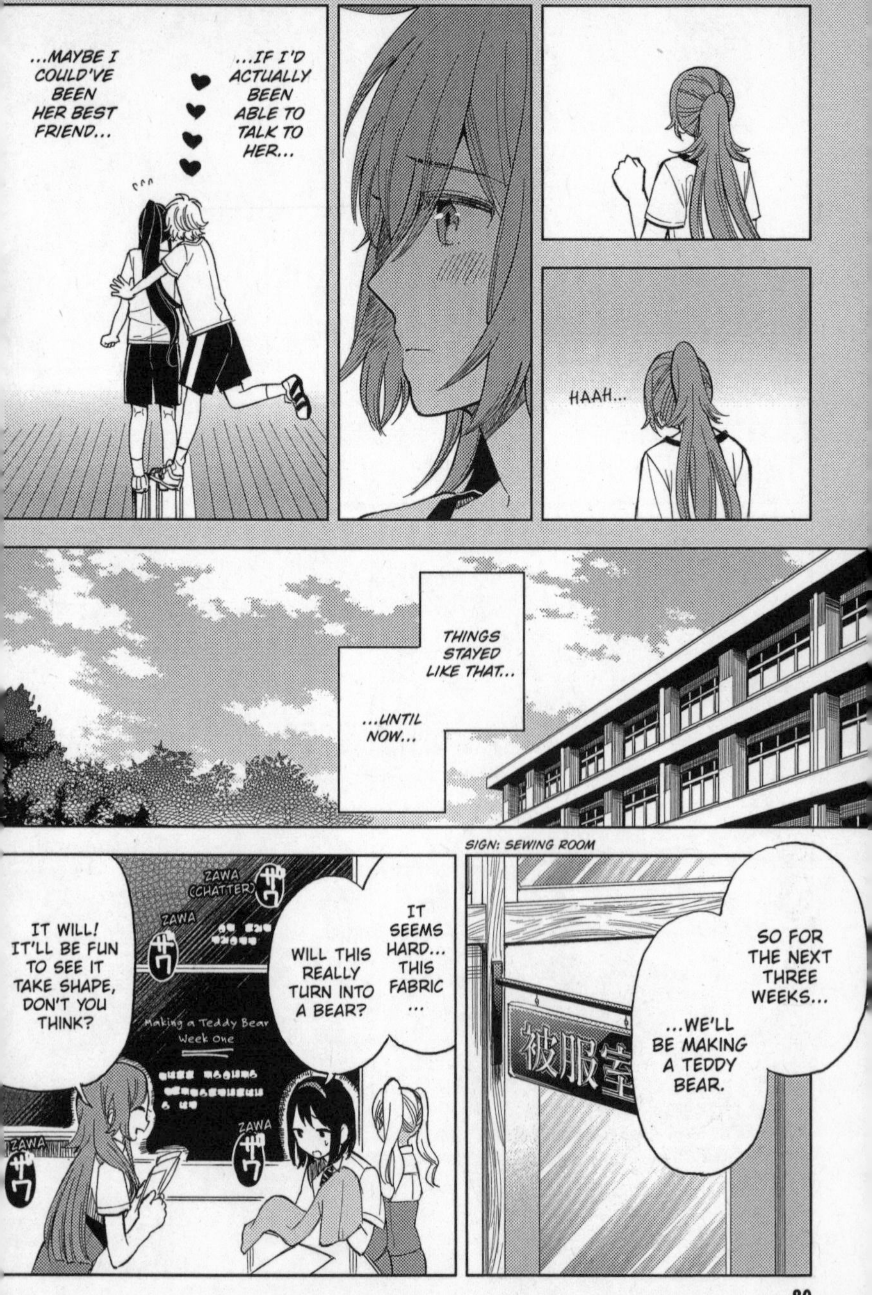
HAAH...
...IF I'D ACTUALLY BEEN ABLE TO TALK TO HER...
...MAYBE I COULD'VE BEEN HER BEST FRIEND...
THINGS STAYED LIKE THAT...
...UNTIL NOW...
SIGN: SEWING ROOM
被服室
SO FOR THE NEXT THREE WEEKS...
...WE'LL BE MAKING A TEDDY BEAR.
ZAWA (CHATTER)
ザワ
ZAWA
ザワ
IT SEEMS HARD... THIS FABRIC ...
WILL THIS REALLY TURN INTO A BEAR?
IT WILL! IT'LL BE FUN TO SEE IT TAKE SHAPE, DON'T YOU THINK?
Making a Teddy Bear Week One
ZAWA
ザワ
ZAWA
ザワ

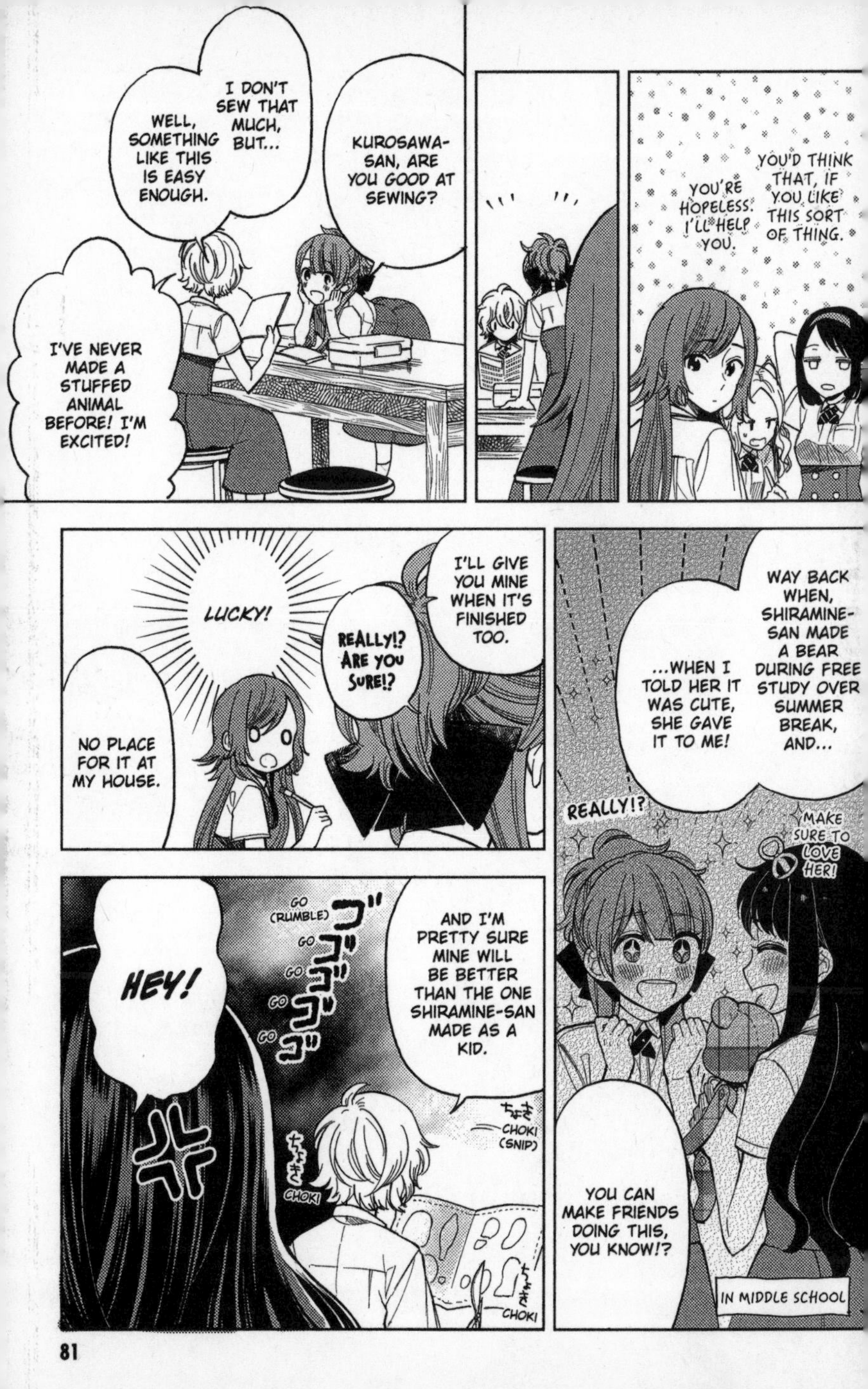
YOU'D THINK THAT, IF YOU LIKE THIS SORT OF THING.
YOU'RE HOPELESS. I'LL HELP YOU.
KUROSAWA-SAN, ARE YOU GOOD AT SEWING?
I DON'T SEW THAT MUCH, BUT...
WELL, SOMETHING LIKE THIS IS EASY ENOUGH.
I'VE NEVER MADE A STUFFED ANIMAL BEFORE! I'M EXCITED!
WAY BACK WHEN, SHIRAMINE-SAN MADE A BEAR DURING FREE STUDY OVER SUMMER BREAK, AND...
...WHEN I TOLD HER IT WAS CUTE, SHE GAVE IT TO ME!
MAKE SURE TO LOVE HER!
REALLY!?
YOU CAN MAKE FRIENDS DOING THIS, YOU KNOW!?
IN MIDDLE SCHOOL
I'LL GIVE YOU MINE WHEN IT'S FINISHED TOO.
REALLY!? ARE YOU SURE!?
LUCKY!
NO PLACE FOR IT AT MY HOUSE.
AND I'M PRETTY SURE MINE WILL BE BETTER THAN THE ONE SHIRAMINE-SAN MADE AS A KID.
GO (RUMBLE)
GO
GO
GO
GO
HEY!
CHOKI (SNIP)
CHOKI
CHOKI

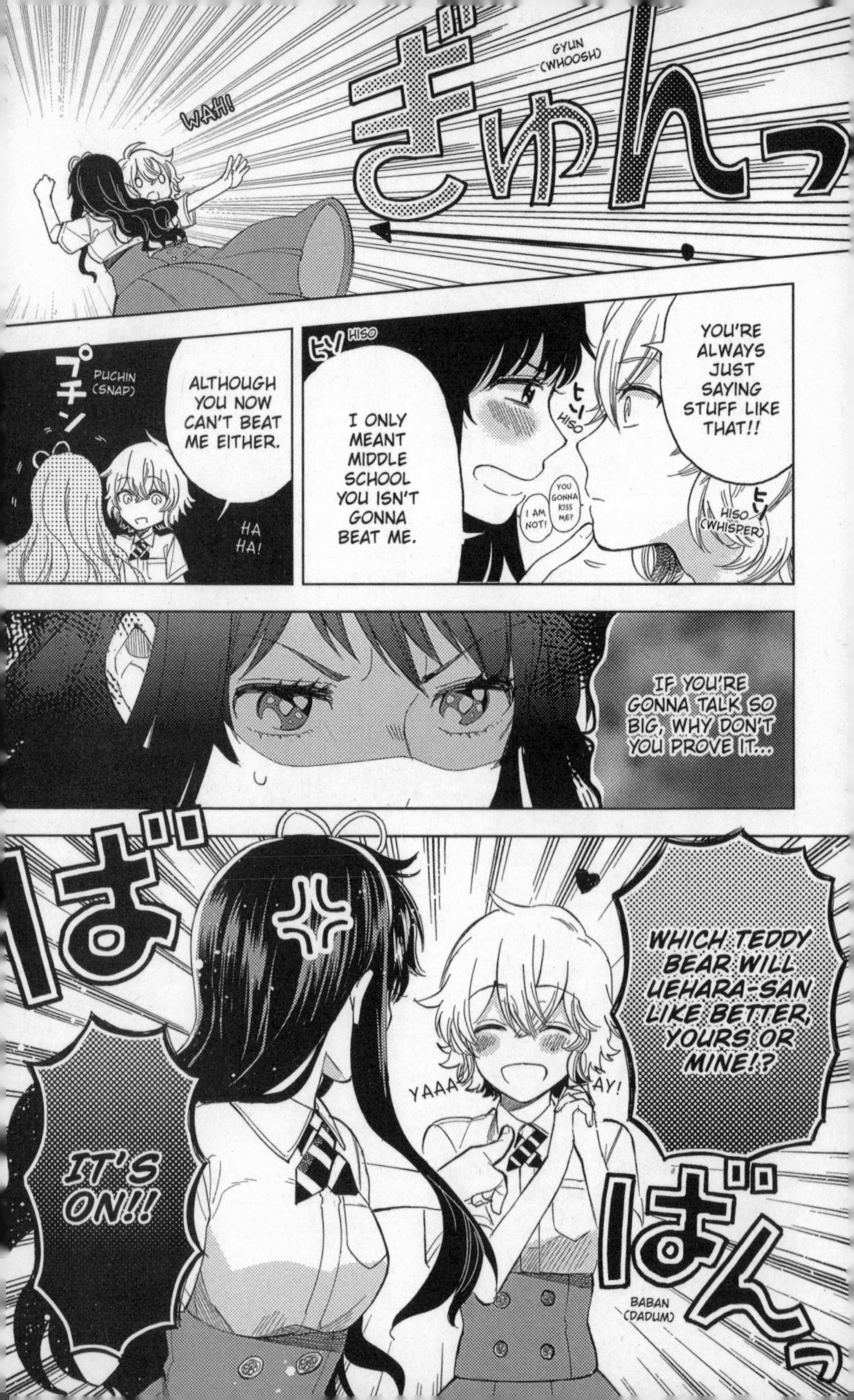
ぎゅんっ
GYUN (WHOOSH)
WAH!
YOU'RE ALWAYS JUST SAYING STUFF LIKE THAT!!
ヒソ
HISO (WHISPER)
YOU GONNA KISS ME?
I AM NOT!
ヒソ HISO
ヒソ HISO
I ONLY MEANT MIDDLE SCHOOL YOU ISN'T GONNA BEAT ME.
ALTHOUGH YOU NOW CAN'T BEAT ME EITHER.
HA HA!
プチン
PUCHIN (SNAP)
IF YOU'RE GONNA TALK SO BIG, WHY DON'T YOU PROVE IT...
WHICH TEDDY BEAR WILL UEHARA-SAN LIKE BETTER, YOURS OR MINE!?
YAAAAY!
IT'S ON!!
ばばんっ
BABAN (DADUM)

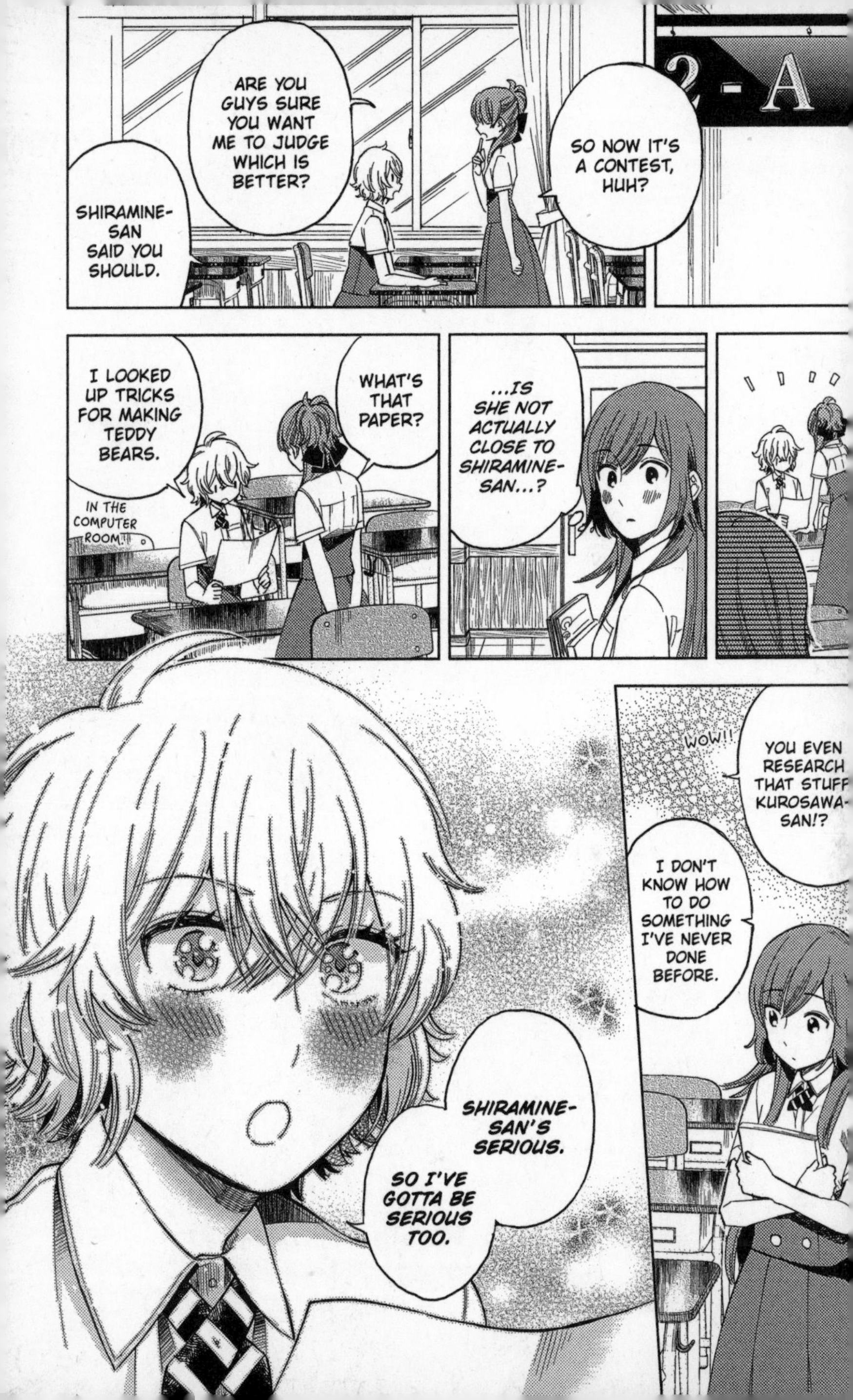
2-A
SO NOW IT'S A CONTEST, HUH?
ARE YOU GUYS SURE YOU WANT ME TO JUDGE WHICH IS BETTER?
SHIRAMINE-SAN SAID YOU SHOULD.
...IS SHE NOT ACTUALLY CLOSE TO SHIRAMINE-SAN...?
WHAT'S THAT PAPER?
I LOOKED UP TRICKS FOR MAKING TEDDY BEARS.
IN THE COMPUTER ROOM!
YOU EVEN RESEARCH THAT STUFF KUROSAWA-SAN!?
WOW!!
I DON'T KNOW HOW TO DO SOMETHING I'VE NEVER DONE BEFORE.
SHIRAMINE-SAN'S SERIOUS.
SO I'VE GOTTA BE SERIOUS TOO.

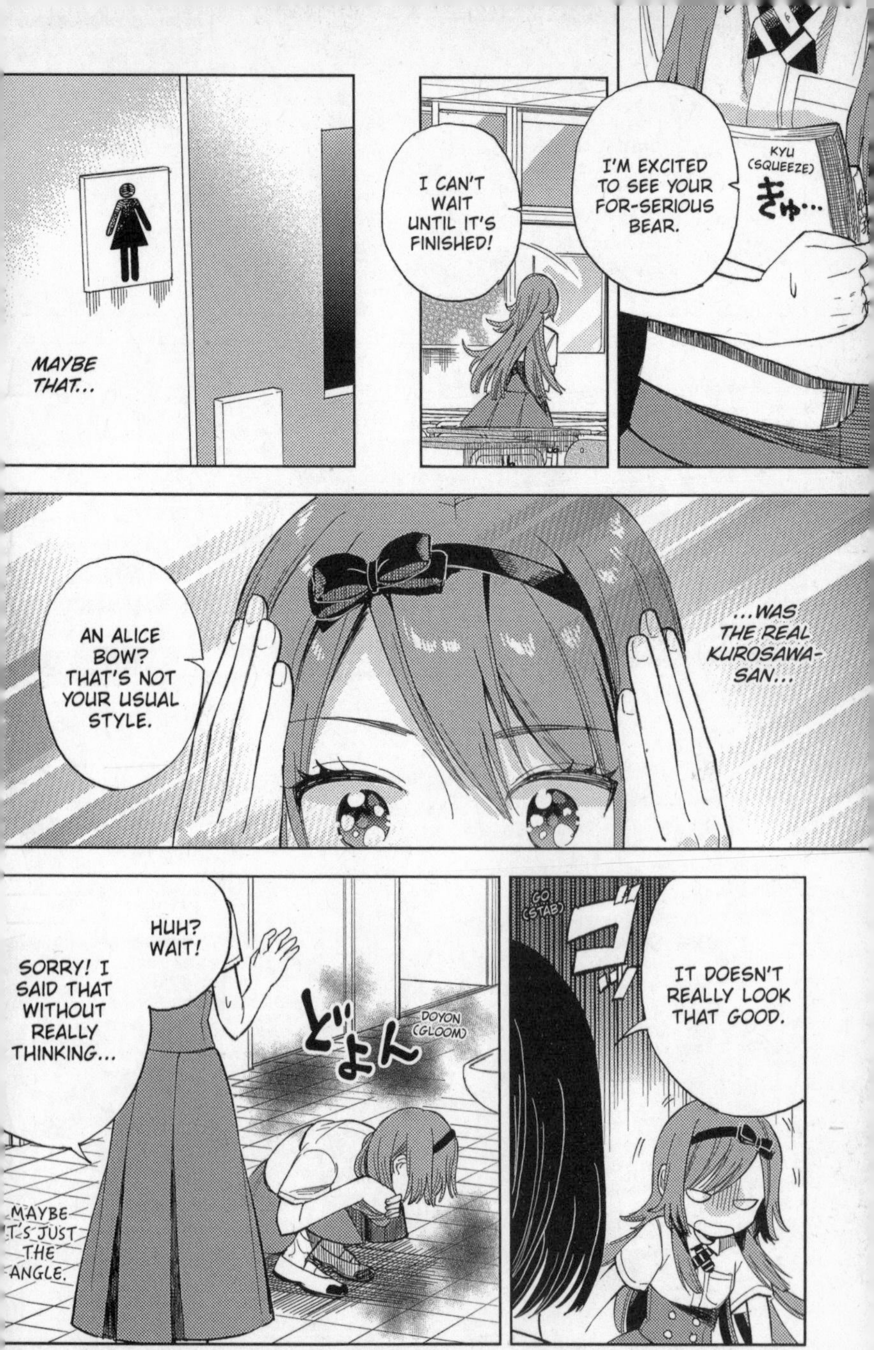
KYU (SQUEEZE)
ぎゅ…
I'M EXCITED TO SEE YOUR FOR-SERIOUS BEAR.
I CAN'T WAIT UNTIL IT'S FINISHED!
MAYBE THAT...
...WAS THE REAL KUROSAWA-SAN...
AN ALICE BOW? THAT'S NOT YOUR USUAL STYLE.
GO (STAB)
IT DOESN'T REALLY LOOK THAT GOOD.
HUH? WAIT!
どよん
DOYON (GLOOM)
SORRY! I SAID THAT WITHOUT REALLY THINKING...
MAYBE IT'S JUST THE ANGLE.

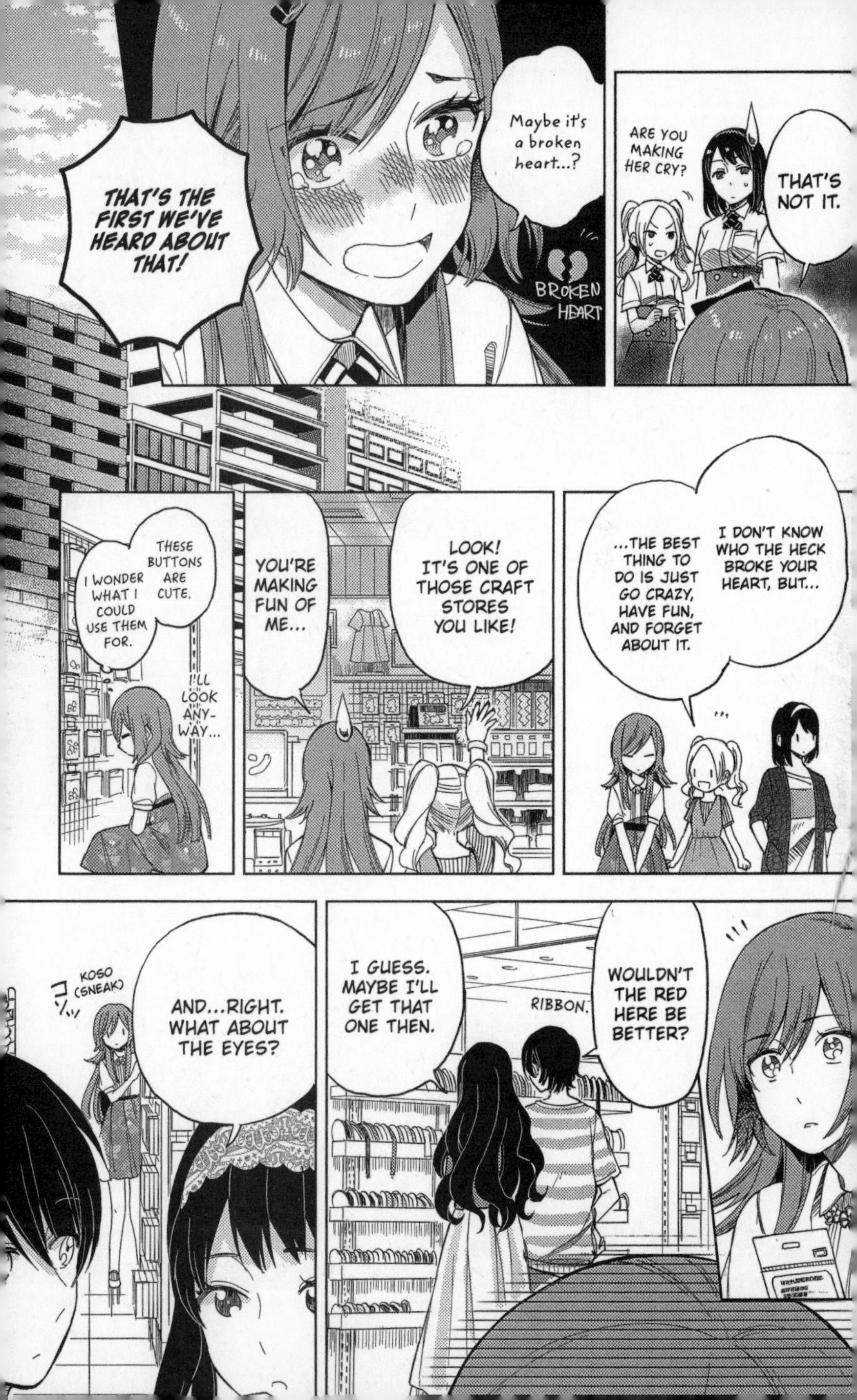
ARE YOU MAKING HER CRY?
THAT'S NOT IT.
Maybe it's a broken heart...?
BROKEN HEART
THAT'S THE FIRST WE'VE HEARD ABOUT THAT!
I DON'T KNOW WHO THE HECK BROKE YOUR HEART, BUT...
...THE BEST THING TO DO IS JUST GO CRAZY, HAVE FUN, AND FORGET ABOUT IT.
...
LOOK! IT'S ONE OF THOSE CRAFT STORES YOU LIKE!
YOU'RE MAKING FUN OF ME...
THESE BUTTONS ARE CUTE.
I WONDER WHAT I COULD USE THEM FOR.
I'LL LOOK ANYWAY...
WOULDN'T THE RED HERE BE BETTER?
RIBBON.
I GUESS. MAYBE I'LL GET THAT ONE THEN.
AND...RIGHT. WHAT ABOUT THE EYES?
KOSO (SNEAK)

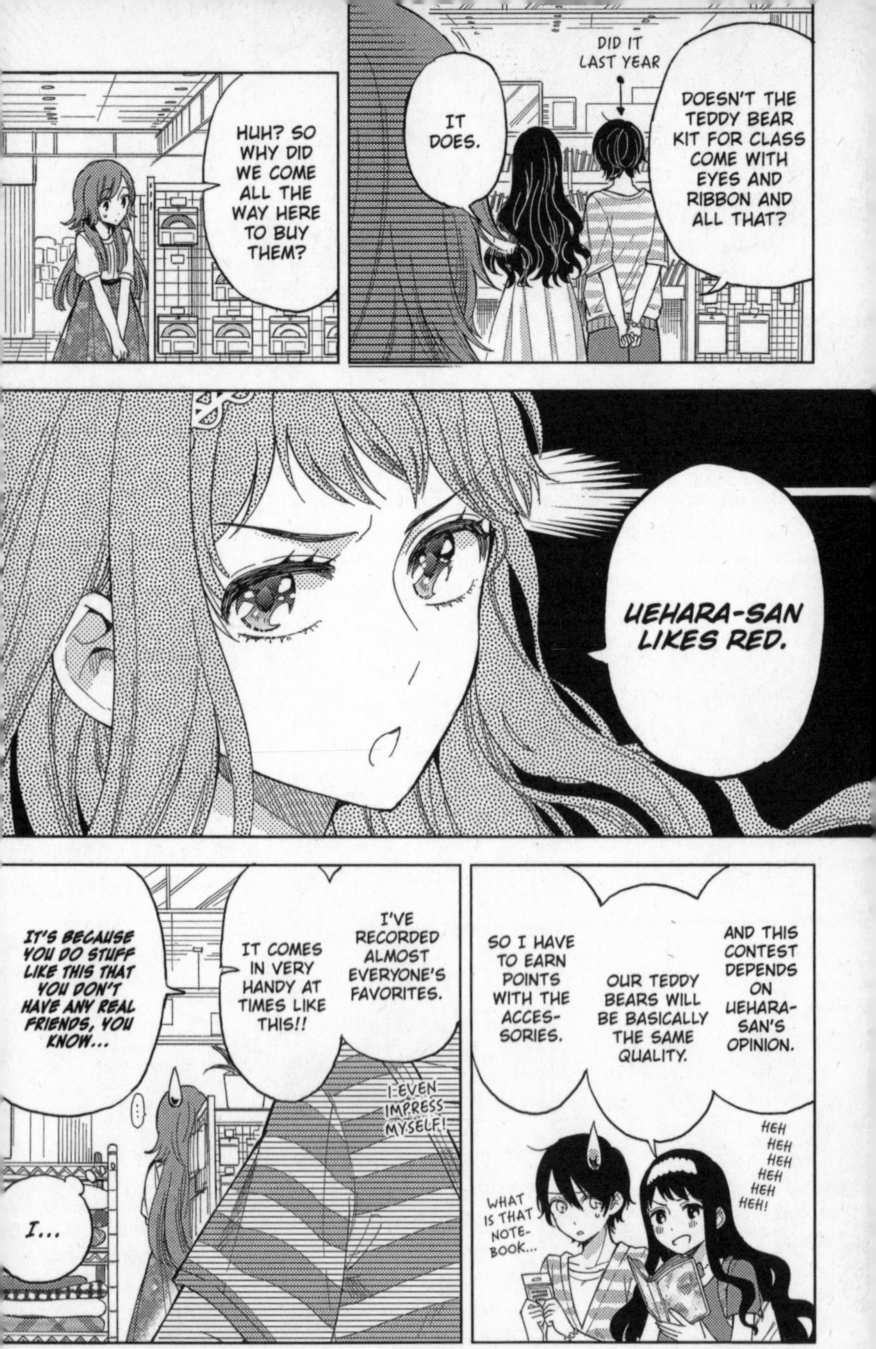
DOESN'T THE TEDDY BEAR KIT FOR CLASS COME WITH EYES AND RIBBON AND ALL THAT?
DID IT LAST YEAR
IT DOES.
HUH? SO WHY DID WE COME ALL THE WAY HERE TO BUY THEM?
UEHARA-SAN LIKES RED.
AND THIS CONTEST DEPENDS ON UEHARA-SAN'S OPINION.
OUR TEDDY BEARS WILL BE BASICALLY THE SAME QUALITY.
SO I HAVE TO EARN POINTS WITH THE ACCES-SORIES.
HEH HEH HEH HEH HEH HEH!
WHAT IS THAT NOTE-BOOK...
I'VE RECORDED ALMOST EVERYONE'S FAVORITES.
IT COMES IN VERY HANDY AT TIMES LIKE THIS!!
I EVEN IMPRESS MYSELF!
IT'S BECAUSE YOU DO STUFF LIKE THIS THAT YOU DON'T HAVE ANY REAL FRIENDS, YOU KNOW...
...
I...

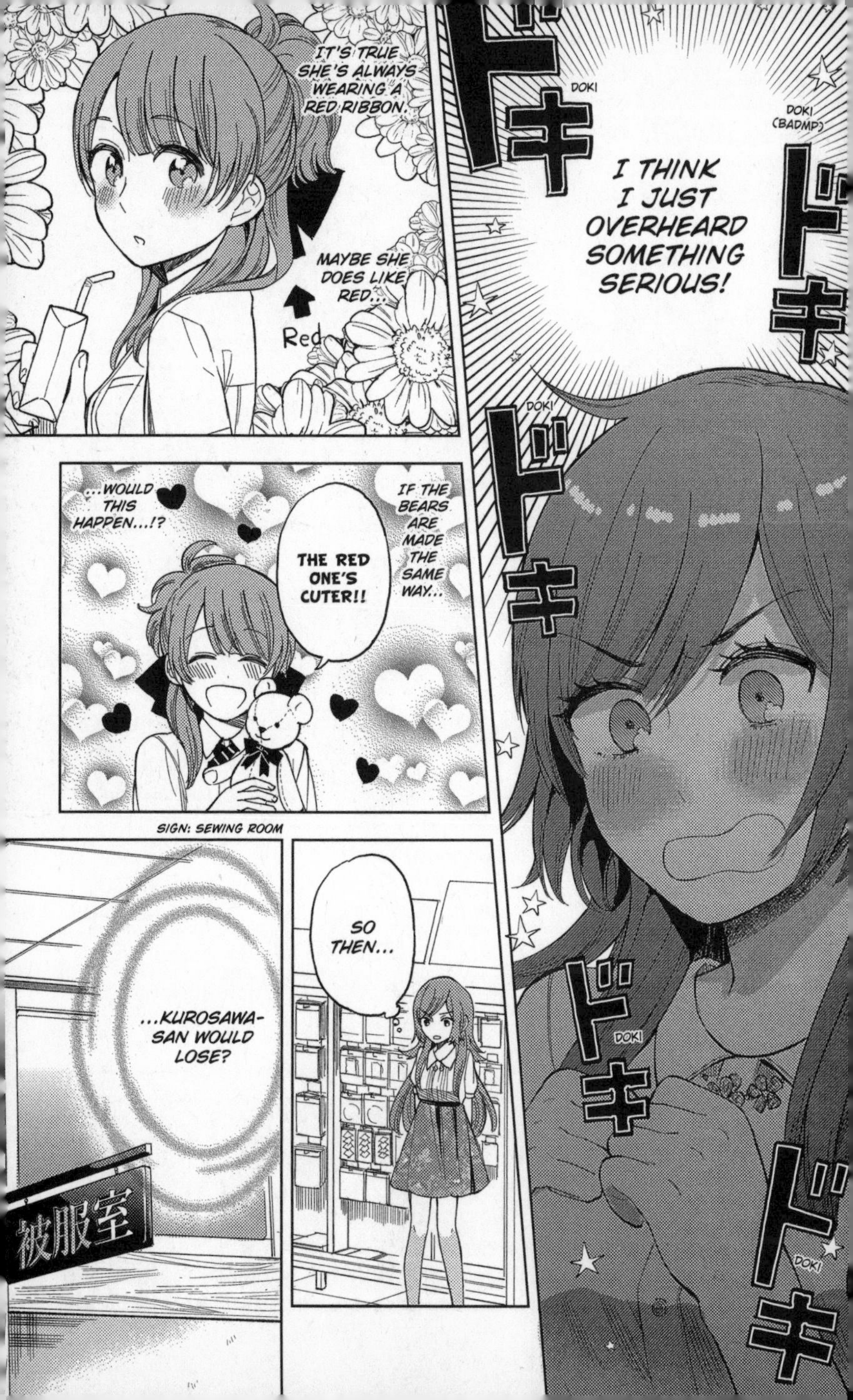
DOKI
DOKI (BADMP)
I THINK I JUST OVERHEARD SOMETHING SERIOUS!
DOKI
DOKI
DOKI
IT'S TRUE SHE'S ALWAYS WEARING A RED RIBBON.
MAYBE SHE DOES LIKE RED...
Red
IF THE BEARS ARE MADE THE SAME WAY...
THE RED ONE'S CUTER!!
...WOULD THIS HAPPEN...!?
SIGN: SEWING ROOM
SO THEN...
...KUROSAWA-SAN WOULD LOSE?
被服室

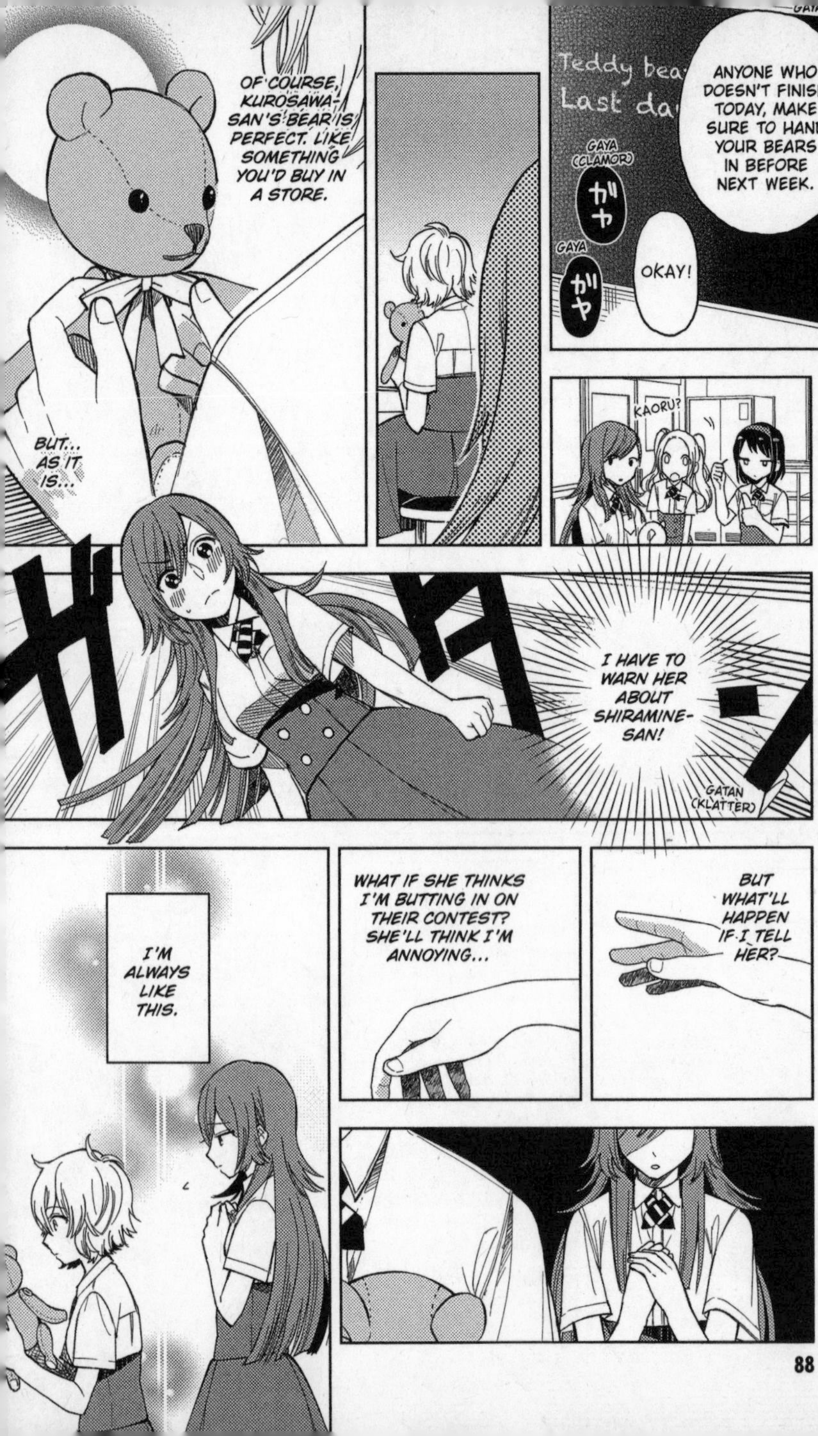
GAYA
Teddy bea
Last da
ANYONE WHO DOESN'T FINISH TODAY, MAKE SURE TO HAND YOUR BEARS IN BEFORE NEXT WEEK.
GAYA (CLAMOR)
ガヤ
GAYA
ガヤ
OKAY!
KAORU?
OF COURSE, KUROSAWA-SAN'S BEAR IS PERFECT. LIKE SOMETHING YOU'D BUY IN A STORE.
BUT... AS IT IS...
I HAVE TO WARN HER ABOUT SHIRAMINE-SAN!
GATAN (KLATTER)
BUT WHAT'LL HAPPEN IF I TELL HER?
WHAT IF SHE THINKS I'M BUTTING IN ON THEIR CONTEST? SHE'LL THINK I'M ANNOYING...
I'M ALWAYS LIKE THIS.

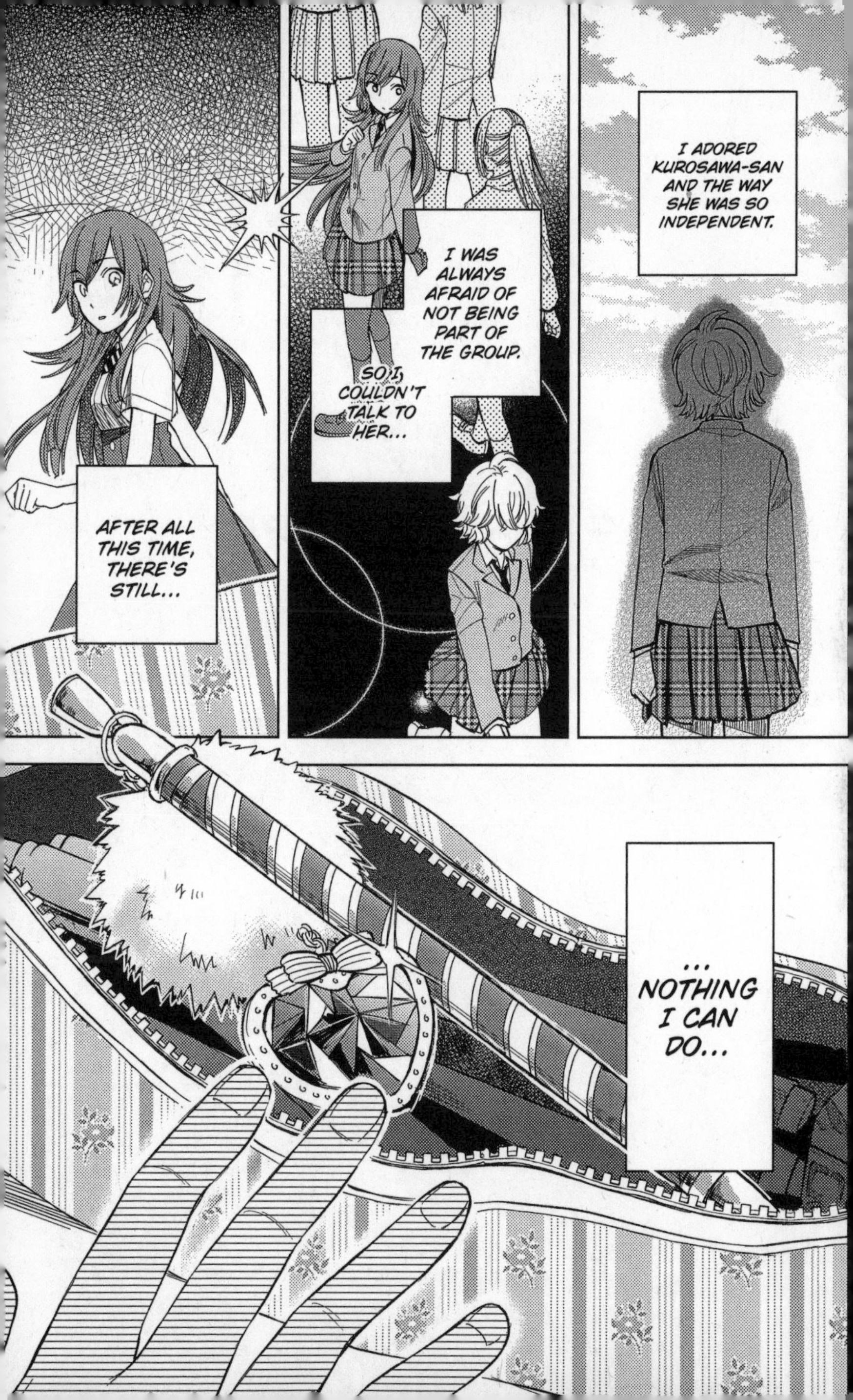
I ADORED KUROSAWA-SAN AND THE WAY SHE WAS SO INDEPENDENT.
I WAS ALWAYS AFRAID OF NOT BEING PART OF THE GROUP.
SO I, COULDN'T TALK TO HER...
AFTER ALL THIS TIME, THERE'S STILL...
...NOTHING I CAN DO...

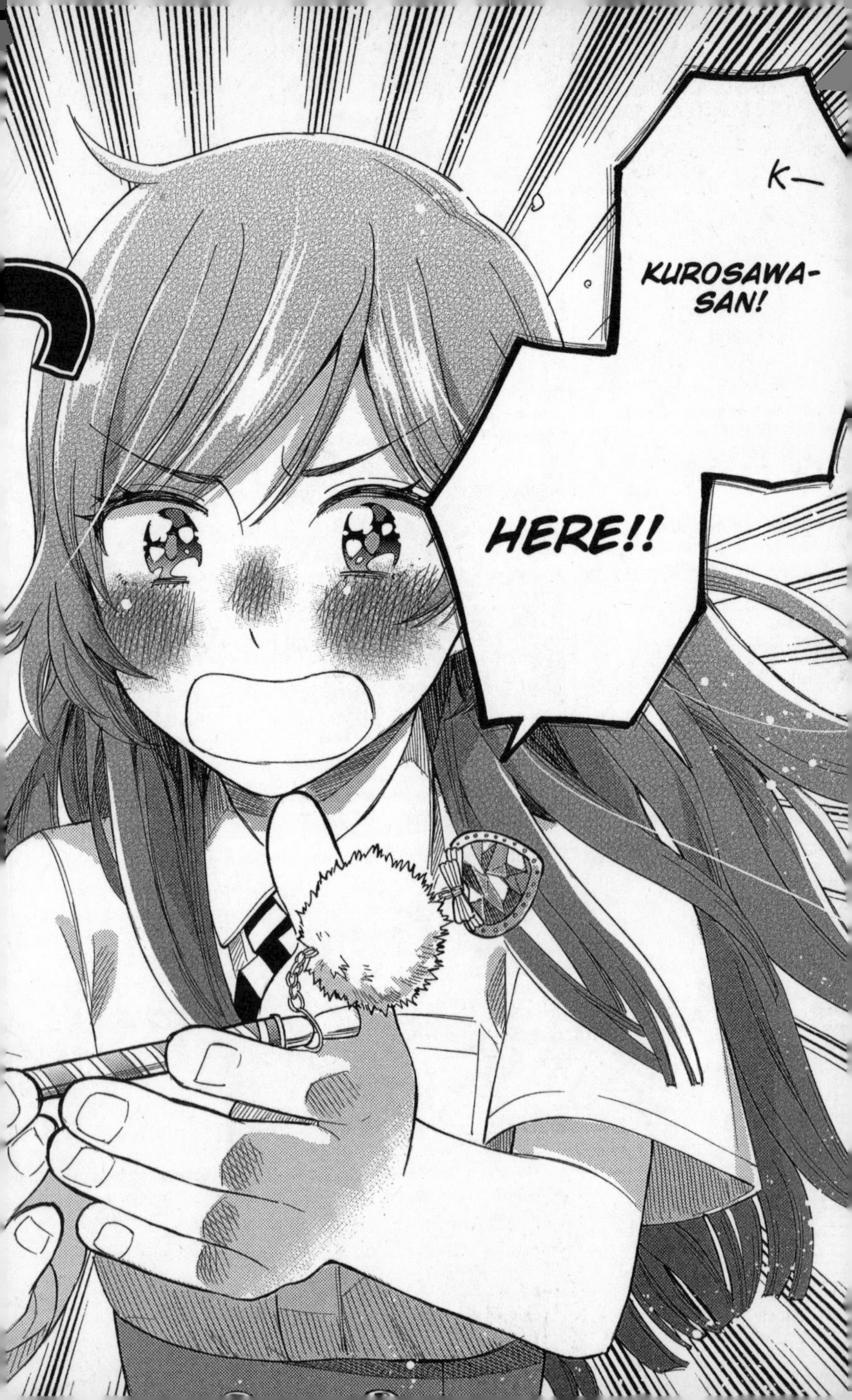
K—
KUROSAWA-SAN!
HERE!!

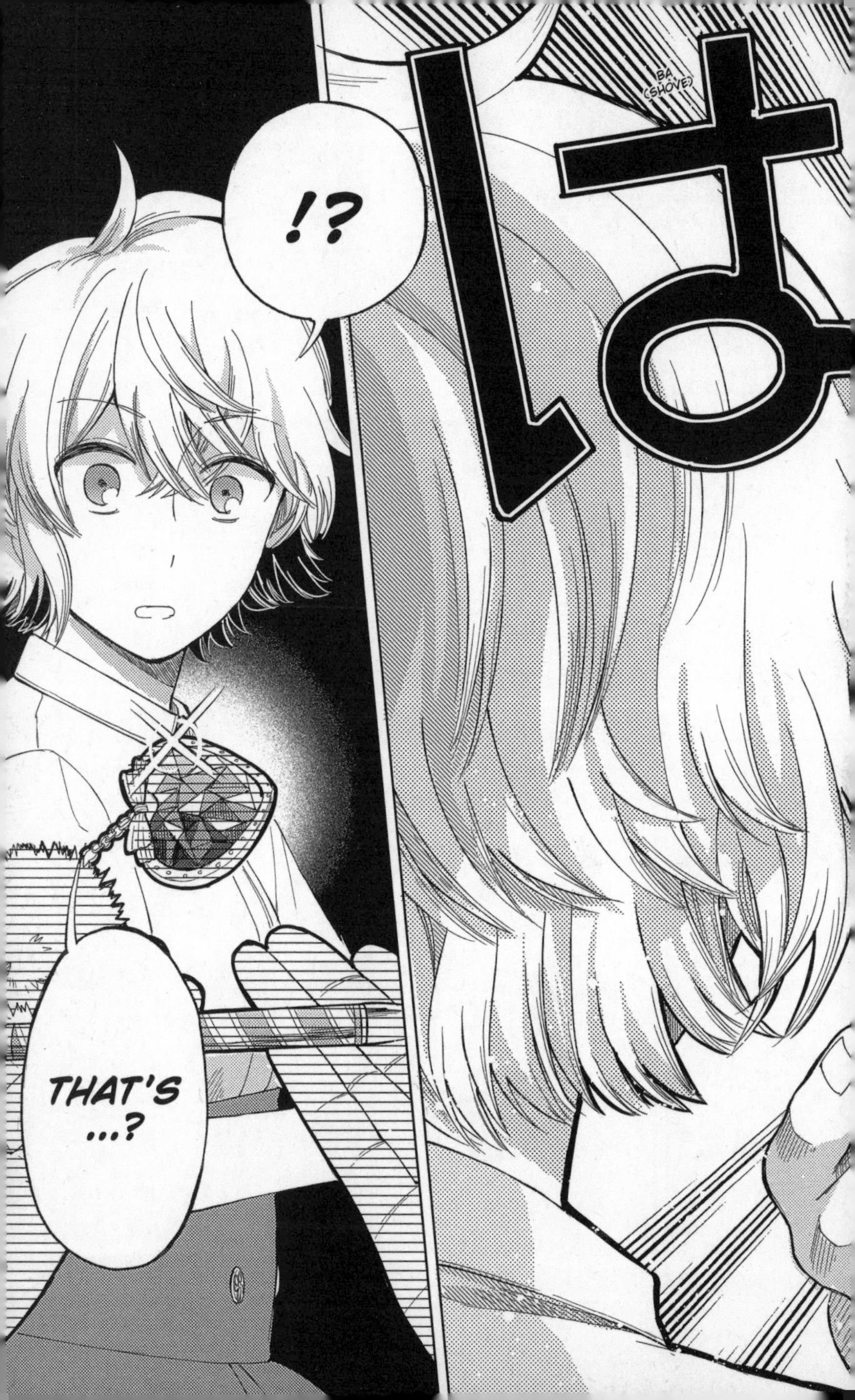
BA (SHOVE)
!?
THAT'S ...?

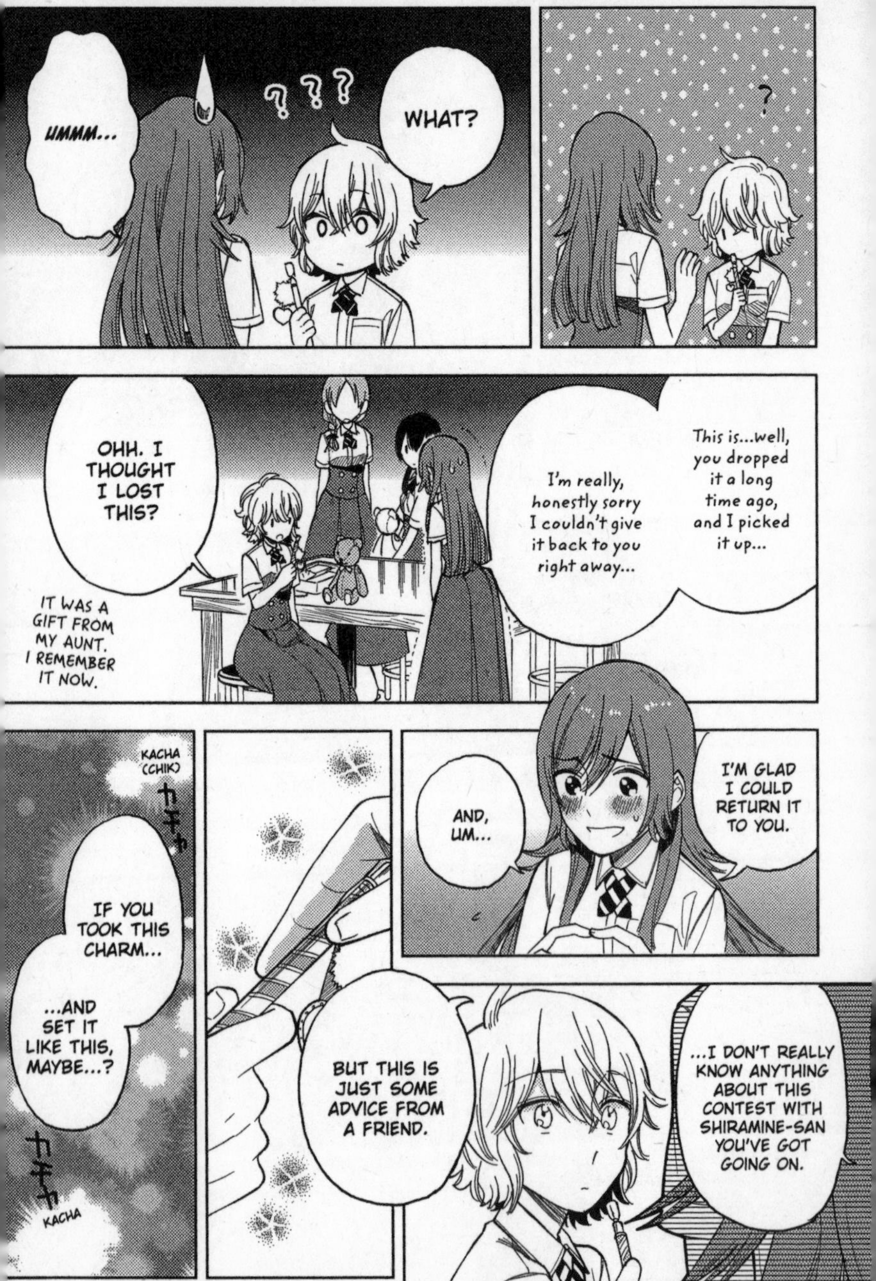
?
WHAT?
? ? ?
UMMM...
This is...well, you dropped it a long time ago, and I picked it up...
I'm really, honestly sorry I couldn't give it back to you right away...
OHH. I THOUGHT I LOST THIS?
IT WAS A GIFT FROM MY AUNT. I REMEMBER IT NOW.
I'M GLAD I COULD RETURN IT TO YOU.
AND, UM...
...I DON'T REALLY KNOW ANYTHING ABOUT THIS CONTEST WITH SHIRAMINE-SAN YOU'VE GOT GOING ON.
BUT THIS IS JUST SOME ADVICE FROM A FRIEND.
KACHA (CHIK)
IF YOU TOOK THIS CHARM...
...AND SET IT LIKE THIS, MAYBE...?
KACHA

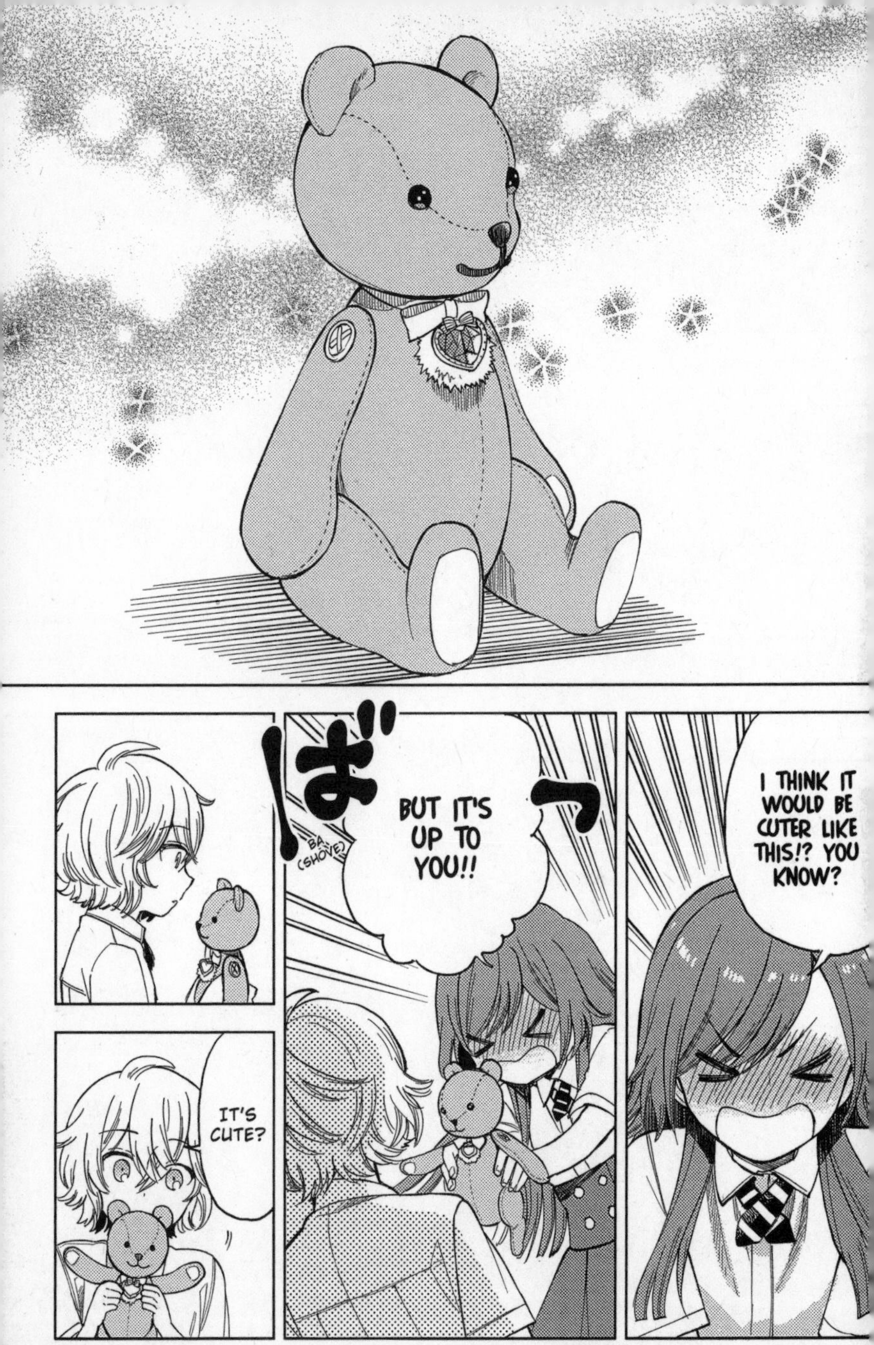
I THINK IT WOULD BE CUTER LIKE THIS!? YOU KNOW?
BUT IT'S UP TO YOU!!
ばーっ
BA (SHOVE)
IT'S CUTE?

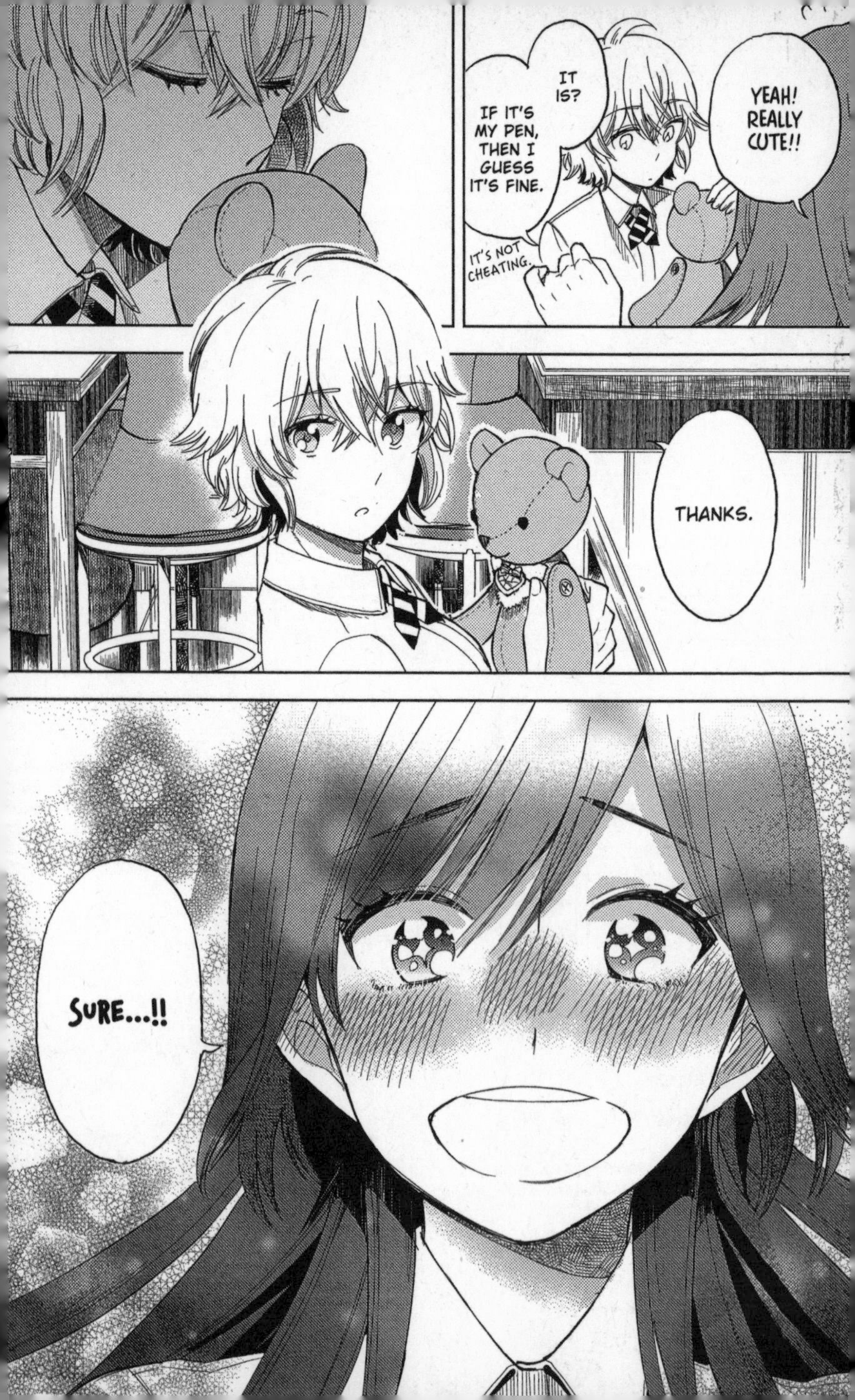
YEAH! REALLY CUTE!!
IT IS?
IF IT'S MY PEN, THEN I GUESS IT'S FINE.
IT'S NOT CHEATING.
THANKS.
SURE...!!

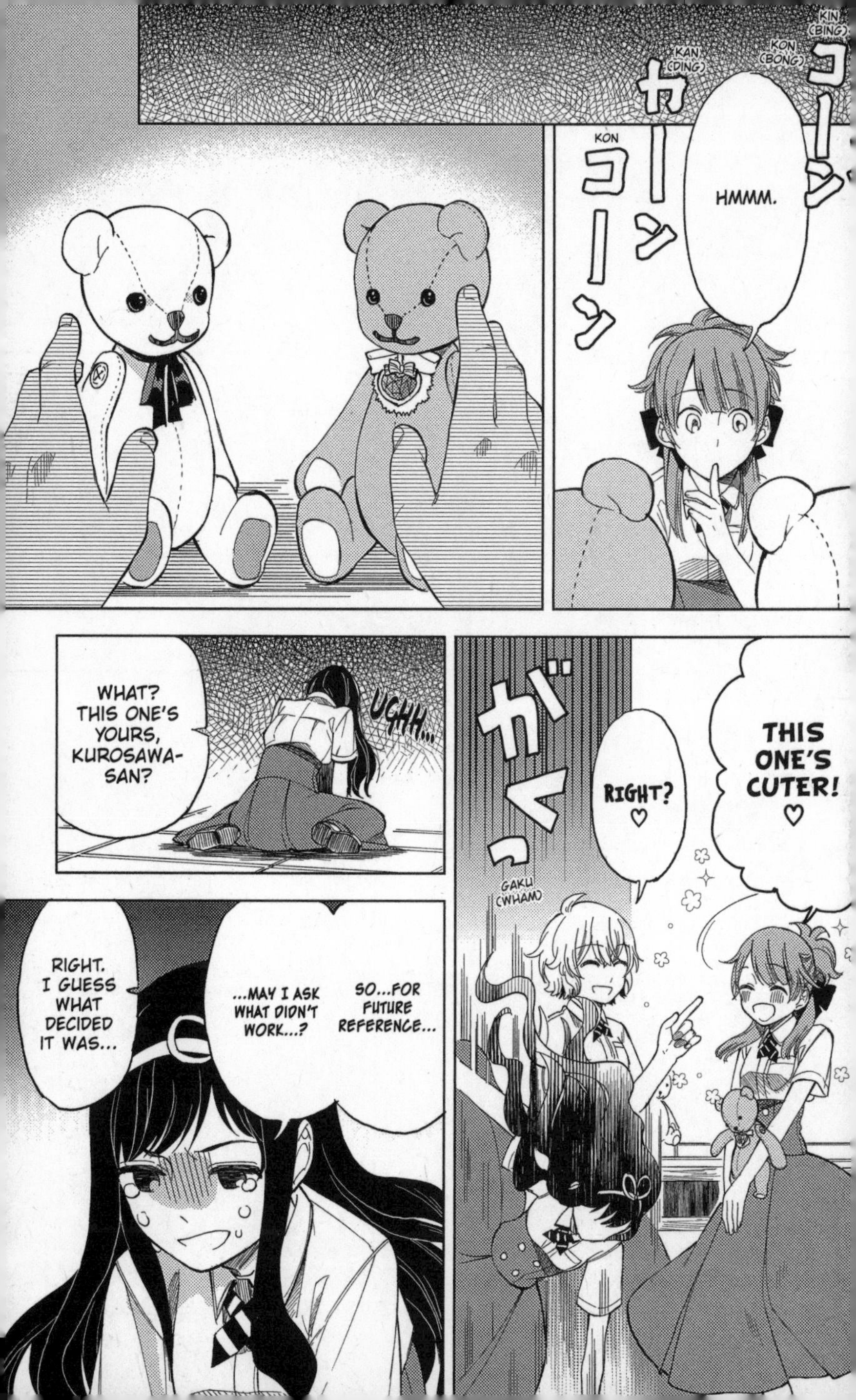
KIN (BING)
KON (BONG)
KAN (DING)
KON
HMMM.
THIS ONE'S CUTER! ♡
RIGHT? ♡
GAKU (WHAM)
WHAT? THIS ONE'S YOURS, KUROSAWA-SAN?
UGHH...
SO...FOR FUTURE REFERENCE...
...MAY I ASK WHAT DIDN'T WORK...?
RIGHT. I GUESS WHAT DECIDED IT WAS...

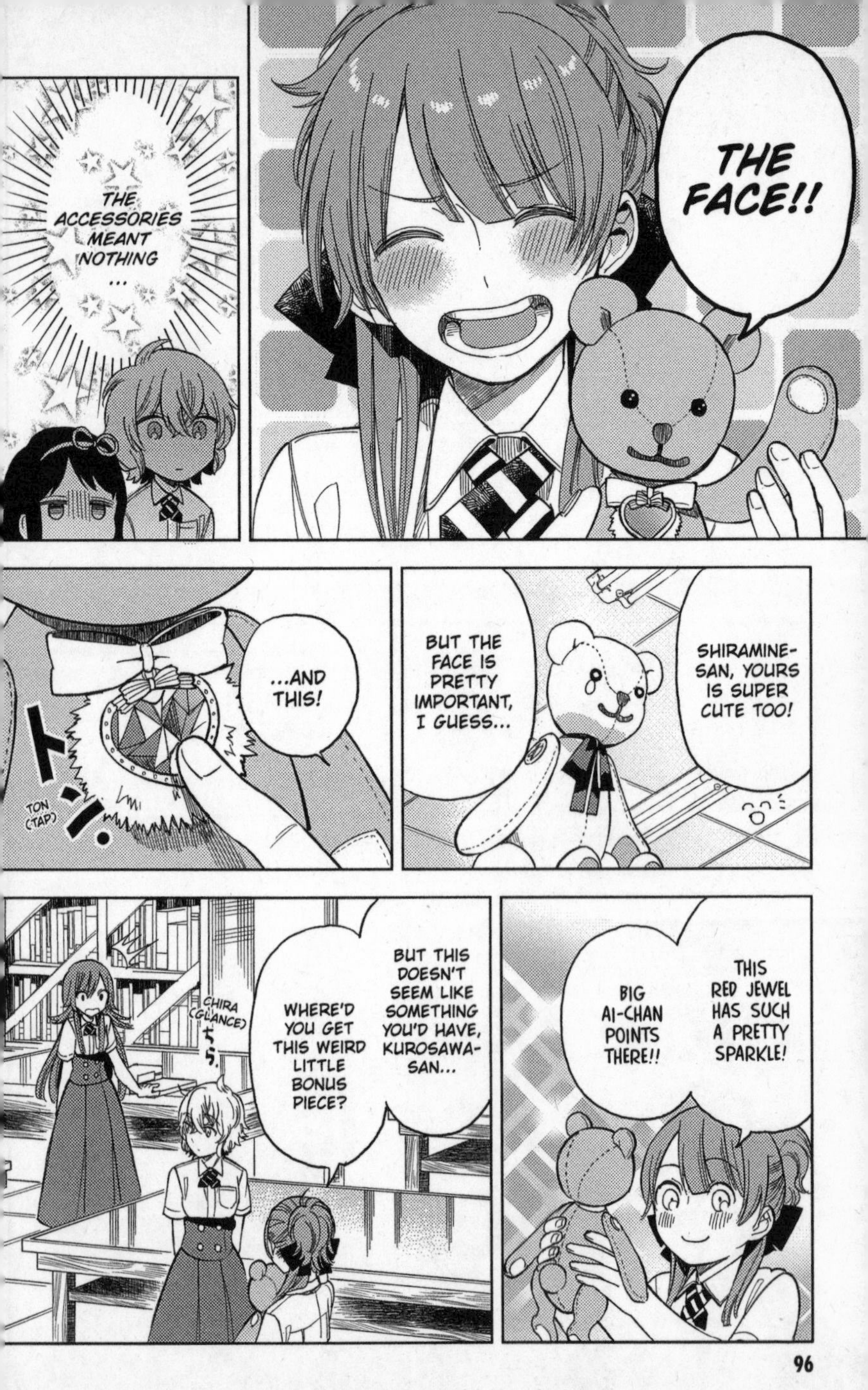
THE FACE!!
THE ACCESSORIES MEANT NOTHING...
SHIRAMINE-SAN, YOURS IS SUPER CUTE TOO!
BUT THE FACE IS PRETTY IMPORTANT, I GUESS...
...AND THIS!
TON (TAP)
THIS RED JEWEL HAS SUCH A PRETTY SPARKLE!
BIG AI-CHAN POINTS THERE!!
BUT THIS DOESN'T SEEM LIKE SOMETHING YOU'D HAVE, KUROSAWA-SAN...
WHERE'D YOU GET THIS WEIRD LITTLE BONUS PIECE?
CHIRA (GLANCE)

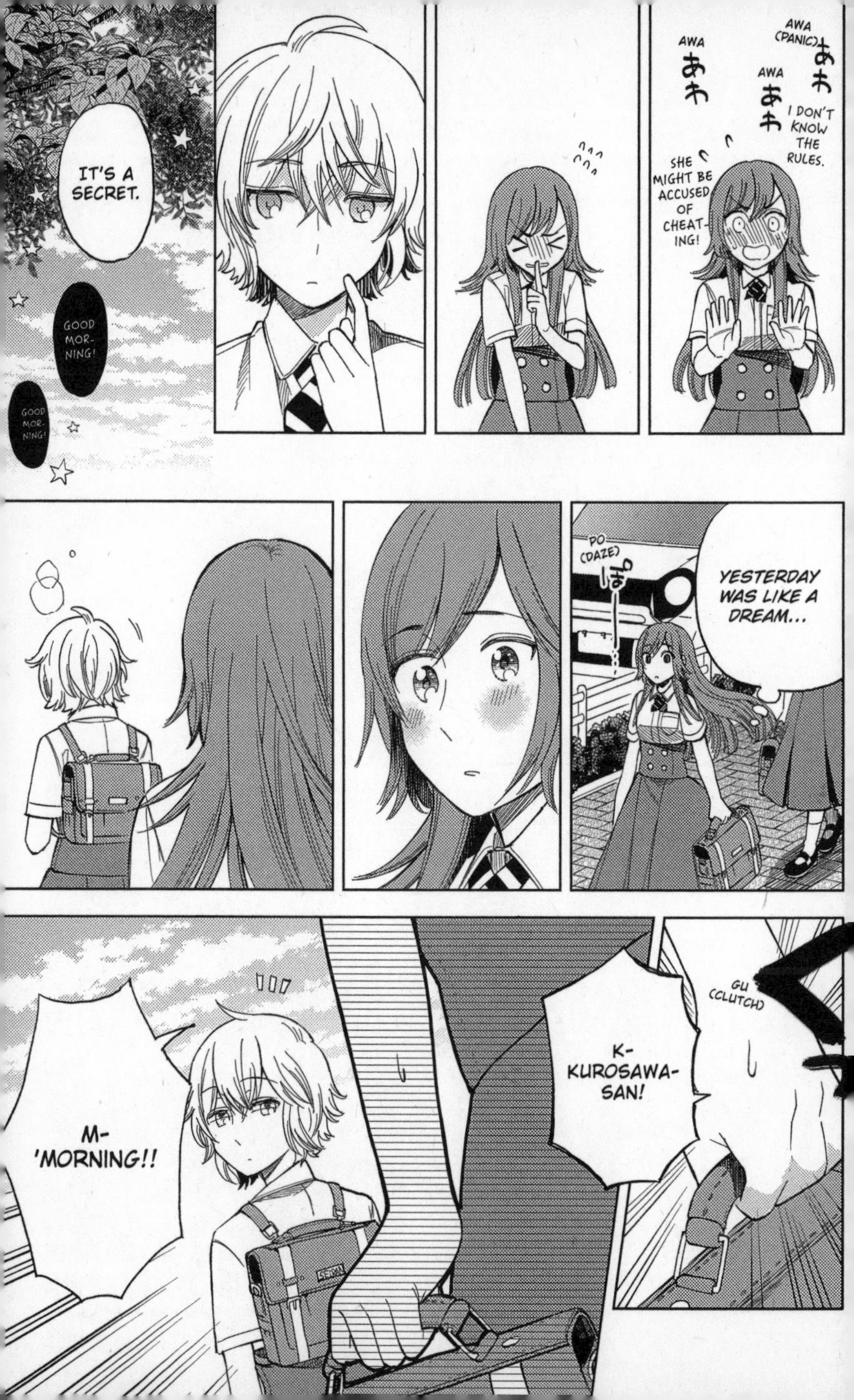
AWA (PANIC)
あわ
AWA
あわ
AWA
あわ
I DON'T KNOW THE RULES.
SHE MIGHT BE ACCUSED OF CHEAT-ING!
IT'S A SECRET.
GOOD MOR-NING!
GOOD MOR-NING!
PO (DAZE)
ぽー…
YESTERDAY WAS LIKE A DREAM...
GU (CLUTCH)
K-KUROSAWA-SAN!
M-'MORNING!!

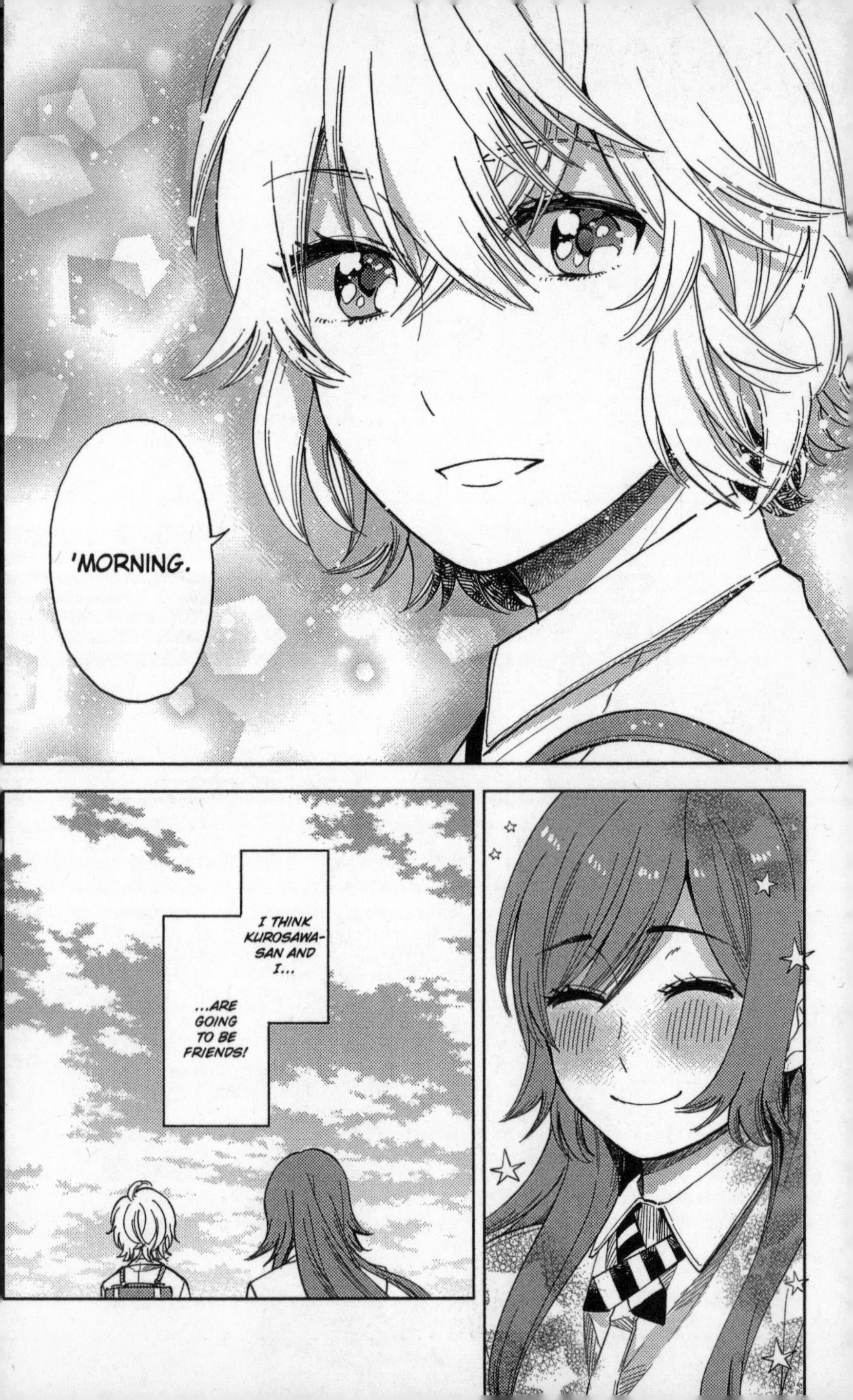
'MORNING.
I THINK KUROSAWA-SAN AND I...
...ARE GOING TO BE FRIENDS!

A Proposed Solution

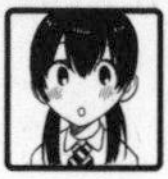

RIKA

SECOND-YEAR. NOT GOOD WITH HER HANDS.

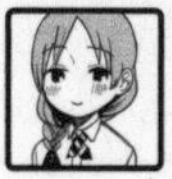

KOKORO

SECOND-YEAR. CRAFT CLUB. DOMESTIC TYPE.

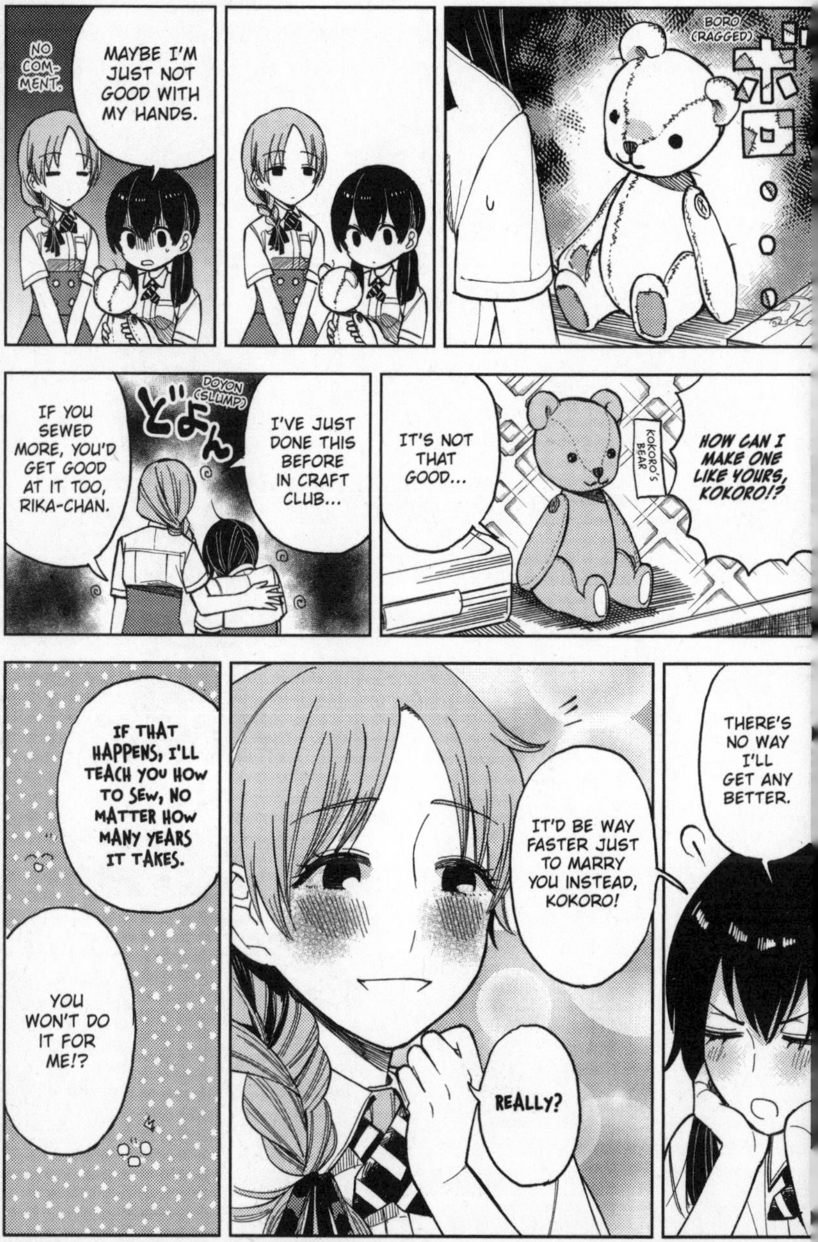
BORO (RAGGED)
MAYBE I'M JUST NOT GOOD WITH MY HANDS.
NO COMMENT.
HOW CAN I MAKE ONE LIKE YOURS, KOKORO!?
KOKORO'S BEAR
IT'S NOT THAT GOOD...
DOYON (SLUMP)
I'VE JUST DONE THIS BEFORE IN CRAFT CLUB...
IF YOU SEWED MORE, YOU'D GET GOOD AT IT TOO, RIKA-CHAN.
THERE'S NO WAY I'LL GET ANY BETTER.
IT'D BE WAY FASTER JUST TO MARRY YOU INSTEAD, KOKORO!
REALLY?
IF THAT HAPPENS, I'LL TEACH YOU HOW TO SEW, NO MATTER HOW MANY YEARS IT TAKES.
YOU WON'T DO IT FOR ME!?

PEOPLE OTHER THAN THE MAIN CHARACTERS HAVE STORIES TOO. HERE, WE PRESENT THE "LITTLE LOVE" STORIES HAPPENING BEHIND THE SCENES.

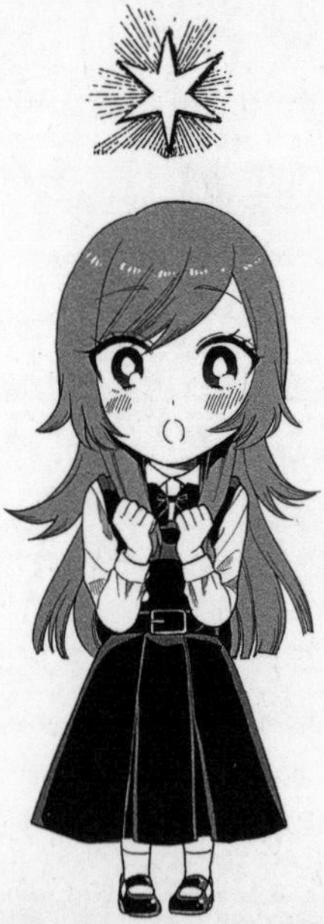

Kaoru Machida

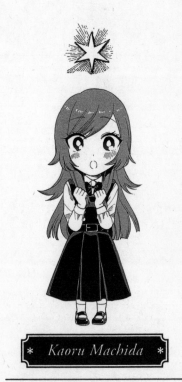

Kaoru Machida

Second-year student at Seiran Academy High School. Member of the craft club. She went to public school until the fall of the first year of middle school and was a classmate of Yurine Kurosawa. Introvert. Although she adored Kurosawa, she couldn't bring herself to approach her. She's an average girl who likes crafts.

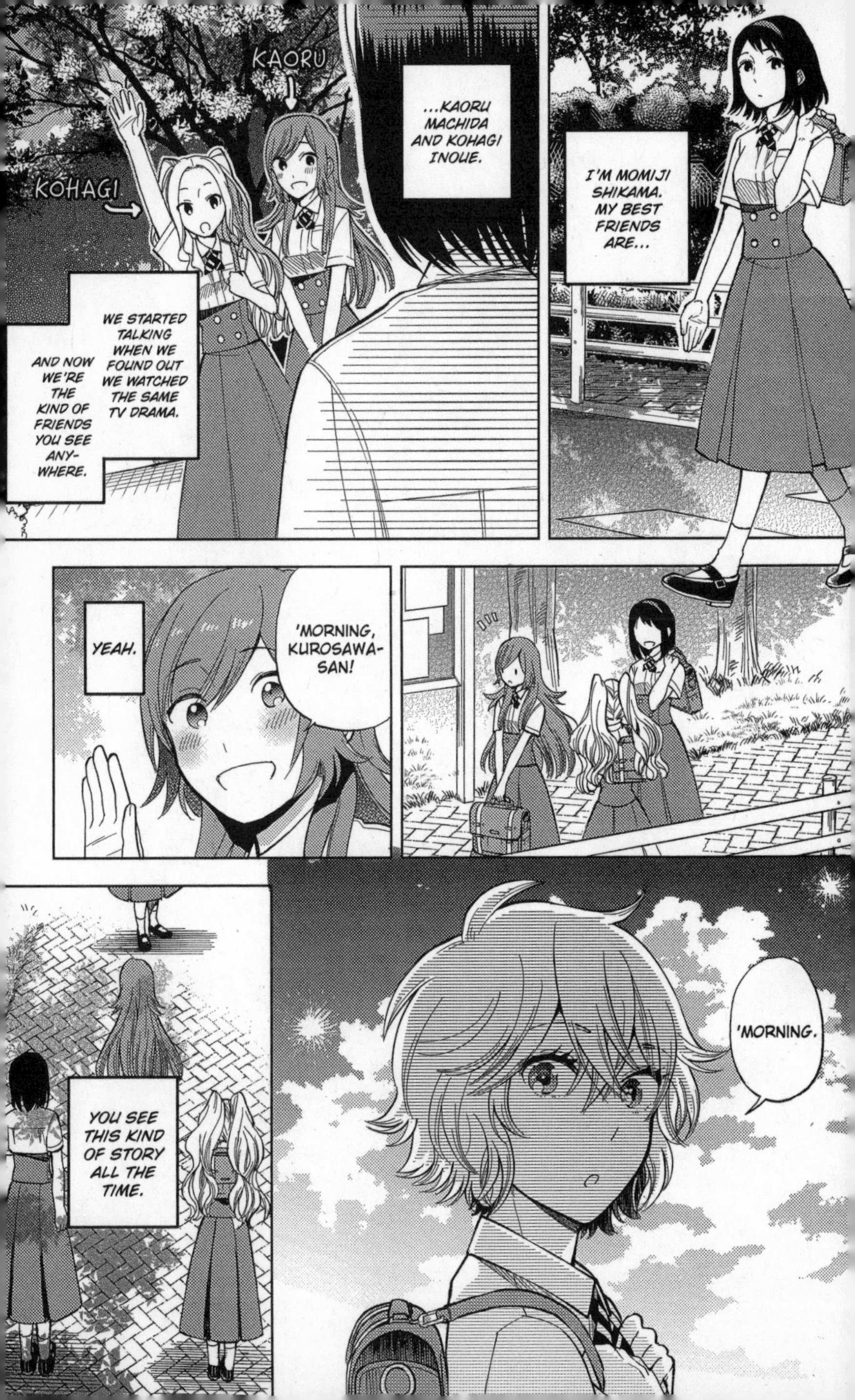
I'M MOMIJI SHIKAMA. MY BEST FRIENDS ARE...
...KAORU MACHIDA AND KOHAGI INOUE.
KAORU
KOHAGI
WE STARTED TALKING WHEN WE FOUND OUT WE WATCHED THE SAME TV DRAMA.
AND NOW WE'RE THE KIND OF FRIENDS YOU SEE ANY-WHERE.
'MORNING, KUROSAWA-SAN!
YEAH.
'MORNING.
YOU SEE THIS KIND OF STORY ALL THE TIME.

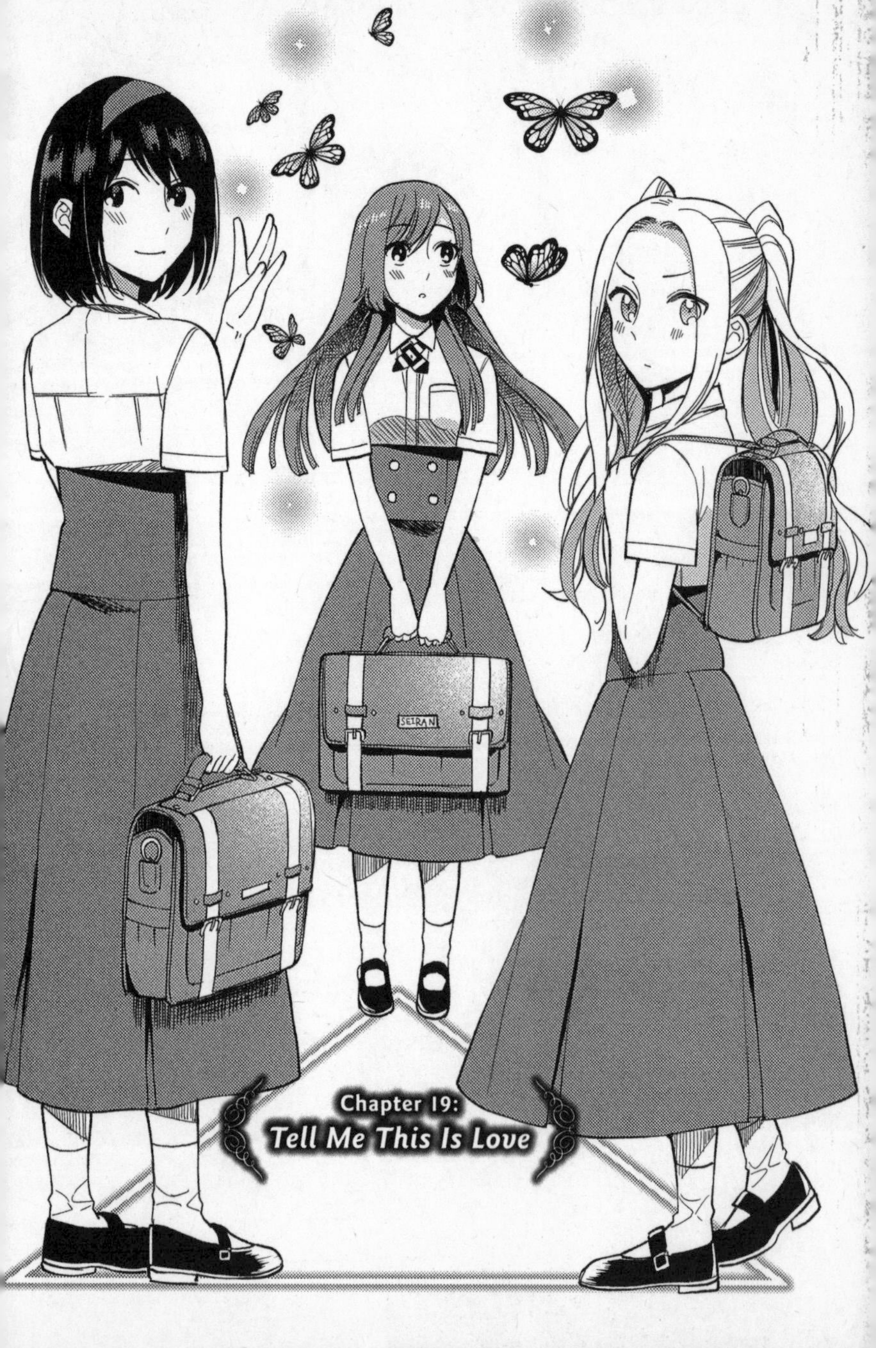
SEIRAN
Chapter 19:
Tell Me This Is Love

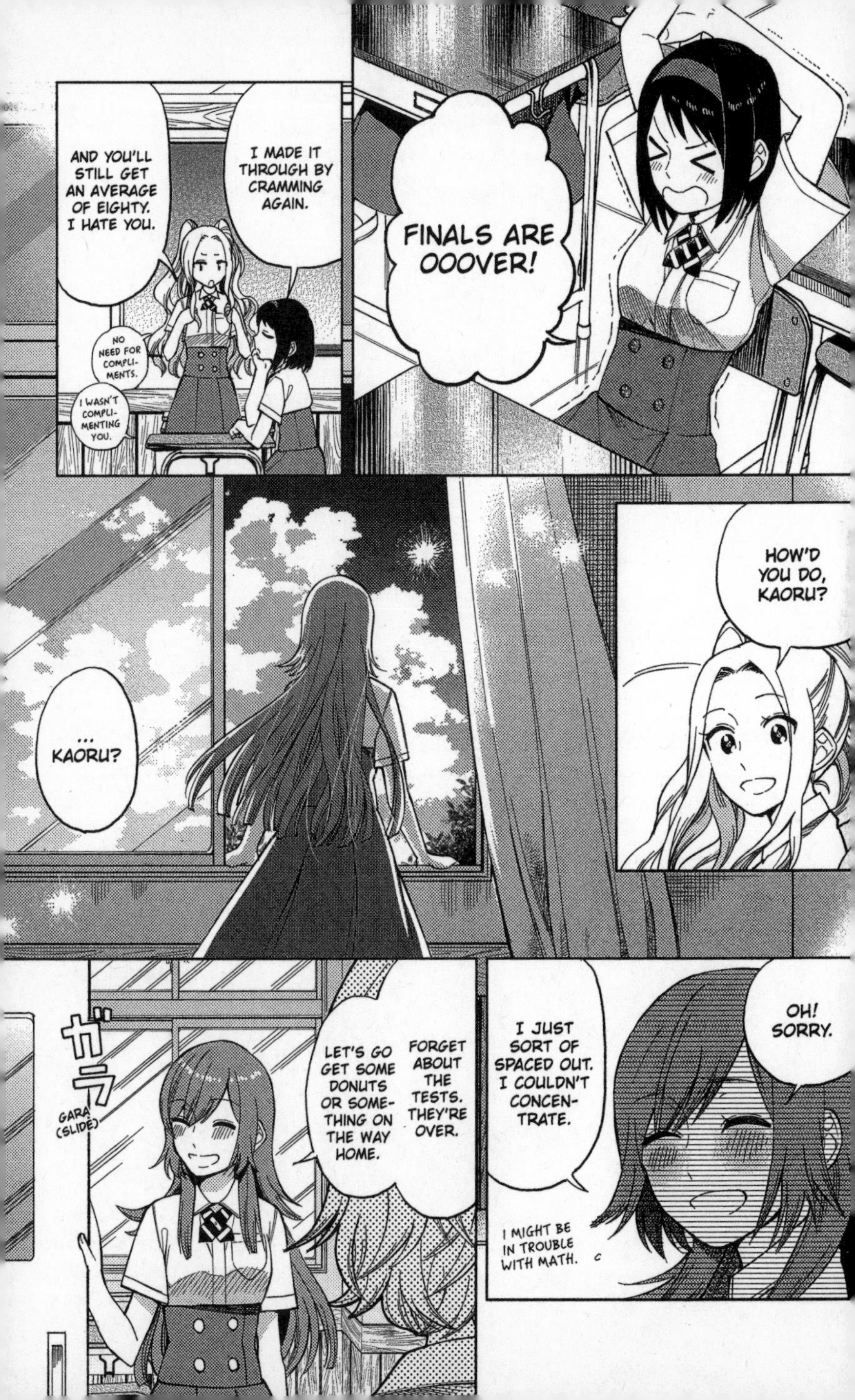
FINALS ARE OOOVER!
I MADE IT THROUGH BY CRAMMING AGAIN.
AND YOU'LL STILL GET AN AVERAGE OF EIGHTY. I HATE YOU.
NO NEED FOR COMPLI-MENTS.
I WASN'T COMPLI-MENTING YOU.
HOW'D YOU DO, KAORU?
... KAORU?
OH! SORRY.
I JUST SORT OF SPACED OUT. I COULDN'T CONCEN-TRATE.
I MIGHT BE IN TROUBLE WITH MATH.
FORGET ABOUT THE TESTS. THEY'RE OVER.
LET'S GO GET SOME DONUTS OR SOME-THING ON THE WAY HOME.
ガラ
GARA (SLIDE)

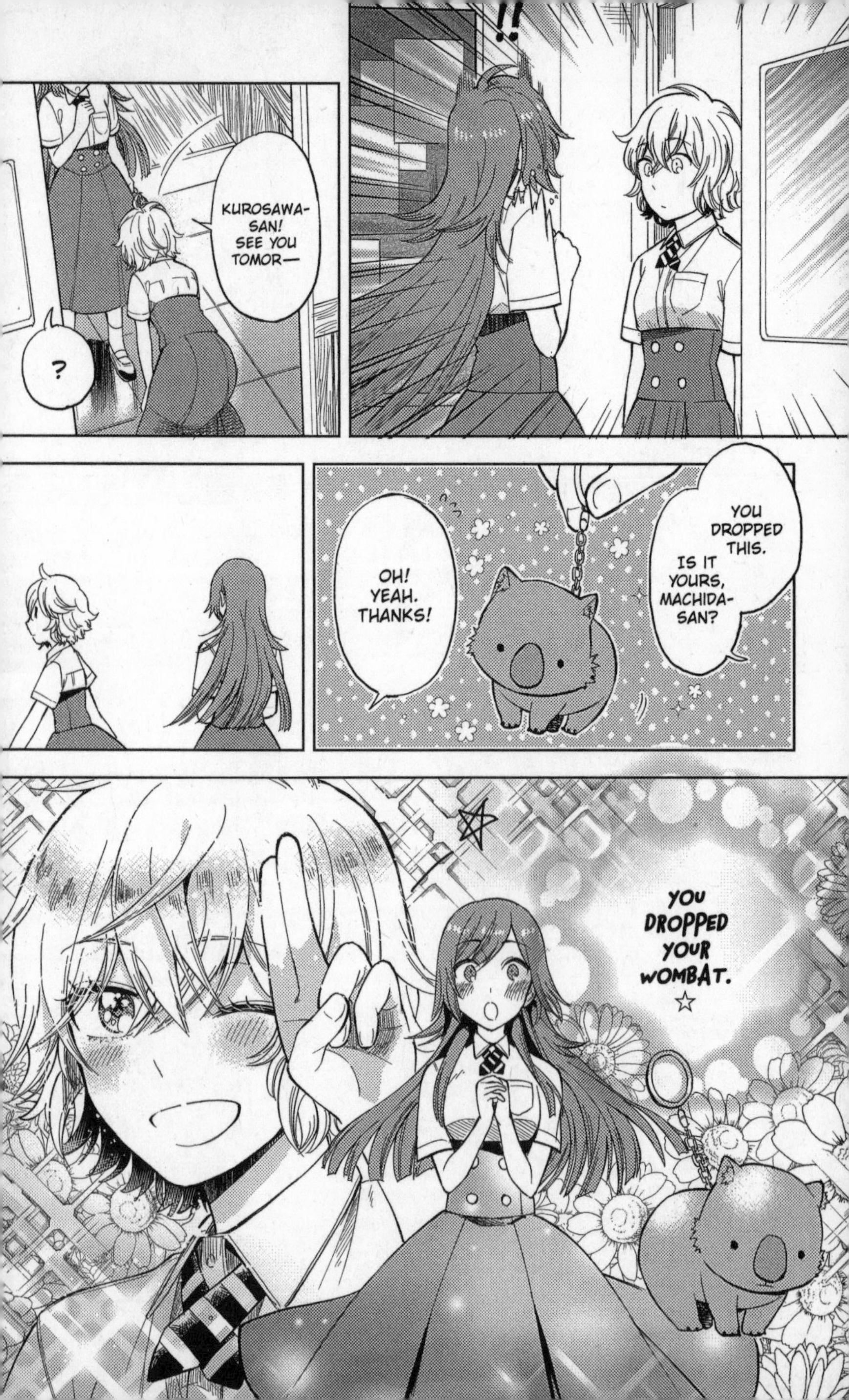
!!
KUROSAWA-SAN! SEE YOU TOMOR—
?
YOU DROPPED THIS. IS IT YOURS, MACHIDA-SAN?
OH! YEAH. THANKS!
YOU DROPPED YOUR WOMBAT. ☆

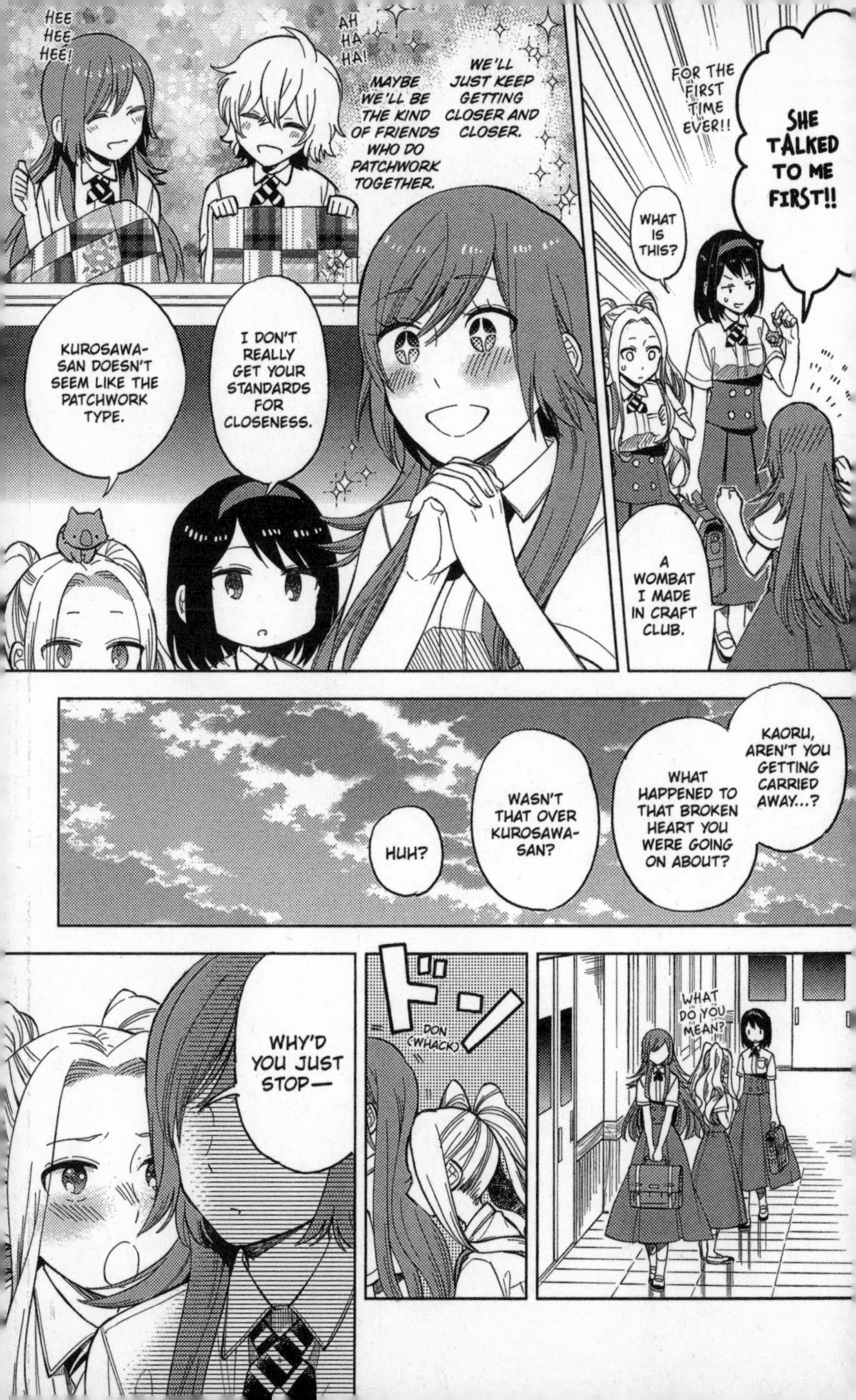

SHE TALKED TO ME FIRST!!
FOR THE FIRST TIME EVER!!
WHAT IS THIS?
A WOMBAT I MADE IN CRAFT CLUB.
WE'LL JUST KEEP GETTING CLOSER AND CLOSER.
MAYBE WE'LL BE THE KIND OF FRIENDS WHO DO PATCHWORK TOGETHER.
AH HA HA!
HEE HEE HEE!
I DON'T REALLY GET YOUR STANDARDS FOR CLOSENESS.
KUROSAWA-SAN DOESN'T SEEM LIKE THE PATCHWORK TYPE.
KAORU, AREN'T YOU GETTING CARRIED AWAY...?
WHAT HAPPENED TO THAT BROKEN HEART YOU WERE GOING ON ABOUT?
WASN'T THAT OVER KUROSAWA-SAN?
HUH?
WHAT DO YOU MEAN?
ドン
DON (WHACK)
WHY'D YOU JUST STOP—

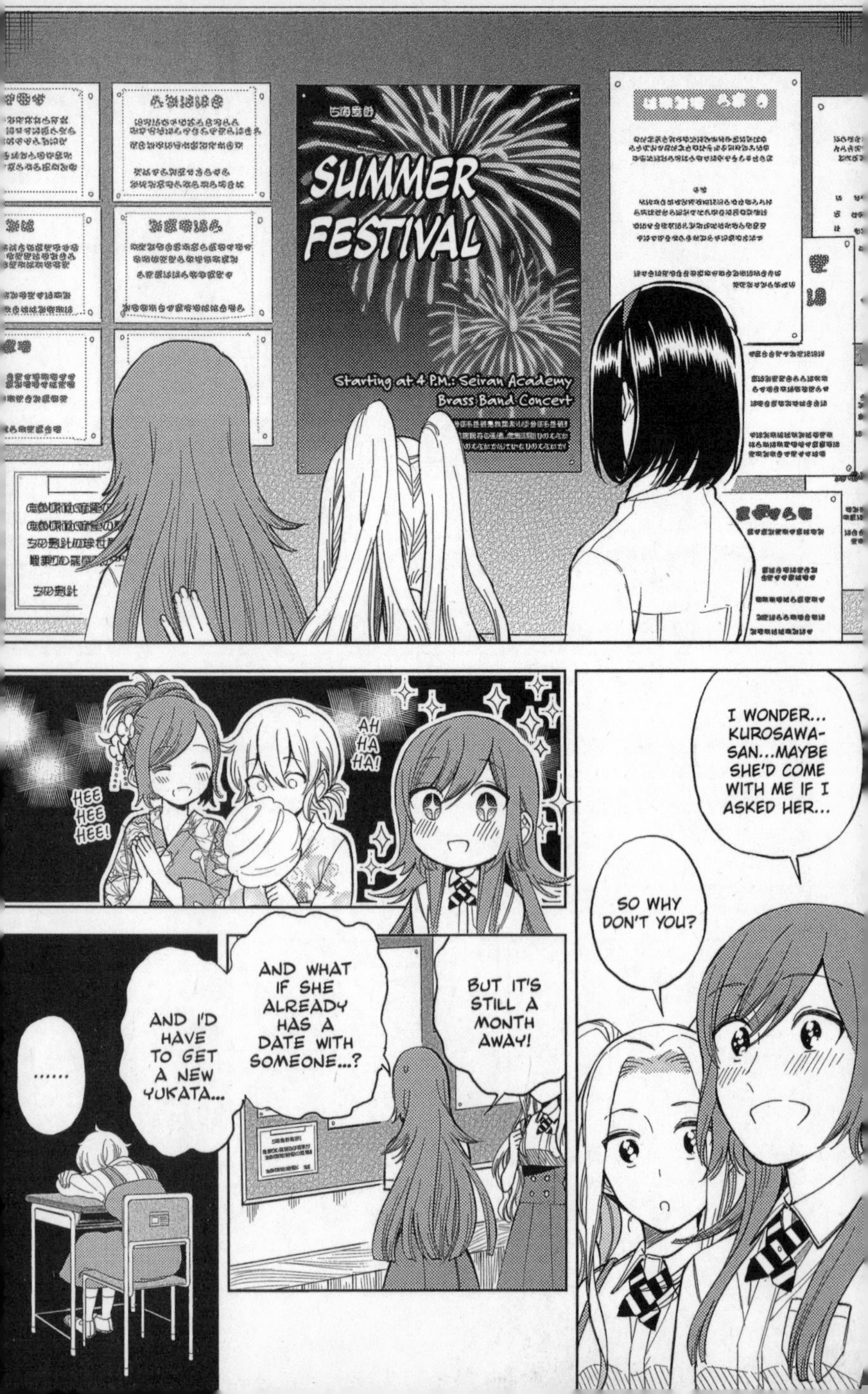
SUMMER FESTIVAL
Starting at 4 P.M.: Seiran Academy Brass Band Concert
I WONDER... KUROSAWA-SAN...MAYBE SHE'D COME WITH ME IF I ASKED HER...
SO WHY DON'T YOU?
AH HA HA!
HEE HEE HEE!
BUT IT'S STILL A MONTH AWAY!
AND WHAT IF SHE ALREADY HAS A DATE WITH SOMEONE...?
AND I'D HAVE TO GET A NEW YUKATA...
......

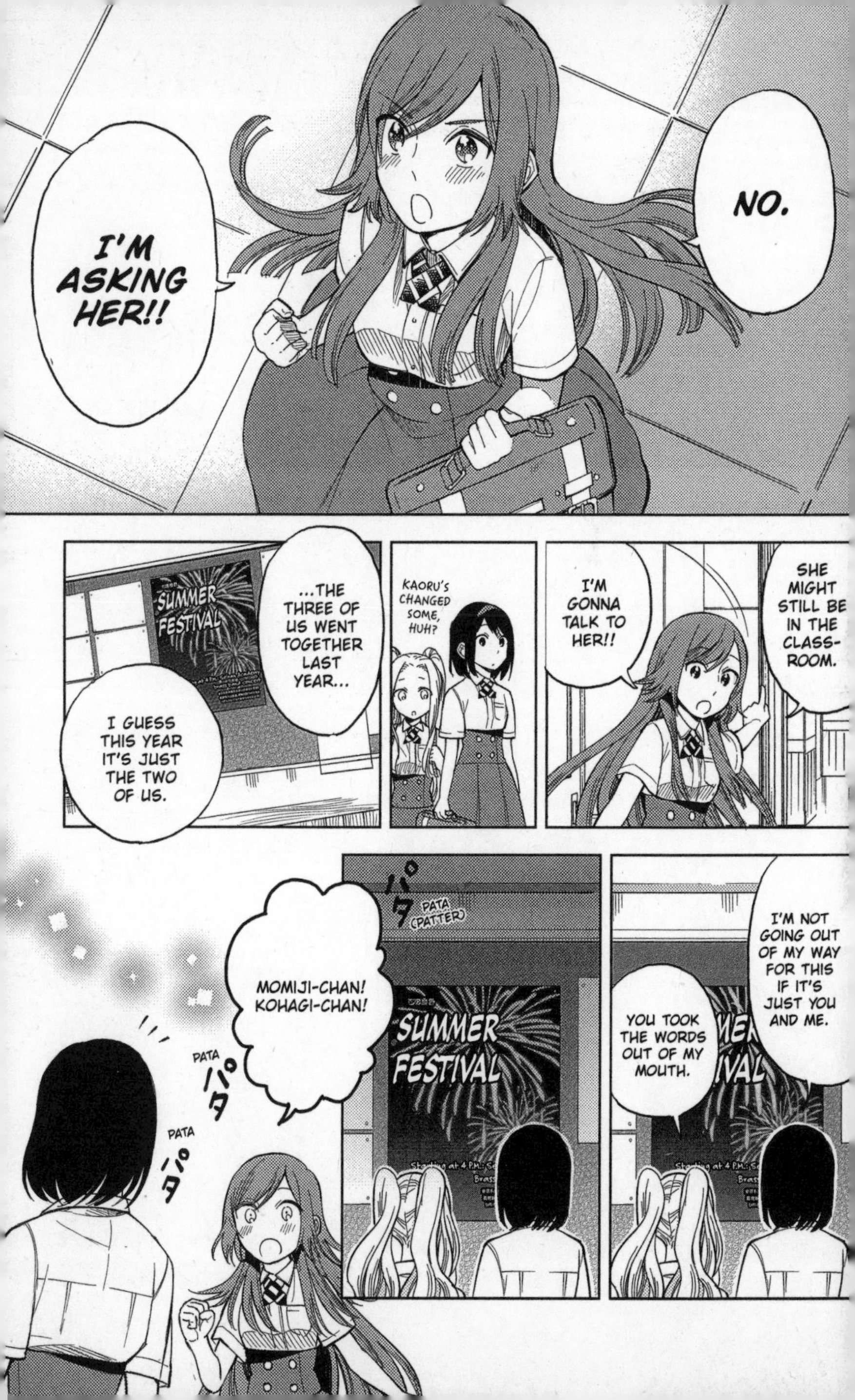
NO.
I'M ASKING HER!!
SHE MIGHT STILL BE IN THE CLASSROOM.
I'M GONNA TALK TO HER!!
KAORU'S CHANGED SOME, HUH?
SUMMER FESTIVAL
...THE THREE OF US WENT TOGETHER LAST YEAR...
I GUESS THIS YEAR IT'S JUST THE TWO OF US.
I'M NOT GOING OUT OF MY WAY FOR THIS IF IT'S JUST YOU AND ME.
YOU TOOK THE WORDS OUT OF MY MOUTH.
パタ
PATA (PATTER)
SUMMER FESTIVAL
MOMIJI-CHAN! KOHAGI-CHAN!
PATA
PATA

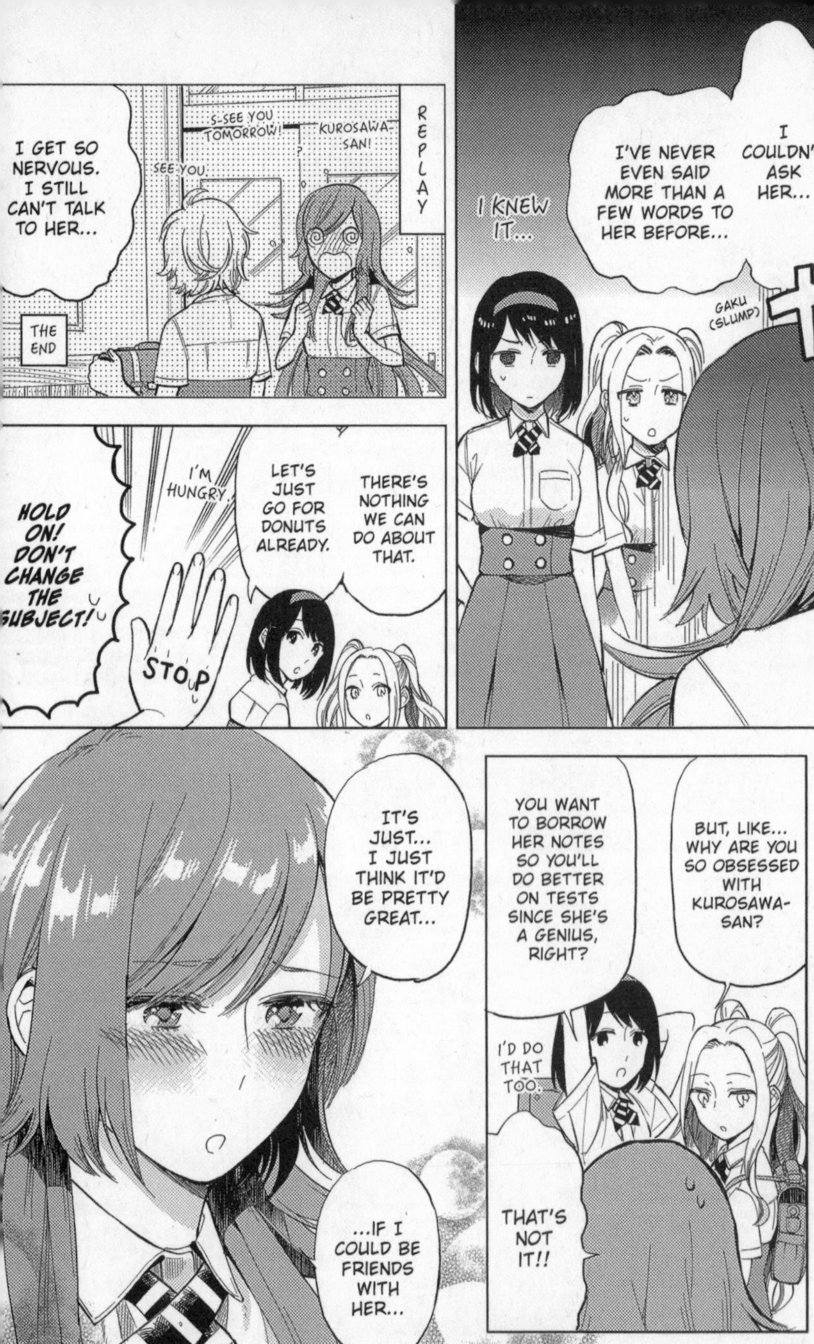
I COULDN'T ASK HER...
I'VE NEVER EVEN SAID MORE THAN A FEW WORDS TO HER BEFORE...
I KNEW IT...
GAKU (SLUMP)
ガク
REPLAY
KUROSAWA-SAN!
S-SEE YOU TOMORROW!
?
SEE YOU.
I GET SO NERVOUS. I STILL CAN'T TALK TO HER...
THE END
THERE'S NOTHING WE CAN DO ABOUT THAT.
LET'S JUST GO FOR DONUTS ALREADY.
I'M HUNGRY.
HOLD ON! DON'T CHANGE THE SUBJECT!
STOP
BUT, LIKE... WHY ARE YOU SO OBSESSED WITH KUROSAWA-SAN?
YOU WANT TO BORROW HER NOTES SO YOU'LL DO BETTER ON TESTS SINCE SHE'S A GENIUS, RIGHT?
I'D DO THAT TOO.
THAT'S NOT IT!!
IT'S JUST... I JUST THINK IT'D BE PRETTY GREAT...
...IF I COULD BE FRIENDS WITH HER...

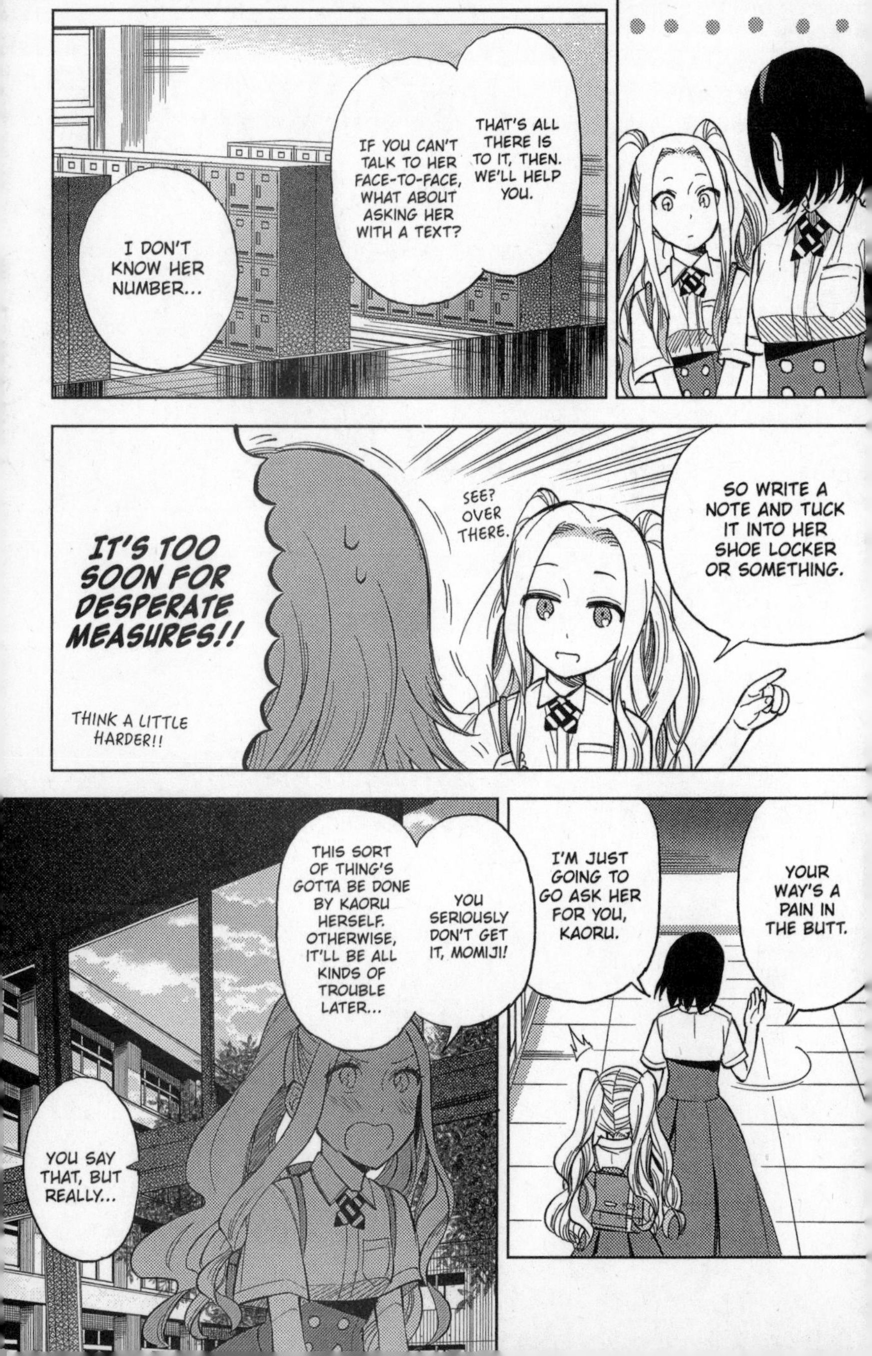
• • • • • •
THAT'S ALL THERE IS TO IT, THEN. WE'LL HELP YOU.
IF YOU CAN'T TALK TO HER FACE-TO-FACE, WHAT ABOUT ASKING HER WITH A TEXT?
I DON'T KNOW HER NUMBER...
SO WRITE A NOTE AND TUCK IT INTO HER SHOE LOCKER OR SOMETHING.
SEE? OVER THERE.
IT'S TOO SOON FOR DESPERATE MEASURES!!
THINK A LITTLE HARDER!!
YOUR WAY'S A PAIN IN THE BUTT.
I'M JUST GOING TO GO ASK HER FOR YOU, KAORU.
YOU SERIOUSLY DON'T GET IT, MOMIJI!
THIS SORT OF THING'S GOTTA BE DONE BY KAORU HERSELF. OTHERWISE, IT'LL BE ALL KINDS OF TROUBLE LATER...
YOU SAY THAT, BUT REALLY...

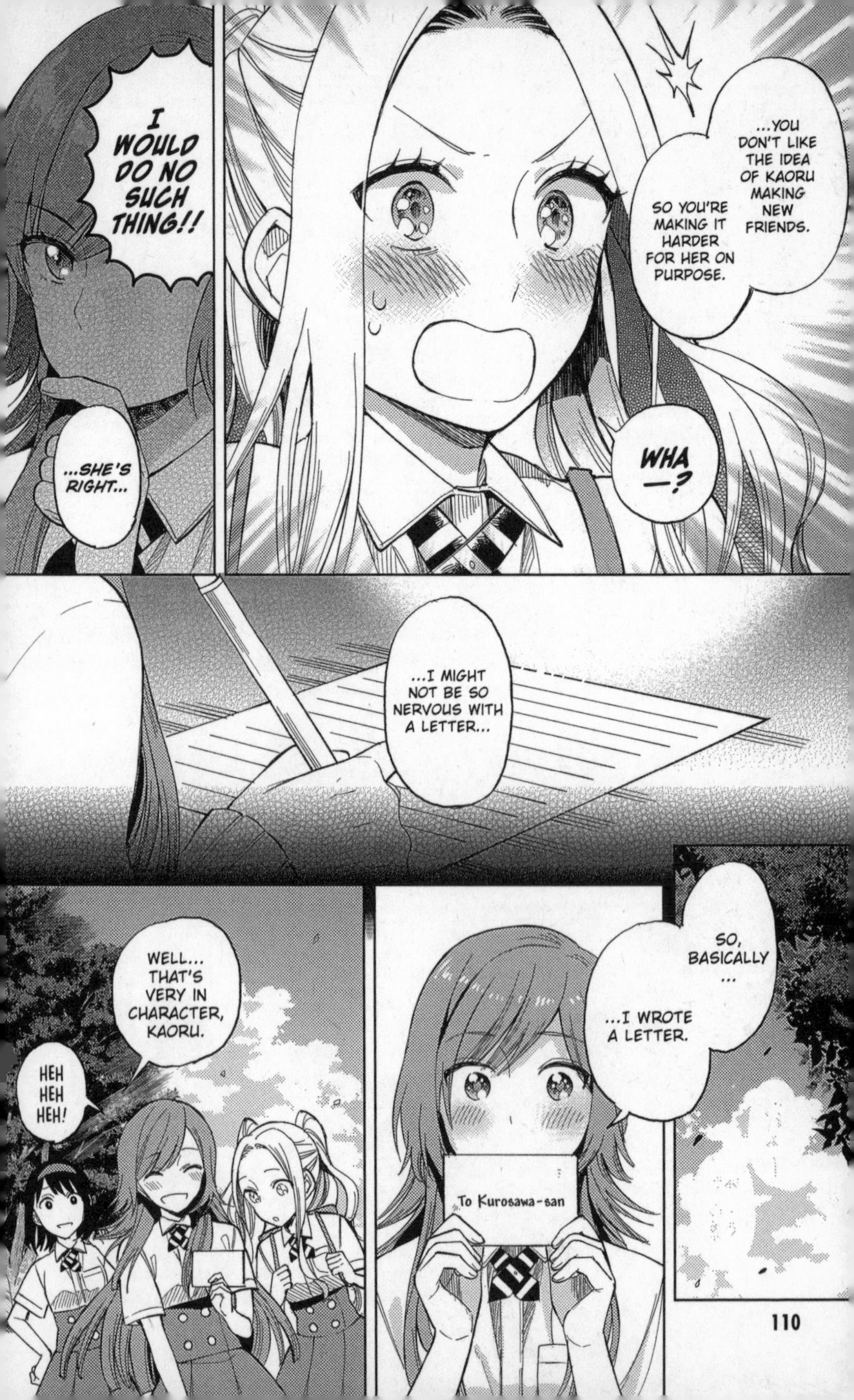

...YOU DON'T LIKE THE IDEA OF KAORU MAKING NEW FRIENDS.
SO YOU'RE MAKING IT HARDER FOR HER ON PURPOSE.
WHA—?
I WOULD DO NO SUCH THING!!
...SHE'S RIGHT...
...I MIGHT NOT BE SO NERVOUS WITH A LETTER...
SO, BASICALLY...
...I WROTE A LETTER.
To Kurosawa-san
WELL... THAT'S VERY IN CHARACTER, KAORU.
HEH HEH HEH!

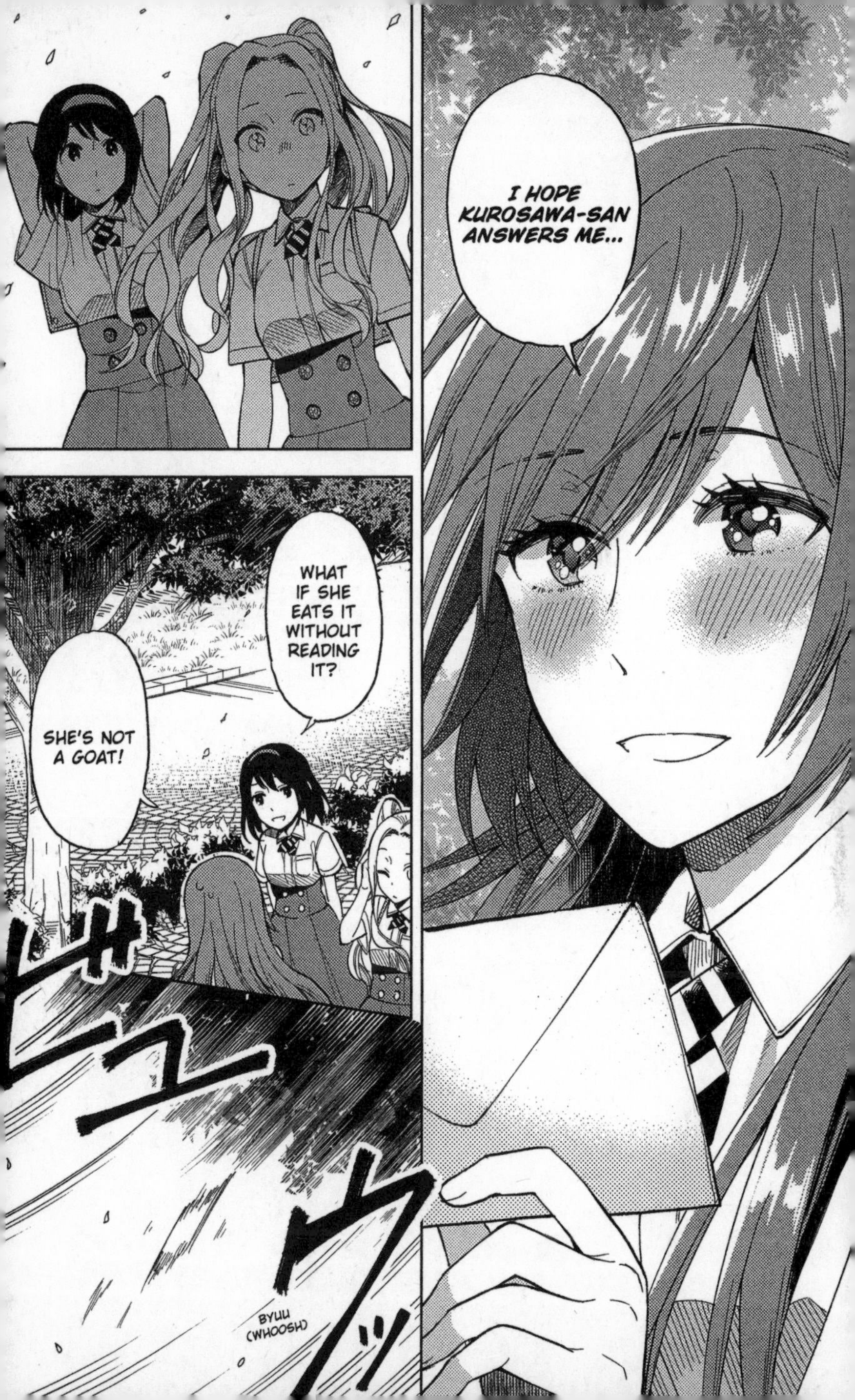
I HOPE KUROSAWA-SAN ANSWERS ME...
WHAT IF SHE EATS IT WITHOUT READING IT?
SHE'S NOT A GOAT!
BYUU (WHOOSH)

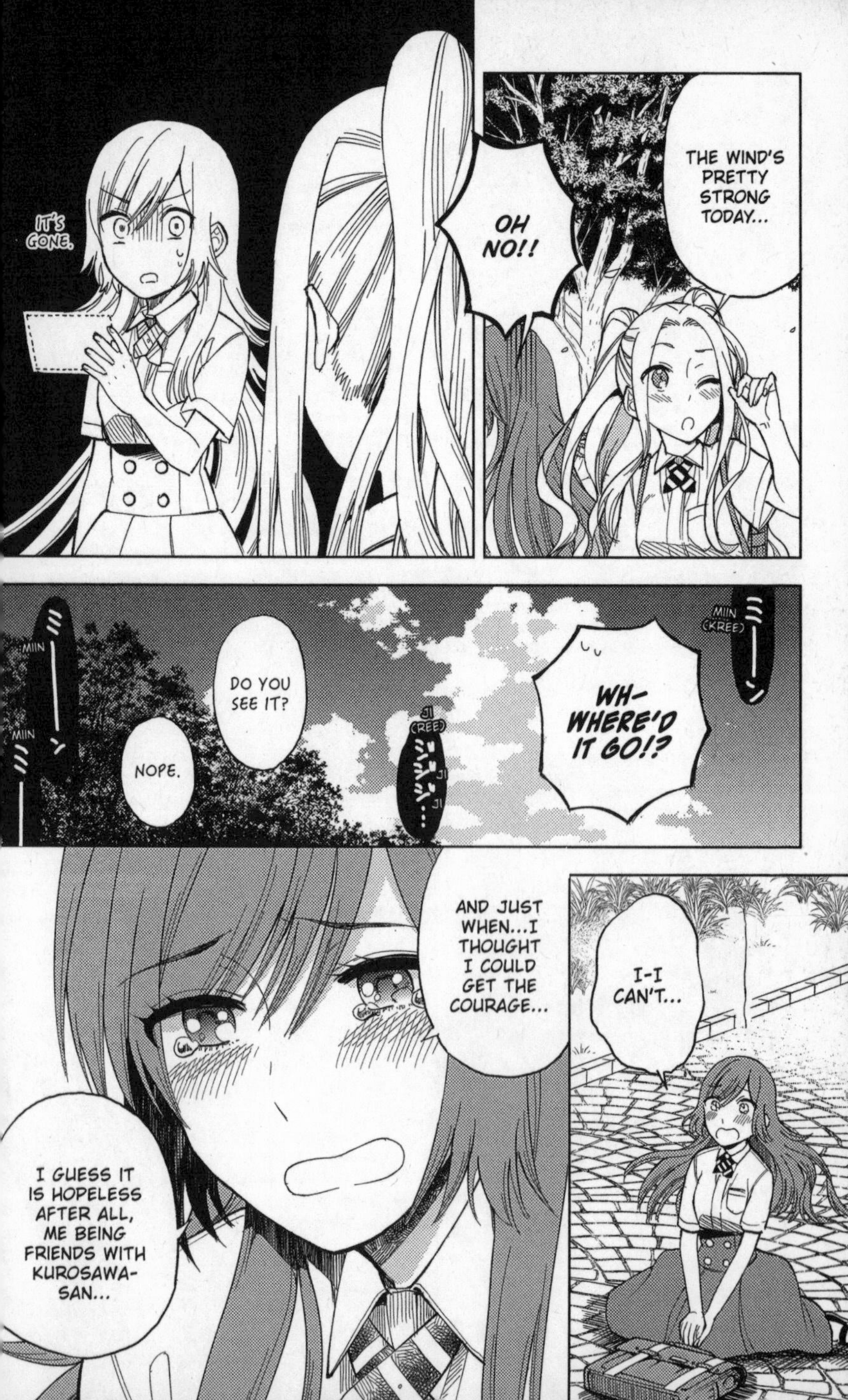
THE WIND'S PRETTY STRONG TODAY...
OH NO!!
IT'S GONE.
MIIN (KREE)
WH-WHERE'D IT GO!?
JI (REE)
JI
JI
DO YOU SEE IT?
NOPE.
MIIN
MIIN
I-I CAN'T...
AND JUST WHEN...I THOUGHT I COULD GET THE COURAGE...
I GUESS IT IS HOPELESS AFTER ALL, ME BEING FRIENDS WITH KUROSAWA-SAN...

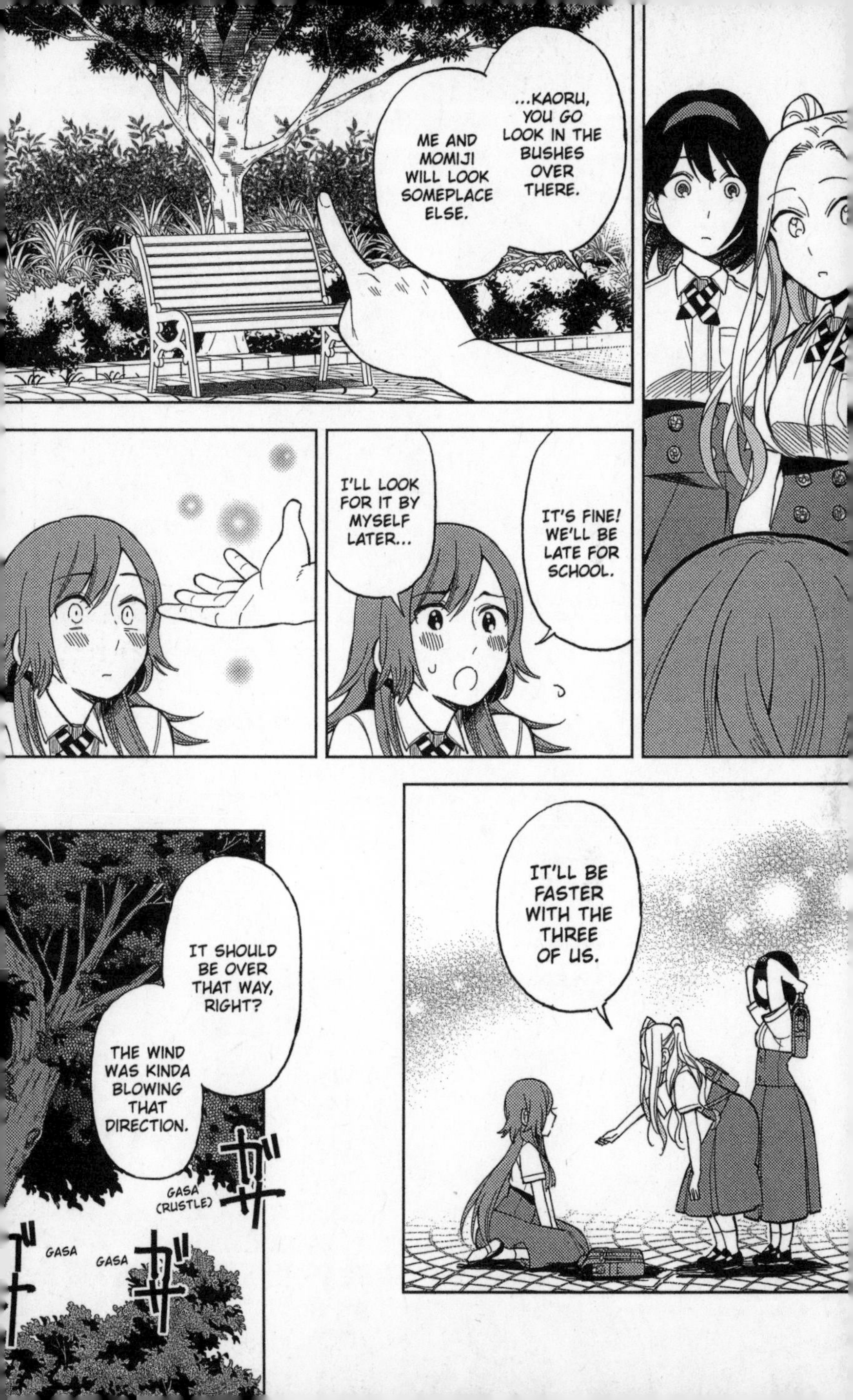
...KAORU, YOU GO LOOK IN THE BUSHES OVER THERE.
ME AND MOMIJI WILL LOOK SOMEPLACE ELSE.
IT'S FINE! WE'LL BE LATE FOR SCHOOL.
I'LL LOOK FOR IT BY MYSELF LATER...
IT'LL BE FASTER WITH THE THREE OF US.
IT SHOULD BE OVER THAT WAY, RIGHT?
THE WIND WAS KINDA BLOWING THAT DIRECTION.
GASA (RUSTLE)
GASA
GASA

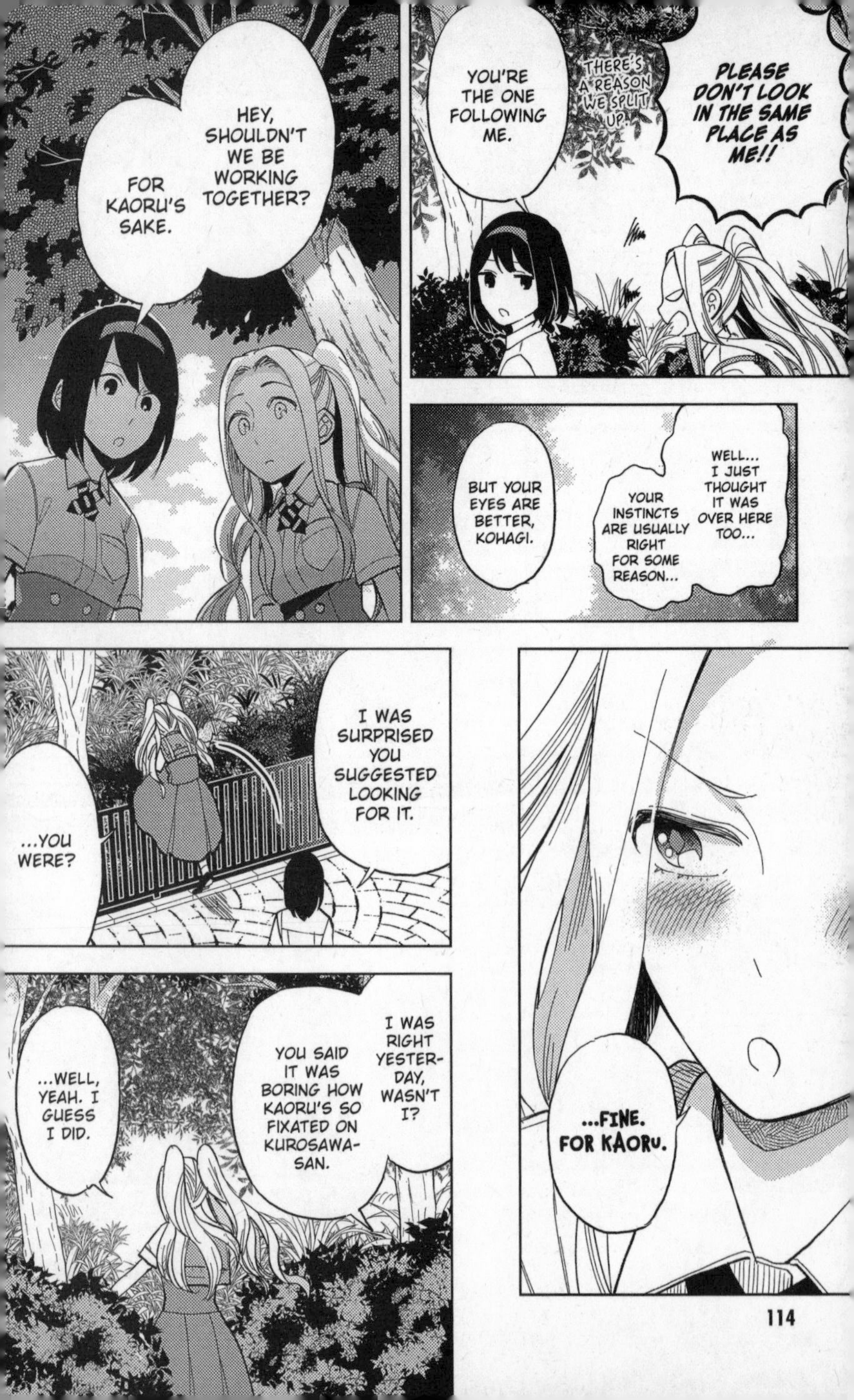
PLEASE DON'T LOOK IN THE SAME PLACE AS ME!!
THERE'S A REASON WE SPLIT UP.
YOU'RE THE ONE FOLLOWING ME.
WELL... I JUST THOUGHT IT WAS OVER HERE TOO...
YOUR INSTINCTS ARE USUALLY RIGHT FOR SOME REASON...
BUT YOUR EYES ARE BETTER, KOHAGI.
HEY, SHOULDN'T WE BE WORKING TOGETHER?
FOR KAORU'S SAKE.
...FINE. FOR KAORU.
I WAS SURPRISED YOU SUGGESTED LOOKING FOR IT.
...YOU WERE?
I WAS RIGHT YESTERDAY, WASN'T I?
YOU SAID IT WAS BORING HOW KAORU'S SO FIXATED ON KUROSAWA-SAN.
...WELL, YEAH. I GUESS I DID.

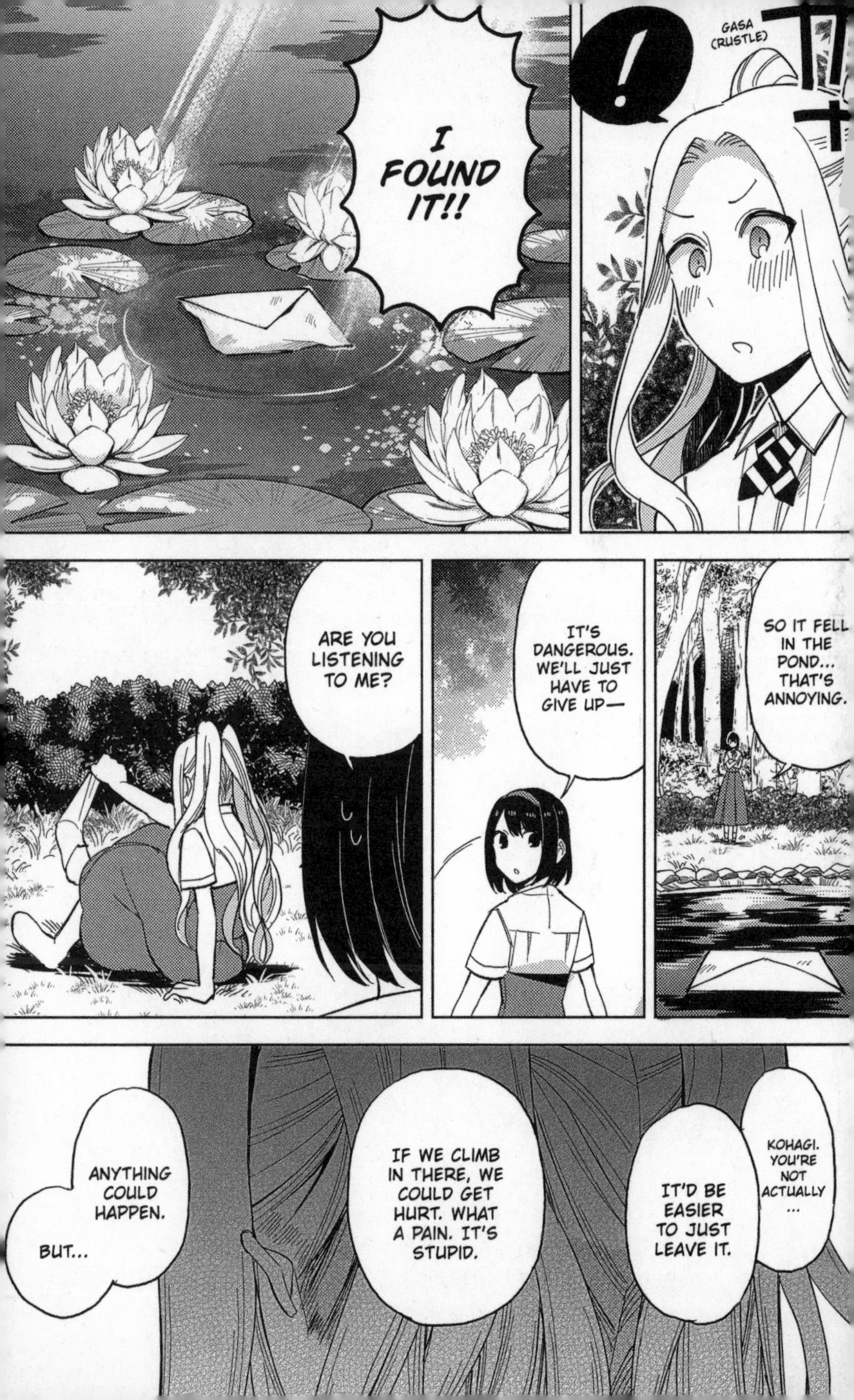
!
GASA (RUSTLE)
I FOUND IT!!
SO IT FELL IN THE POND... THAT'S ANNOYING.
IT'S DANGEROUS. WE'LL JUST HAVE TO GIVE UP—
ARE YOU LISTENING TO ME?
KOHAGI. YOU'RE NOT ACTUALLY ...
IT'D BE EASIER TO JUST LEAVE IT.
IF WE CLIMB IN THERE, WE COULD GET HURT. WHAT A PAIN. IT'S STUPID.
ANYTHING COULD HAPPEN.
BUT...

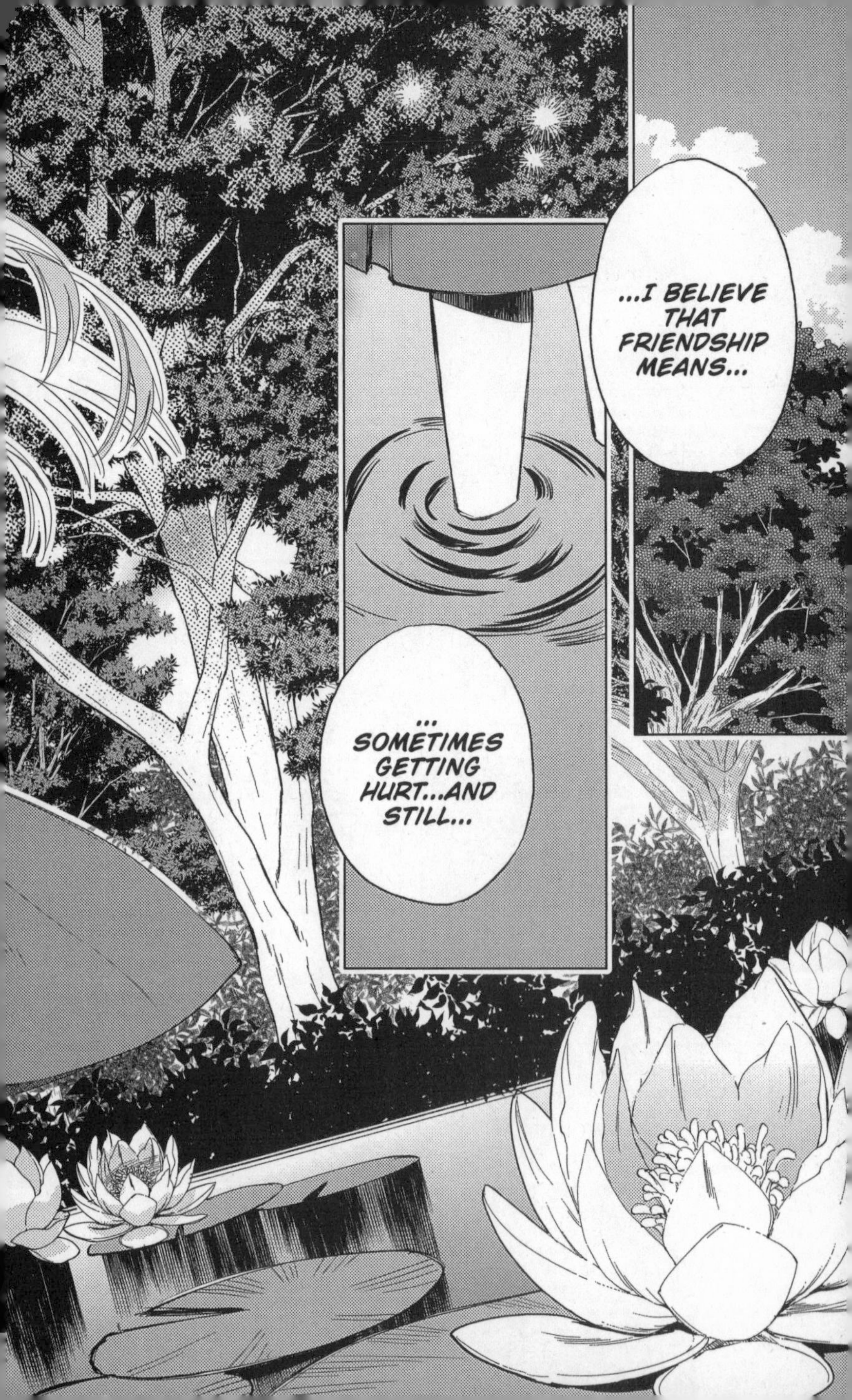
...I BELIEVE THAT FRIENDSHIP MEANS...
... SOMETIMES GETTING HURT...AND STILL...

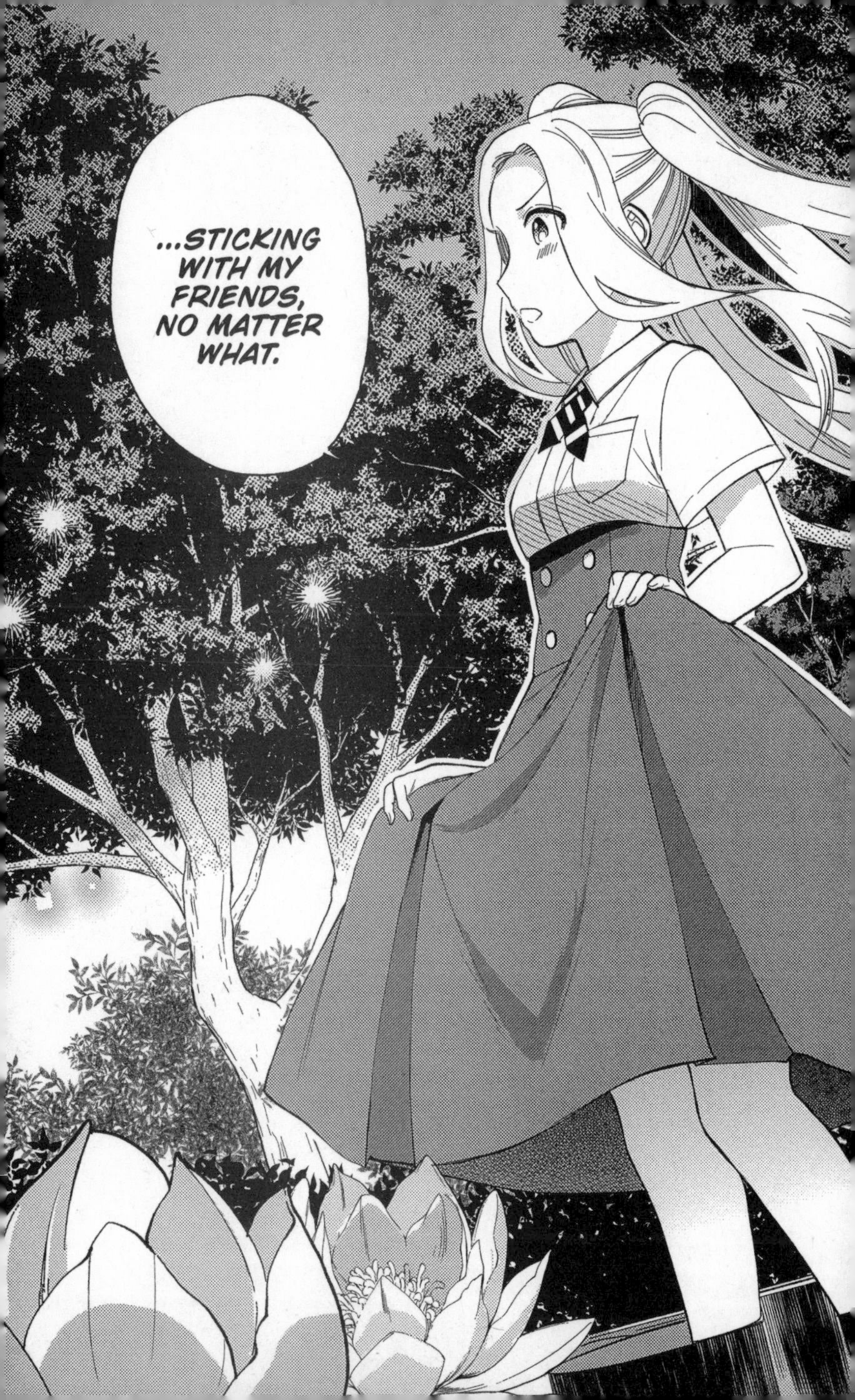
...STICKING WITH MY FRIENDS, NO MATTER WHAT.

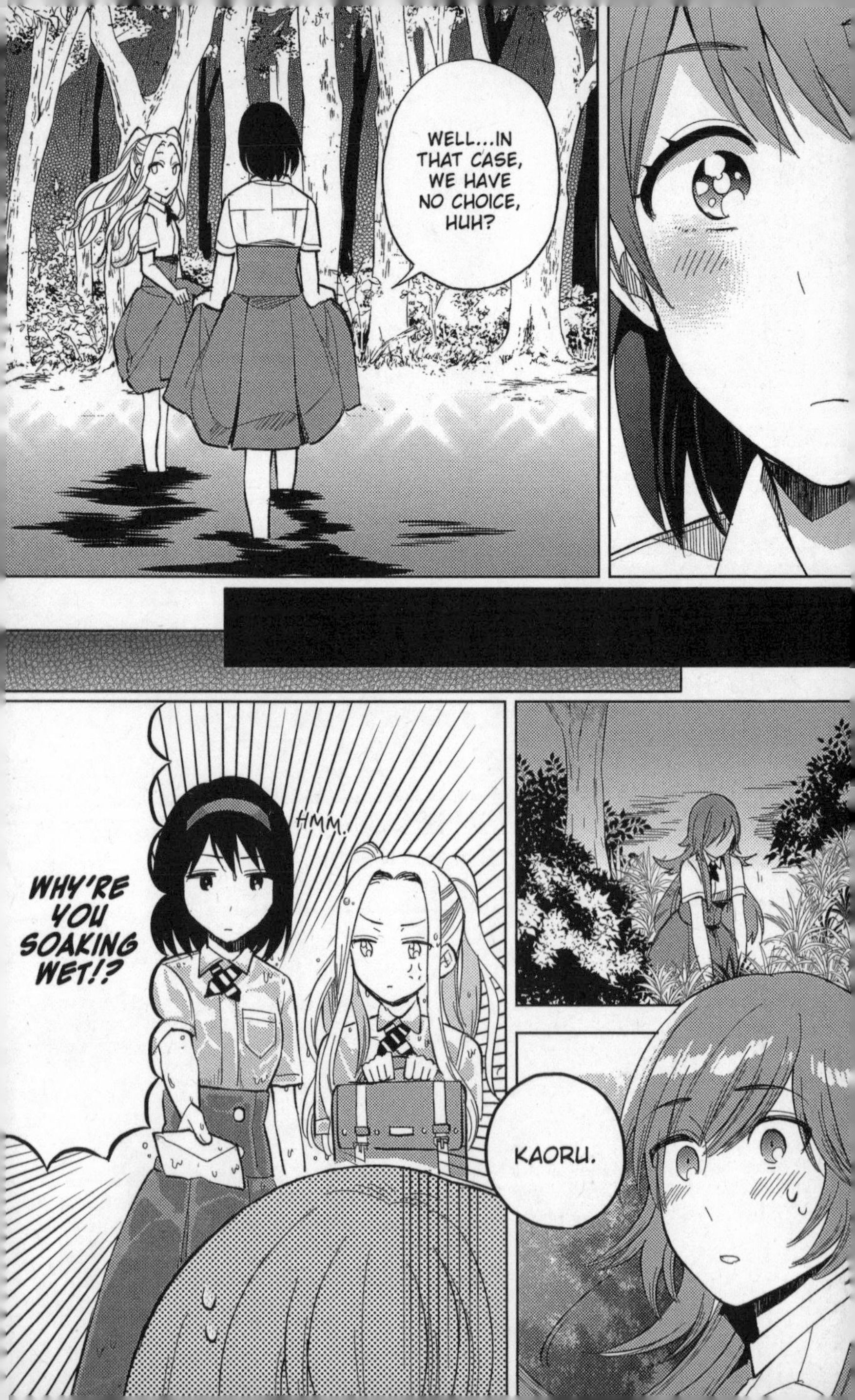
WELL...IN THAT CASE, WE HAVE NO CHOICE, HUH?
KAORU.
HMM.
WHY'RE YOU SOAKING WET!?

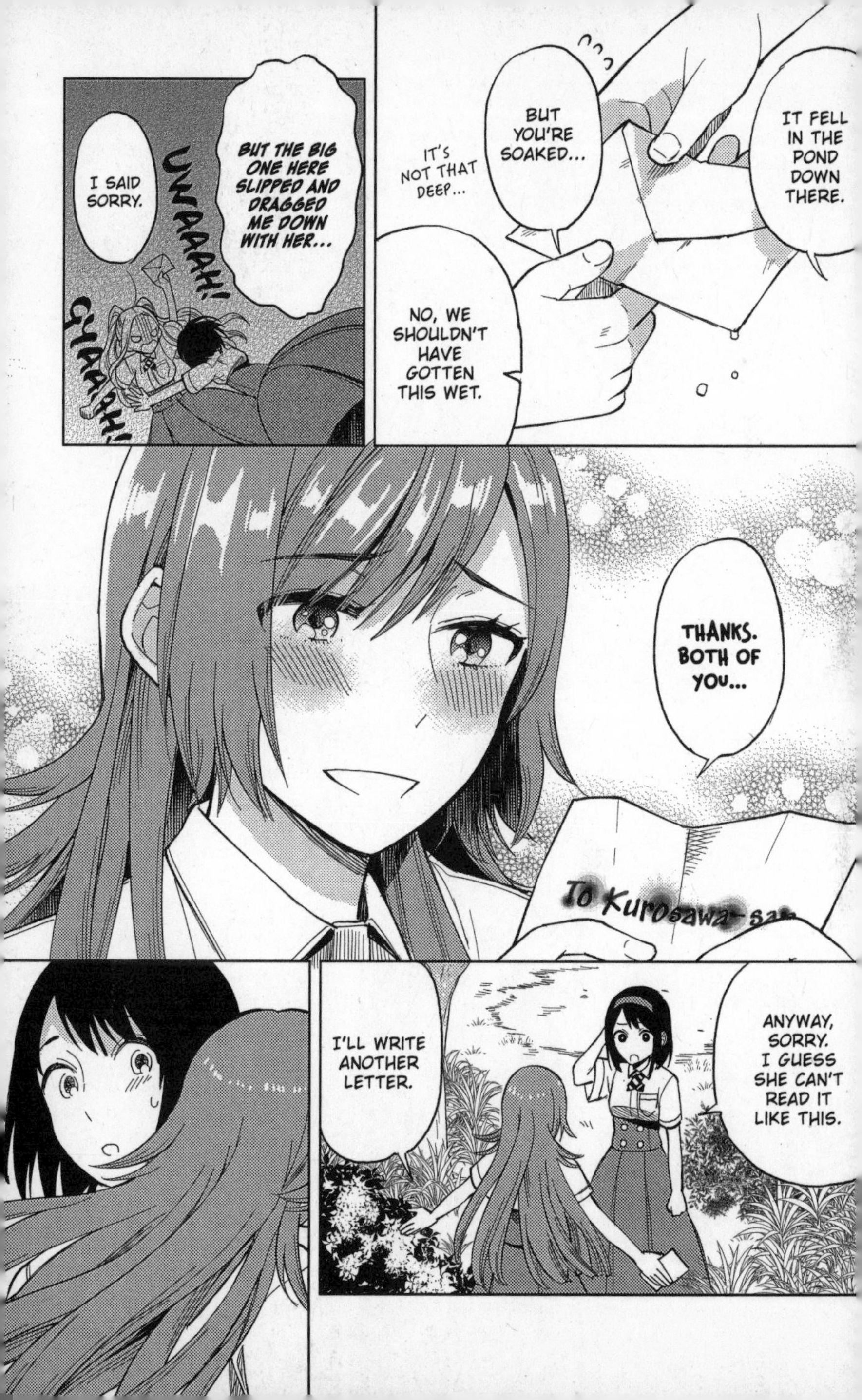
IT FELL IN THE POND DOWN THERE.
BUT YOU'RE SOAKED...
IT'S NOT THAT DEEP...
NO, WE SHOULDN'T HAVE GOTTEN THIS WET.
BUT THE BIG ONE HERE SLIPPED AND DRAGGED ME DOWN WITH HER...
I SAID SORRY.
UWAAAAH!
GYAAAAH!
THANKS. BOTH OF YOU...
To Kurosawa-sa
ANYWAY, SORRY. I GUESS SHE CAN'T READ IT LIKE THIS.
I'LL WRITE ANOTHER LETTER.

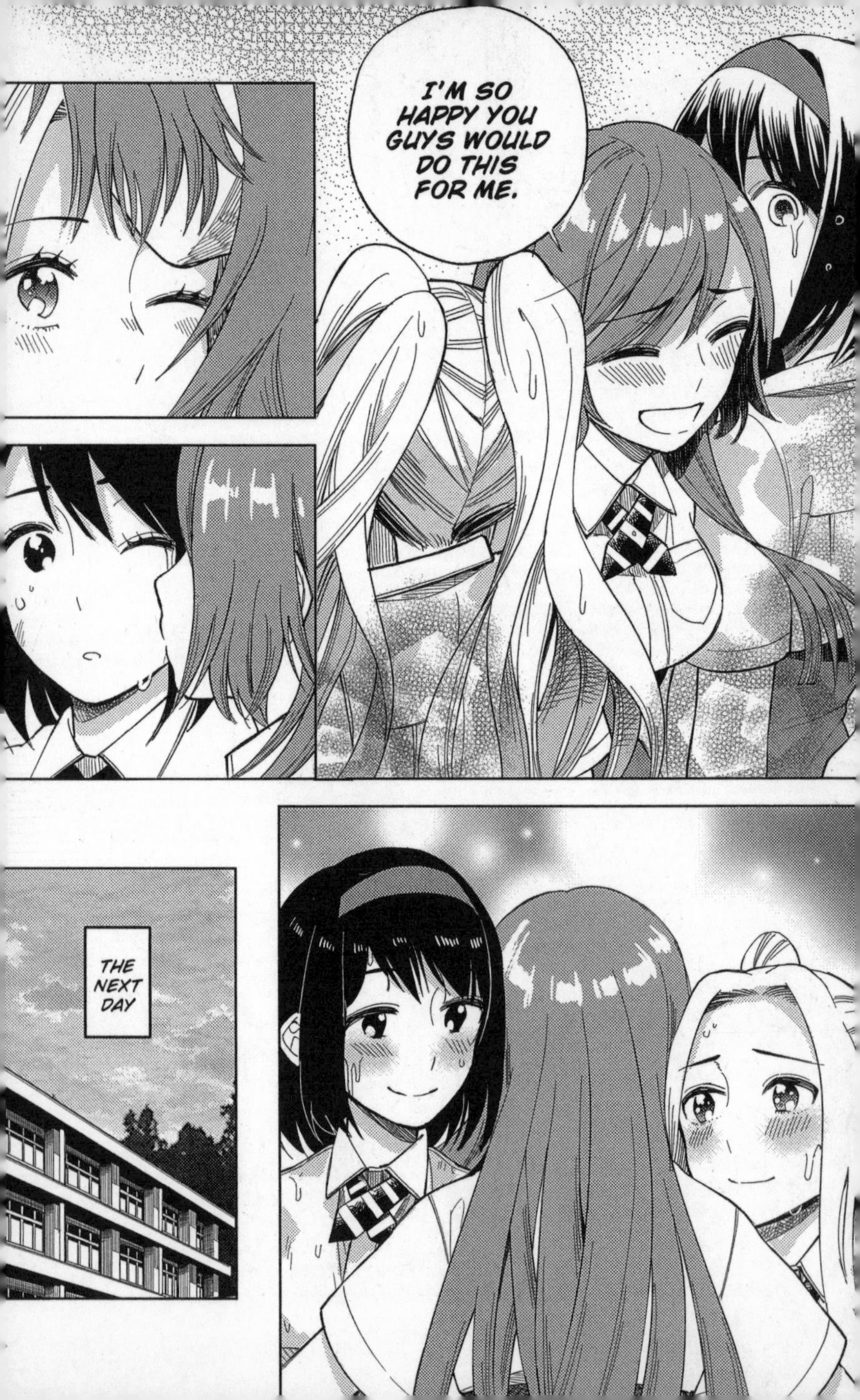
I'M SO HAPPY YOU GUYS WOULD DO THIS FOR ME.
THE NEXT DAY

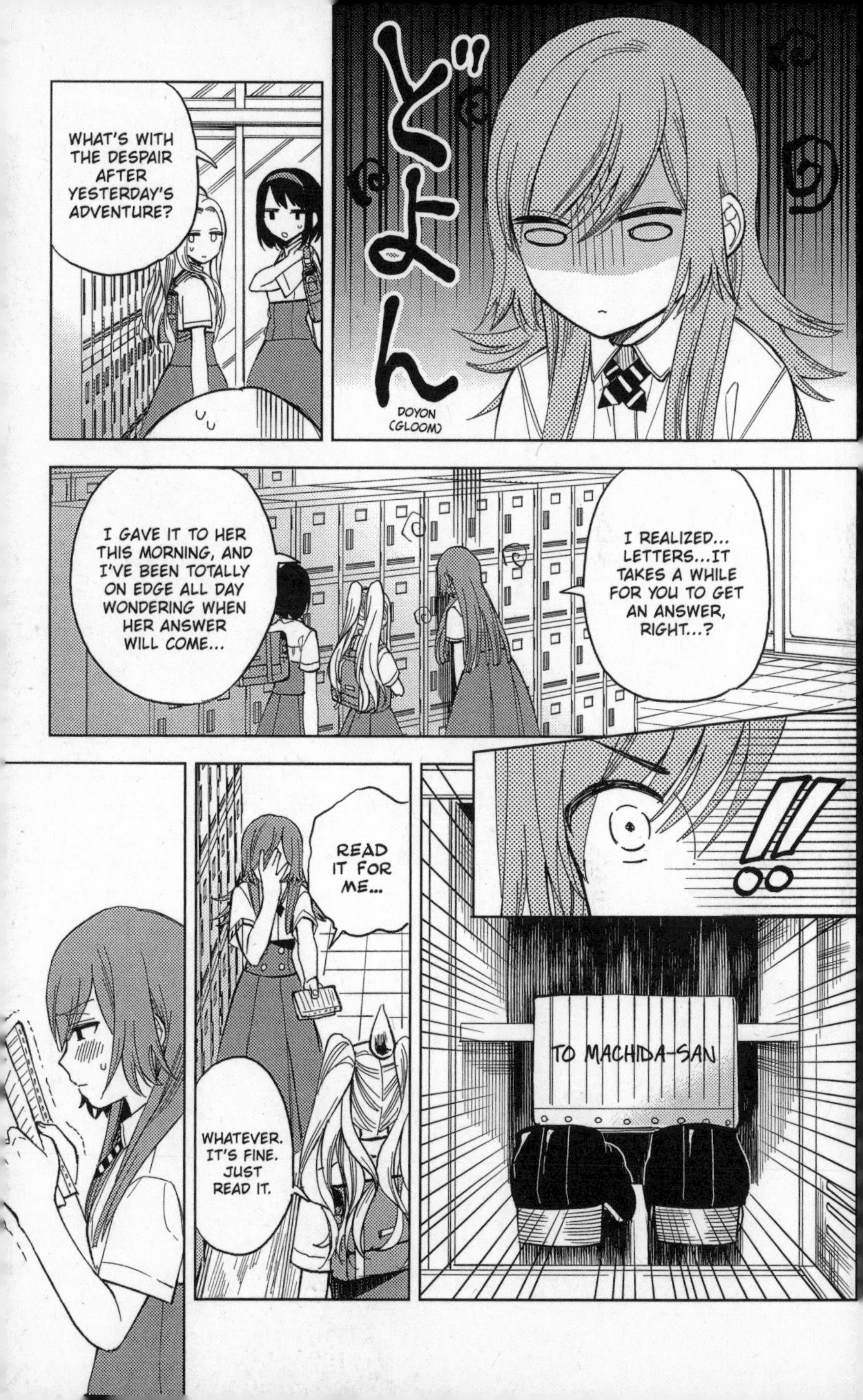
どよん
DOYON (GLOOM)
WHAT'S WITH THE DESPAIR AFTER YESTERDAY'S ADVENTURE?
I REALIZED... LETTERS...IT TAKES A WHILE FOR YOU TO GET AN ANSWER, RIGHT...?
I GAVE IT TO HER THIS MORNING, AND I'VE BEEN TOTALLY ON EDGE ALL DAY WONDERING WHEN HER ANSWER WILL COME...
!!
TO MACHIDA-SAN
READ IT FOR ME...
WHATEVER. IT'S FINE. JUST READ IT.

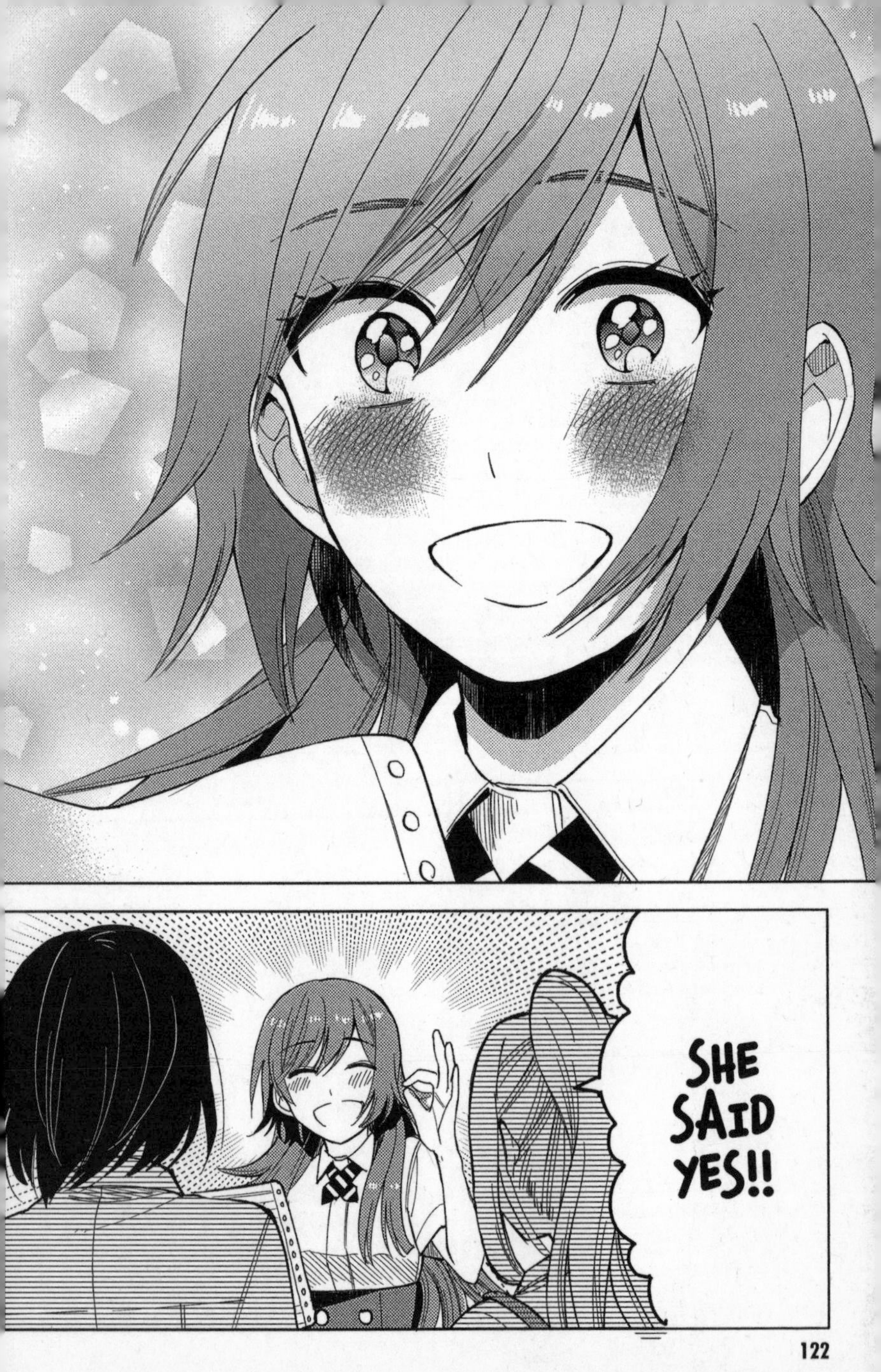
SHE SAID YES!!

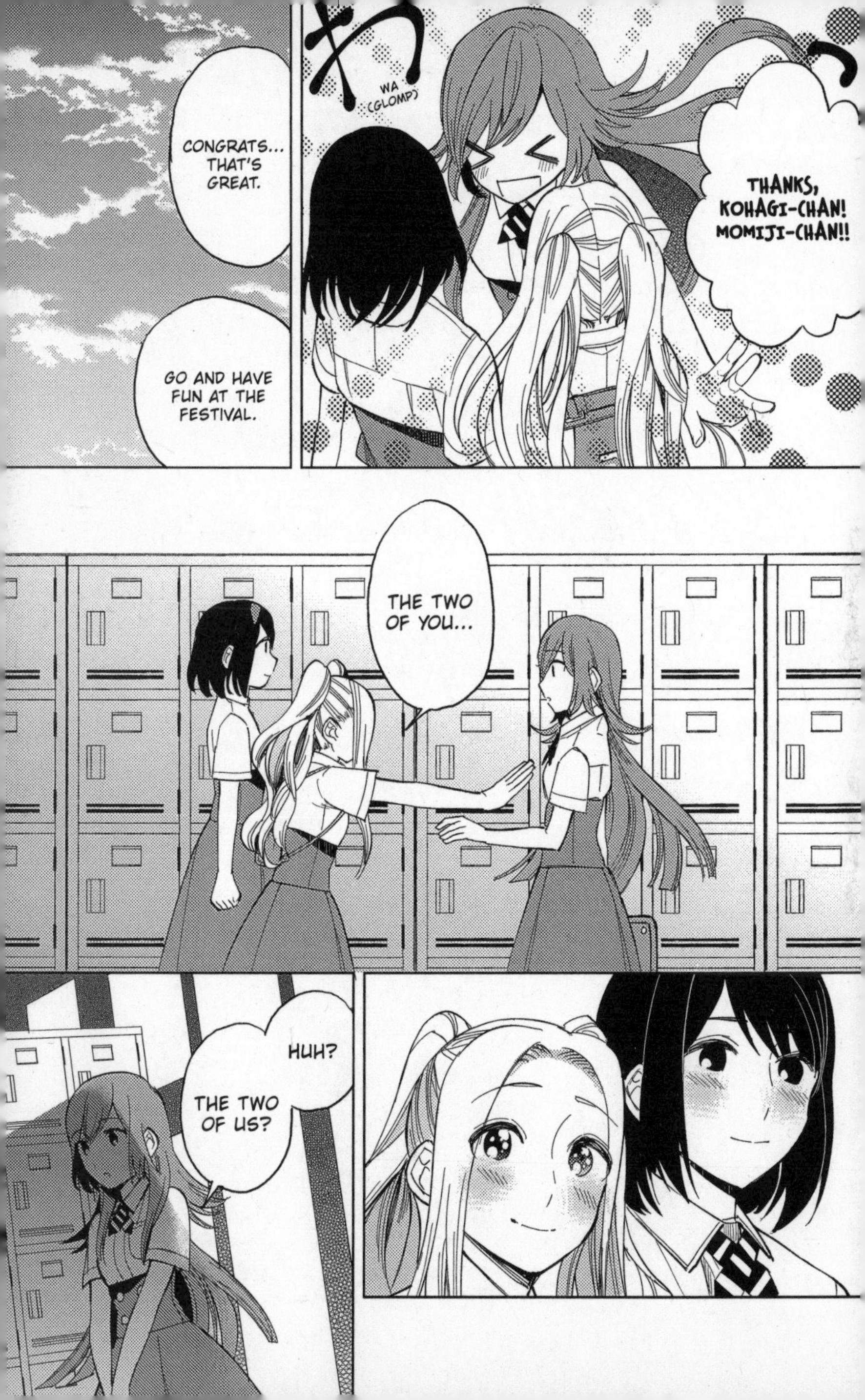
WA (GLOMP)
THANKS, KOHAGI-CHAN! MOMIJI-CHAN!!
CONGRATS... THAT'S GREAT.
GO AND HAVE FUN AT THE FESTIVAL.
THE TWO OF YOU...
HUH?
THE TWO OF US?

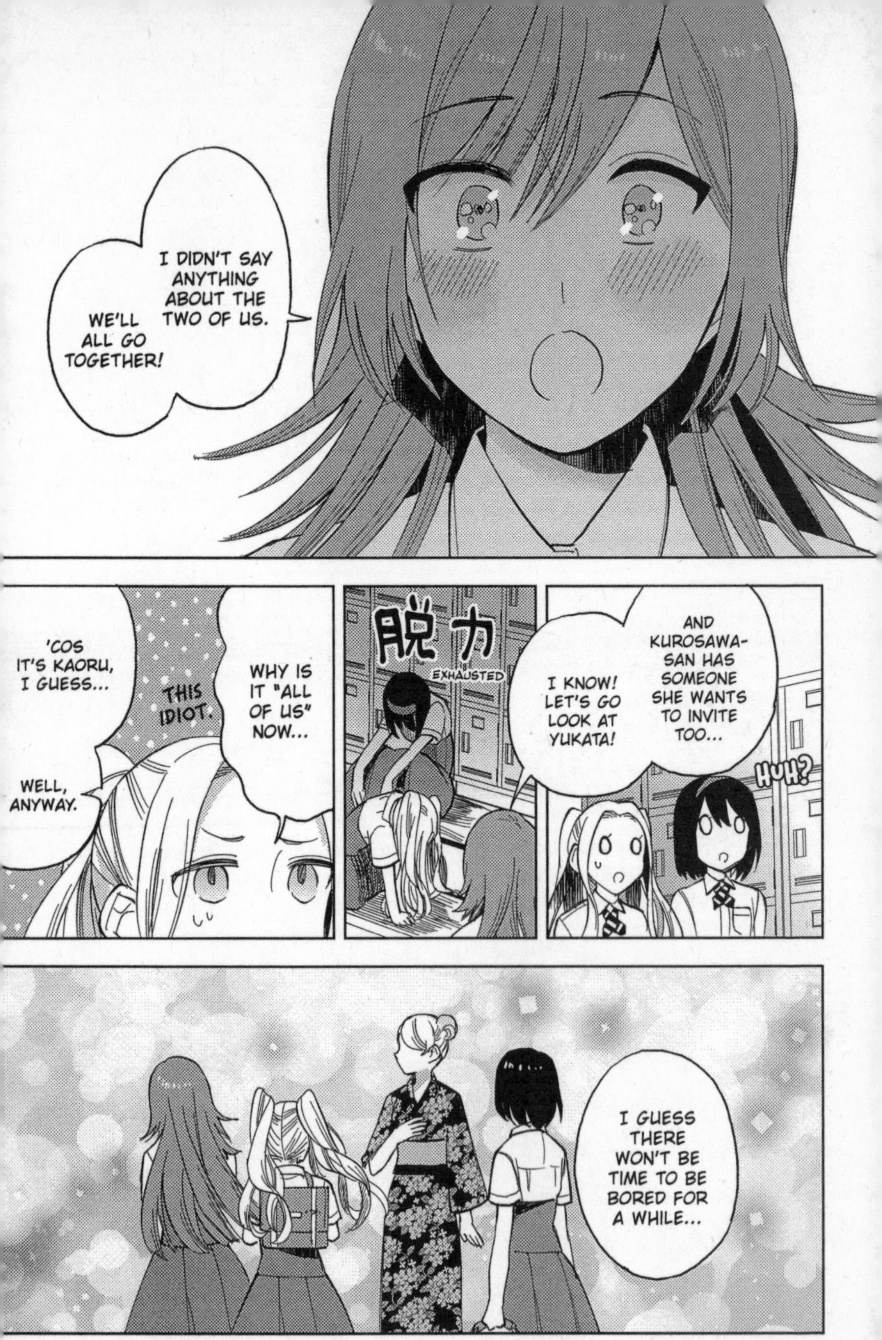
I DIDN'T SAY ANYTHING ABOUT THE TWO OF US.
WE'LL ALL GO TOGETHER!
AND KUROSAWA-SAN HAS SOMEONE SHE WANTS TO INVITE TOO...
I KNOW! LET'S GO LOOK AT YUKATA!
HUH?
脱力
EXHAUSTED
WHY IS IT "ALL OF US" NOW...
THIS IDIOT.
'COS IT'S KAORU, I GUESS...
WELL, ANYWAY.
I GUESS THERE WON'T BE TIME TO BE BORED FOR A WHILE...

Chisato's Road

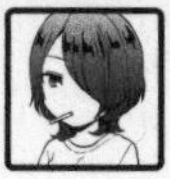

CHISATO

TWENTY-FIVE. GRADUATED VOCATIONAL COLLEGE, STILL HAS NO FULL-TIME JOB. ALL SHE'S GOT ARE HER LOOKS.

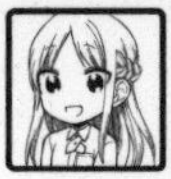

AYUMI

MIDDLE SCHOOL THIRD-YEAR, FIFTEEN YEARS OLD. SHE'S AN ONLY CHILD, AND HER PARENTS CHERISH HER.

KISS THEATER: WHAT'S BEHIND THE STORY!?

PEOPLE OTHER THAN THE MAIN CHARACTERS HAVE STORIES TOO. HERE, WE PRESENT THE "LITTLE LOVE" STORIES HAPPENING BEHIND THE SCENES.

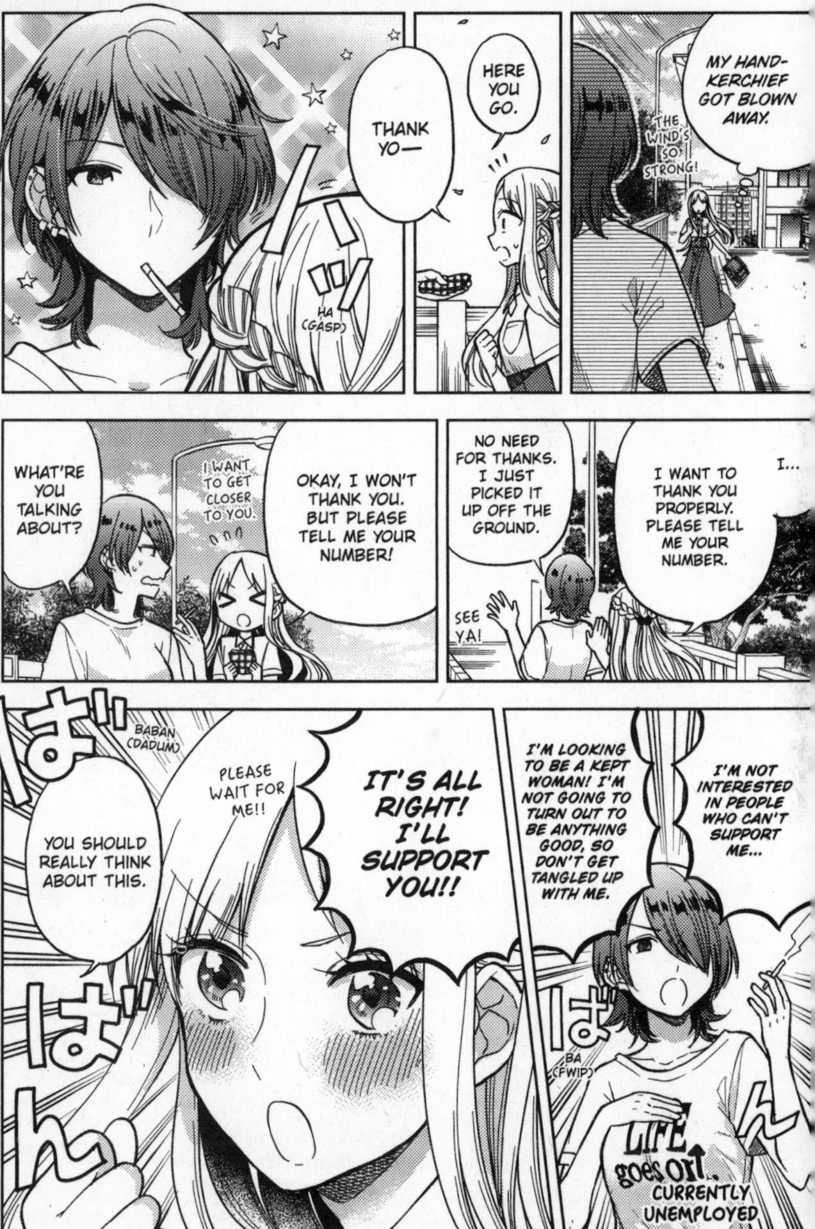
MY HAND-KERCHIEF GOT BLOWN AWAY.
THE WIND'S SO STRONG!
HERE YOU GO.
THANK YO—
HA (GASP)
I...
I WANT TO THANK YOU PROPERLY. PLEASE TELL ME YOUR NUMBER.
NO NEED FOR THANKS. I JUST PICKED IT UP OFF THE GROUND.
SEE YA!
OKAY, I WON'T THANK YOU. BUT PLEASE TELL ME YOUR NUMBER!
I WANT TO GET CLOSER TO YOU.
WHAT'RE YOU TALKING ABOUT?
I'M NOT INTERESTED IN PEOPLE WHO CAN'T SUPPORT ME...
I'M LOOKING TO BE A KEPT WOMAN! I'M NOT GOING TO TURN OUT TO BE ANYTHING GOOD, SO DON'T GET TANGLED UP WITH ME.
ば
BA (FWIP)
LIFE goes on.
CURRENTLY UNEMPLOYED
IT'S ALL RIGHT! I'LL SUPPORT YOU!!
PLEASE WAIT FOR ME!!
ばばん
BABAN (DADUM)
YOU SHOULD REALLY THINK ABOUT THIS.

❋ *Kohagi Inoue* ❋

K o h a g i   I n o u e

Second-year student at Seiran Academy High School. Kaoru's friend. Short. Having been at Seiran Academy since the beginning of middle school, she happened to become close with Kaoru when she transferred in. Later on, Momiji joined them, and now the three are usually together. Kohagi likes to meddle, while Momiji finds most things not worth the hassle, so they have a give-and-take relationship with the introverted Kaoru.

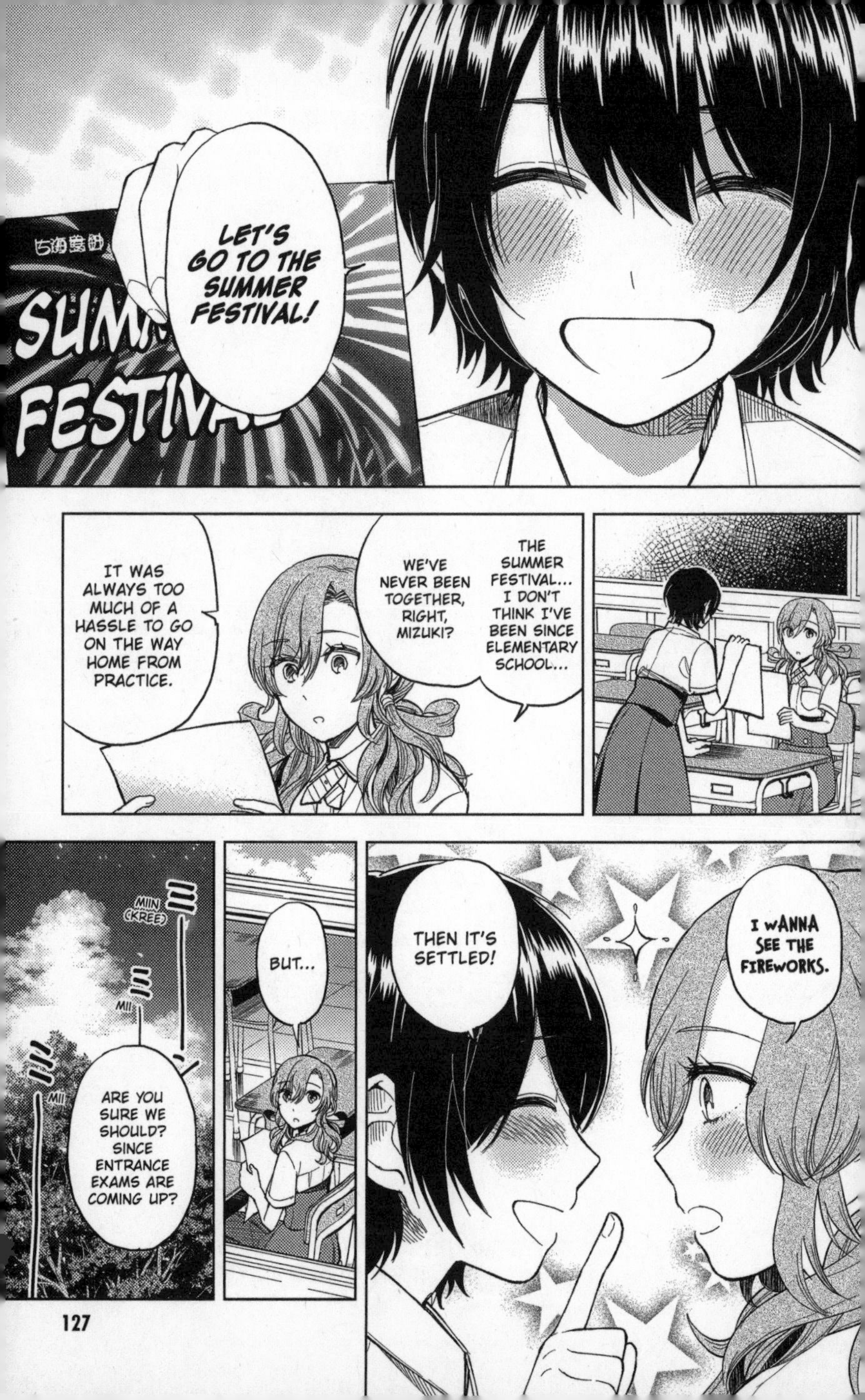
LET'S GO TO THE SUMMER FESTIVAL!
THE SUMMER FESTIVAL... I DON'T THINK I'VE BEEN SINCE ELEMENTARY SCHOOL...
WE'VE NEVER BEEN TOGETHER, RIGHT, MIZUKI?
IT WAS ALWAYS TOO MUCH OF A HASSLE TO GO ON THE WAY HOME FROM PRACTICE.
I wANNA SEE THE FIREWORKS.
THEN IT'S SETTLED!
BUT...
ARE YOU SURE WE SHOULD? SINCE ENTRANCE EXAMS ARE COMING UP?
MIIN (KREE)
MII
MII

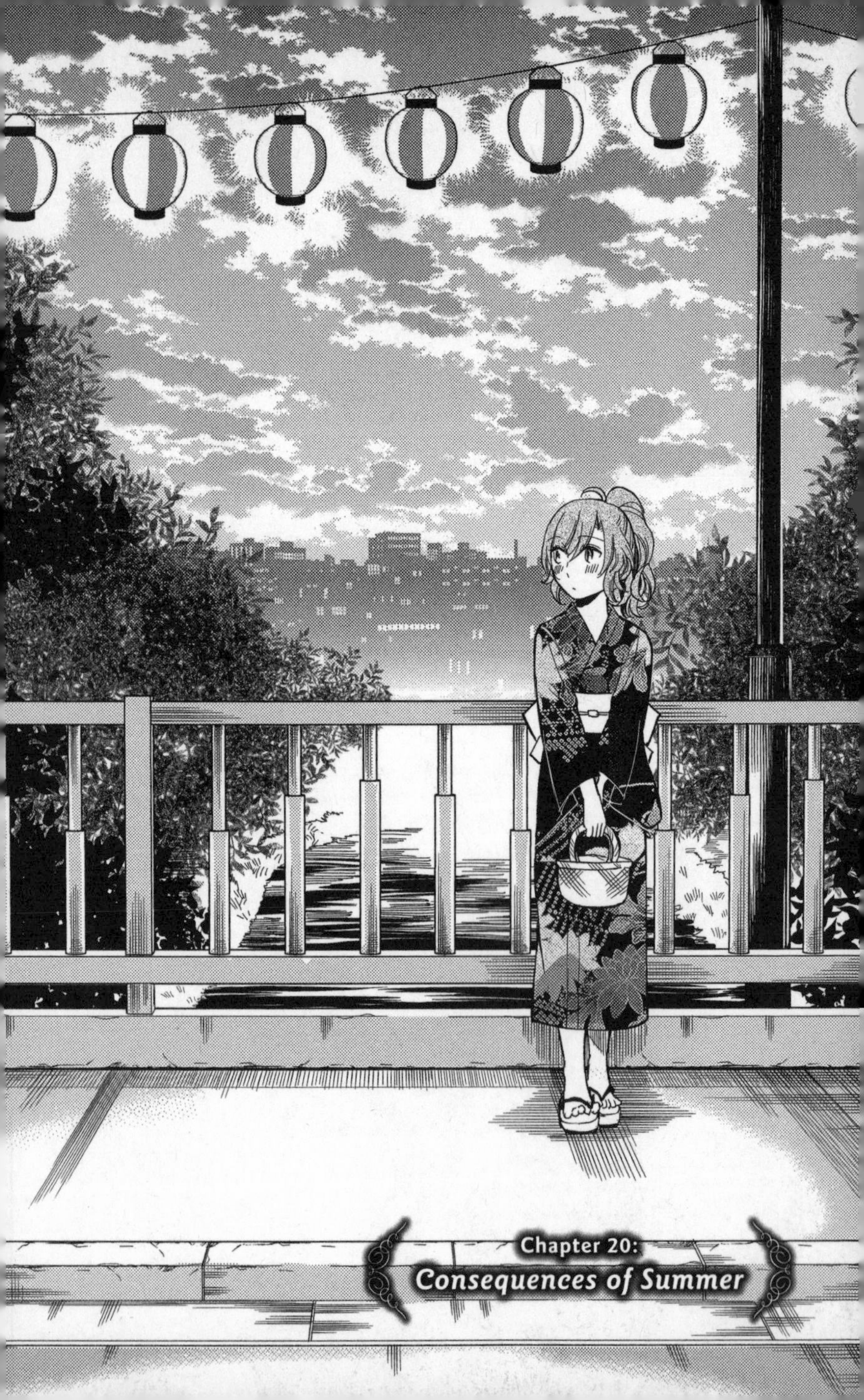
Chapter 20:
Consequences of Summer

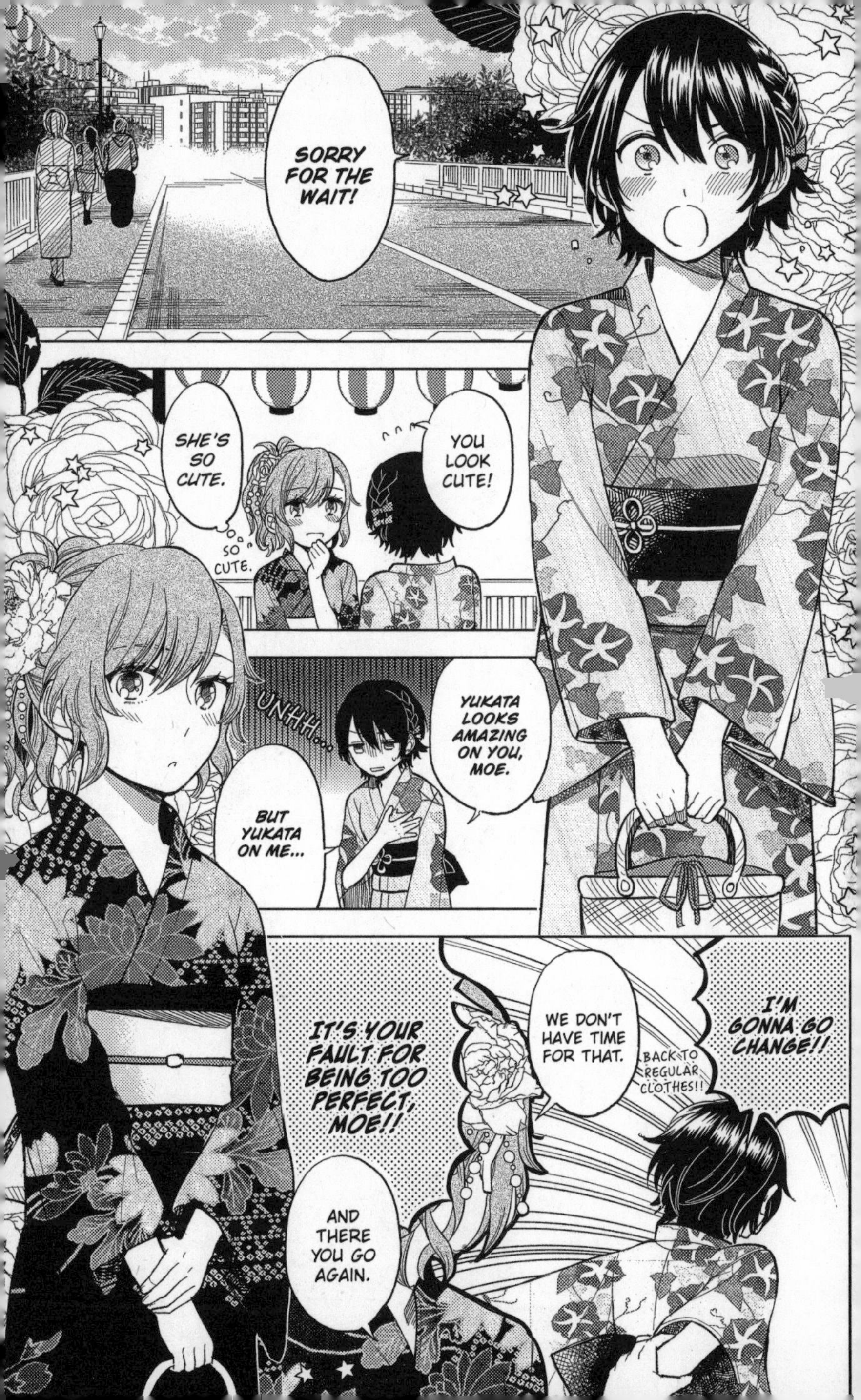
SORRY FOR THE WAIT!
YOU LOOK CUTE!
SHE'S SO CUTE.
SO CUTE.
YUKATA LOOKS AMAZING ON YOU, MOE.
UNHH...
BUT YUKATA ON ME...
I'M GONNA GO CHANGE!!
BACK TO REGULAR CLOTHES!!
WE DON'T HAVE TIME FOR THAT.
IT'S YOUR FAULT FOR BEING TOO PERFECT, MOE!!
AND THERE YOU GO AGAIN.

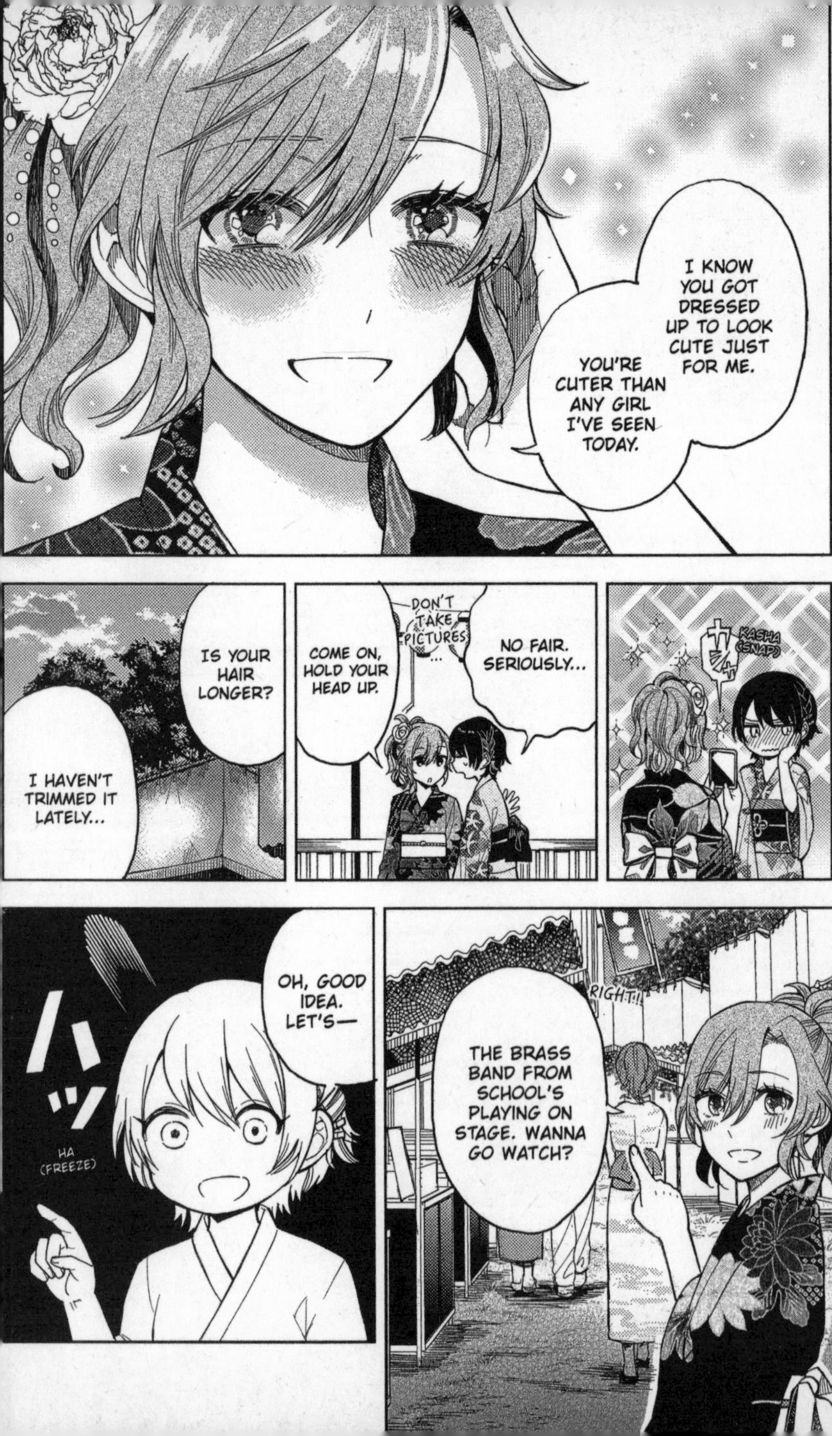
I KNOW YOU GOT DRESSED UP TO LOOK CUTE JUST FOR ME.
YOU'RE CUTER THAN ANY GIRL I'VE SEEN TODAY.
KASHA (SNAP)
NO FAIR. SERIOUSLY...
DON'T TAKE PICTURES...
COME ON, HOLD YOUR HEAD UP.
IS YOUR HAIR LONGER?
I HAVEN'T TRIMMED IT LATELY...
RIGHT!!
THE BRASS BAND FROM SCHOOL'S PLAYING ON STAGE. WANNA GO WATCH?
OH, GOOD IDEA. LET'S—
ハッ
HA (FREEZE)

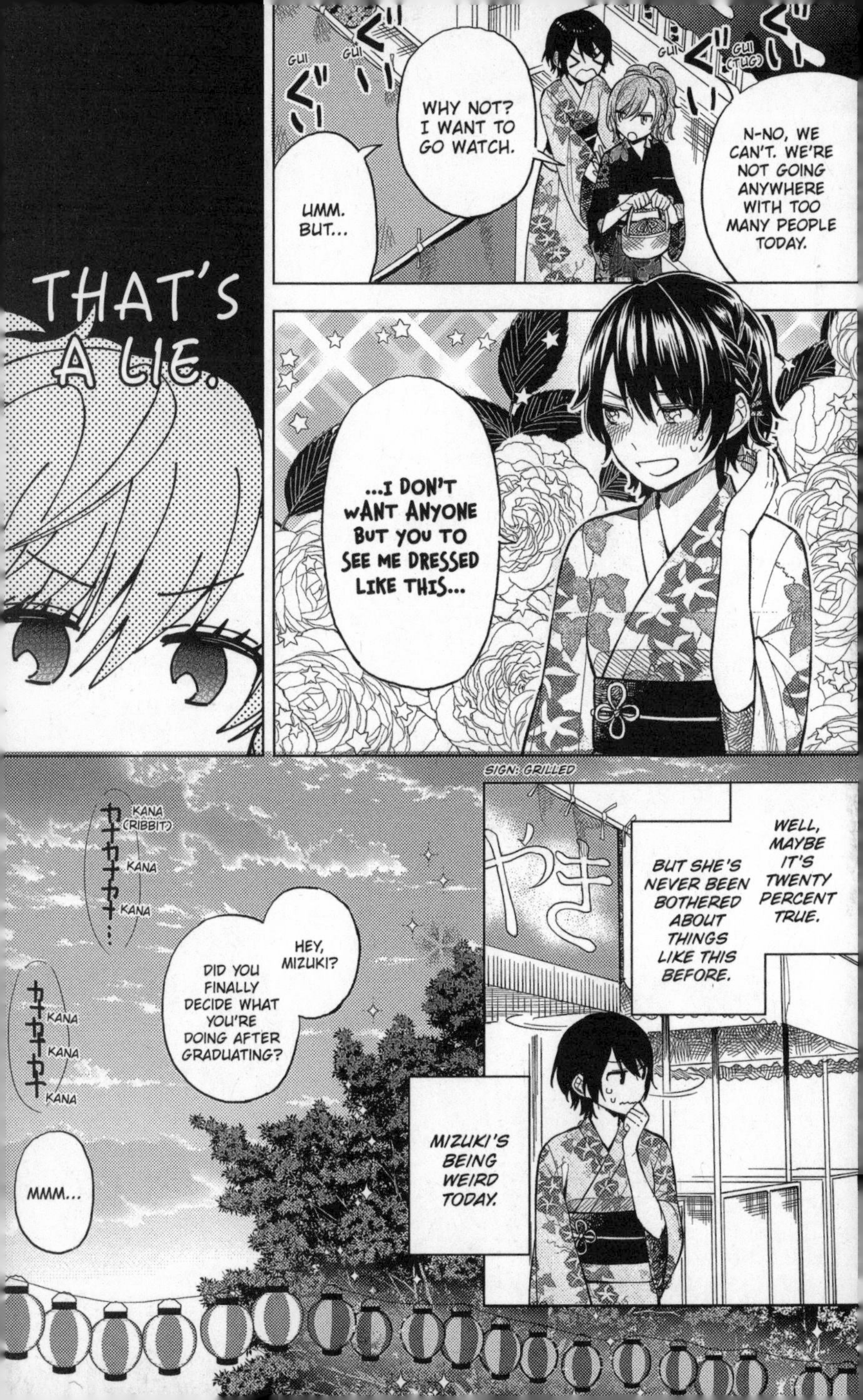
GUI (TUG)
GUI
N-NO, WE CAN'T. WE'RE NOT GOING ANYWHERE WITH TOO MANY PEOPLE TODAY.
WHY NOT? I WANT TO GO WATCH.
GUI
GUI
UMM. BUT...
...I DON'T WANT ANYONE BUT YOU TO SEE ME DRESSED LIKE THIS...
THAT'S A LIE.
SIGN: GRILLED
WELL, MAYBE IT'S TWENTY PERCENT TRUE.
BUT SHE'S NEVER BEEN BOTHERED ABOUT THINGS LIKE THIS BEFORE.
MIZUKI'S BEING WEIRD TODAY.
KANA (RIBBIT)
KANA
KANA
HEY, MIZUKI?
DID YOU FINALLY DECIDE WHAT YOU'RE DOING AFTER GRADUATING?
KANA
KANA
KANA
MMM...

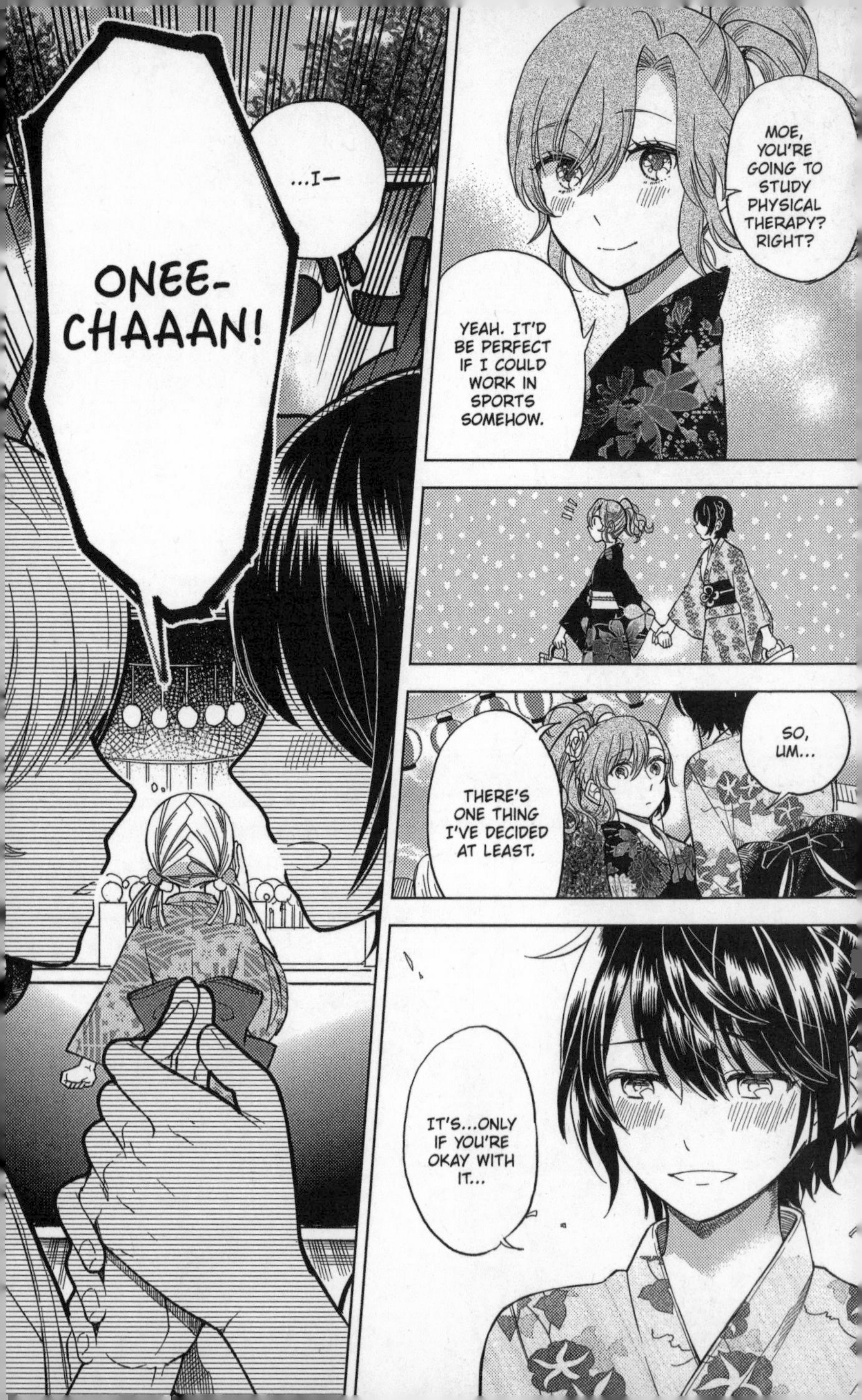
MOE, YOU'RE GOING TO STUDY PHYSICAL THERAPY? RIGHT?
YEAH. IT'D BE PERFECT IF I COULD WORK IN SPORTS SOMEHOW.
SO, UM...
THERE'S ONE THING I'VE DECIDED AT LEAST.
IT'S...ONLY IF YOU'RE OKAY WITH IT...
...I—
ONEE-CHAAAN!

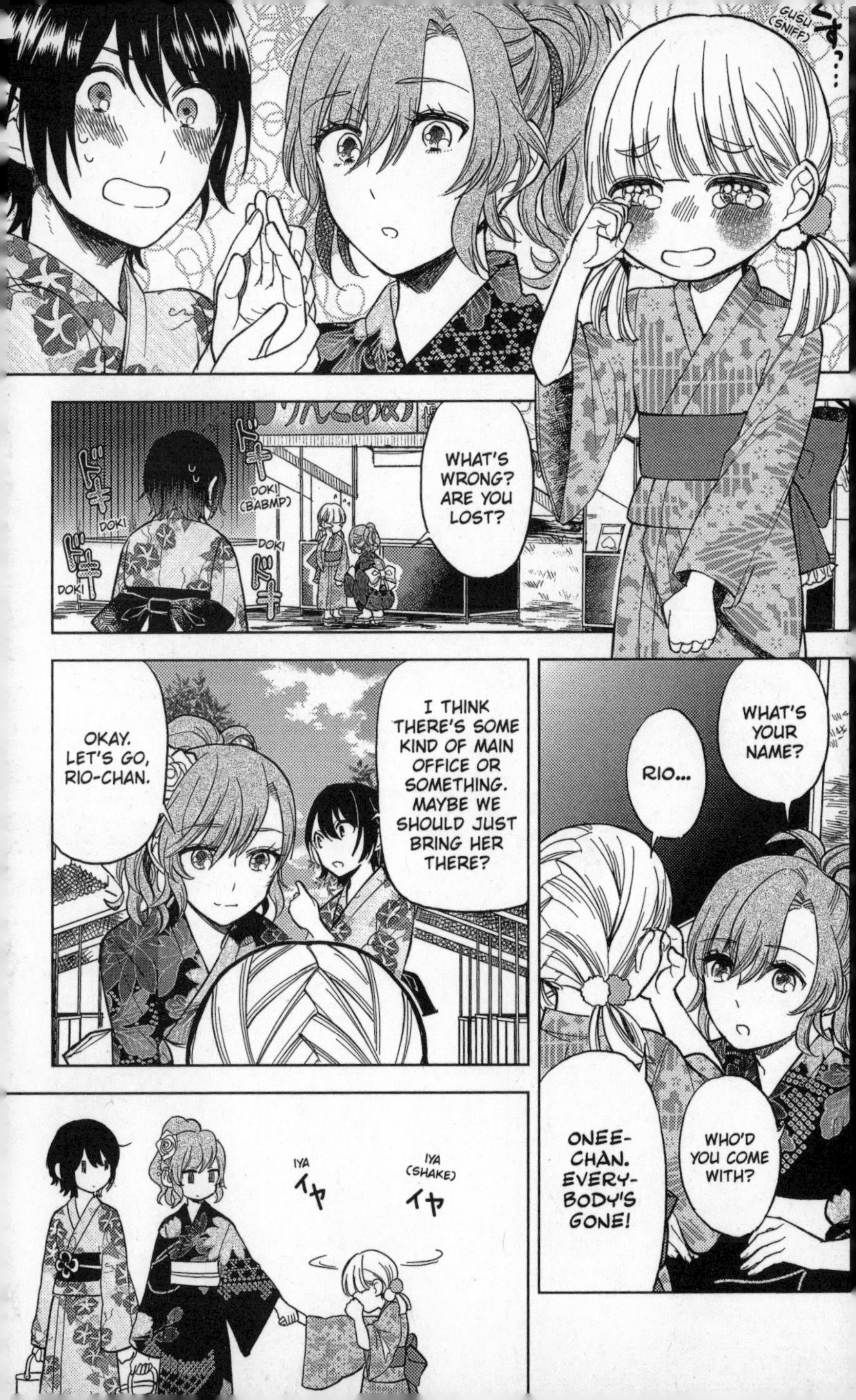
ぐすっ…
GUSU (SNIFF)
WHAT'S WRONG? ARE YOU LOST?
ドキ
DOKI (BABMP)
DOKI
ドキ
DOKI
DOKI
WHAT'S YOUR NAME?
RIO...
WHO'D YOU COME WITH?
ONEE-CHAN. EVERYBODY'S GONE!
I THINK THERE'S SOME KIND OF MAIN OFFICE OR SOMETHING. MAYBE WE SHOULD JUST BRING HER THERE?
OKAY. LET'S GO, RIO-CHAN.
イヤ
IYA (SHAKE)
イヤ
IYA

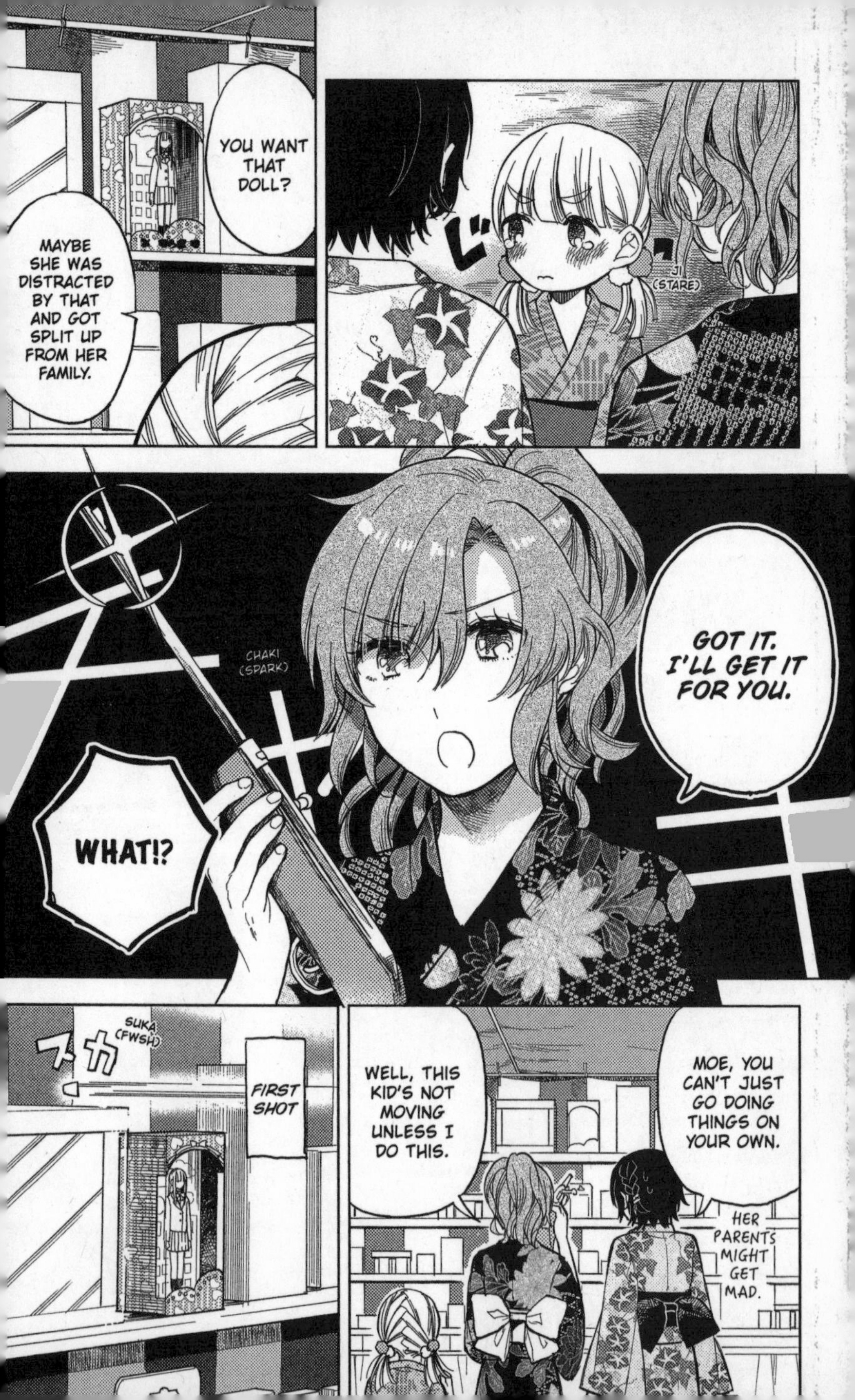
JI
(STARE)
YOU WANT THAT DOLL?
MAYBE SHE WAS DISTRACTED BY THAT AND GOT SPLIT UP FROM HER FAMILY.
GOT IT. I'LL GET IT FOR YOU.
CHAKI
(SPARK)
WHAT!?
MOE, YOU CAN'T JUST GO DOING THINGS ON YOUR OWN.
HER PARENTS MIGHT GET MAD.
WELL, THIS KID'S NOT MOVING UNLESS I DO THIS.
FIRST SHOT
SUKA
(FWSH)

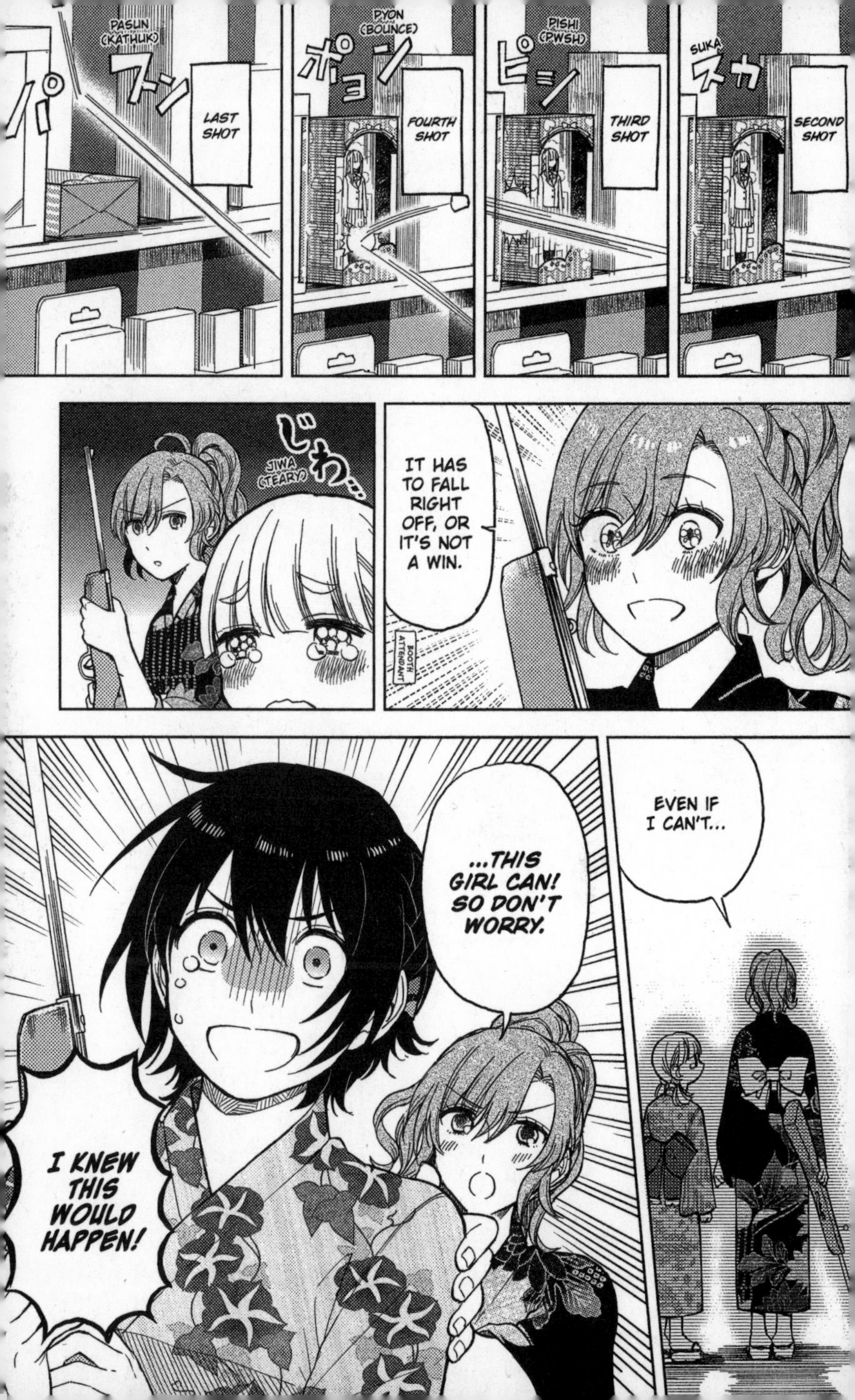

SUKA
SECOND SHOT
PISHI (PWSH)
THIRD SHOT
PYON (BOUNCE)
FOURTH SHOT
PASUN (KATHUK)
LAST SHOT
IT HAS TO FALL RIGHT OFF, OR IT'S NOT A WIN.
BOOTH ATTENDANT
JIWA (TEARY)
EVEN IF I CAN'T...
...THIS GIRL CAN! SO DON'T WORRY.
I KNEW THIS WOULD HAPPEN!

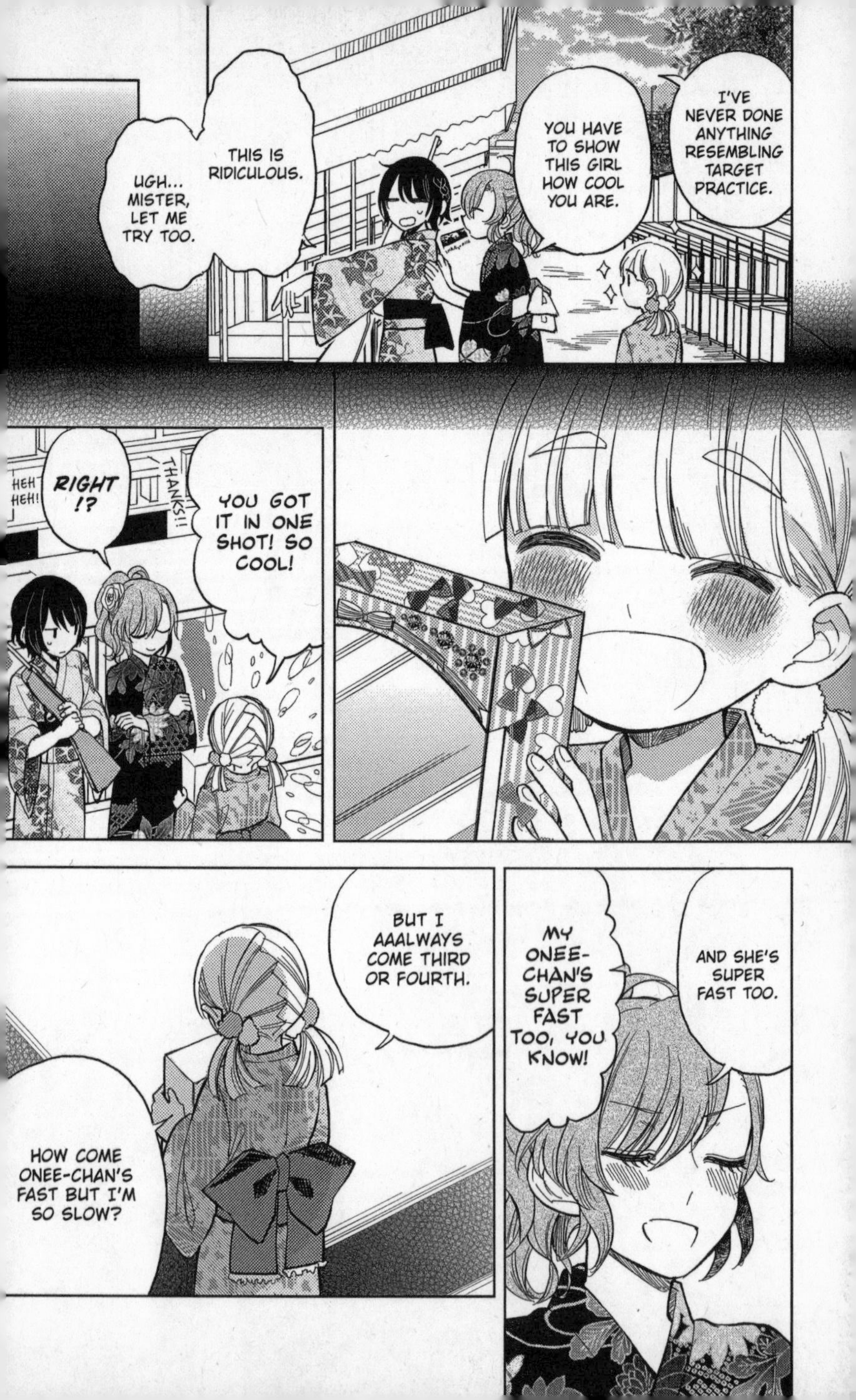
I'VE NEVER DONE ANYTHING RESEMBLING TARGET PRACTICE.
YOU HAVE TO SHOW THIS GIRL HOW COOL YOU ARE.
THIS IS RIDICULOUS.
UGH... MISTER, LET ME TRY TOO.
YOU GOT IT IN ONE SHOT! SO COOL!
THANKS!!
RIGHT!?
HEH HEH!
AND SHE'S SUPER FAST TOO.
MY ONEE-CHAN'S SUPER FAST TOO, YOU KNOW!
BUT I AAALWAYS COME THIRD OR FOURTH.
HOW COME ONEE-CHAN'S FAST BUT I'M SO SLOW?

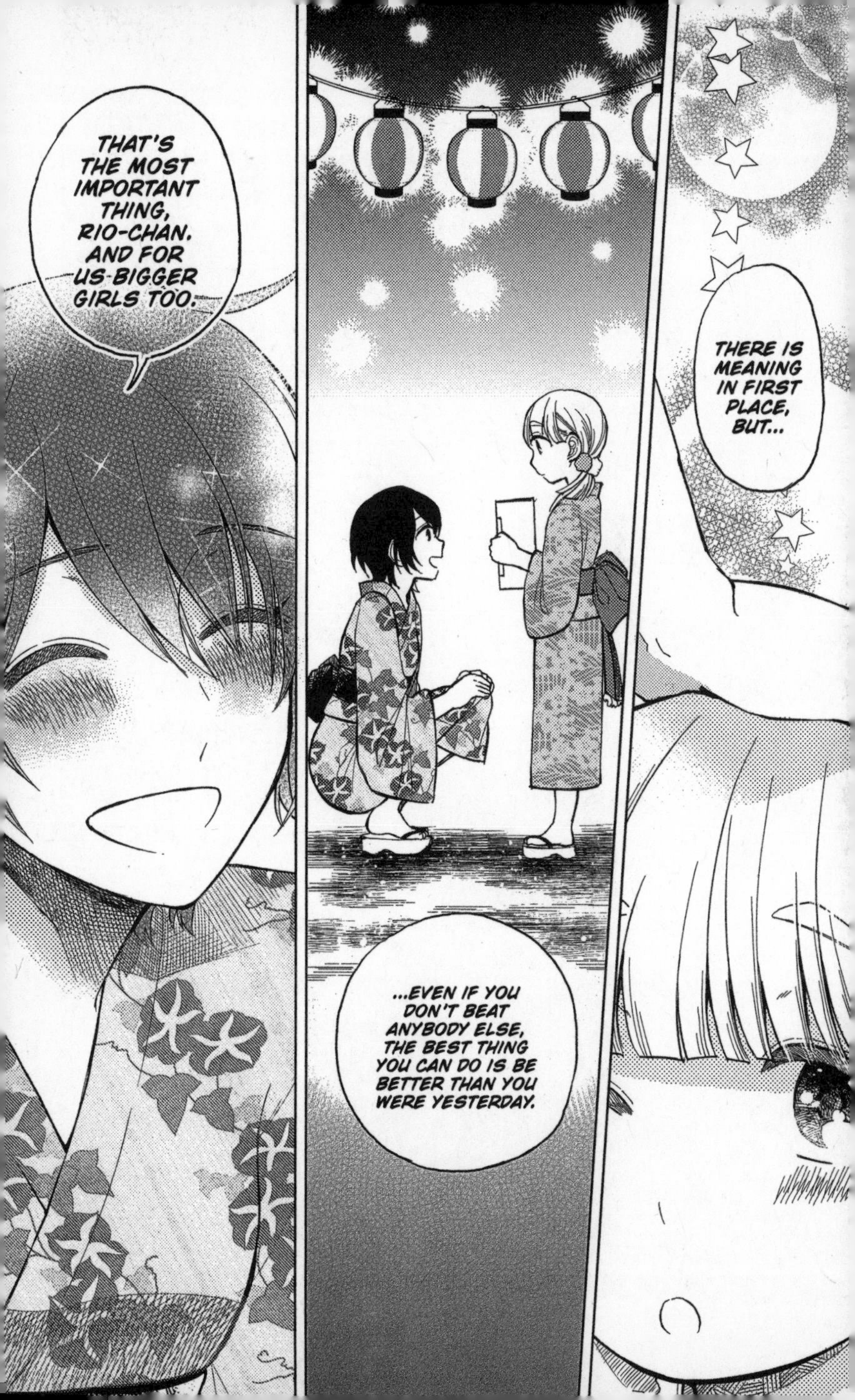
THERE IS MEANING IN FIRST PLACE, BUT...
...EVEN IF YOU DON'T BEAT ANYBODY ELSE, THE BEST THING YOU CAN DO IS BE BETTER THAN YOU WERE YESTERDAY.
THAT'S THE MOST IMPORTANT THING, RIO-CHAN. AND FOR US BIGGER GIRLS TOO.

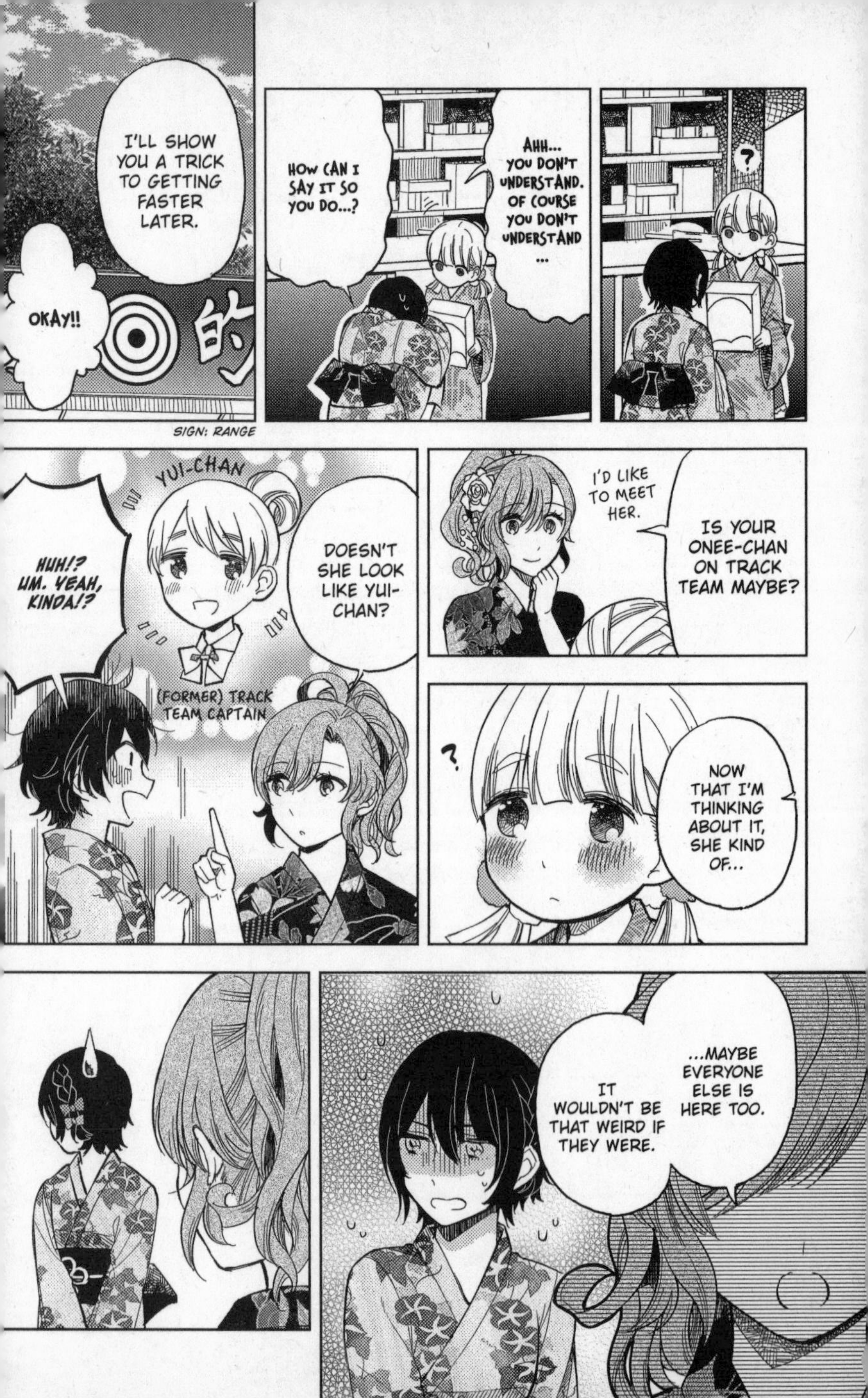
?
AHH... YOU DON'T UNDERSTAND. OF COURSE YOU DON'T UNDERSTAND ...
HOW CAN I SAY IT SO YOU DO...?
I'LL SHOW YOU A TRICK TO GETTING FASTER LATER.
OKAY!!
SIGN: RANGE
IS YOUR ONEE-CHAN ON TRACK TEAM MAYBE?
I'D LIKE TO MEET HER.
?
NOW THAT I'M THINKING ABOUT IT, SHE KIND OF...
DOESN'T SHE LOOK LIKE YUI-CHAN?
YUI-CHAN
(FORMER) TRACK TEAM CAPTAIN
HUH!? UM. YEAH, KINDA!?
...MAYBE EVERYONE ELSE IS HERE TOO.
IT WOULDN'T BE THAT WEIRD IF THEY WERE.

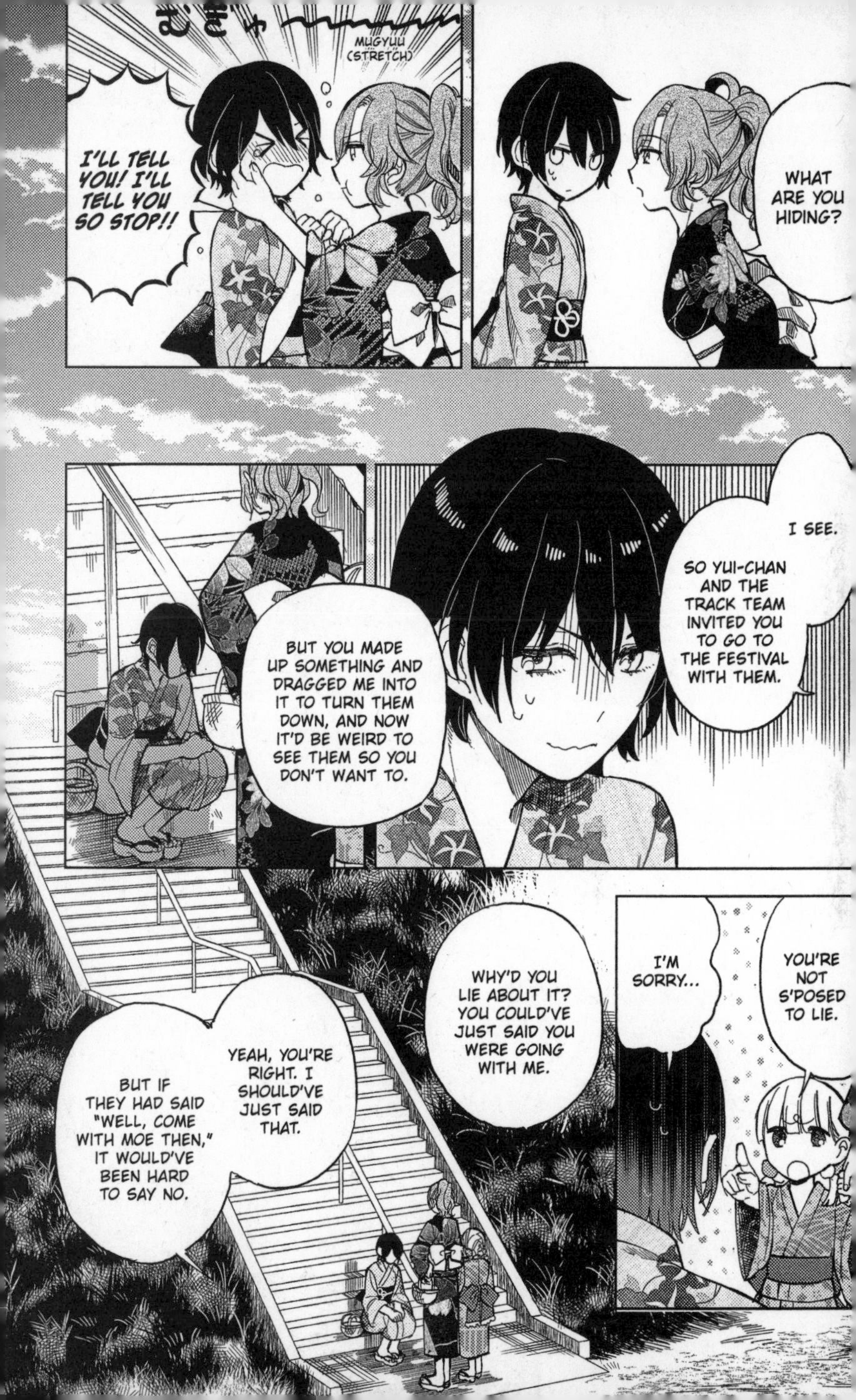
WHAT ARE YOU HIDING?
むぎゅ〜
MUGYUU (STRETCH)
I'LL TELL YOU! I'LL TELL YOU SO STOP!!
I SEE.
SO YUI-CHAN AND THE TRACK TEAM INVITED YOU TO GO TO THE FESTIVAL WITH THEM.
BUT YOU MADE UP SOMETHING AND DRAGGED ME INTO IT TO TURN THEM DOWN, AND NOW IT'D BE WEIRD TO SEE THEM SO YOU DON'T WANT TO.
YOU'RE NOT S'POSED TO LIE.
I'M SORRY...
WHY'D YOU LIE ABOUT IT? YOU COULD'VE JUST SAID YOU WERE GOING WITH ME.
YEAH, YOU'RE RIGHT. I SHOULD'VE JUST SAID THAT.
BUT IF THEY HAD SAID "WELL, COME WITH MOE THEN," IT WOULD'VE BEEN HARD TO SAY NO.

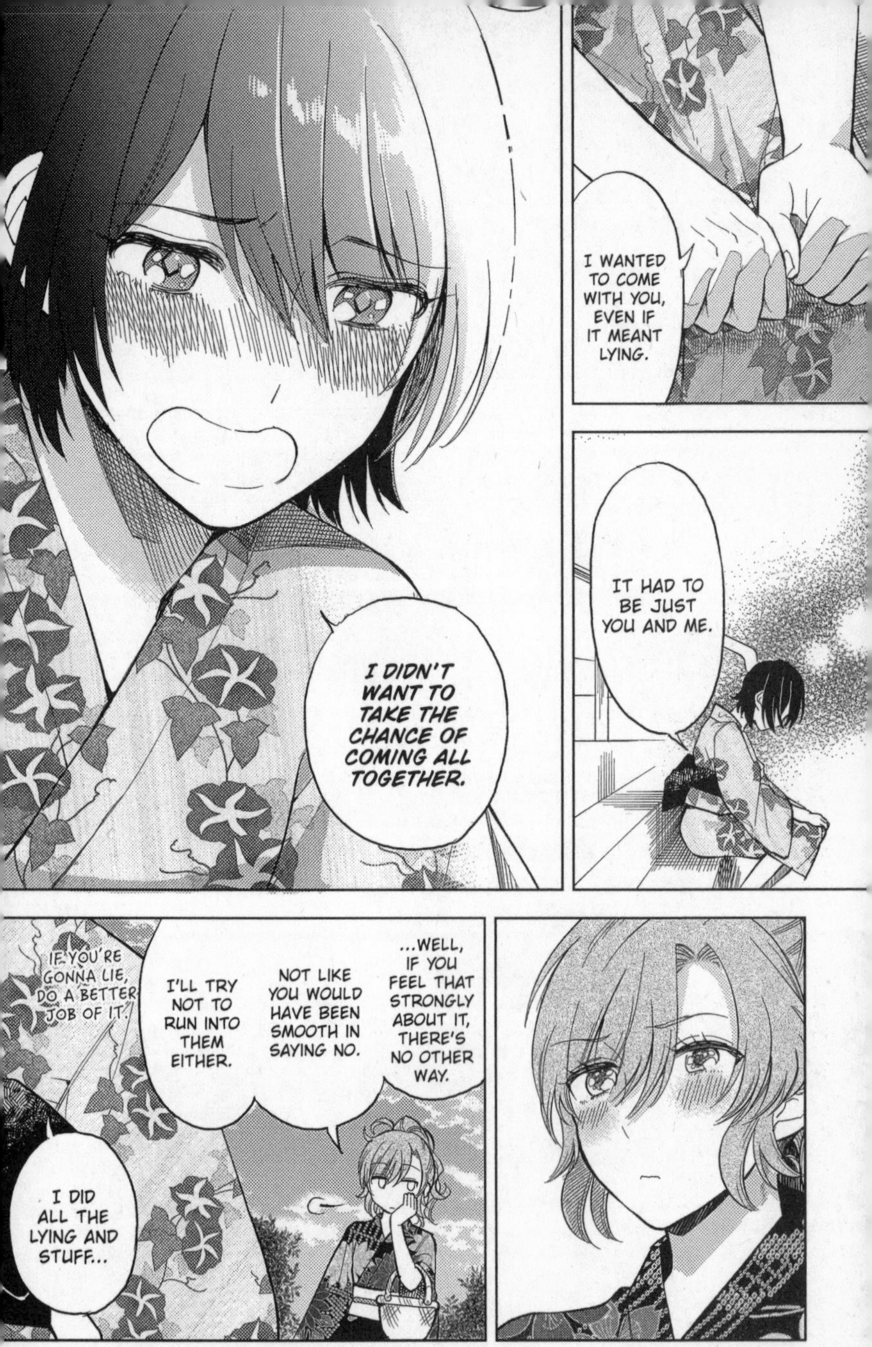
I WANTED TO COME WITH YOU, EVEN IF IT MEANT LYING.
IT HAD TO BE JUST YOU AND ME.
I DIDN'T WANT TO TAKE THE CHANCE OF COMING ALL TOGETHER.
...WELL, IF YOU FEEL THAT STRONGLY ABOUT IT, THERE'S NO OTHER WAY.
NOT LIKE YOU WOULD HAVE BEEN SMOOTH IN SAYING NO.
I'LL TRY NOT TO RUN INTO THEM EITHER.
IF YOU'RE GONNA LIE, DO A BETTER JOB OF IT.
I DID ALL THE LYING AND STUFF...

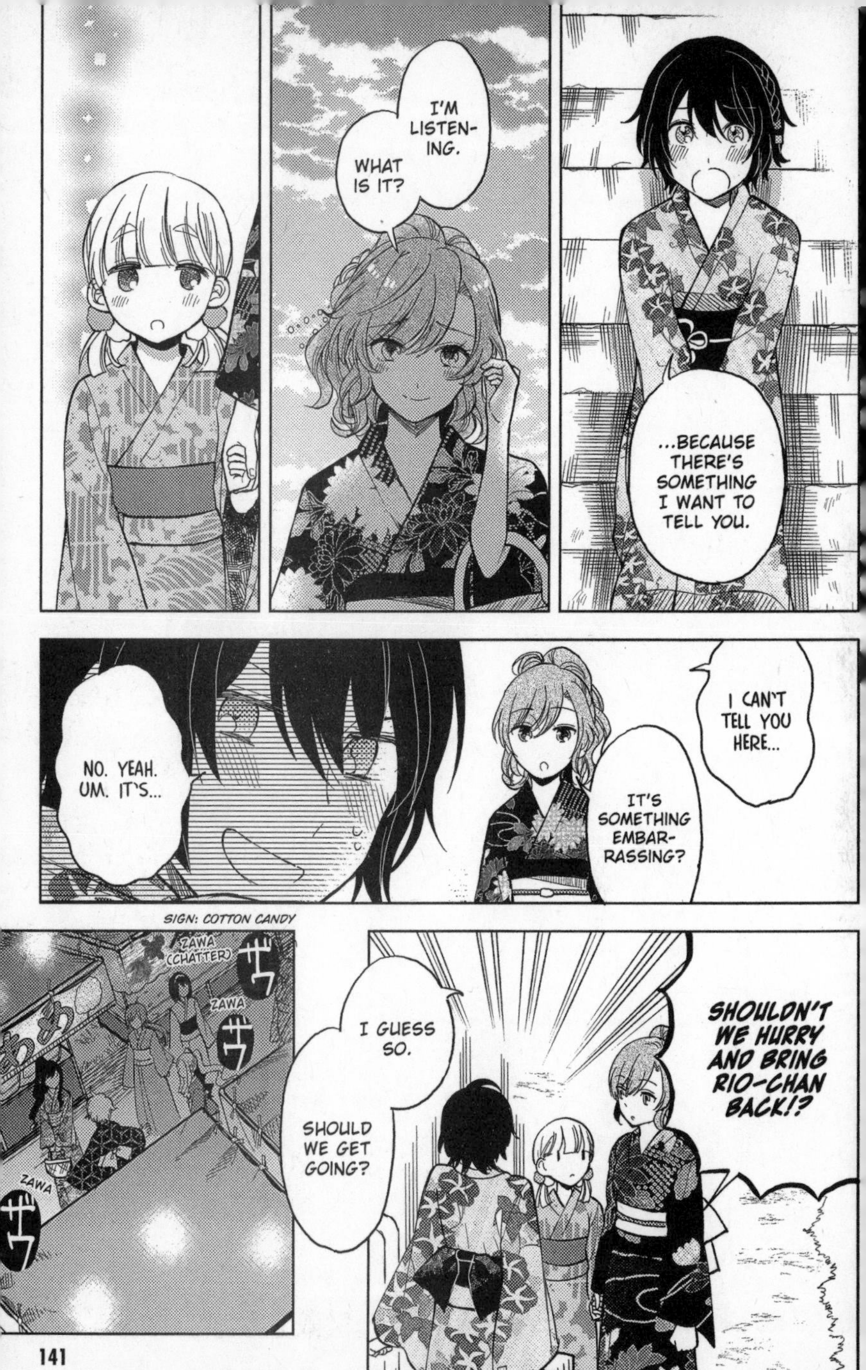
...BECAUSE THERE'S SOMETHING I WANT TO TELL YOU.
I'M LISTEN-ING.
WHAT IS IT?
I CAN'T TELL YOU HERE...
IT'S SOMETHING EMBAR-RASSING?
NO. YEAH. UM. IT'S...
SHOULDN'T WE HURRY AND BRING RIO-CHAN BACK!?
I GUESS SO.
SHOULD WE GET GOING?
SIGN: COTTON CANDY
ZAWA (CHATTER)
ザワ
ZAWA
ザワ
ZAWA
ザワ

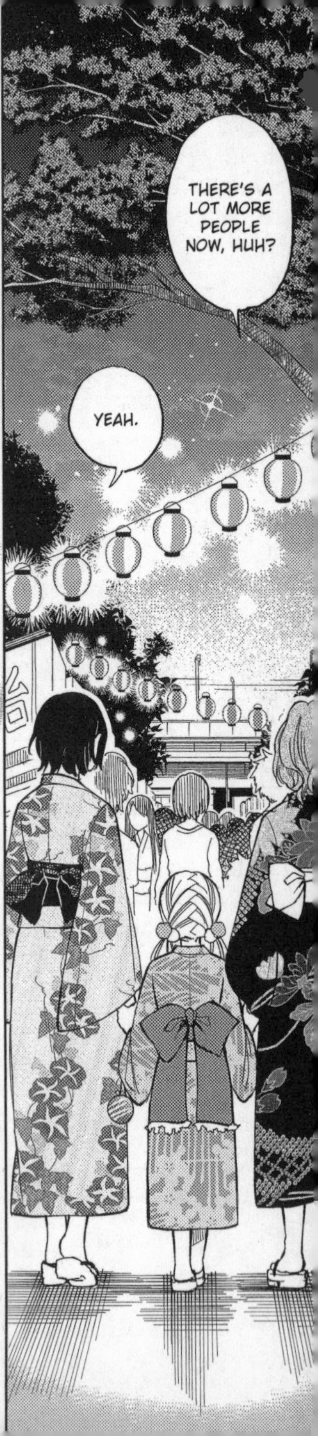
THERE'S A LOT MORE PEOPLE NOW, HUH?
YEAH.

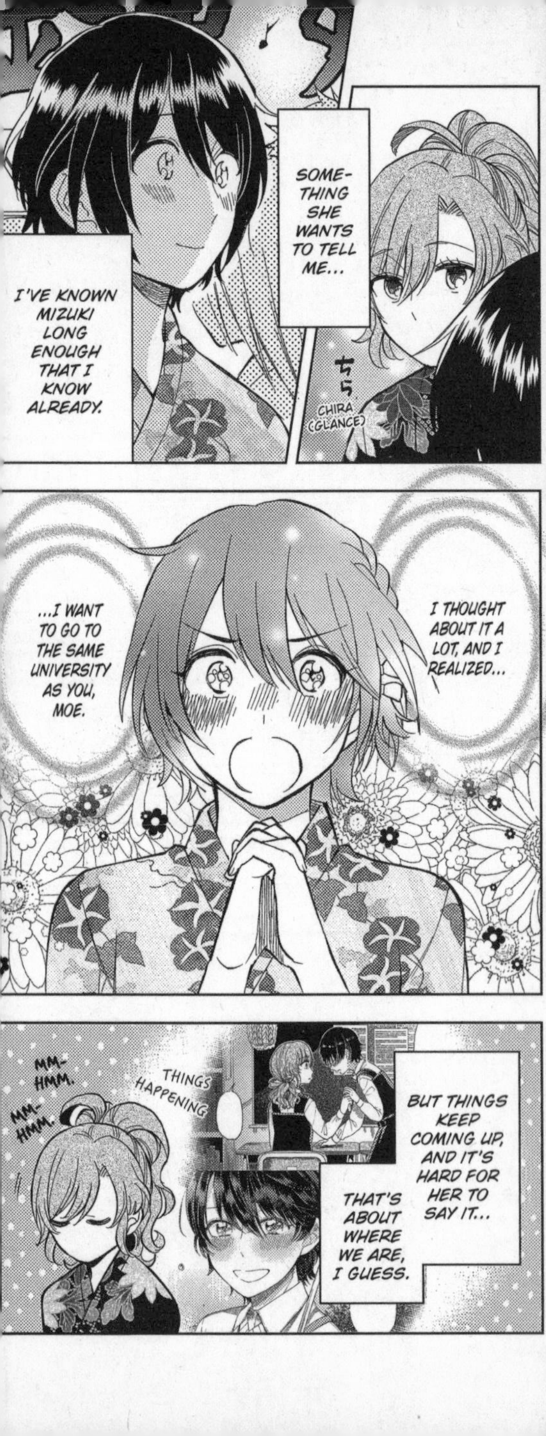
SOME-THING SHE WANTS TO TELL ME...
ちら
CHIRA (GLANCE)
I'VE KNOWN MIZUKI LONG ENOUGH THAT I KNOW ALREADY.
I THOUGHT ABOUT IT A LOT, AND I REALIZED...
...I WANT TO GO TO THE SAME UNIVERSITY AS YOU, MOE.
BUT THINGS KEEP COMING UP, AND IT'S HARD FOR HER TO SAY IT...
THINGS HAPPENING
MM-HMM.
MM-HMM.
THAT'S ABOUT WHERE WE ARE, I GUESS.

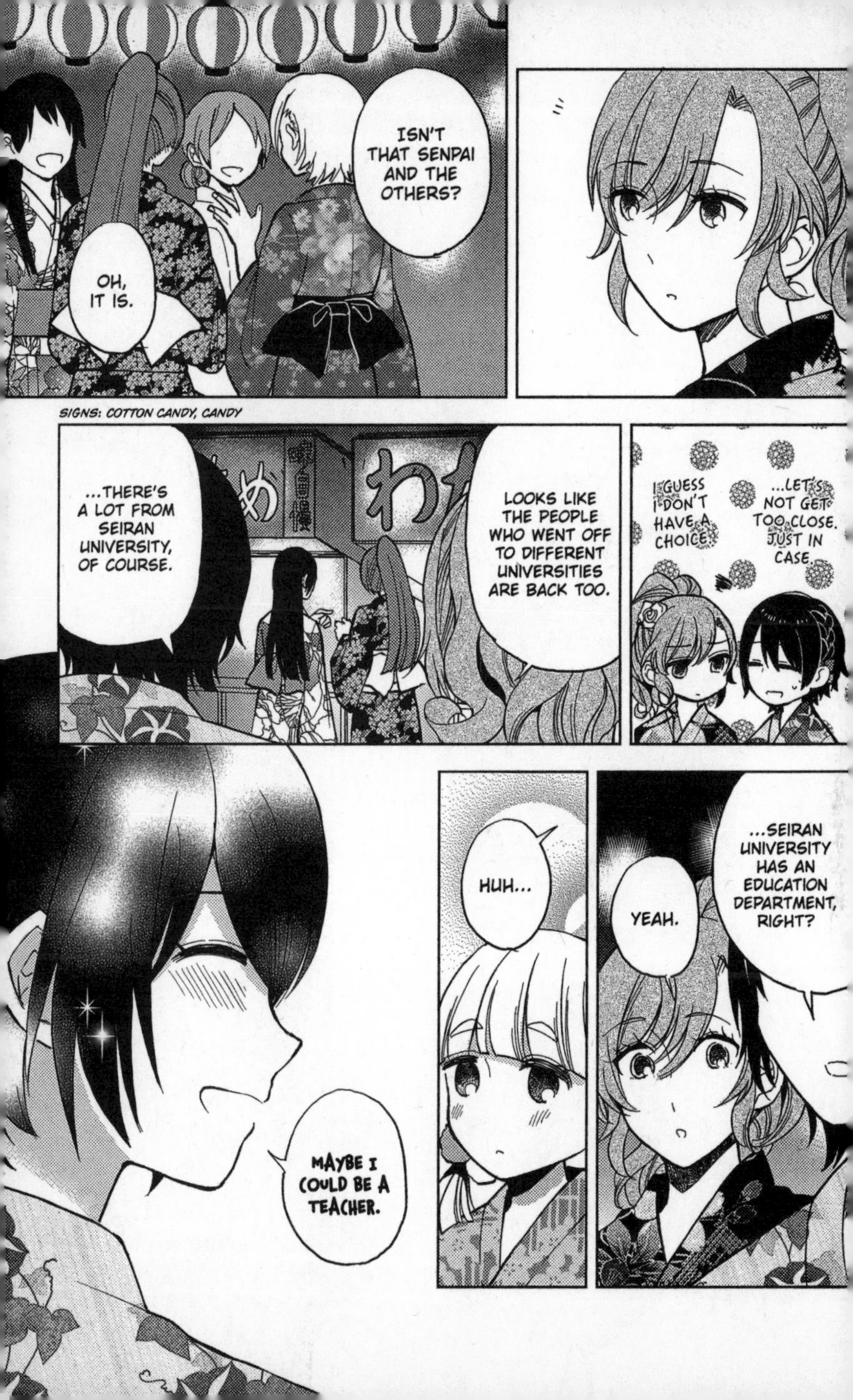
ISN'T THAT SENPAI AND THE OTHERS?
OH, IT IS.
SIGNS: COTTON CANDY, CANDY
...LET'S NOT GET TOO CLOSE. JUST IN CASE.
I GUESS I DON'T HAVE A CHOICE.
LOOKS LIKE THE PEOPLE WHO WENT OFF TO DIFFERENT UNIVERSITIES ARE BACK TOO.
...THERE'S A LOT FROM SEIRAN UNIVERSITY, OF COURSE.
...SEIRAN UNIVERSITY HAS AN EDUCATION DEPARTMENT, RIGHT?
YEAH.
HUH...
MAYBE I COULD BE A TEACHER.

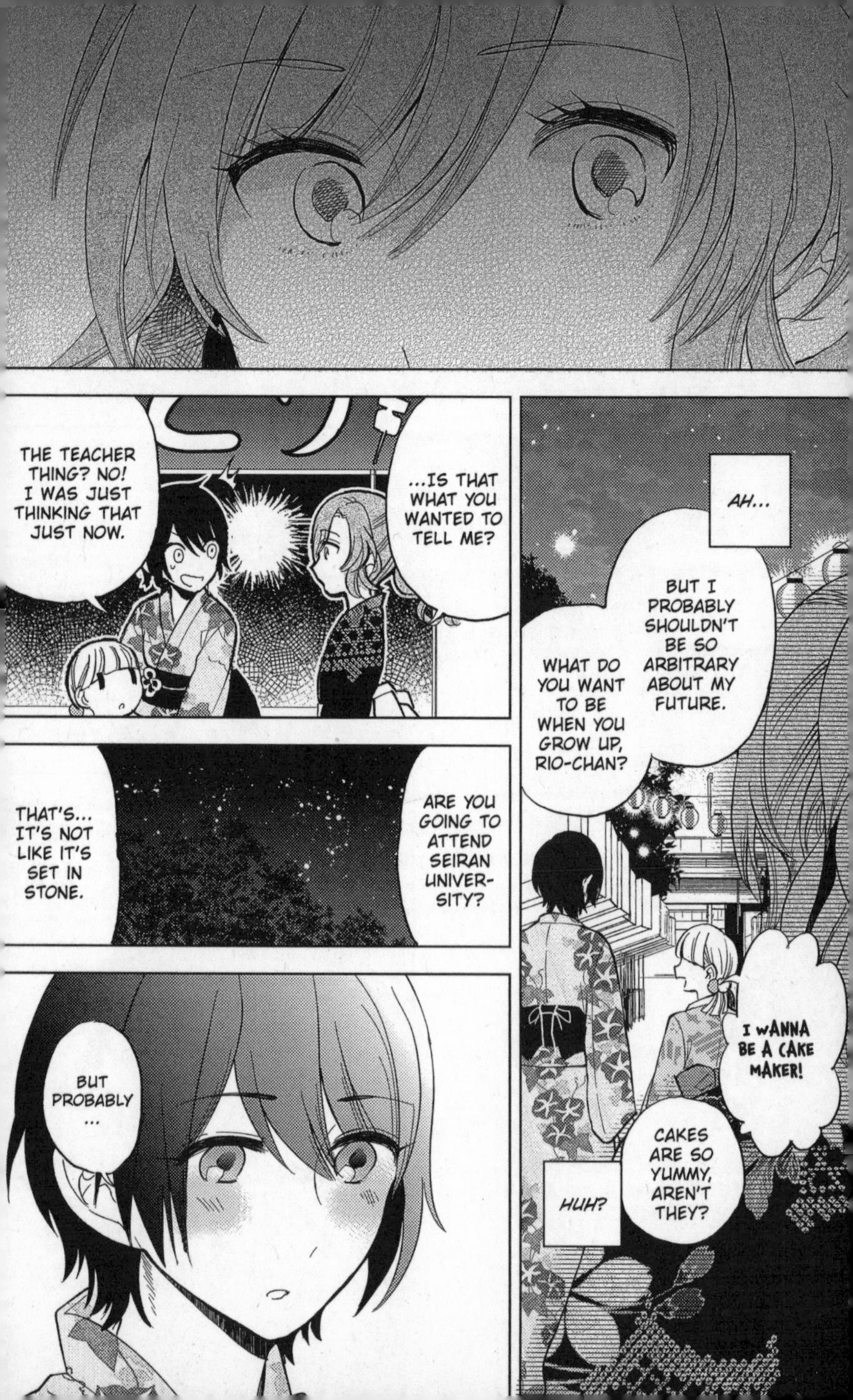
AH...
BUT I PROBABLY SHOULDN'T BE SO ARBITRARY ABOUT MY FUTURE.
WHAT DO YOU WANT TO BE WHEN YOU GROW UP, RIO-CHAN?
I WANNA BE A CAKE MAKER!
CAKES ARE SO YUMMY, AREN'T THEY?
HUH?
...IS THAT WHAT YOU WANTED TO TELL ME?
THE TEACHER THING? NO! I WAS JUST THINKING THAT JUST NOW.
ARE YOU GOING TO ATTEND SEIRAN UNIVERSITY?
THAT'S... IT'S NOT LIKE IT'S SET IN STONE.
BUT PROBABLY ...

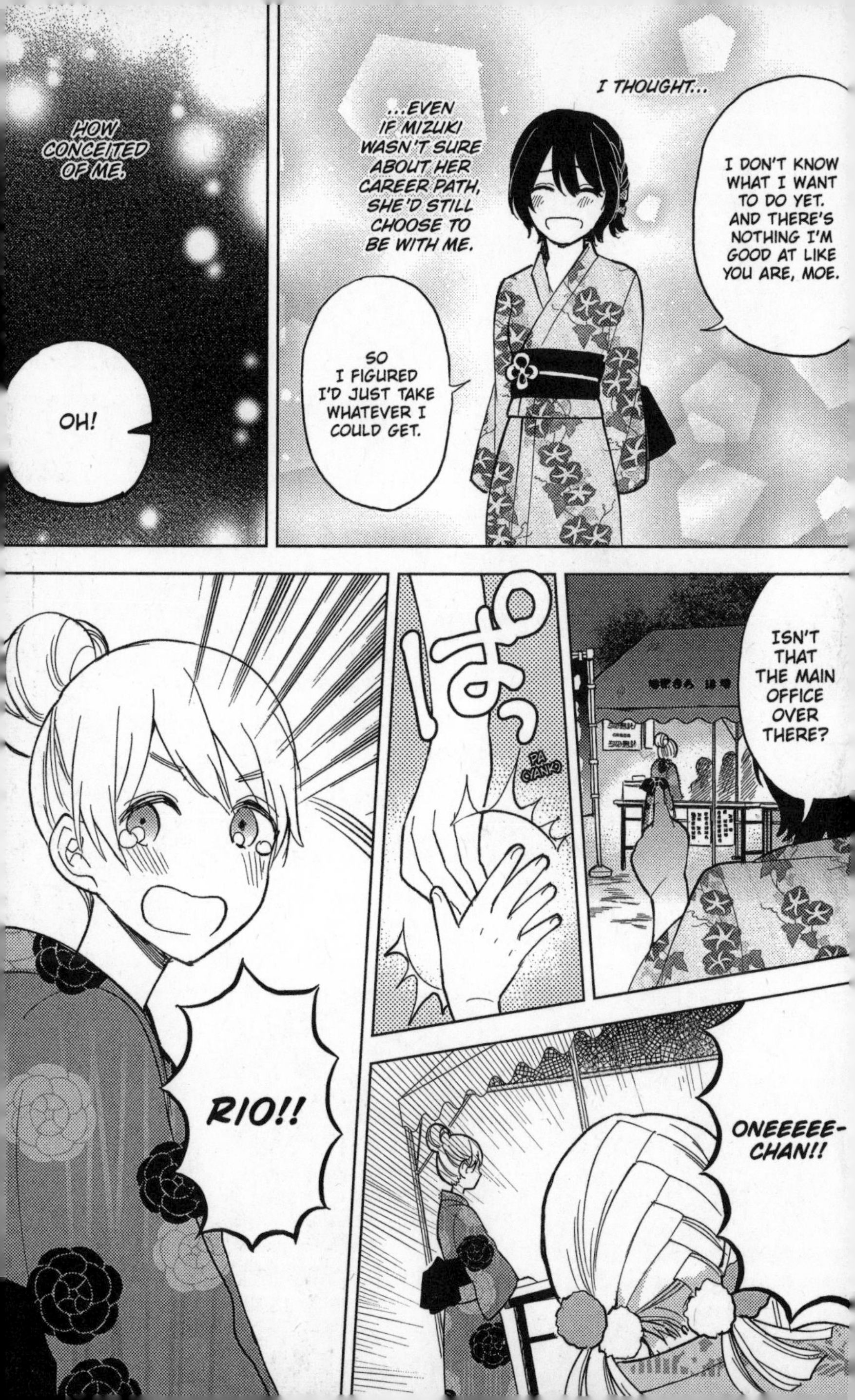
I THOUGHT...
I DON'T KNOW WHAT I WANT TO DO YET. AND THERE'S NOTHING I'M GOOD AT LIKE YOU ARE, MOE.
...EVEN IF MIZUKI WASN'T SURE ABOUT HER CAREER PATH, SHE'D STILL CHOOSE TO BE WITH ME.
SO I FIGURED I'D JUST TAKE WHATEVER I COULD GET.
HOW CONCEITED OF ME.
OH!
ISN'T THAT THE MAIN OFFICE OVER THERE?
ぱっ
PA GYANK
ONEEEEE-CHAN!!
RIO!!

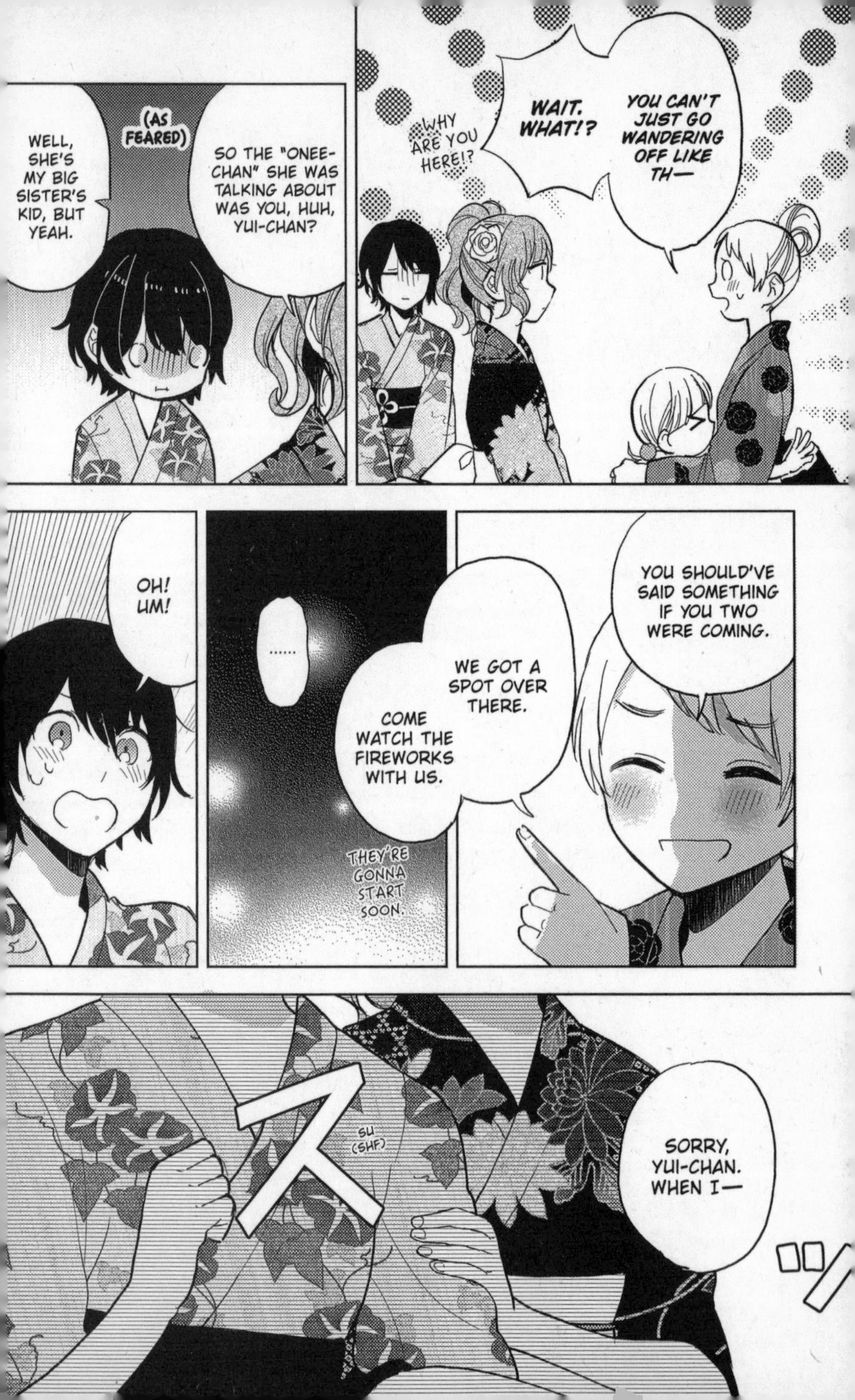
YOU CAN'T JUST GO WANDERING OFF LIKE TH—
WAIT. WHAT!?
WHY ARE YOU HERE!?
SO THE "ONEE-CHAN" SHE WAS TALKING ABOUT WAS YOU, HUH, YUI-CHAN?
(AS FEARED)
WELL, SHE'S MY BIG SISTER'S KID, BUT YEAH.
YOU SHOULD'VE SAID SOMETHING IF YOU TWO WERE COMING.
WE GOT A SPOT OVER THERE.
COME WATCH THE FIREWORKS WITH US.
......
THEY'RE GONNA START SOON.
OH! UM!
SORRY, YUI-CHAN. WHEN I—
SU (SHF)
ス

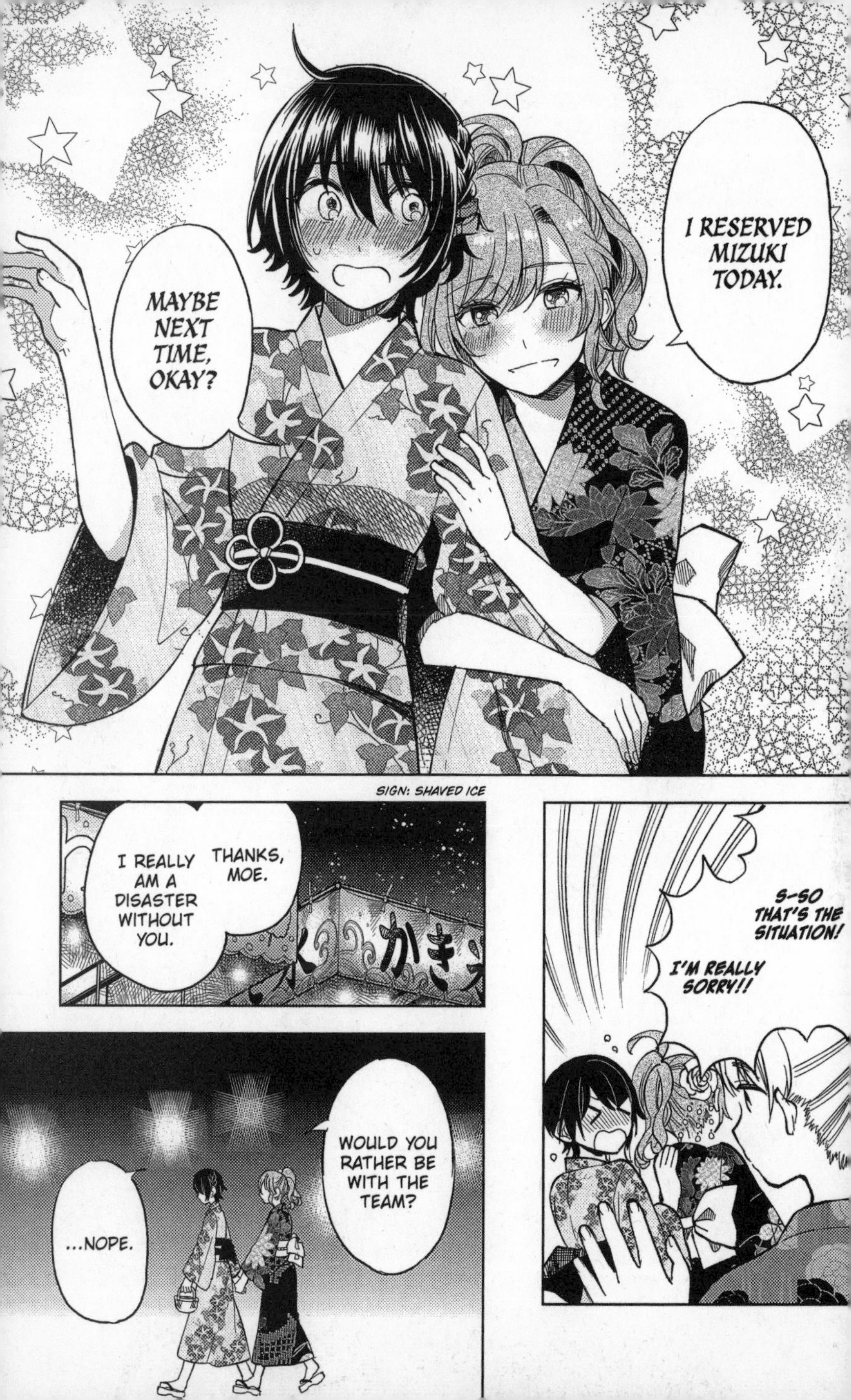
I RESERVED MIZUKI TODAY.
MAYBE NEXT TIME, OKAY?
S-SO THAT'S THE SITUATION!
I'M REALLY SORRY!!
SIGN: SHAVED ICE
THANKS, MOE.
I REALLY AM A DISASTER WITHOUT YOU.
WOULD YOU RATHER BE WITH THE TEAM?
...NOPE.

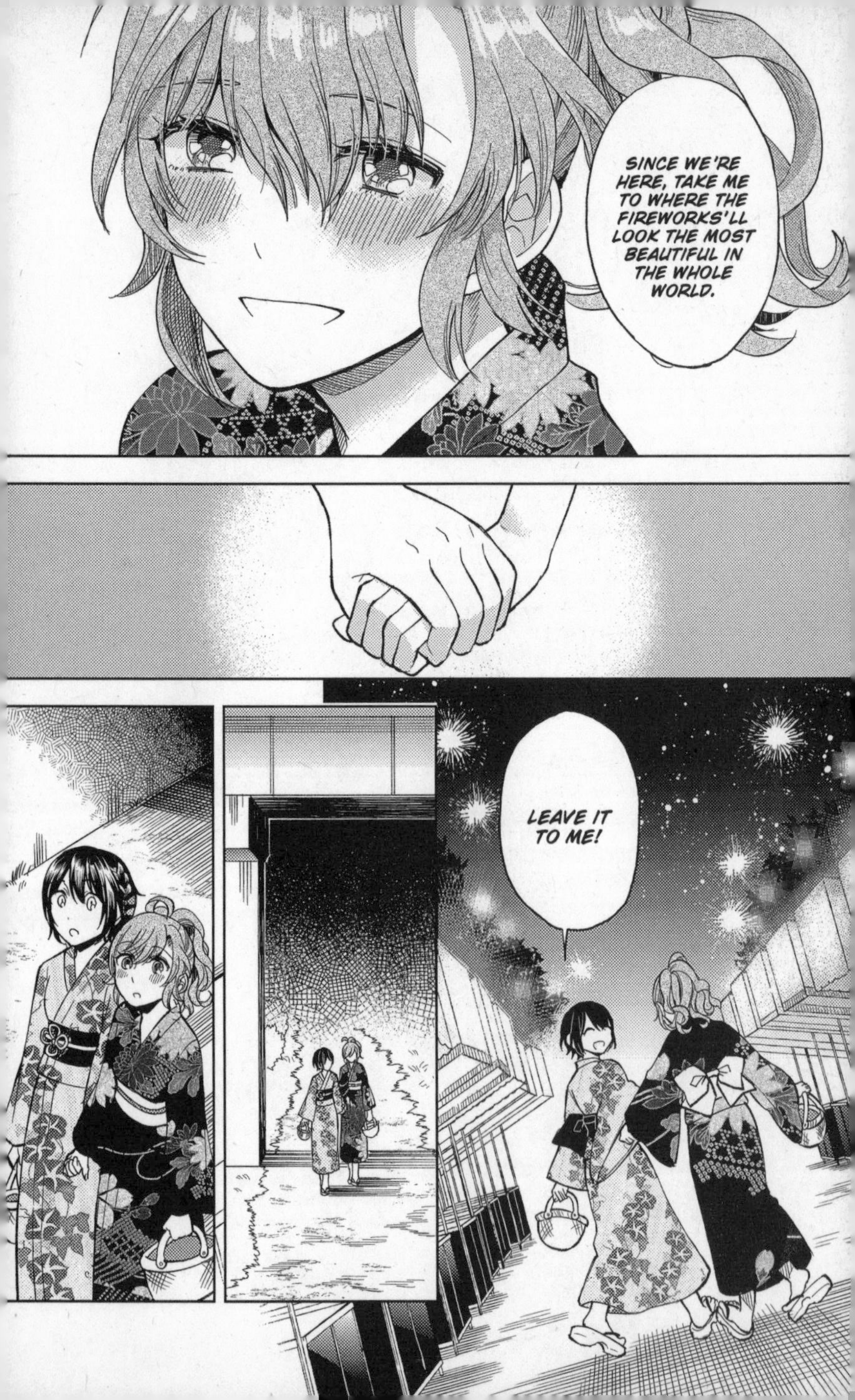
SINCE WE'RE HERE, TAKE ME TO WHERE THE FIREWORKS'LL LOOK THE MOST BEAUTIFUL IN THE WHOLE WORLD.
LEAVE IT TO ME!

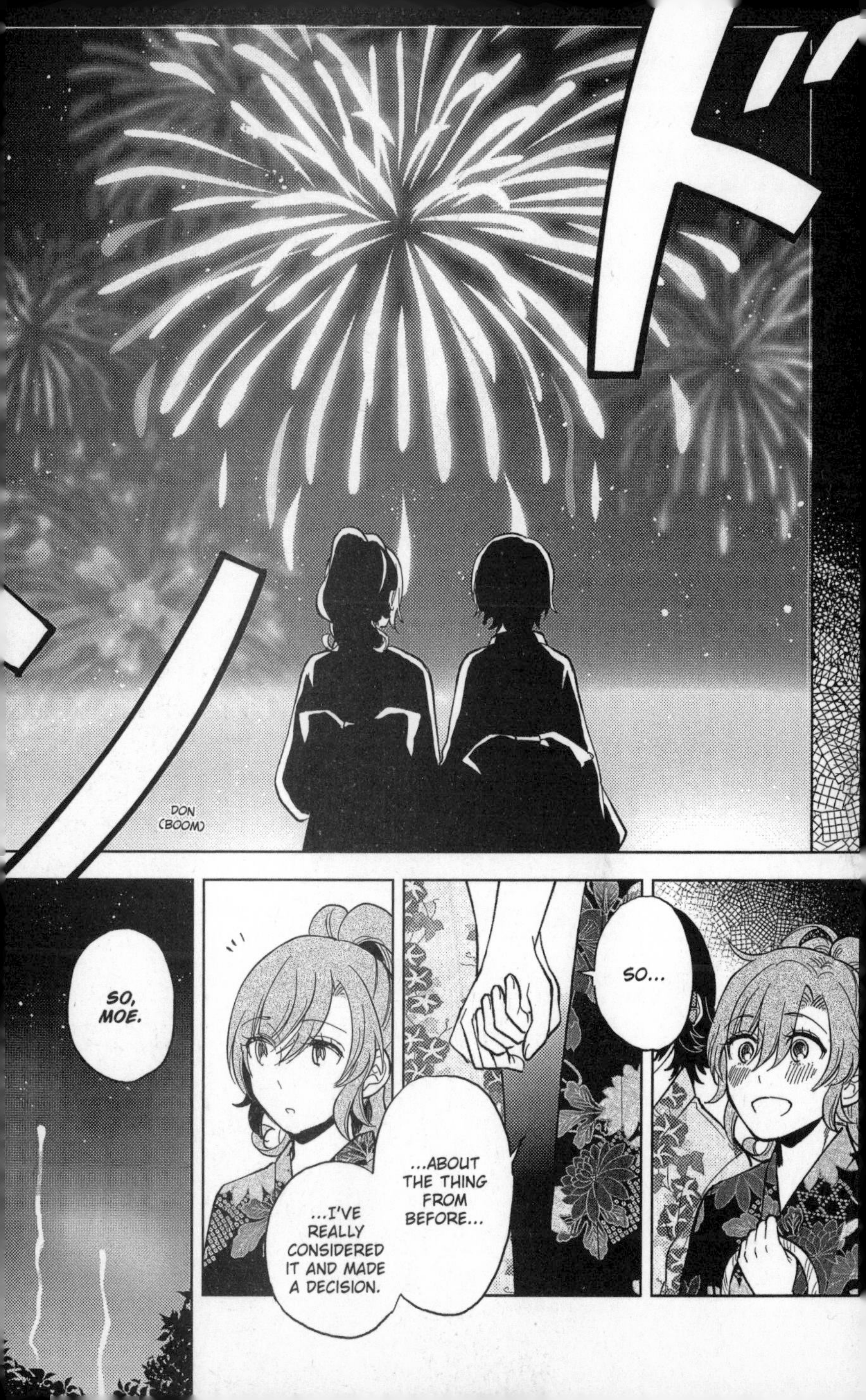
DON (BOOM)
SO...
...ABOUT THE THING FROM BEFORE...
...I'VE REALLY CONSIDERED IT AND MADE A DECISION.
SO, MOE.

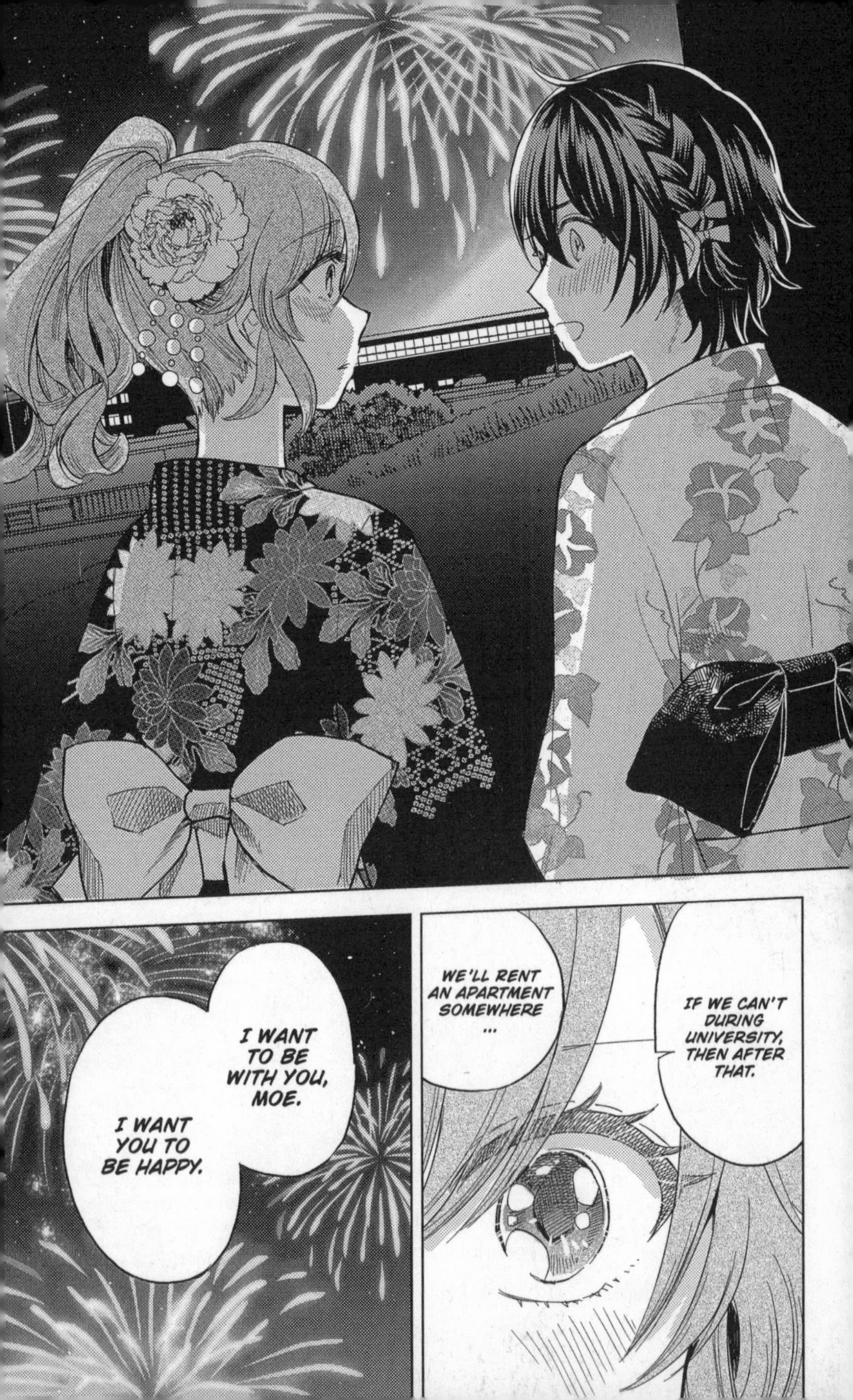
IF WE CAN'T DURING UNIVERSITY, THEN AFTER THAT.
WE'LL RENT AN APARTMENT SOMEWHERE ...
I WANT TO BE WITH YOU, MOE.
I WANT YOU TO BE HAPPY.

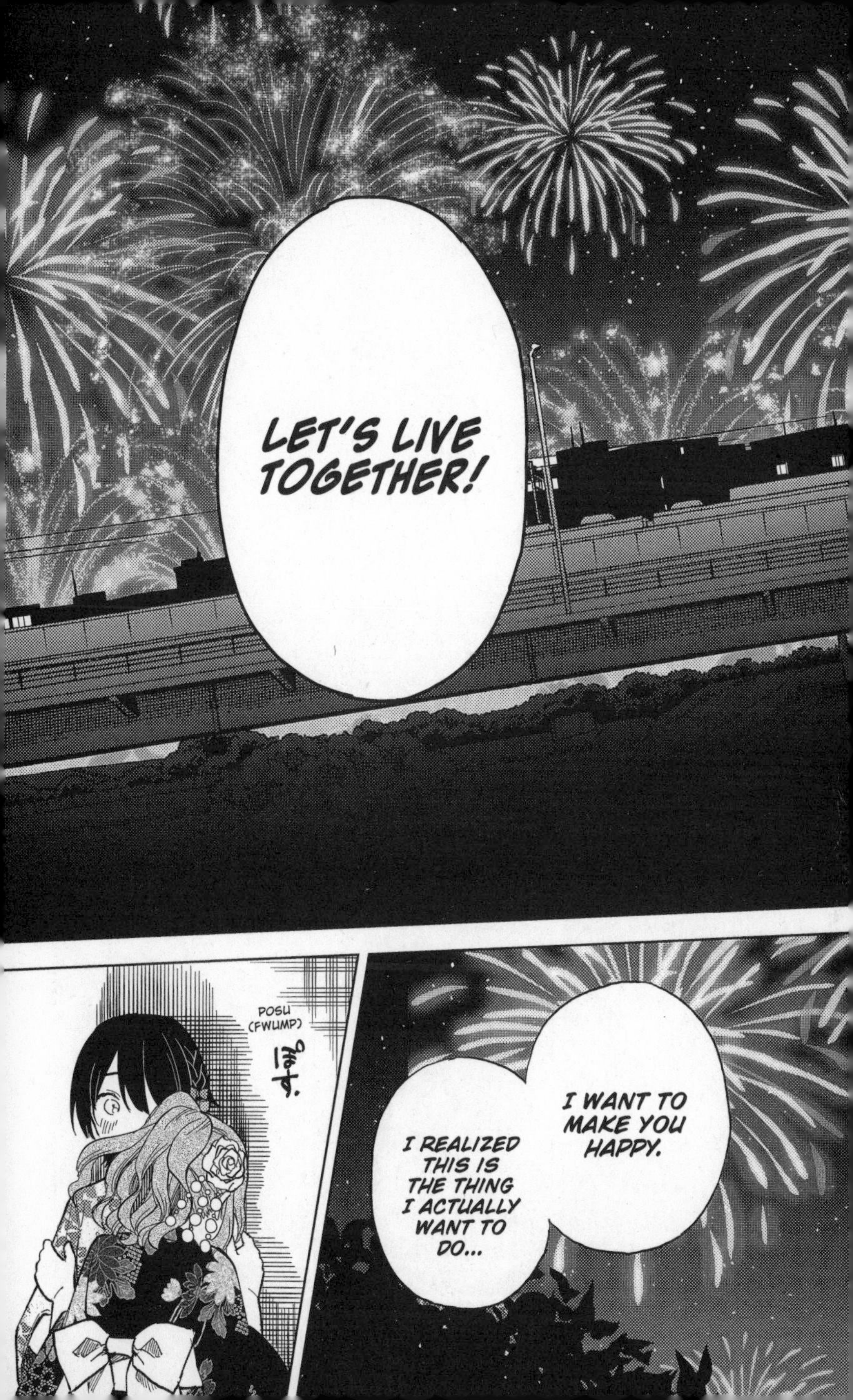
LET'S LIVE TOGETHER!
I WANT TO MAKE YOU HAPPY.
I REALIZED THIS IS THE THING I ACTUALLY WANT TO DO...
POSU (FWUMP)

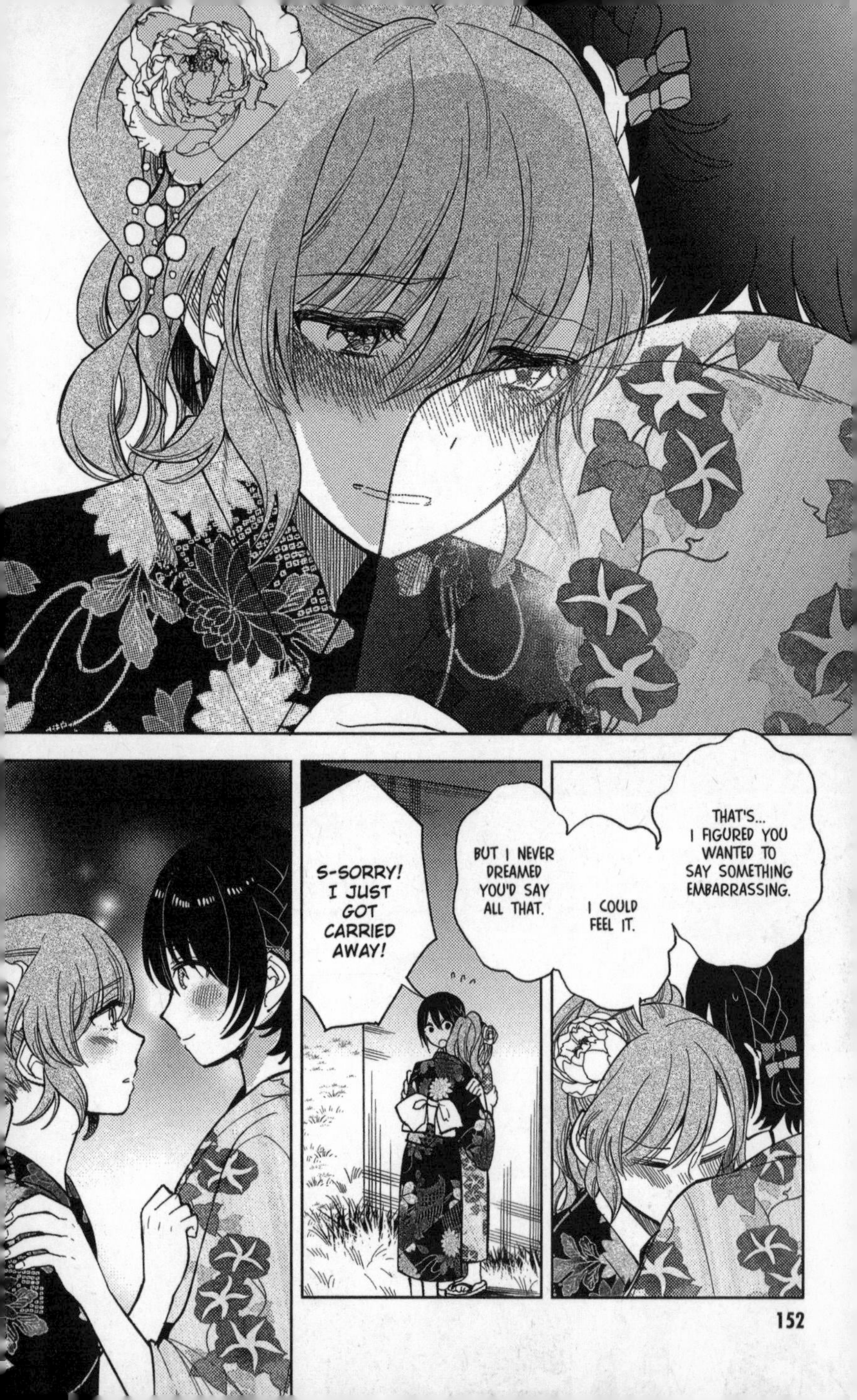
THAT'S... I FIGURED YOU WANTED TO SAY SOMETHING EMBARRASSING.
I COULD FEEL IT.
BUT I NEVER DREAMED YOU'D SAY ALL THAT.
S-SORRY! I JUST GOT CARRIED AWAY!

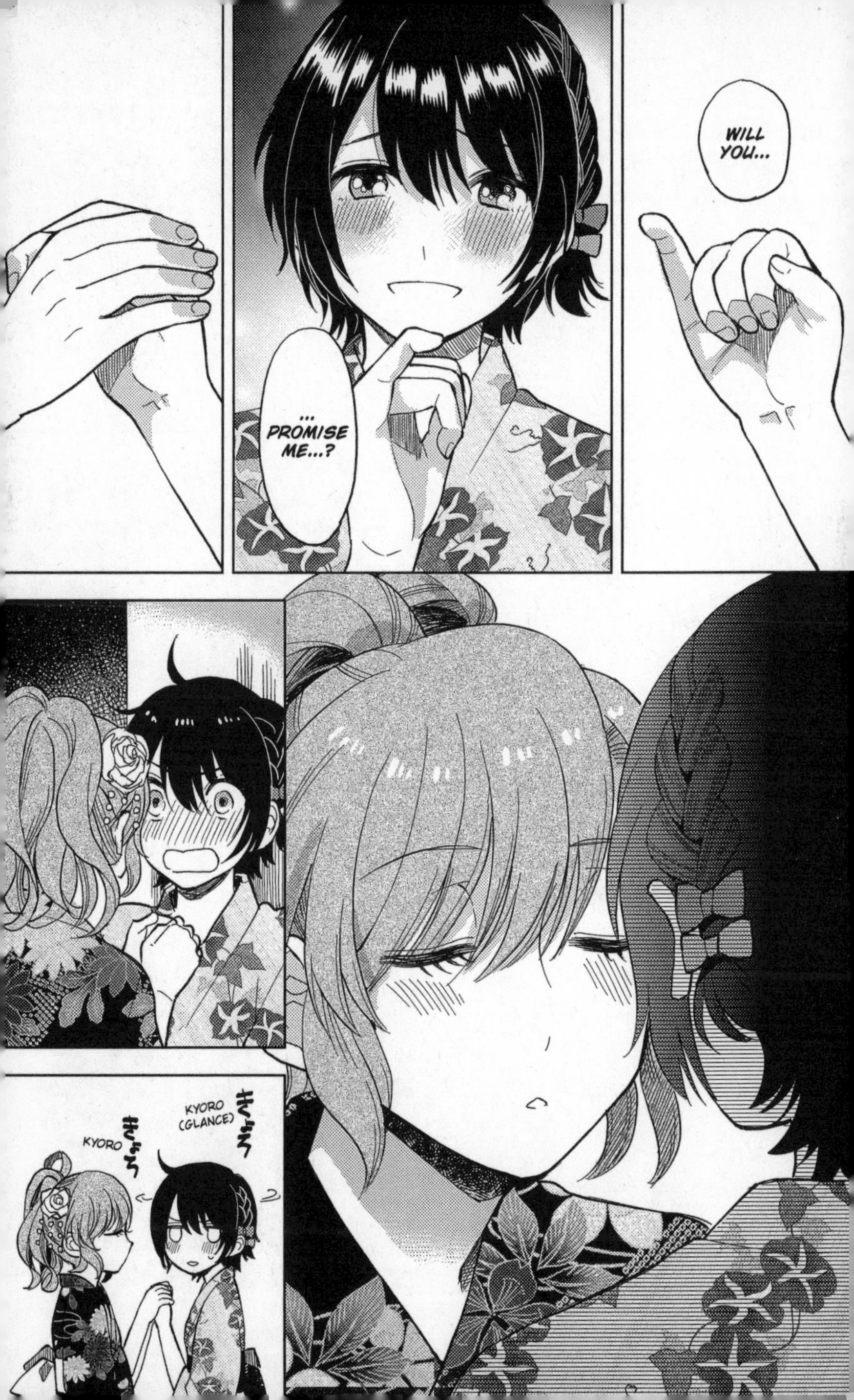
WILL YOU...
... PROMISE ME...?
きょろ
KYORO (GLANCE)
きょろ
KYORO

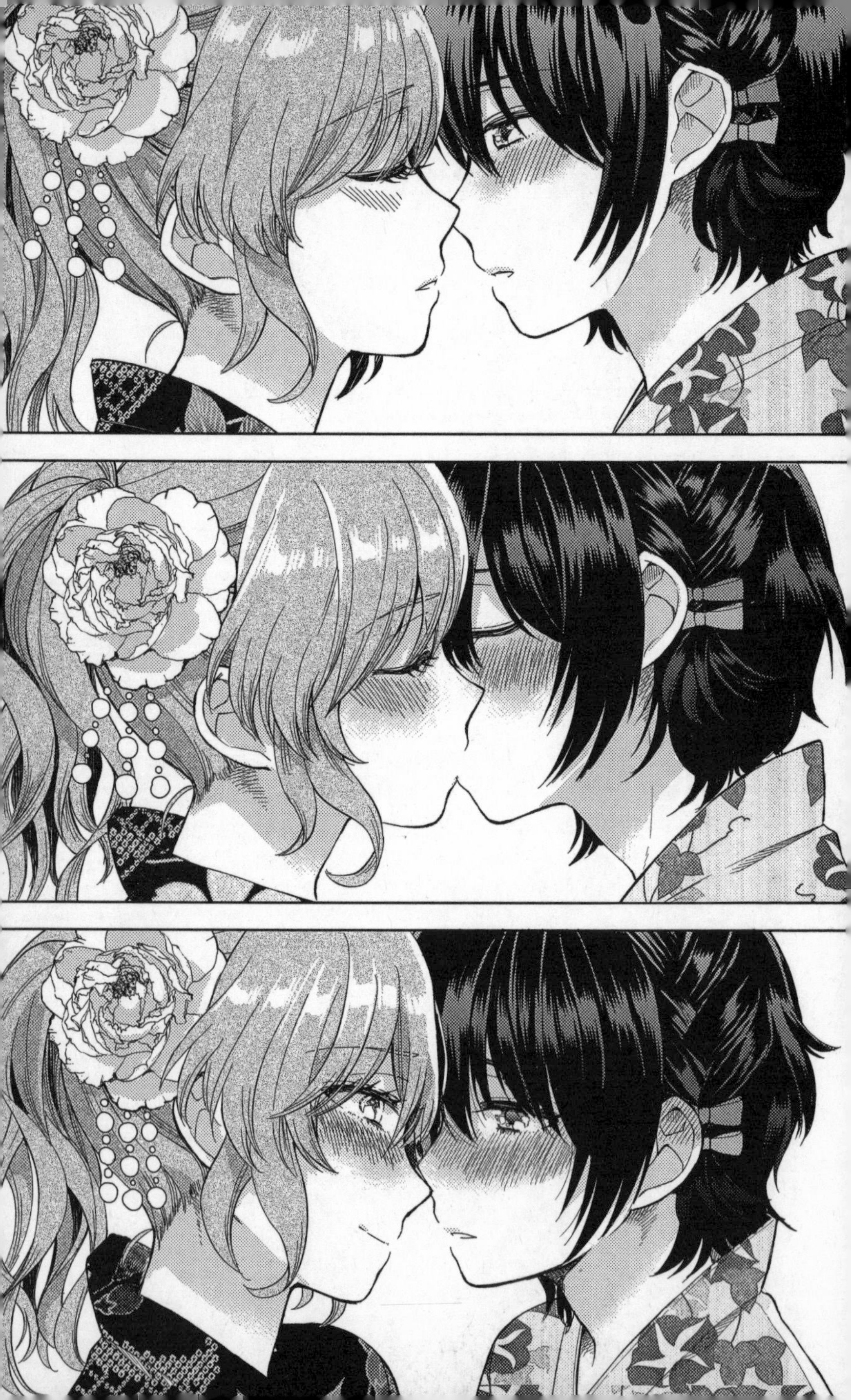

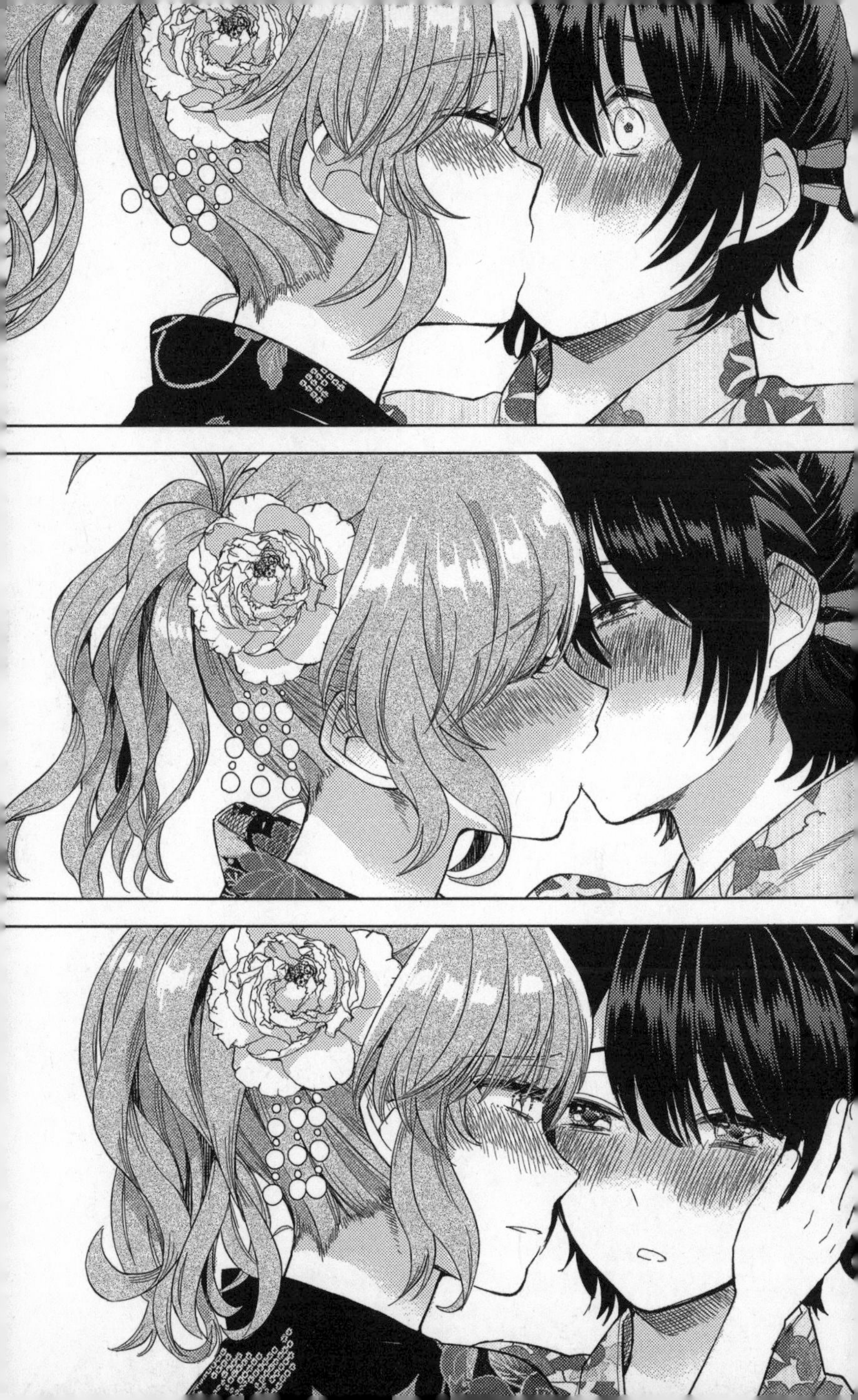

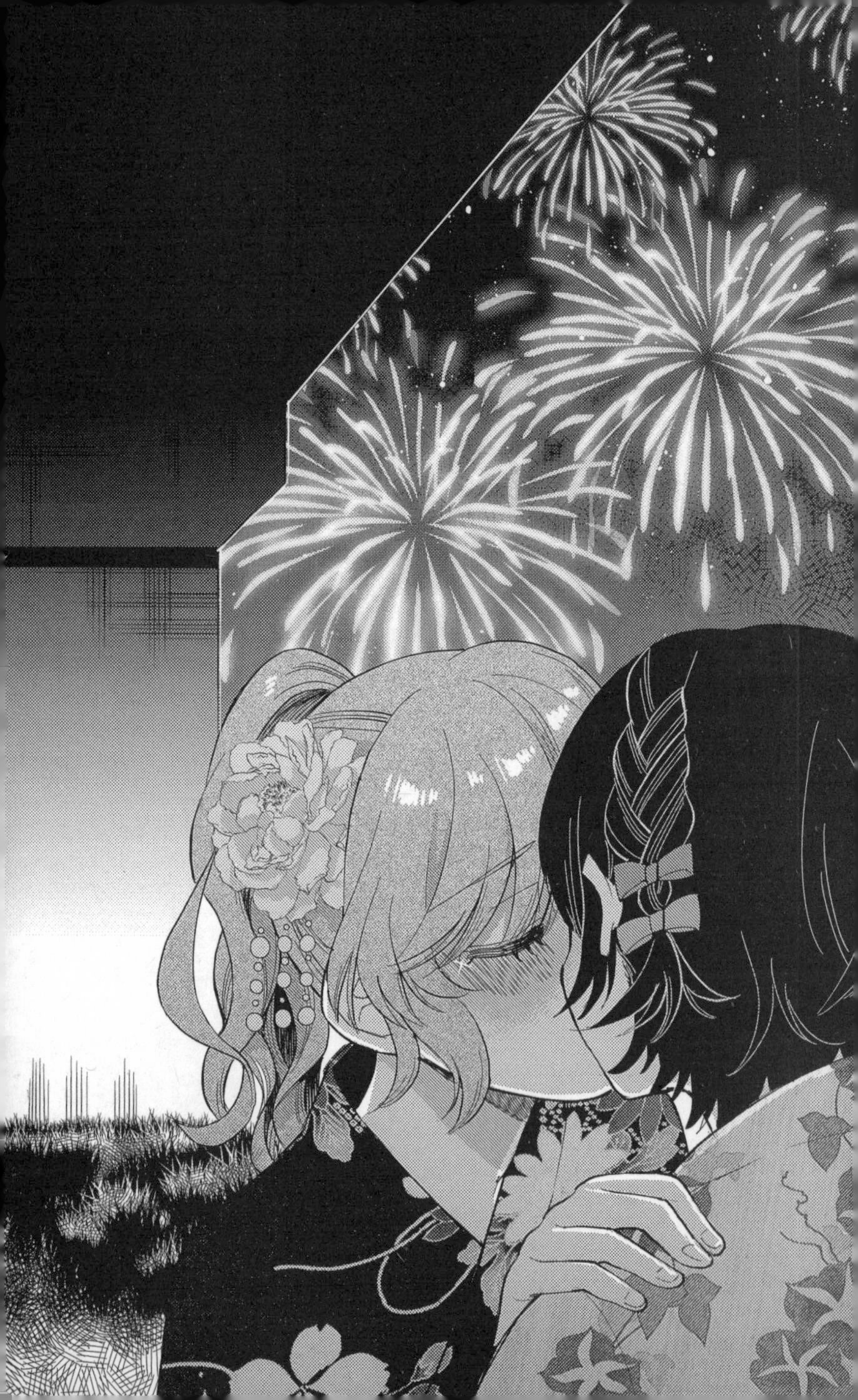

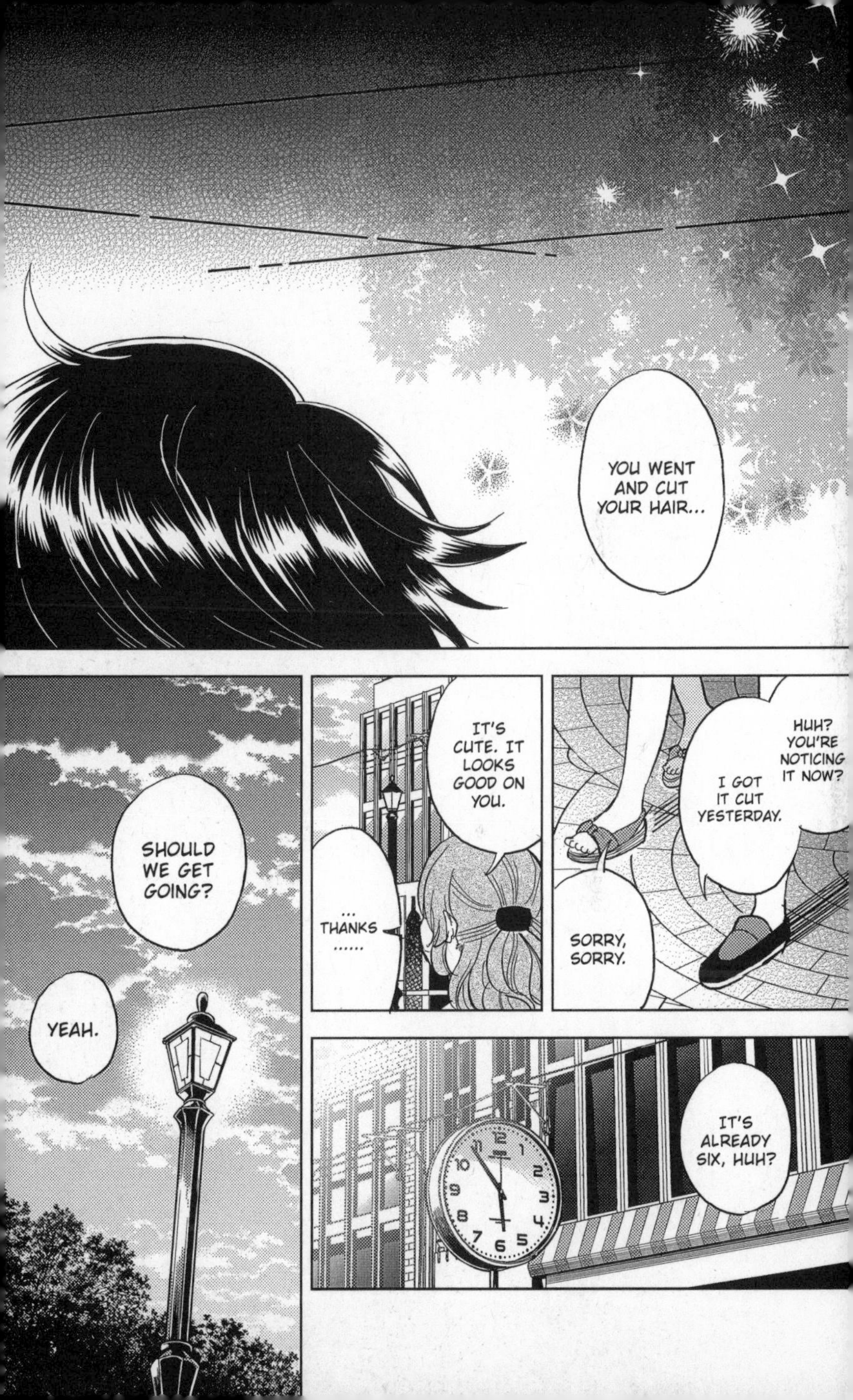

YOU WENT AND CUT YOUR HAIR...
HUH? YOU'RE NOTICING IT NOW?
I GOT IT CUT YESTERDAY.
SORRY, SORRY.
IT'S CUTE. IT LOOKS GOOD ON YOU.
...THANKS......
IT'S ALREADY SIX, HUH?
SHOULD WE GET GOING?
YEAH.

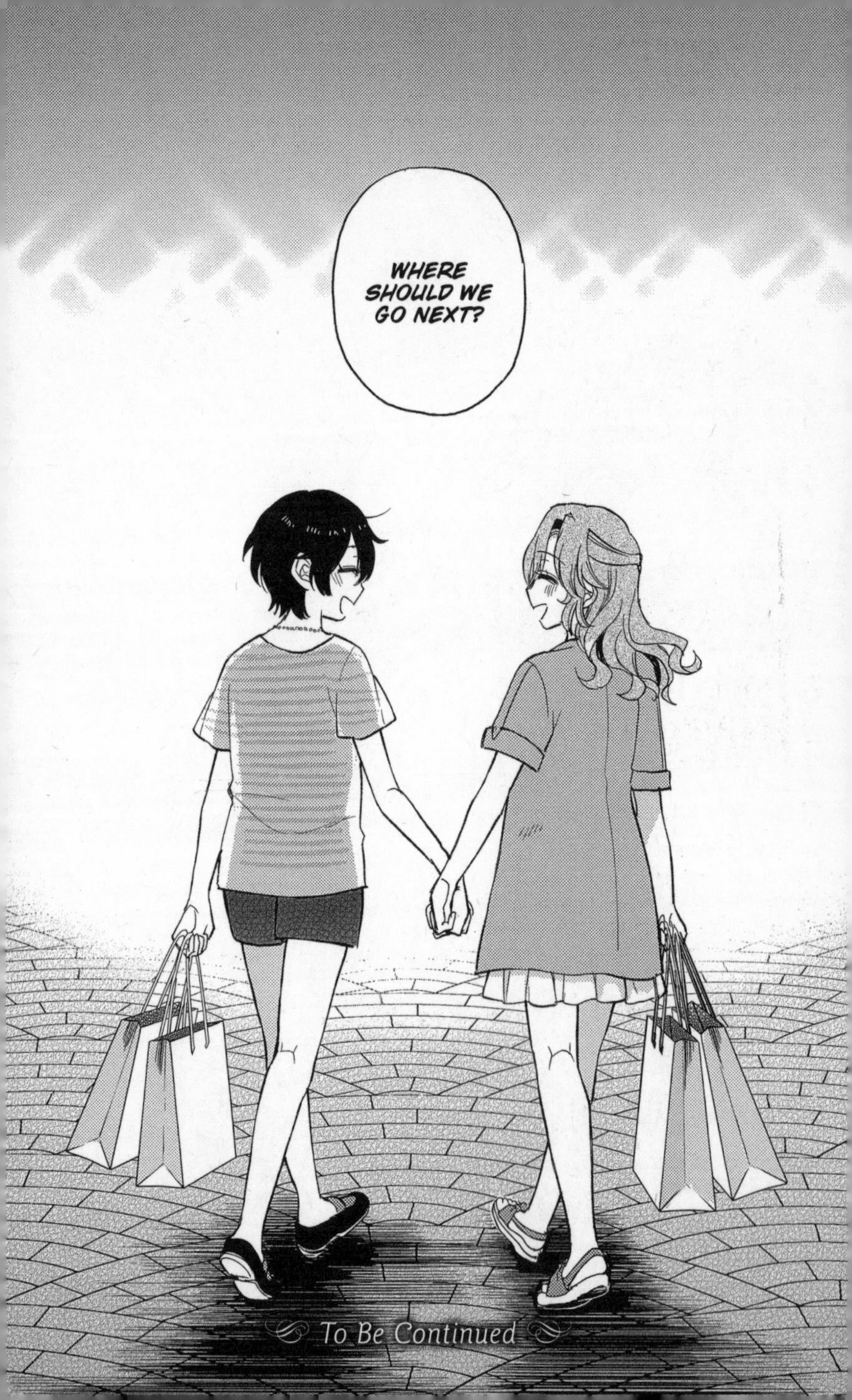
WHERE SHOULD WE GO NEXT?
To Be Continued

After the Festival

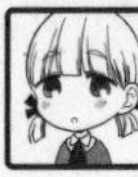

RIO

YUI'S NIECE. FIVE YEARS OLD. STILL CLINGS TO HER MOTHER. SHE OFTEN COMES OVER TO YUI'S HOUSE.

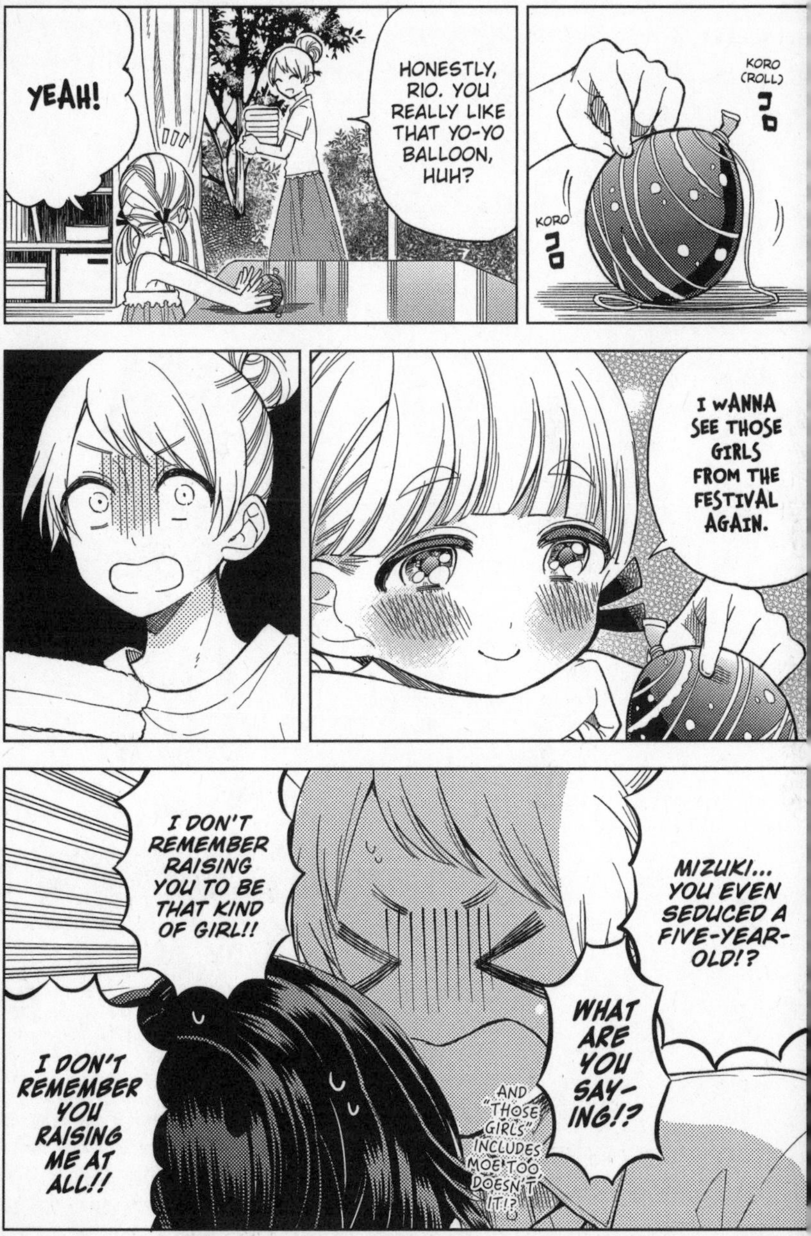
KORO (ROLL)
コロ
KORO
コロ
HONESTLY, RIO. YOU REALLY LIKE THAT YO-YO BALLOON, HUH?
YEAH!
I WANNA SEE THOSE GIRLS FROM THE FESTIVAL AGAIN.
MIZUKI... YOU EVEN SEDUCED A FIVE-YEAR-OLD!?
I DON'T REMEMBER RAISING YOU TO BE THAT KIND OF GIRL!!
WHAT ARE YOU SAYING!?
AND "THOSE GIRLS" INCLUDES MOE TOO, DOESN'T IT!?
I DON'T REMEMBER YOU RAISING ME AT ALL!!

KISS THEATER: WHAT'S BEHIND THE STORY!? ✶ PEOPLE OTHER THAN THE MAIN CHARACTERS HAVE STORIES TOO. HERE, WE PRESENT THE "LITTLE LOVE" STORIES HAPPENING BEHIND THE SCENES.

Momiji Shikama

Momiji Shikama

Second-year student at Seiran Academy High School. Friends with Kaoru and Kohagi. Tall. There's nothing she's particularly bad at, but since she doesn't really care, she slips by in all her subjects with just a passing mark. She has an older sister who works, and perhaps because she talks with her sister's friends, she seems mature somehow.

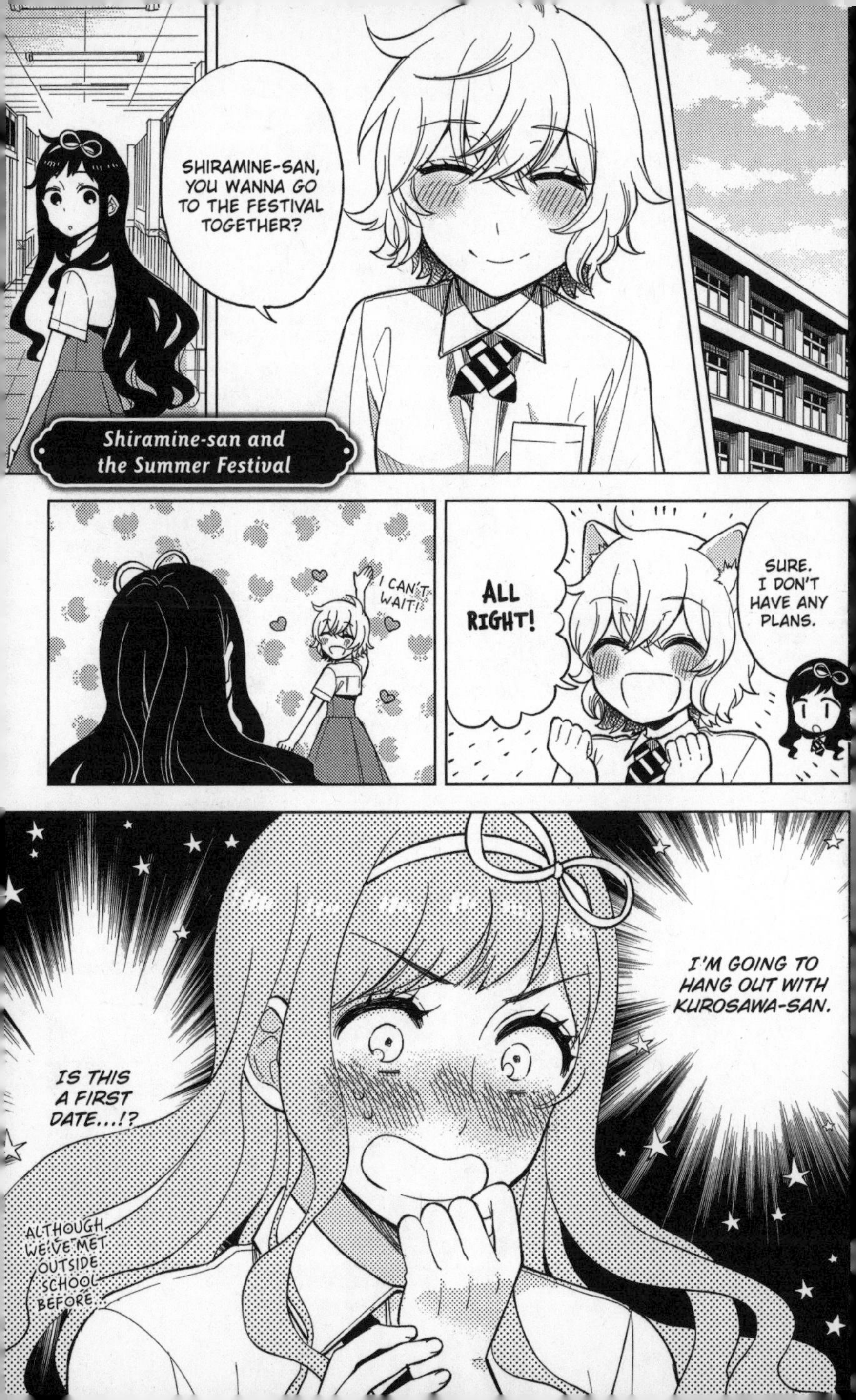
SHIRAMINE-SAN, YOU WANNA GO TO THE FESTIVAL TOGETHER?
Shiramine-san and the Summer Festival
SURE. I DON'T HAVE ANY PLANS.
ALL RIGHT!
I CAN'T WAIT!
I'M GOING TO HANG OUT WITH KUROSAWA-SAN.
IS THIS A FIRST DATE...!?
ALTHOUGH WE'VE MET OUTSIDE SCHOOL BEFORE.

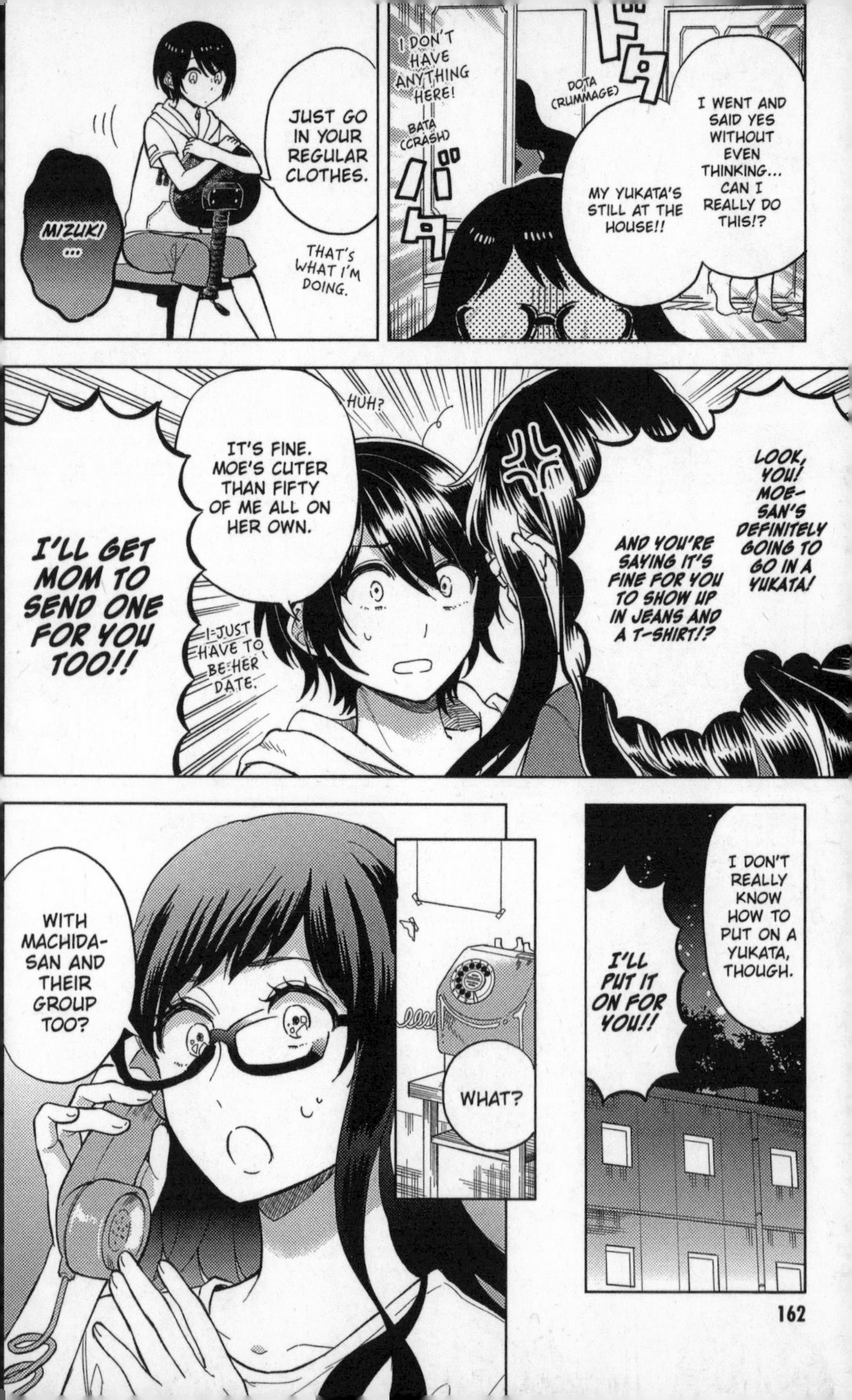
I WENT AND SAID YES WITHOUT EVEN THINKING... CAN I REALLY DO THIS!?
MY YUKATA'S STILL AT THE HOUSE!!
DOTA (RUMMAGE)
I DON'T HAVE ANYTHING HERE!
BATA (CRASH)
JUST GO IN YOUR REGULAR CLOTHES.
THAT'S WHAT I'M DOING.
MIZUKI...
LOOK, YOU! MOE-SAN'S DEFINITELY GOING TO GO IN A YUKATA!
AND YOU'RE SAYING IT'S FINE FOR YOU TO SHOW UP IN JEANS AND A T-SHIRT!?
HUH?
IT'S FINE. MOE'S CUTER THAN FIFTY OF ME ALL ON HER OWN.
I JUST HAVE TO BE HER DATE.
I'LL GET MOM TO SEND ONE FOR YOU TOO!!
I DON'T REALLY KNOW HOW TO PUT ON A YUKATA, THOUGH.
I'LL PUT IT ON FOR YOU!!
WHAT?
WITH MACHIDA-SAN AND THEIR GROUP TOO?

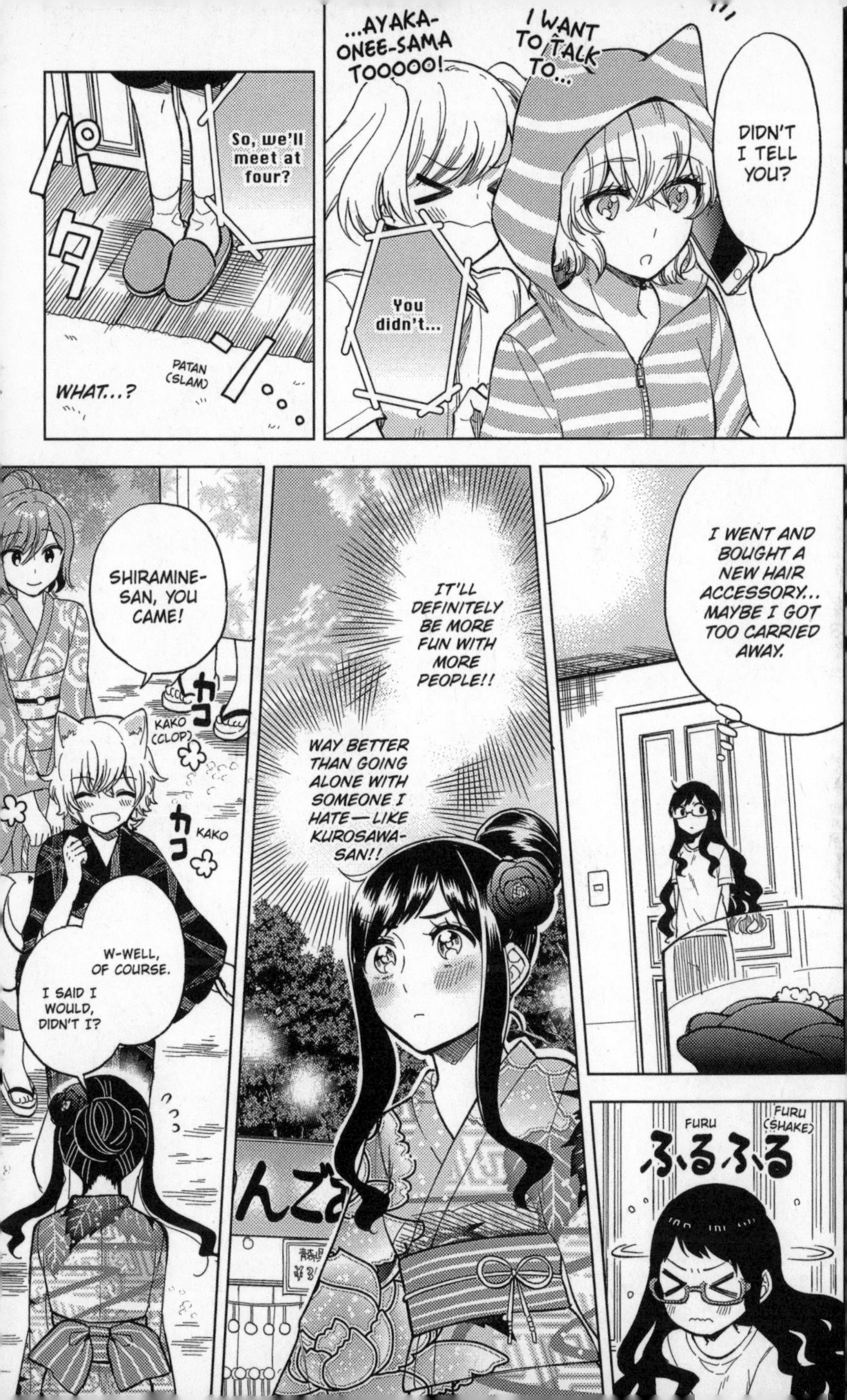
DIDN'T I TELL YOU?
I WANT TO TALK TO...
...AYAKA-ONEE-SAMA TOOOOO!
You didn't...
So, we'll meet at four?
PATAN (SLAM)
WHAT...?
I WENT AND BOUGHT A NEW HAIR ACCESSORY... MAYBE I GOT TOO CARRIED AWAY.
FURU FURU (SHAKE)
ふるふる
IT'LL DEFINITELY BE MORE FUN WITH MORE PEOPLE!!
WAY BETTER THAN GOING ALONE WITH SOMEONE I HATE—LIKE KUROSAWA-SAN!!
SHIRAMINE-SAN, YOU CAME!
KAKO (CLOP)
KAKO
W-WELL, OF COURSE.
I SAID I WOULD, DIDN'T I?

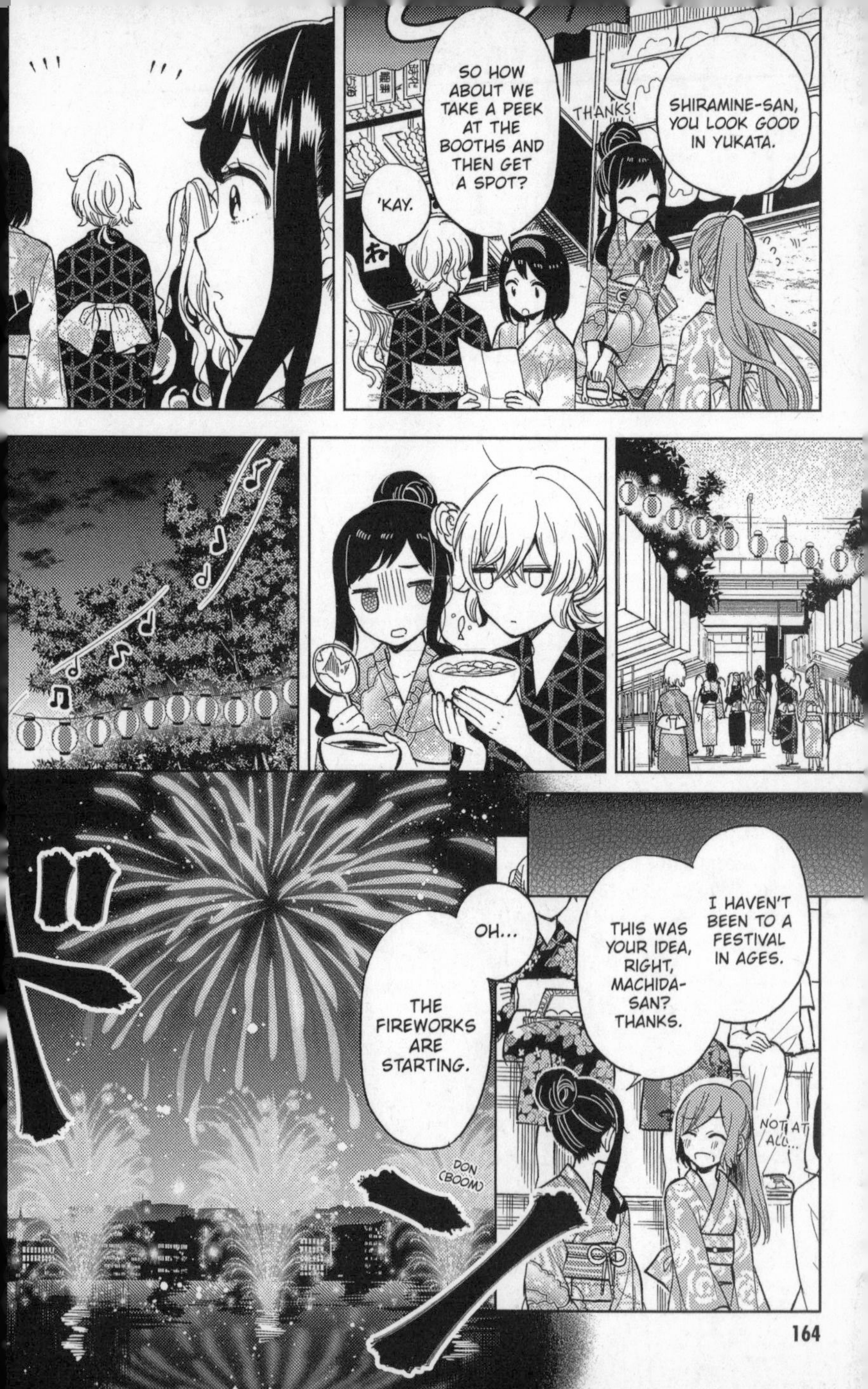
SHIRAMINE-SAN, YOU LOOK GOOD IN YUKATA.
THANKS!
SO HOW ABOUT WE TAKE A PEEK AT THE BOOTHS AND THEN GET A SPOT?
'KAY.
I HAVEN'T BEEN TO A FESTIVAL IN AGES.
THIS WAS YOUR IDEA, RIGHT, MACHIDA-SAN? THANKS.
NOT AT ALL...
OH...
THE FIREWORKS ARE STARTING.
DON (BOOM)

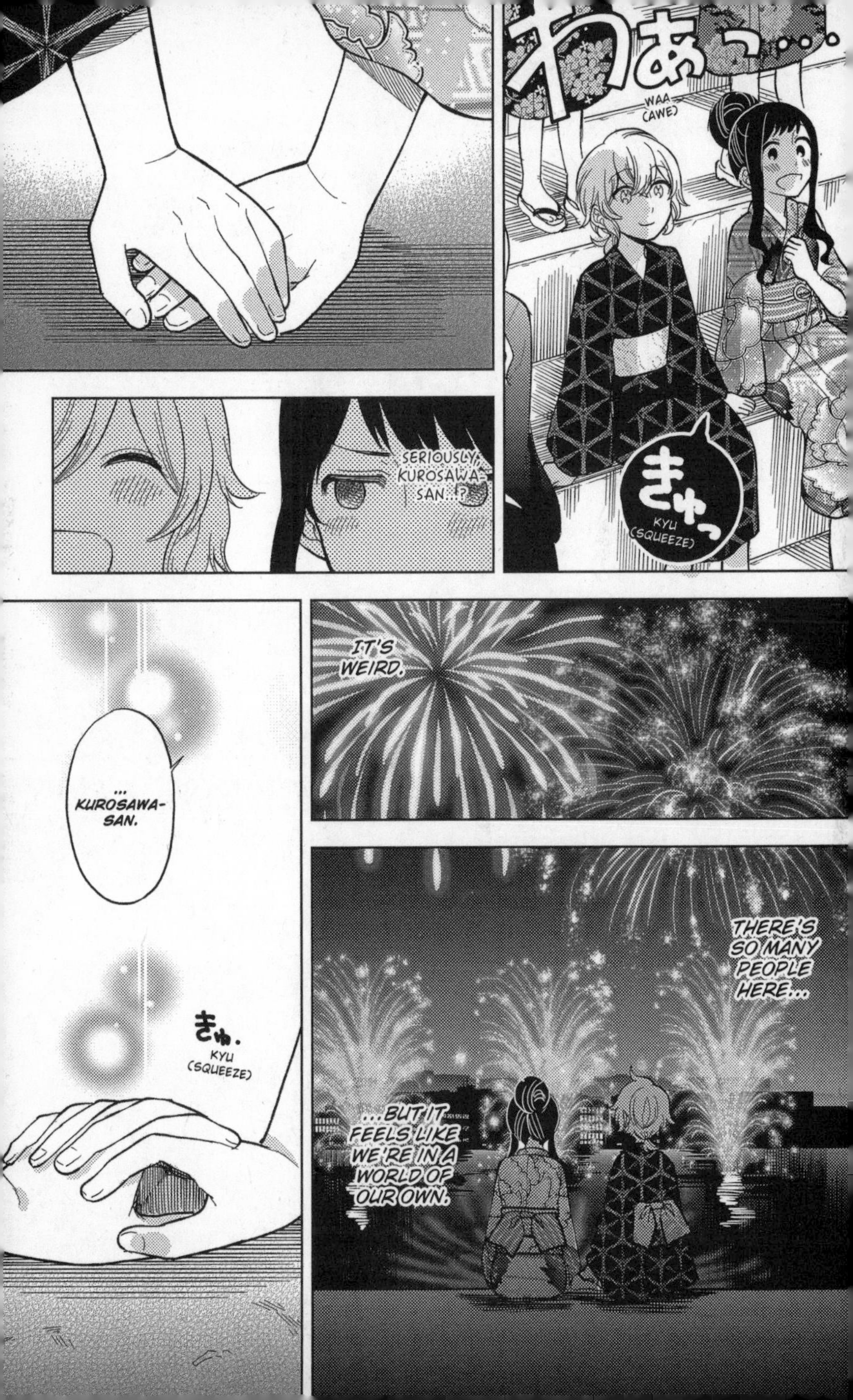
わぁっ…
WAA (AWE)
きゅっ
KYU (SQUEEZE)
SERIOUSLY, KUROSAWA-SAN...?
IT'S WEIRD.
THERE'S SO MANY PEOPLE HERE...
...BUT IT FEELS LIKE WE'RE IN A WORLD OF OUR OWN.
... KUROSAWA-SAN.
きゅ.
KYU (SQUEEZE)

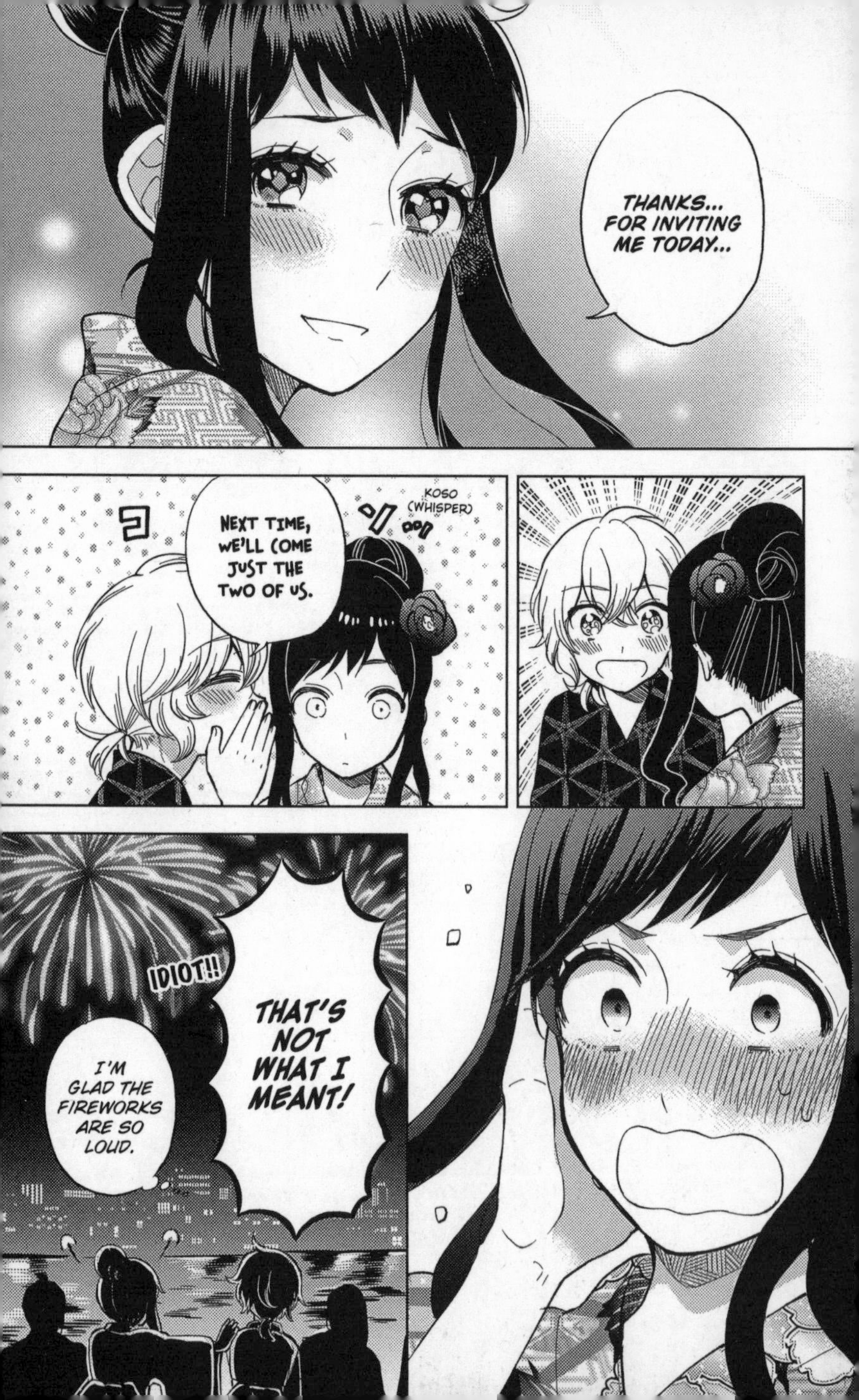
THANKS... FOR INVITING ME TODAY...
KOSO (WHISPER)
NEXT TIME, WE'LL COME JUST THE TWO OF US.
THAT'S NOT WHAT I MEANT!
IDIOT!!
I'M GLAD THE FIREWORKS ARE SO LOUD.

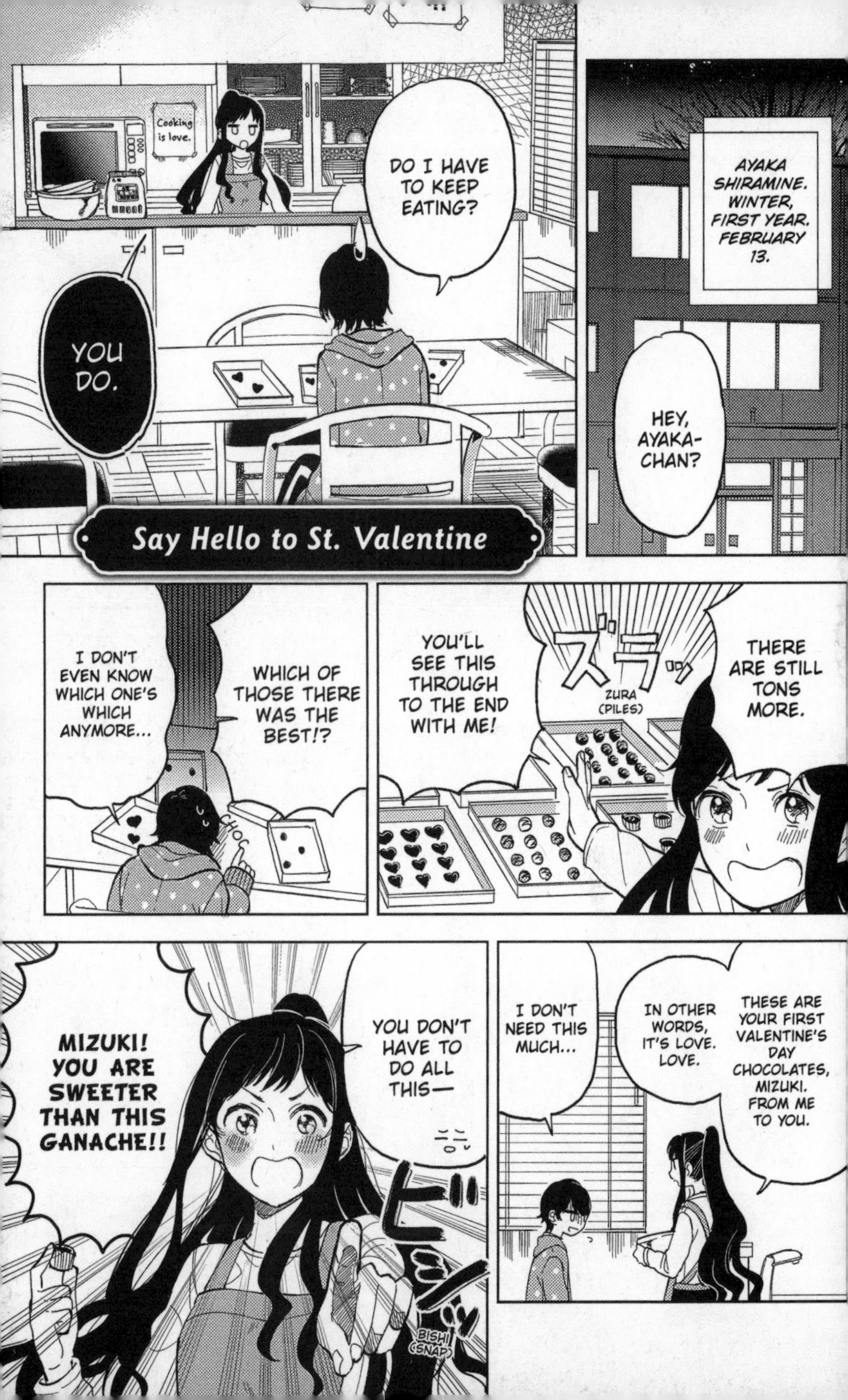
AYAKA SHIRAMINE. WINTER, FIRST YEAR. FEBRUARY 13.
HEY, AYAKA-CHAN?
Cooking is love.
DO I HAVE TO KEEP EATING?
YOU DO.
Say Hello to St. Valentine
THERE ARE STILL TONS MORE.
ZURA (PILES)
YOU'LL SEE THIS THROUGH TO THE END WITH ME!
WHICH OF THOSE THERE WAS THE BEST!?
I DON'T EVEN KNOW WHICH ONE'S WHICH ANYMORE...
CHOC
THESE ARE YOUR FIRST VALENTINE'S DAY CHOCOLATES, MIZUKI. FROM ME TO YOU.
IN OTHER WORDS, IT'S LOVE. LOVE.
I DON'T NEED THIS MUCH...
YOU DON'T HAVE TO DO ALL THIS—
MIZUKI! YOU ARE SWEETER THAN THIS GANACHE!!
BISHI (SNAP)

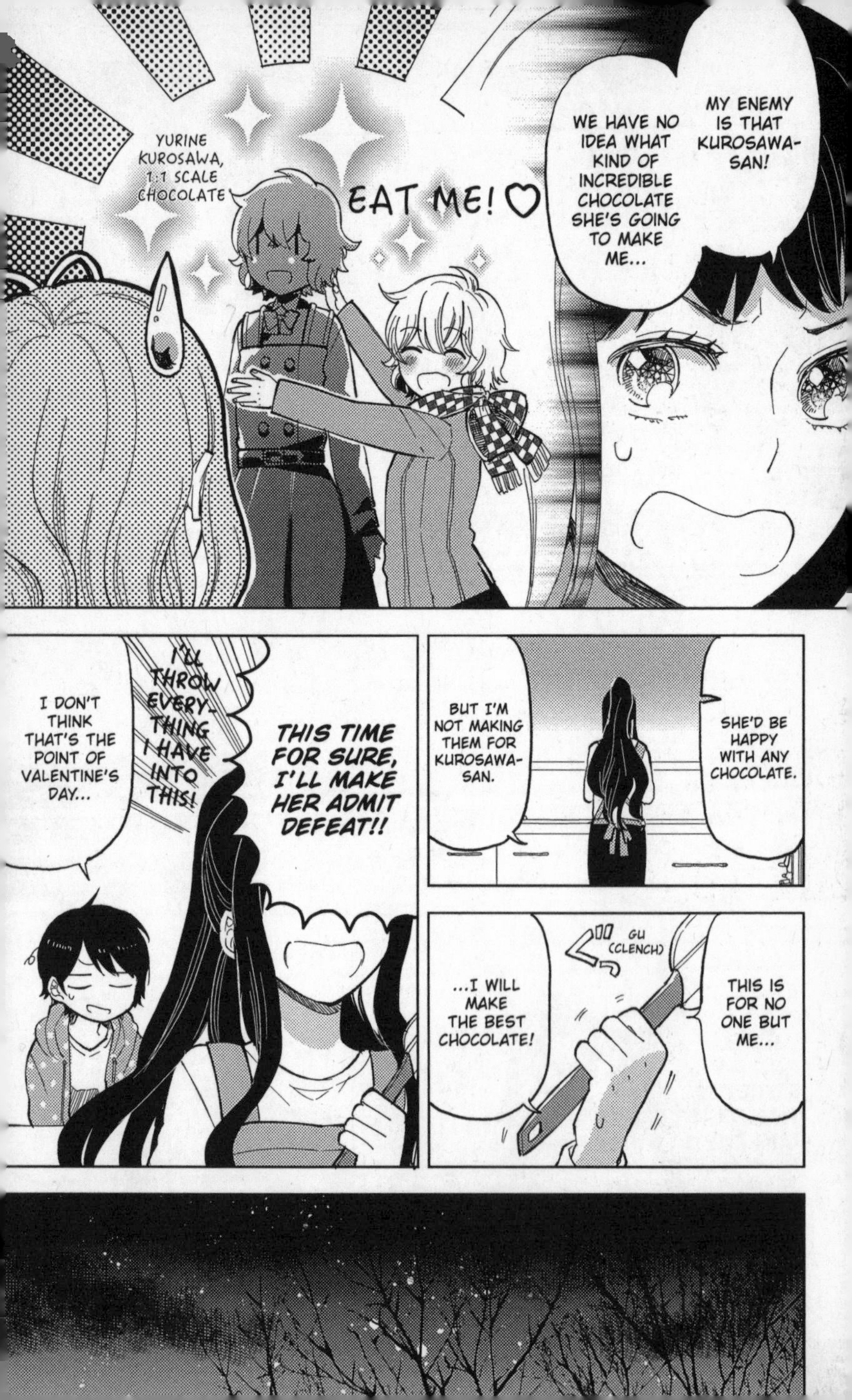
MY ENEMY IS THAT KUROSAWA-SAN!
WE HAVE NO IDEA WHAT KIND OF INCREDIBLE CHOCOLATE SHE'S GOING TO MAKE ME...
EAT ME! ♡
YURINE KUROSAWA, 1:1 SCALE CHOCOLATE
SHE'D BE HAPPY WITH ANY CHOCOLATE.
BUT I'M NOT MAKING THEM FOR KUROSAWA-SAN.
THIS IS FOR NO ONE BUT ME...
GU (CLENCH)
...I WILL MAKE THE BEST CHOCOLATE!
THIS TIME FOR SURE, I'LL MAKE HER ADMIT DEFEAT!!
I'LL THROW EVERYTHING I HAVE INTO THIS!
I DON'T THINK THAT'S THE POINT OF VALENTINE'S DAY...

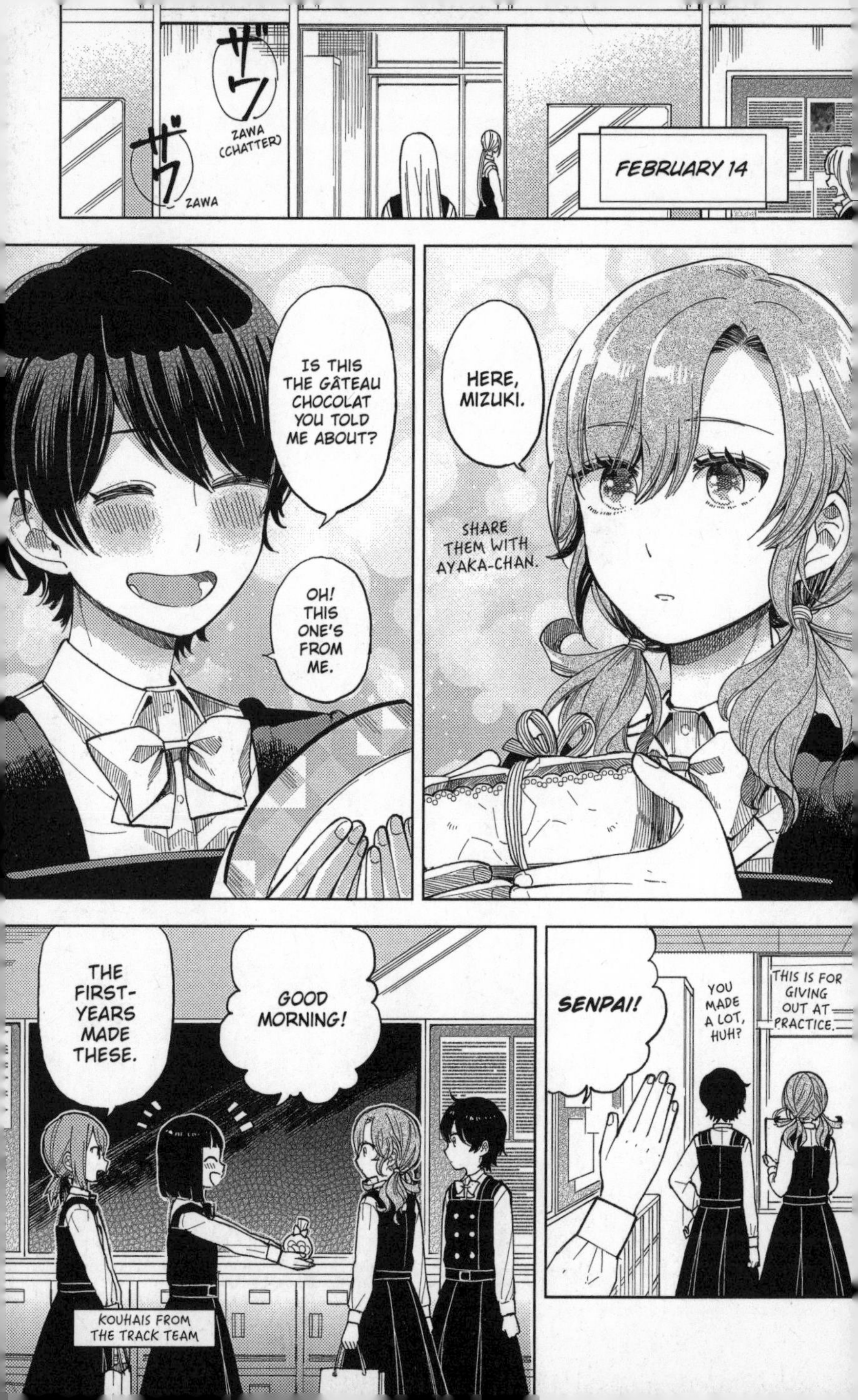
FEBRUARY 14
ZAWA (CHATTER)
ZAWA
HERE, MIZUKI.
SHARE THEM WITH AYAKA-CHAN.
IS THIS THE GÂTEAU CHOCOLAT YOU TOLD ME ABOUT?
OH! THIS ONE'S FROM ME.
THIS IS FOR GIVING OUT AT PRACTICE.
YOU MADE A LOT, HUH?
SENPAI!
GOOD MORNING!
THE FIRST-YEARS MADE THESE.
KOUHAIS FROM THE TRACK TEAM

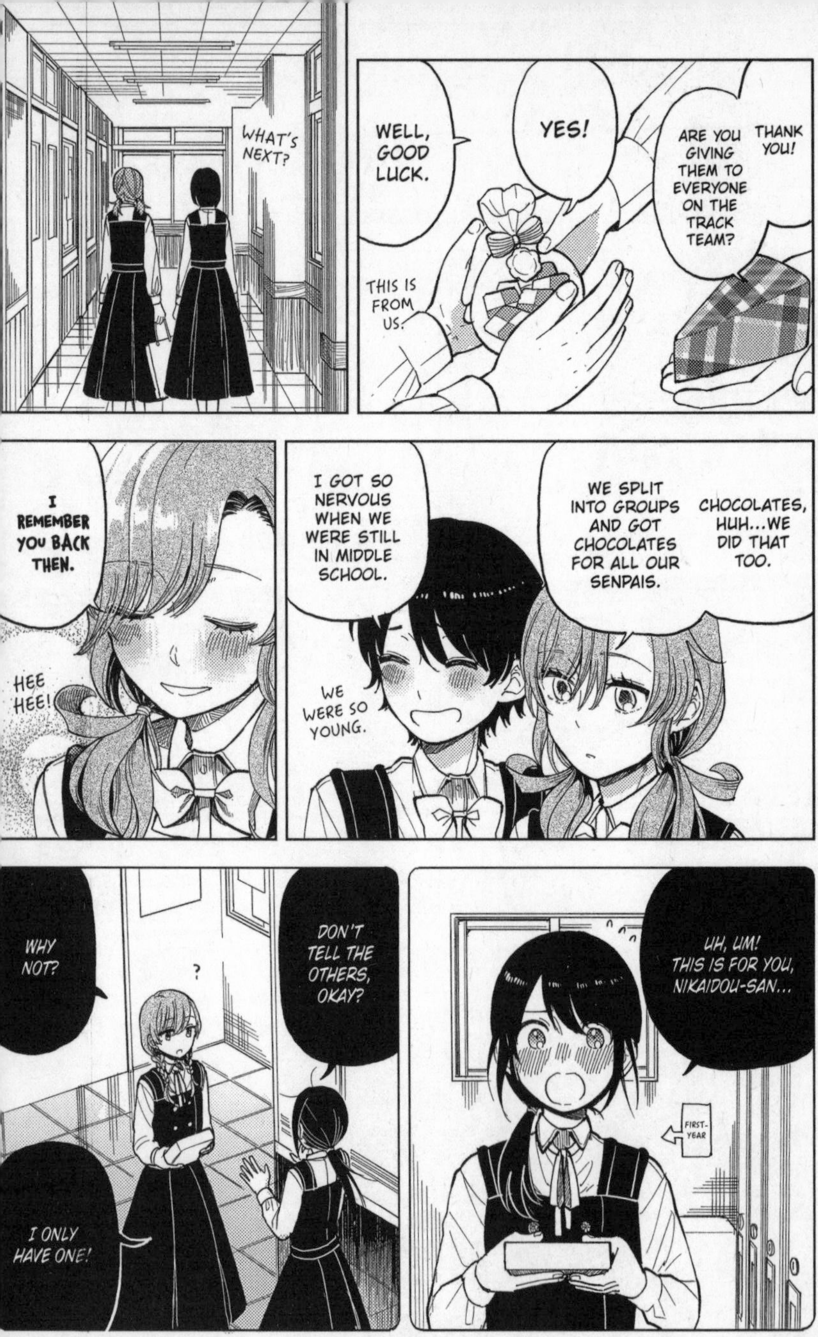
THANK YOU!
ARE YOU GIVING THEM TO EVERYONE ON THE TRACK TEAM?
YES!
WELL, GOOD LUCK.
THIS IS FROM US.
WHAT'S NEXT?
CHOCOLATES, HUH...WE DID THAT TOO.
WE SPLIT INTO GROUPS AND GOT CHOCOLATES FOR ALL OUR SENPAIS.
I GOT SO NERVOUS WHEN WE WERE STILL IN MIDDLE SCHOOL.
WE WERE SO YOUNG.
I REMEMBER YOU BACK THEN.
HEE HEE!
UH, UM! THIS IS FOR YOU, NIKAIDOU-SAN...
FIRST-YEAR
DON'T TELL THE OTHERS, OKAY?
?
WHY NOT?
I ONLY HAVE ONE!

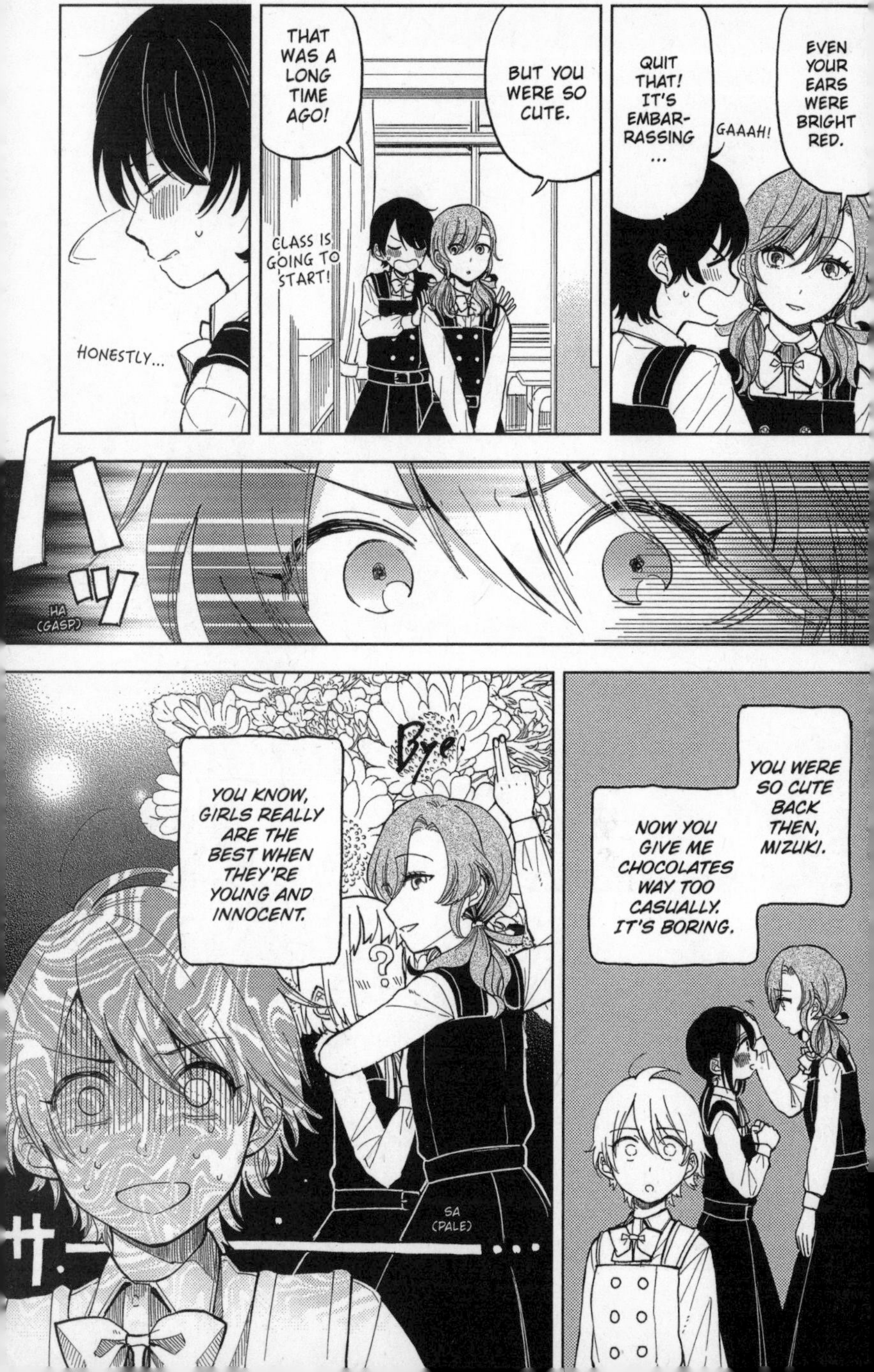
EVEN YOUR EARS WERE BRIGHT RED.
GAAAH!
QUIT THAT! IT'S EMBARRASSING...
BUT YOU WERE SO CUTE.
THAT WAS A LONG TIME AGO!
CLASS IS GOING TO START!
HONESTLY...
HA (GASP)
YOU WERE SO CUTE BACK THEN, MIZUKI.
NOW YOU GIVE ME CHOCOLATES WAY TOO CASUALLY. IT'S BORING.
Bye
YOU KNOW, GIRLS REALLY ARE THE BEST WHEN THEY'RE YOUNG AND INNOCENT.
?
SA (PALE)
...

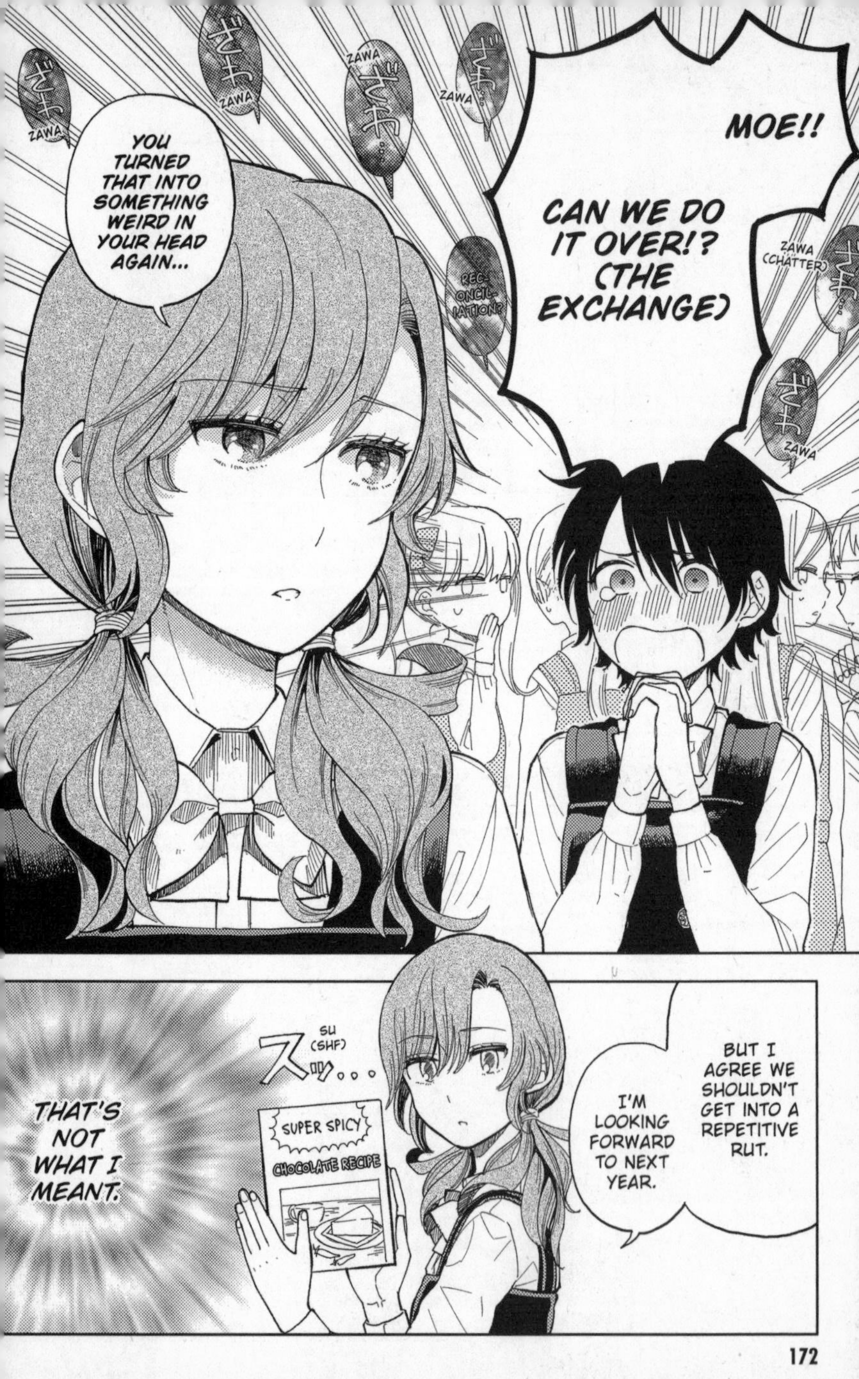

ZAWA
ZAWA (CHATTER)
MOE!!
CAN WE DO IT OVER!? (THE EXCHANGE)
ZAWA
ZAWA
REC-ONCIL-IATION?
ZAWA
ZAWA
YOU TURNED THAT INTO SOMETHING WEIRD IN YOUR HEAD AGAIN...
BUT I AGREE WE SHOULDN'T GET INTO A REPETITIVE RUT.
I'M LOOKING FORWARD TO NEXT YEAR.
SU (SHF)
SUPER SPICY
CHOCOLATE RECIPE
THAT'S NOT WHAT I MEANT.

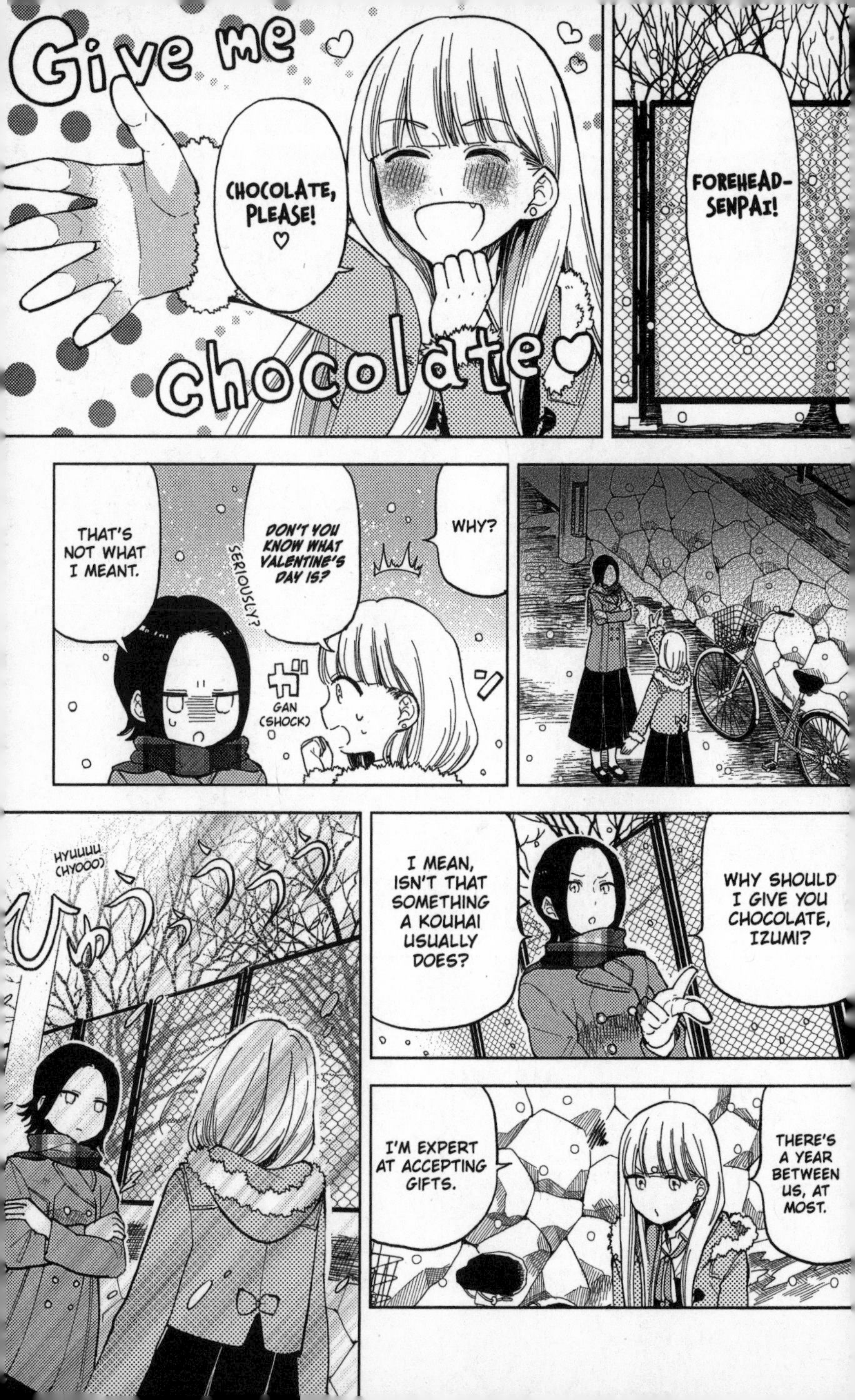
FOREHEAD-SENPAI!
Give me chocolate♥
CHOCOLATE, PLEASE! ♡
WHY?
DON'T YOU KNOW WHAT VALENTINE'S DAY IS?
SERIOUSLY?
ガ
GAN (SHOCK)
THAT'S NOT WHAT I MEANT.
WHY SHOULD I GIVE YOU CHOCOLATE, IZUMI?
I MEAN, ISN'T THAT SOMETHING A KOUHAI USUALLY DOES?
THERE'S A YEAR BETWEEN US, AT MOST.
I'M EXPERT AT ACCEPTING GIFTS.
ひゅう
HYUUUU (HYOOO)

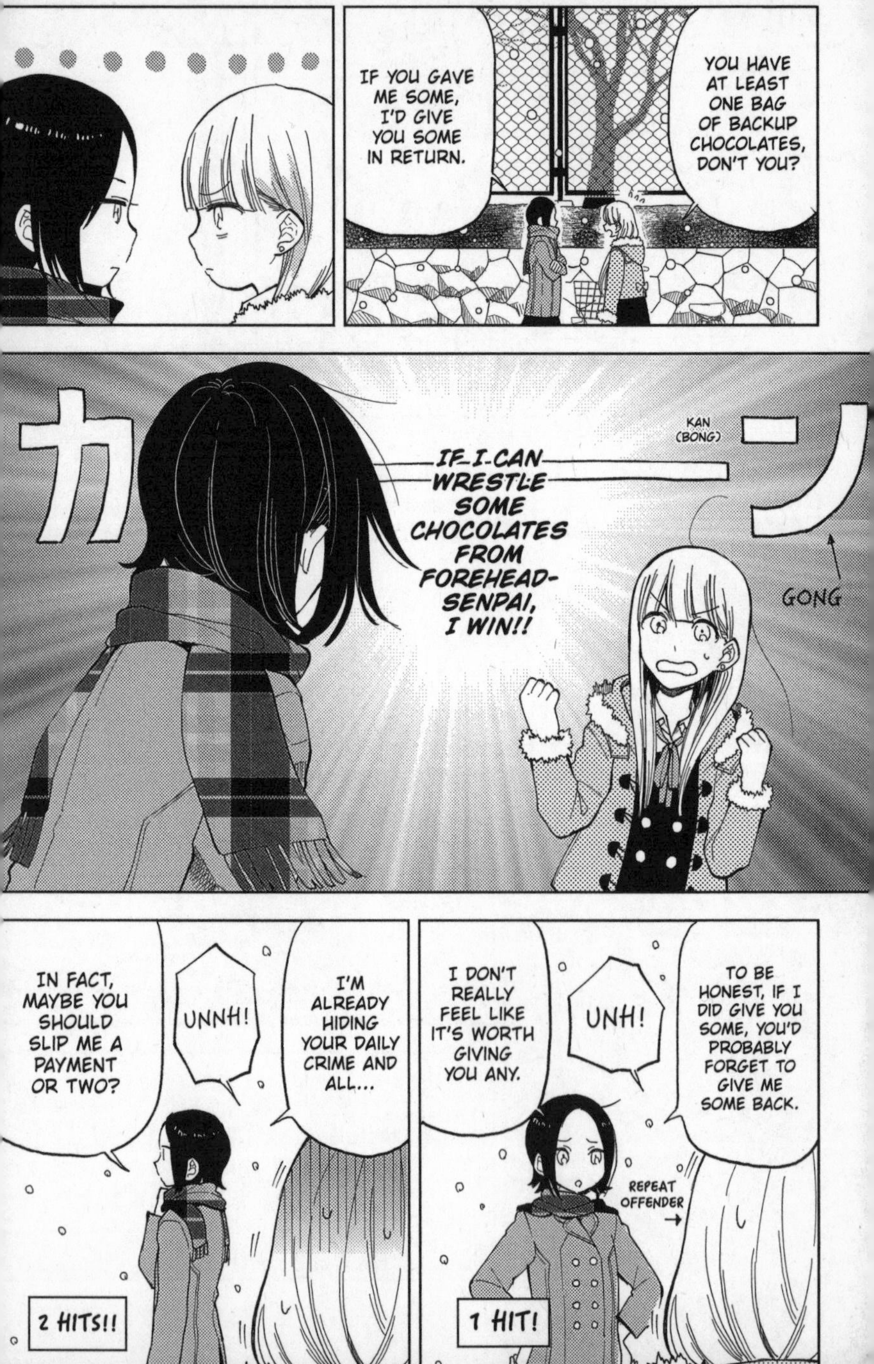
YOU HAVE AT LEAST ONE BAG OF BACKUP CHOCOLATES, DON'T YOU?
IF YOU GAVE ME SOME, I'D GIVE YOU SOME IN RETURN.
カーン
KAN (BONG)
GONG
IF I CAN WRESTLE SOME CHOCOLATES FROM FOREHEAD-SENPAI, I WIN!!
TO BE HONEST, IF I DID GIVE YOU SOME, YOU'D PROBABLY FORGET TO GIVE ME SOME BACK.
UNH!
I DON'T REALLY FEEL LIKE IT'S WORTH GIVING YOU ANY.
REPEAT OFFENDER →
1 HIT!
I'M ALREADY HIDING YOUR DAILY CRIME AND ALL...
UNNH!
IN FACT, MAYBE YOU SHOULD SLIP ME A PAYMENT OR TWO?
2 HITS!!

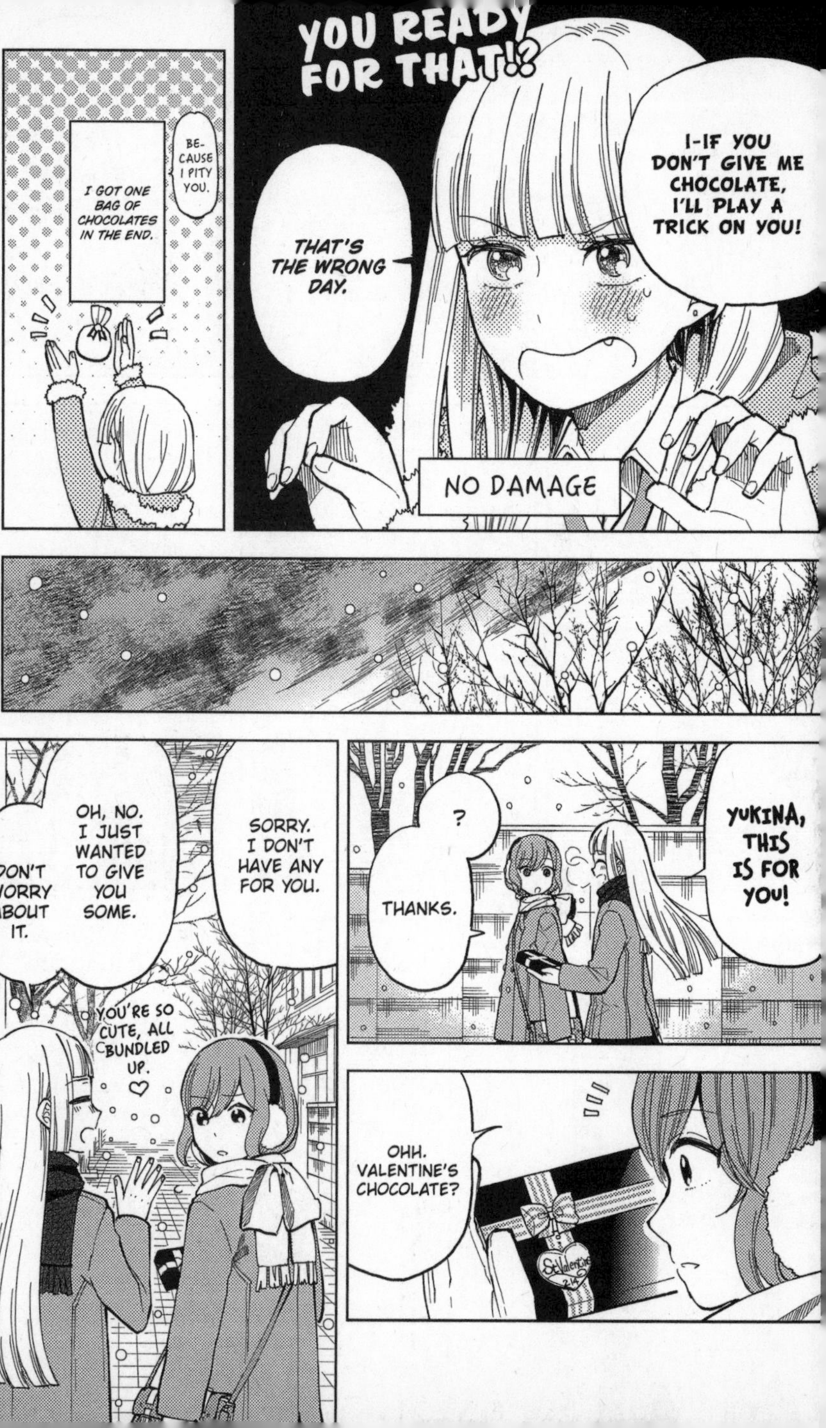
YOU READY FOR THAT!?
I-IF YOU DON'T GIVE ME CHOCOLATE, I'LL PLAY A TRICK ON YOU!
THAT'S THE WRONG DAY.
NO DAMAGE
BE-CAUSE I PITY YOU.
I GOT ONE BAG OF CHOCOLATES IN THE END.
YUKINA, THIS IS FOR YOU!
?
THANKS.
OHH. VALENTINE'S CHOCOLATE?
St.Valentine 2.14
SORRY. I DON'T HAVE ANY FOR YOU.
OH, NO. I JUST WANTED TO GIVE YOU SOME.
DON'T WORRY ABOUT IT.
YOU'RE SO CUTE, ALL BUNDLED UP. ♡

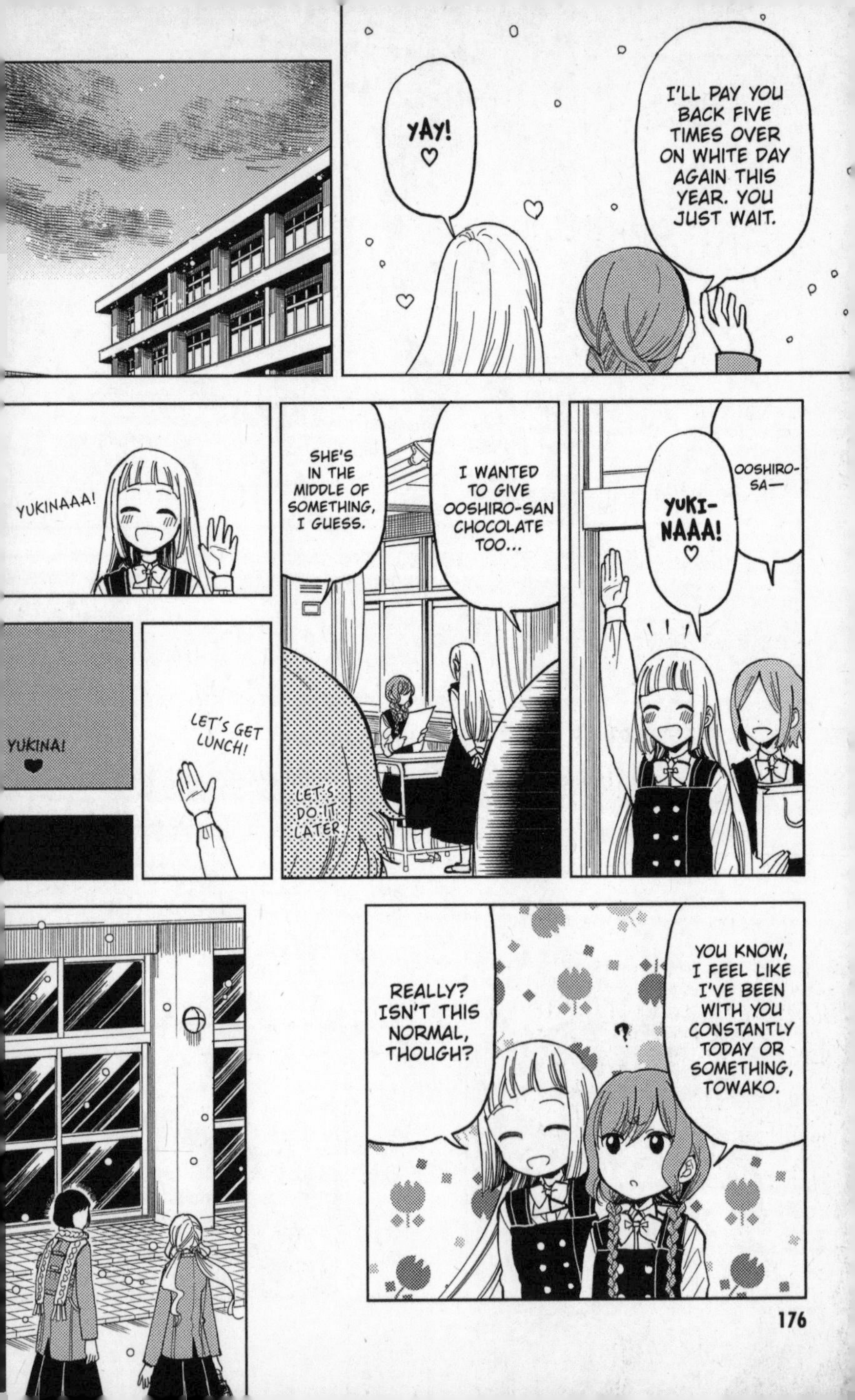
I'LL PAY YOU BACK FIVE TIMES OVER ON WHITE DAY AGAIN THIS YEAR. YOU JUST WAIT.
YAY! ♡
OOSHIRO-SA—
YUKI-NAAA! ♡
I WANTED TO GIVE OOSHIRO-SAN CHOCOLATE TOO...
SHE'S IN THE MIDDLE OF SOMETHING, I GUESS.
LET'S DO IT LATER.
YUKINAAA!
LET'S GET LUNCH!
YUKINA! ♥
YOU KNOW, I FEEL LIKE I'VE BEEN WITH YOU CONSTANTLY TODAY OR SOMETHING, TOWAKO.
REALLY? ISN'T THIS NORMAL, THOUGH?

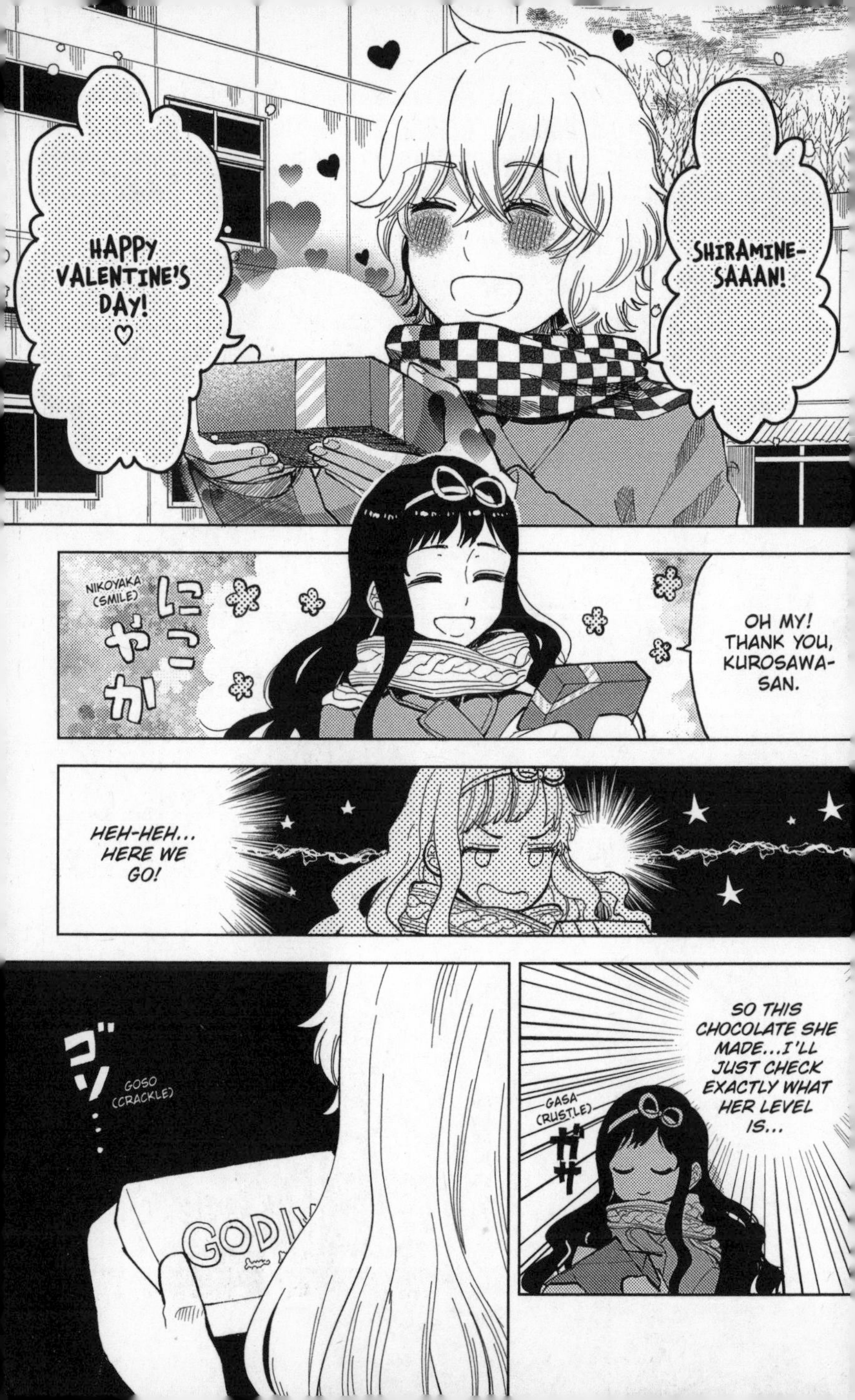
SHIRAMINE-SAAAN!
HAPPY VALENTINE'S DAY! ♡
OH MY! THANK YOU, KUROSAWA-SAN.
にっこやか
NIKOYAKA (SMILE)
HEH-HEH... HERE WE GO!
SO THIS CHOCOLATE SHE MADE...I'LL JUST CHECK EXACTLY WHAT HER LEVEL IS...
ガサ
GASA (RUSTLE)
ゴソ
GOSO (CRACKLE)
GODIV

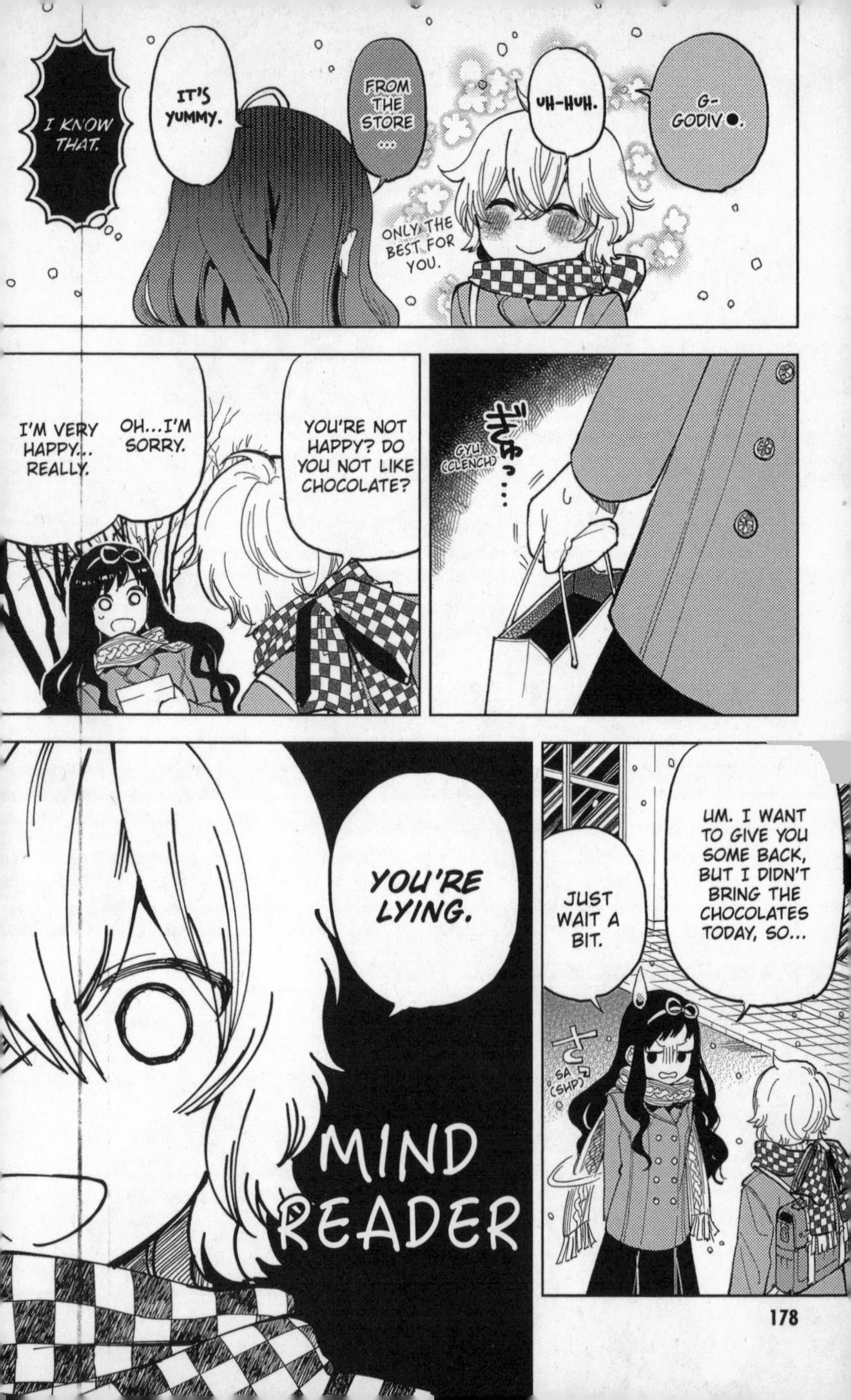

G-GODIV●.
UH-HUH.
ONLY THE BEST FOR YOU.
FROM THE STORE...
IT'S YUMMY.
I KNOW THAT.
ぎゅっ…
GYU (CLENCH)
YOU'RE NOT HAPPY? DO YOU NOT LIKE CHOCOLATE?
OH...I'M SORRY.
I'M VERY HAPPY... REALLY.
UM. I WANT TO GIVE YOU SOME BACK, BUT I DIDN'T BRING THE CHOCOLATES TODAY, SO...
JUST WAIT A BIT.
さっ
SA (SHP)
YOU'RE LYING.
MIND READER

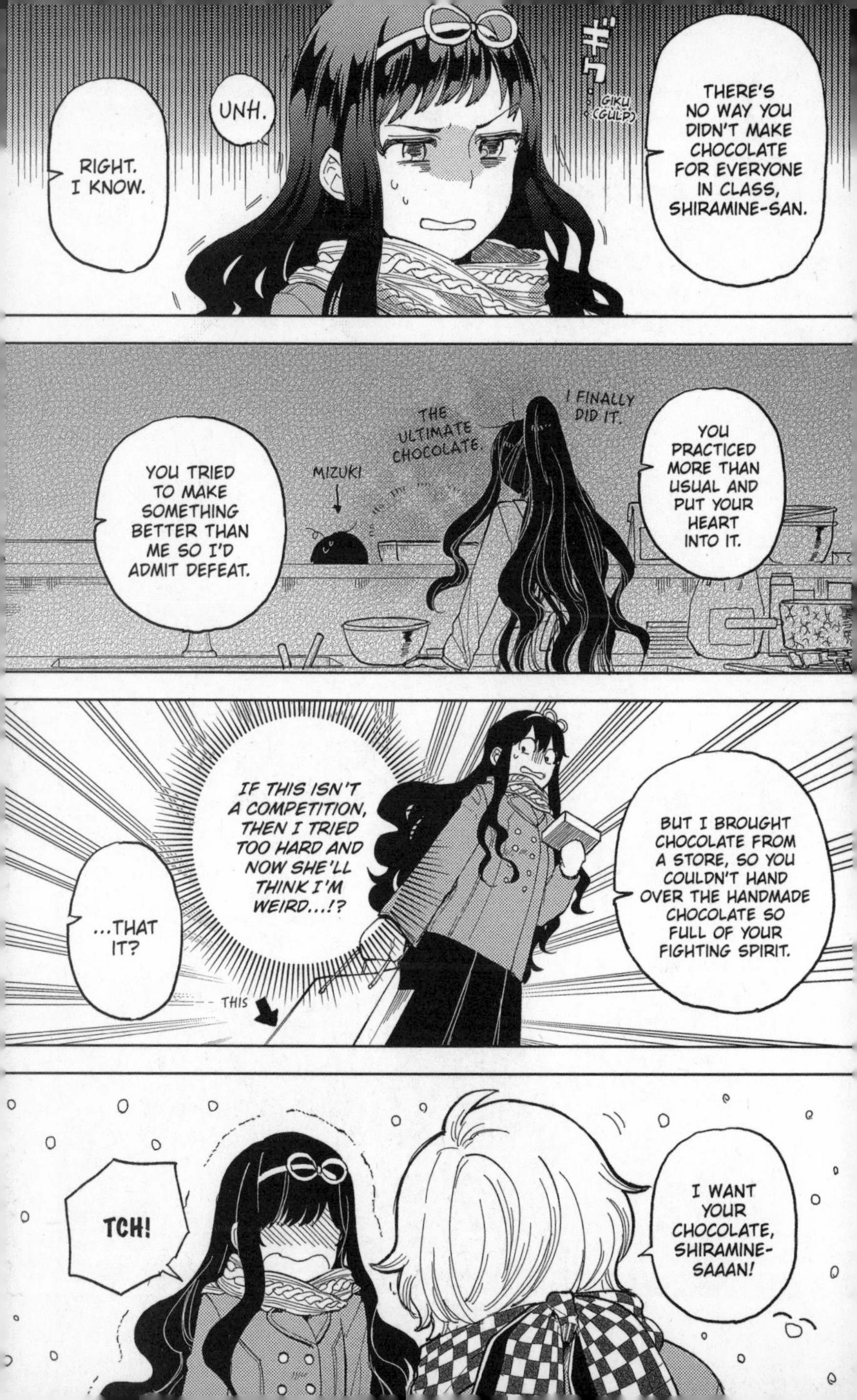
THERE'S NO WAY YOU DIDN'T MAKE CHOCOLATE FOR EVERYONE IN CLASS, SHIRAMINE-SAN.
GIKU (GULP)
UNH.
RIGHT. I KNOW.
I FINALLY DID IT.
YOU PRACTICED MORE THAN USUAL AND PUT YOUR HEART INTO IT.
THE ULTIMATE CHOCOLATE.
MIZUKI
YOU TRIED TO MAKE SOMETHING BETTER THAN ME SO I'D ADMIT DEFEAT.
BUT I BROUGHT CHOCOLATE FROM A STORE, SO YOU COULDN'T HAND OVER THE HANDMADE CHOCOLATE SO FULL OF YOUR FIGHTING SPIRIT.
IF THIS ISN'T A COMPETITION, THEN I TRIED TOO HARD AND NOW SHE'LL THINK I'M WEIRD...!?
...THAT IT?
THIS
I WANT YOUR CHOCOLATE, SHIRAMINE-SAAAN!
TCH!

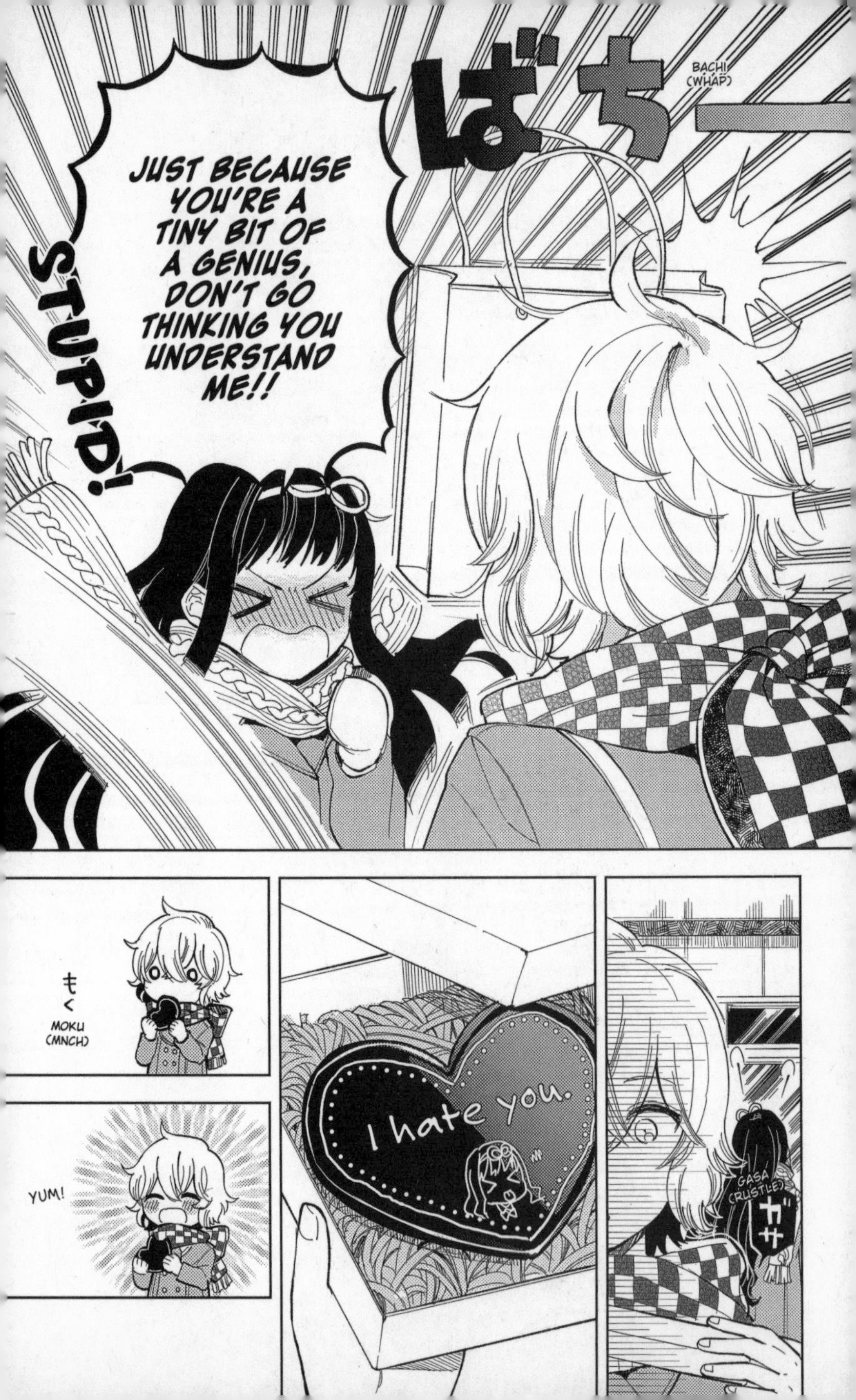
ばちー
BACHI (WHAP)
JUST BECAUSE YOU'RE A TINY BIT OF A GENIUS, DON'T GO THINKING YOU UNDERSTAND ME!!
STUPID!
ガサ
GASA (RUSTLE)
I hate you.
もく
MOKU (MNCH)
YUM!

AFTERWORD

I HAD PERSONALLY SETTLED ON A THEME OF "LOVE COMEDY" FOR VOLUME FOUR, BUT MY EDITOR INSISTED THAT THIS WAS THE STORY OF THE FUTURE, AND I THOUGHT THAT SOUNDED BETTER, SO THE THEME FOR THIS VOLUME IS "FUTURE." I HOPE YOU LIKE IT! CANNO HERE. THANK YOU FOR READING ALL THE WAY TO THE END!

AGAIN, MY EDITOR, EVERYONE IN THE ALIVE EDITORIAL DEPARTMENT, THE DESIGNER, KANARASHI-SAN AND KAWAUCHI-KUN WHO SAVED ME WHEN I BEGGED FOR HELP IN TEARS, AND MY FRIENDS AND FAMILY WERE SO IMPORTANT IN HELPING MAKE THIS BOOK. THANK YOU SO VERY MUCH!! LIKE I MENTIONED IN THE AFTERWORD IN THE LAST VOLUME, THEY DID MAKE A DRAMA CD, AND THANKS TO P-SAN, THE SCRIPTWRITER, THE VOICE ACTORS, AND EVERYONE ELSE INVOLVED, THE WORLD OF KISS HAS GROWN BIGGER THAN I IMAGINED. THANK YOU! MORE THAN ANYTHING, WHAT MADE IT POSSIBLE FOR ME TO COME THIS FAR IS YOU READING KISS AND ROOTING FOR ME ON THE OTHER SIDE OF THE PAGE (OR MONITOR). TRULY, THANK YOU. I WANT TO KEEP EXPANDING THIS WORLD, AND I WOULD LOVE IT IF YOU CAME ALONG WITH ME.

I WANT TO DO A STORY AROUND SHIRAMINE NEXT TIME.
I HOPE WE MEET AGAIN IN VOLUME FIVE!!

CANNO

THERE'S NO CONNECTION BETWEEN MIZUKI AND MOE'S NAMES BECAUSE I CREATED THEIR CHARACTERS AT A DIFFERENT TIME FROM THE OTHERS.

Kiss & White Lily for My Dearest Girl

CANNO

TRANSLATION: JOCELYNE ALLEN
LETTERING: ALEXIS ECKERMAN

ANOKO NI KISS TO SHIRAYURI WO Vol. 4
©CANNO 2016
First published in Japan in 2016 by KADOKAWA CORPORATION, Tokyo.
English translation rights arranged with KADOKAWA CORPORATION, Tokyo through Tuttle-Mori Agency, Inc., Tokyo.

English translation © 2017 by Yen Press, LLC

Yen Press
1290 Avenue of the Americas
New York, NY 10104

Visit us at yenpress.com
facebook.com/yenpress
twitter.com/yenpress
yenpress.tumblr.com
instagram.com/yenpress

First Yen Press Edition: November 2017

Yen Press is an imprint of Yen Press, LLC.
The Yen Press name and logo are trademarks of Yen Press, LLC.

The publisher is not responsible for websites (or their content) that are not owned by the publisher.

Library of Congress Control Number: 2016958499

ISBNs: 978-0-316-47052-0 (paperback)
978-0-316-47053-7 (ebook)

10 9 8 7 6 5 4 3 2 1

BVG

Printed in the United States of America